by graham edmonds and deborah gray
consultant: patrick stirling

A Dorling Kindersley Book

LONDON, NEW YORK, MUNICH, MELBOURNE, DELHI

Project Editor: Clare Lister
Editors: Brian Cooper and James Harrison
Designers: Dan Green, Adrienne Hutchinson, and Michael Yeowell
Assistant Editor: Sarah Goulding
Assistant Designer: Joanne Little
Senior Design Co-ordinator: Sophia M Tampakopoulos Turner
Category Publisher: Sue Grabham
Production Controller: Nicola Torode

Published in Great Britain in 2002
by Dorling Kindersley,
80 Strand, London WC2R 0RL
A Penguin company

ISBN 0 7513 4407 9

Printed and bound in
Italy by Legoprint

See our complete catalogue at
www.dk.com

Contents

How To Use This Book

The Internet Dictionary is alphabetical, with over 5,000 definitions. Many of the definitions are cross-referenced, and have web site links. There are also useful feature boxes on key areas of the Internet. The six appendices provide extra information, including text messaging acronyms, emoticons, domain name suffixes, number definitions, file extensions, and useful web sites.

Alphabetical order – Each alphabetical section is introduced by a full picture.

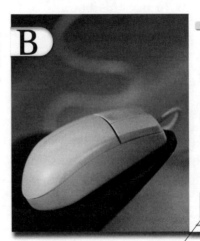

Cross references – The words in *italics* can also be found as headwords in the dictionary.

back door – This provides a means of access to a program, online service or entire computer system. Sometimes known only by the original *programmer*, and intended

Web site addresses – Where there is a relevant web site, it will be listed at the bottom of the definition so you can visit it on the Web.

America Online (AOL) – AOL is one of the leading *Internet Service Providers* in the world.
Go to: www.aol.com

AOLAnywhere

Company Logos – Each company logo shows the picture you will see upon opening their web site.

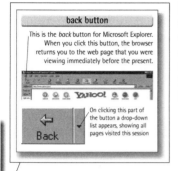

back button

This is the *back* button for Microsoft Explorer. When you click this button, the browser returns you to the web page that you were viewing immediately before the present.

On clicking this part of the button a drop-down list appears, showing all pages visited this session

Feature boxes – There are over 150 special features on key areas of the Internet to give you extra information on everything from downloading files to finding the most appropriate Internet Service Provider. If a definition has a feature box, you will be directed to it by **SEE: FEATURE BOX.**

annotations

AND operator – Used in searching, it finds entries that match both search words linked with the word "AND"; e.g. ham AND

Running Head – The first and last headwords on the page are shown at the top of each page to help you navigate around the book.

angel – An investor in Internet or computer start-up companies.

Headword – Each headword is in bold to make it easy to find.

Ananova's video reports have an area devoted to them on the company's web site.

animated GIF – Graphics Interchange Format. An animated image produced by a series of computer-drawn graphic images, which when played in succession give the appearance of movement; e.g. a moving diagram or cartoon. Animated GIFs require much less memory that a graphic image and can be played by major web browsers without the need for additional software.
SEE ALSO: GRAPHICS INTERCHANGE FORMAT

See also – These references direct you to other definitions that may interest you or enhance your knowledge on the topic you are looking up.

The Dictionary is designed to be read by everyone, from Internet newbies to technological experts, and across all age groups, from the youngest Generation Y member to the oldest silver surfer.

PCs and Apple Mac computers –

Almost all of the definitions within the dictionary apply to both Macintosh computers and PCs. Where the definitions apply to one or the other, this will be made clear in the text.

Power Mac

PC

US language – It is standard for computer dictionaries to be written using American English language. This is to avoid any confusion, as most software packages are written in American English.

Software and browsers – Many of the definitions refer to Microsoft Windows, and either Netscape Navigator or Internet Explorer because they are the most widely-used.

 **Netscape**

About the authors

Graham Edmonds has written three books on the Internet, *The Good Web Site Guide 2001*, and *The Good Web Site Guide 2002*, as well as *The Cool Web Site Guide*. He lives near Cirencester with a fat cat.

Deborah Gray began her publishing career in California during the 1980s. She now lives and works in a Wiltshire village surrounded by cows, and linked up to the real world via the Internet. She has edited *The Good Web Site Guides* and *The Cool Web Site Guide*.

Website content – The Internet is ever-changing and we cannot control what people put on their sites. It is possible that material we do not condone has been posted since we published this book. Please use discretion when you access the Internet, especially with your children. The publishers and authors have done their best to ensure the accuracy and currency of the information in this book, however, we cannot accept responsibility for any loss, injury, or inconvenience you may sustain as a result of the information or advice contained in this book.

@ – The symbol used to link a person's name and address in e-mail. It was chosen because it has an appropriate meaning that does not appear in postal addresses. Many companies have chosen to insert it into their name.

A2A – **A**pplication-to-**A**pplication. Allows people within a *chat* facility to collaborate by having joint control over a program running on a computer. Also referred to as *Application Sharing*.

AAC – See: **A**dvanced **A**udio **C**oding

abandonware – Software no longer sold or supported by the manufacturer. Unless such a program has been re-launched as freeware, it is usually considered to be illegal.
SEE ALSO: FREEWARE

ABEND – The **ab**normal **end** of an operation due to software or hardware failure. It may occasionally be used in e-mail subject lines alerting others to the loss of Internet access. It derives from an error message on the IBM350.
SEE ALSO: CRASH

abort – To stop or end an operation or program before completion, usually suddenly. It can either be intentional (e.g. when the user decides to abort a printing operation that is in progress) or unintentional, owing to program failure caused by an electrical shortage.

About.com – A web site that uses experts from around the world to provide information on a wide range of topics from shopping and travel to arts and science. There are opportunities to become guides, as well to receive advice. Each guide is screened and given training by About.com.
GO TO: www.about.com

About. The Human Internet.

absolute address – A fixed address at which data is stored in the computer's memory. The address has a numerical location, unlike a relative address, which indicates one location only in relation to another. In HTML the absolute address usually refers to the hyperlink's complete address including protocol, (e.g. http://www.madeuplink.com/pageno.htm).
SEE ALSO: MACHINE ADDRESS, RELATIVE ADDRESS

absolute link – A hyperlink on a web page that gives the full path to the link. This can be a problem if the linked web page still exists, but has moved its position on the web site into a different folder. Most web sites use relative links instead, which take the user straight to the linked web page.

AC-3 – The sound coding system used by Dolby Digital.

ACAP – See: **A**pplication **C**onfiguration **A**ccess **P**rotocol

Accelerated Graphics Port (AGP) – The socket or *expansion slot* into which a high speed graphics adapter card can be added. This port provides a special route (*bus*) from the PC's processor to the memory, which can cope with the demands of 3D graphic material. It was developed by Intel Corporation.

accelerator – 1. An expansion board that makes a computer faster by adding a faster central processing unit.
2. Short for graphics accelerator.
3. A shortcut of keys that the computer user can use to replace the menu and mouse operation.

Acceptable Use Policy (AUP) – Contract specifying what a subscriber can and cannot do while using a particular online service; e.g. some Internet Service Providers may restrict part or all of their networks to non-commercial use.

Access – A *database*-handling program from Microsoft, particularly useful for web designers. It can be used to store searchable data and can be integrated easily into web page construction.
Go to: www.microsoft.com/office/access

access – To log on to the Internet (or any other network) in order to surf the World Wide Web, send and receive e-mail, and download files. Internet access is gained via a modem and Internet Service Provider or an office network.

access code – A password or series of characters and numbers that enables a user to log on and use the Internet.
See also: access

access control – A security system is able to protect a computer from unauthorized access.

Access Control List (ACL) – A list attached to an object (commonly a file) that contains a list of users and specifies the access permissions each user has to that object.

access log – Record maintained on a computer indicating the time and duration of Internet access logged over a specified period of time.

access number – The telephone number(s) supplied by the Internet Service Provider to provide users with access to their service.

access provider – **See:** Internet Service Provider

access speed – The time taken for the screen to update while connected to the Internet, expressed in *bits* per second. It is dependent on type of phone line, modem, and ISP transmission rate.

access time – The amount of time between requesting a page on the Internet and the screen displaying that page. This can vary depending on speed of connection and *network congestion*.

accessories – A group of small programs designed to perform a limited task; for instance, desktop accessories for most operating systems will usually include an address book, a notepad, and some disk management programs.
SEE: FEATURE BOX

accessware – Programs that provide security systems for Internet access to authorize usage and guarantee privacy.

account – Data about a user stored on a computer; it includes username, password, and the location of the user's data.

ACK – Acknowledge. A signal sent by the receiving modem to the sending modem to acknowledge receipt of a *packet* of data. The signal indicates that the computer is ready to receive the next package.

ACM – See: Association for Computing Machinery

acoustic coupler – A device onto which a telephone handset is placed, connecting a computer with a network. Since the 1970s, it has generally been replaced by the electronic modem connection.

ACPI – See: Advanced Configuration and Power Interface

Acrobat – See: Adobe Acrobat

acronym – Word formed from the first letters of other words e.g. ARPA or *ASCII*.
SEE: APPENDIX 1 for use in e-mail text.

action games – Computer games that involve the use of *joystick* or *arrow keys*.

activate – To initiate an Internet connection, program, or function.

Active Channel – A Microsoft standard that allows the user to receive web content to their browser in real time.

active desktop –The part of the *desktop* that is receiving commands.
SEE: FEATURE BOX

active directory – A Windows 2000 product enabling the creation of a single

accessories

The accessories menu should be easy to find regardless of the operating system you are using. The accessories menu for Windows ME is available when you click the Start button and choose Accessories from the Programs menu.

Windows ME accessories include several Internet-related applications, such as Telnet Chat, and Hyperterminal.

- Communications ►
- Hyperterminal ►
- Multimedia ►
- Address Book
- Calculator
- Character Map
- Chat
- Clipboard Viewer
- Clock
- Dial-Up Networking
- Imaging
- Notepad
- Object Packager
- Paint
- Phone Dialer
- Synchronize
- Telnet
- WordPad

searchable directory for a *network*, reducing the number of directories needed.

active matrix display – A type of flat panel display in which the screen is refreshed and updated more frequently than in conventional displays.
See also: **TFT**

Active Movie – A Microsoft video application providing online and desktop multimedia tools.

Active Server Page (ASP) .asp – A Microsoft product used for the building of interactive web pages and applications. These run on a web server, generating the HTML pages sent to browsers. Server-produced pages cannot be easily copied.
Go to: www.microsoft.com

Active Template Library (ATL) – Microsoft-supplied templates that can help create objects within their programs.

ActiveX – A term covering a number of programs and technologies from Microsoft that enable the running of multimedia effects within a web page. For example, web pages can be enhanced by audio, animation, or video clips.
See also: **Object Linking & Embedding**

ActiveX Control – A small, very flexible program enabling web pages to use ActiveX components. It only works with Windows.

adapter card – See: expansion card

Adaptive Differential Pulse Code Modulation (ADPCM) – Converts an analog or voice signal into a compressed digital signal. This method of encoding data is more economical than the method used for the PCM data format used in *.wav* files, for example.
See also: **analog, digital**

Adaptive Technology – A standard setting PC introduced in 1984 by IBM. The most advanced PC of the time, it had an Intel 80286 processor, 16-bit bus, 1.2MB floppy drive, and used the 84-key keyboard with alphanumeric keys, number pad, F keys, and arrow keys. Also known as AT.

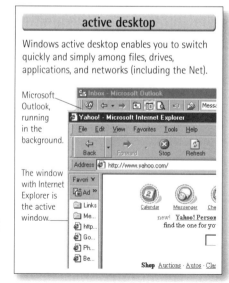

active desktop

Windows active desktop enables you to switch quickly and simply among files, drives, applications, and networks (including the Net).

Microsoft Outlook, running in the background.

The window with Internet Explorer is the active window.

A/D Converter – **See: A**nalog to **D**igital Converter

ad banner – **See:** banner ad

ad click – A user's click on a *banner ad,* which usually directs the user to the advertiser's web site. Some ads are charged by the number of user clicks generated.

ad click rate – The average number of times an ad is viewed before a response, in the form of a click, is made.

ad server – A server that specializes in accounts with advertising sites. These servers often control which *banner ad*s appear on a user's computer, as well as the rotation of adverts on-screen, depending on the input from the visitor. Some servers work by selecting adverts on the basis of which keywords the user types into the search engine.

ADB – **A**pple **D**esktop **B**us. This kind of communications port is found mainly on older Apple computers and was commonly used for keyboard-to-mouse connections.

ADC – **See: A**nalog to **D**igital **C**onverter

add to – To increase the computer's functions by adding new hardware devices or software programs.

add to cart – An instruction on a shopping web site to show that the user wants to buy the selected item. The item is then placed in the shopping cart,

and the price to the cart total is added.
SEE ALSO: CART

add-in – A peripheral device that usually fits inside the computer as opposed to one plugged in on the outside. An example would be an *expansion board.*

add-ons – A device or program that is designed to enhance the functioning of an existing device or program.

address – 1. Like postal addresses, Internet addresses are individual and make personal communication possible through the computer. There are two types:
i. An Internet address also known as Uniform Resource Locator (URL) such as www.dk.com. This URL is translated by the computer into a set of numbers, which is transmitted to a *Domain Name Server's* (DNS) computer, which in turn finds the requested page and sends it back to the computer.
SEE ALSO: **URL**
ii. E-mail addresses such as john@dk.com enable messages to be routed to an individual. They consist of a *username* linked by an *@ sign* to a *host name.* The host is commonly an ISP or a company domain name.
2. The number that identifies a storage area within the computer's memory where one byte of data is located; so for 32Mb of memory there will be approximately 32 million different addresses.

address book – A personal collection of names and Internet addresses. This is usually part of the main e-mail application, e.g. Microsoft Outlook, or may constitute part of the Internet browser. It enables quick addressing for individual or group e-mails. Other stored information can include "snail mail" addresses, telephone numbers, and other personal information.
SEE: FEATURE BOX

address bus – The electronic lines used to connect the processor to the memory, which enable data to be retrieved. The higher the number of lines (usually 24 or 32), the faster the retrieval.
SEE ALSO: BUS

Address Resolution Protocol (ARP) – This is part of the system that is used to carry data across the Internet. Every *host* computer is assigned a unique number. ARP reads this number and finds the *network* address of the computer to which it refers. Data is then directed to the destination computer.
SEE ALSO: IP (INTERNET PROTOCOL), ASSIGN

Administrator – Sometimes abbreviated to admin.
SEE ALSO: SYSTEMS ADMINISTRATOR

ADN – Advanced Digital Network. A dedicated telephone line capable of transmitting data, video, and other digital signals very fast and reliably. Usually transmits at 56 kbps or above.

ADO – **A**ctiveX **D**ata **O**bjects. An *interface* used to access a variety of data objects, including web pages, spreadsheets, and databases.

 Adobe – Adobe Systems is probably the leading company in producing programs used in the design and editing of images and text.
GO TO: www.adobe.com

Adobe After Effects –
A set of *tools* that are used to deliver a wide range of multimedia, motion picture, and animation effects on web pages.

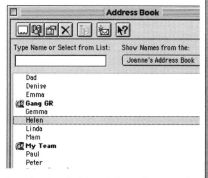

address book

In Microsoft Outlook's address book, names can be stored, organized, and viewed in groups or lists, according to preference.

The address book for Microsoft Outlook (Mac version).

Adobe Acrobat – A suite of programs, developed by Adobe Systems, for creating and distributing documents. They allow you to create a Portable Document File (PDF) for a document. You can then distribute the PDF file electronically to people who view the document with the Acrobat Reader (freely distributed). Its main advantage is that you can see exactly the layout intended by the author.

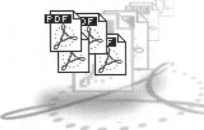

 Adobe Photoshop – A class-leading image editing program from Adobe Systems, widely used in the production of web graphics.

Adobe PostScript – Industry-standard program and language used for printing on laser printers and, more recently, desktop publishing.

ADPCM – Adaptive Differential Pulse Code Modulation. The process of converting analog voice samples into high-quality digital signals.

ADSL – **See:** Asymmetric Digital Subscriber Line

Advanced Audio Coding (AAC) – An audio compression format defined by the MPEG-2 standard. Claims to produce higher quality audio reproduction and requires less data than MP3. It is not compatible with the MPEG-1 coding scheme.

Advanced Configuration and Power Interface (ACPI) – A communication mode between the operating system, motherboard, and other devices such as hard drive and CD drive, that ensures electrical power to all devices is available on demand.

Advanced Intelligent Tape (AIT) – A storage tape format that provides 35GB storage per tape. Each tape contains a small memory chip, which records file locations, speeding up the time taken to retrieve a file.

Advanced Micro Devices (AMD) – 1. Used in the flat panel liquid crystal displays of laptop and notebook computers. The electronic "ink" contains millions of microcapsules, each containing a mixture of dye pigment and pigment chips. These capsules then respond to electronic charges to produce the color image.

 2. A global company that produces microprocessors, memory devices, and circuitry. It is in competition with market leaders such as Intel.

Advanced Mobile Phone Service/System – An analog mobile phone system popular throughout the Americas, Asia-Pacific region, and Eastern Europe. It operates in the 800 MHz frequency band.

Advanced Research Projects Agency Network (ARPANet) – Developed by the U.S. Department of Defense, this is the original group of companies that linked computers via leased telephone lines. This formed the prototype for today's Internet, providing its physical *backbone*.

advanced streaming format – A file format designed to store synchronized multimedia data. It is used to produce live broadcasting by sending audio and video data in a continuous stream down the line. SEE ALSO: STREAMING

adventure game – A computer game set in a theme-based environment such as medieval, gothic horror, science fiction, desert war, etc. Some can be played on-line, others need to be *downloaded*.

After Effects® 4.1 – **See:** Adobe After Effects

agent – A program that works in the background, gathering information or processing data. The user can state preferences and interests, then the agent will gather relevant information from the Internet. Also known as web agents and *autonomous agents*.

AGFA (Snapscan etc) – A leading image and photographic development company.

AGP – **See:** **A**ccelerated **G**raphics **P**ort

AI – **See:** **A**rtificial **I**ntelligence

AIFF – **See:** **A**udio **I**nterchange **F**ile **F**ormat

aintitcoolnews.com – A popular movie review web site. GO TO: www.aintitcoolnews.com

airbrush – A graphics tool that creates a soft fill effect.

air cooling – A method of cooling the computer's central processor by way of a heatsink and/or fan.

air gap – A type of network security in which a computer or *network* is secured by keeping it physically separate from other local networks, computers, and the Internet. This can be disadvantageous if the user cannot obtain all the resources needed from a single computer.

AIT – **See:** **A**dvanced **I**ntelligent **T**ape

AIX – **A**dvanced **I**nteractive e**X**ecutive is a version of the *UNIX* operating system, developed by *IBM,* which is popular with web developers.

Aladdin Expander – A program from Aladdin Systems that expands and decodes compressed files that have been downloaded from the Internet, or received via e-mail. It works with most operating systems, including Windows, Macintosh, Solaris, and Linux. It is also known as the *StuffIt Expander*.
Go to: www.aladdinsys.com

algorithm – 1. A method that solves a particular problem or performs a specific task (such as sorting). It comes embedded in a program.
2. A programming term referring to a series of instructions given to the computer.

alias – 1. An *address book* entry that combines a number of addresses that are frequently mailed simultaneously, e.g. "friends", "colleagues." Entries of this kind are known as a "group" in Internet Explorer and "list" in Netscape Navigator.
2. A shortcut link to a file location.

aliasing – 1. The act of using aliases.
2. Describes text that has jagged edges (*jaggies*), often a problem with large text used in graphics images.
3. False frequencies in digitized sound.

alert box – A warning or error message that appears in a box to warn of a system problem, for instance, or network failure. The user must hit the return key or click to acknowledge the message before being allowed to continue.
See: feature box
See also: dialog box

align – To line up the text against the left or right margin or, in freeform, to work against the ruler.
See: feature box
See also: justified

Aloha – A protocol for both satellite and terrestrial radio links that transmits sound in a package. However, transmissions on occasion collide with other transmissions sent over the same frequency, and the package has to be retransmitted. An improvement is "slotted Aloha," which transmits in allotted time slots.

Alpha – A high speed 64-bit processing chip that is used with the Microsoft Windows NT operating system.

---

alert box

This alert box for Microsoft Outlook, containing an exclamation point and three option buttons, is a typical Microsoft Windows alert box.

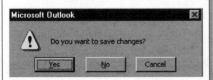

An alert box gives the user three clear options: yes, no, or cancel.

alpha blending - This is when two objects are overlapped. Primarily used to create atmospheric effects such as "fogging," where an image is placed behind a translucent image so that the image appears to be seen though fog.

alpha channel - In a 32-bit graphics system, 8-bits are reserved for the alpha channel. This channel uses information about the *pixel*'s transparency and relates this to how the pixel's colors should be merged with those of another pixel when the two are placed one on top of the other. In practice, it works on color blocks rather than on individual pixels. It is an important tool in animation.

alpha geek - (slang) The most well-informed member of a high-tech group – not necessarily the leader or supervisor of the group. They might only display their expertise in one area of technology.

alphanumeric - A character in the sets A-Z or 0-9, as opposed to punctuation, white space, or non-printable characters.

Alpha processor - A type of processor created by the Digital Equipment Corporation for use in workstations and network servers.

alpha testing - Primary manufacturer's testing of new software products.
SEE ALSO: BETA TESTING

ALS – See: **A**pplication **L**ink **S**oftware

alt. (or .alt) - Newsgroup type covering alternative discussions about a wide range of topics. ISPs may restrict access to alt. newsgroups since some are offensive.

alt text - Text seen momentarily as an image loads or a mouse pointer stops over it. Some web designers add advertising messages and additional keywords to this text to increase the hits for the site.

Altavista - Commonly used *search engine* and *portal* web site.
GO TO: www.altavista.com

altavista

alter ego - The persona adopted by a user for text-based games such as Portal.

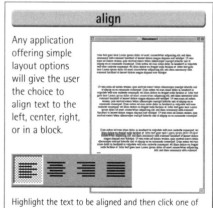

align

Any application offering simple layout options will give the user the choice to align text to the left, center, right, or in a block.

Highlight the text to be aligned and then click one of the alignment buttons (l to r: left, center, right, block).

alternating current (AC) – An electric current that reverses its direction at regular intervals.

ALU – **See:** **A**rithmetic **L**ogic **U**nit

amazon.com. **Amazon.com** – One of the leading online retailers, it started life as a bookstore but has now expanded into other areas of retailing. It has a reputation for excellent service combined with good value and recommendations.
Go to: www.amazon.com

amazoned – (verb) When an established company is blindsided by a Web-based company that has a better understanding of Internet technology. The latter is often an Internet start-up company. This term refers to the huge growth of *Amazon.com* and the consequences of this for conventional booksellers.

AMD – **See:** **A**dvanced **M**icro **D**evices

America Online (AOL) – AOL is one of the leading *Internet Service Providers* in the world.
Go to: www.aol.com

American National Standards Institute (ANSI) – The principle standardizing agency for the computer industry. Developed *ASCII* and *SCSI*.

American Standard Code for Information Interchange (ASCII) – **See:** ASCII

ampere (amp) – The basic unit of measurement of electric current in a circuit. One ampere is the equivalent to a flow of one coulomb per second.

ampersand – The "&" sign meaning "and." Sometimes called "pretzel."

amplitude – The size of a vibration, which is the maximum value of an analog or digital waveform.

AMR – **See:** **A**udio **M**odem **R**iser

analog (analogue UK sp.) – A signal that is represented in a way that is continuously variable. *Digital* signals, on the other hand, are represented in discrete units (the binary digits 1 and 0). The sound waves created by speech and music have traditionally been represented as analog signals. All signals need to be translated from analog to digital to be understood by today's computers.

analog control – Analog devices are controlled by switches and sliding dials as opposed to the digital displays favored by digital systems.

analog monitor – A monitor that works with analog signals and can consequently display an infinite range of colors. Some older types of monitors have a more limited color range.

analog-to-digital converter (ADC) – An electronic circuit that converts data from analog to digital (binary) form. For example, an audio CD is created by converting analog sound signals into digital data. It can be said to work by *sampling* or measuring the height of an analog signal thousands of times per second.

Ananova – One of the leading online news services, famous for its virtual reality newscaster, also called Ananova. Part of the Orange mobile communications group.
Go to: www.ananova.com

Ananova was the world's first virtual newscaster. She made her debut on April 19, 2000.

anchor – The destination of a *link* on a web page that allows the user to jump from one part of the page to another.

AND operator – Used in searching, it finds entries that match both search words linked with the word "AND"; e.g. ham AND eggs will find web pages mentioning the words "ham" and the word "eggs" together.

angel – An investor in Internet or computer start-up companies.

angle brackets – The keyboard symbols <> are used to enclose HTML tags and other codes.

animated GIF – **G**raphics **I**nterchange **F**ormat. An animated image produced by a series of computer-drawn graphic images, which when played in succession give the appearance of movement; e.g. a moving diagram or cartoon. Animated GIFs require much less memory that a graphic image and can be played by major web browsers without the need for additional software.
See also: Graphics Interchange Format

animation – A series of images drawn in several frames (cells), each one slightly different. When played in succession, they give the appearance of movement.

ANNIE – A web page that has been left without changes for some considerable time. Named after orphan Annie, the fictional character who was abandoned.

annotations – Personal notes made relating to a web page that are stored on the user's system and are accessed each time the web page is opened.

anomaly – A fault within a computer or program for which there is no obvious explanation. Also called a *bug*.

anonymizer – A service that allows a user to surf the Web anonymously.
Go to: www.anonymizer.com

anonymous FTP – An Internet site that holds files available for public download by *file transfer protocol*. Such sites can be accessed with users having to give only their e-mail address as a password and the word "guest" or "anonymous" as the user name.

anonymous posting – A message sent to a newsgroup with no disclosure of the sender's identity.

anonymous remailer – A service that hides the identity of the sender of an e-mail. The remailer that receives the e-mail from the sender hides the headers that identify the sender and forwards the message to its destination. This can prevent spammers from knowing a user's e-mail address.

ANSI – **See:** **A**merican **N**ational **S**tandards **I**nstitute

answer-only modem – A modem that can receive calls but cannot send them.

anti-aliasing – A method of making the jagged edges of text or curved lines look smooth by shading in the steps between.

antistatic mat – Floor mat for reducing static electricity around computer equipment. Static can damage computer equipment, which may result in data loss.

antivirus software – A program that detects and removes computer viruses. It should be run on any file that is downloaded or shared on the Internet.

AOL – **See:** **A**merica **O**nline

Apache – A popular free Web server.
Go to: www.apache.org

API – **See:** **A**pplication **P**rogram **I**nterface

app – **See:** **App**lication program

append – To add data to the end of a file or database or extend a character string.

Apple – A personal computer manufacturer renowned for innovation and design. Founded in 1976 by Steve Jobs and Steve Wozniak, it is best known for its Macintosh series of computers first introduced in 1984.
Go to: www.apple.com

The Macintosh 128K was released in 1984. It had a black and white monitor, a keyboard, a mouse, and a floppy disk drive.

Apple Computer - The Apple Macintosh features a user interface that is common to all its computers. This means that familiarity with one Apple Mac ensures that the user can work on any model with relative ease.

The Quicksilver PowerMac G4, released in July 2001. The design has evolved in both technology and design since the first Apple Macintosh in 1984.

Apple Desktop bus (ADB) - A type of communications pathway built into older versions of the Apple Macintosh computer. It is used to connect low-speed input devices such as the keyboard and mouse. A single ADB port can support as many as 16 simultaneous input devices.

Apple key - A key on Apple computers labeled with the Apple logo, it serves as the Command key.
SEE ALSO: COMMAND

Apple menu - Apple's easy-to-use customizable menu feature.
SEE: FEATURE BOX

AppleScript - A scripting language developed by Apple Computers that can provide an easy way for the automation of common tasks.

AppleshareIP - A network program from Apple Computers covering web use, file management, e-mail, and print servers.

AppleTalk - A *local-area network* (LAN) system built into all models of Apple Macintosh computers.

applet - A simple program that is sometimes attached to *HTML* documents. Applets can be quickly downloaded and, since they are written in *Java* or *ActiveX*, can run on most Internet *browsers*. Examples include news tickertape or web page *multimedia* effects.

Apple menu

Clicking the Apple icon will reveal the Apple menu. It can be used to launch programs or files quickly.

This drop-down menu can be customized by editing the contents of the Apple Menu Items folder in the control panels.

File Edit View Window
About This Computer
Extensis Suitcase 9
Mac Assistant
Apple System Profiler
Applications ▶
Calculator
Chooser
Control Panels ▶
Favorites
Key Caps
Network Browser
Note Pad
Recent Applications ▶
Recent Documents ▶
Recent Servers ▶
Scrapbook
Sherlock 2
Stickies
~Open Monthly User Audit

application – A program designed to accomplish a specific task, e.g. word processing, accounting, or desktop publishing. Such programs may be embedded in an *HTML* document and run on the user's computer.
SEE ALSO: SYSTEM SOFTWARE, UTILITY

Application Configuration Access Protocol (ACAP) – An e-mail protocol that allows access to e-mail related services, such as mailboxes and searching for keywords within messages, while they are still on the server. Formerly known as Internet Message Support Protocol (IMSP).

application gateway – Software that maintains security on a secluded *network* but allows selective communication with the outside world. Most commonly used in a business environment that is permanently connected to the Internet.

Application Program Interface (API) – Commands within software that can communicate between an *application* and the computer's *operating system*. These enable programs to run in Windows and to display such things as help files and message boxes.

Application Service Provider (ASP) – A company that runs software programs, which are used by a third party on the Internet (e.g. a search facility on a web-based shopping site, as well as web design or accounting facilities.).

application sharing – See: A2A

application software – See: application

Application-Specific Integrated Circuit (ASIC) – A special microchip that is used for a specific application.

apt–get – Everything sent via the Internet is divided up into small *packets* of data that the computer manages quickly. The term apt-get describes "apt," software automatically checking for new packets that are waiting to be downloaded onto the computer.

ARC – See: **A**ttached **R**esource **C**omputer

arcade games – Games for the home computer that are similar to those formerly found in games arcades.

Archie – The first on-line *search engine*, developed in 1990. It is particularly useful for finding public files on *anonymous FTP* sites when the computer user knows the name of the file for which they are searching rather than simply its content. It is a slow process depending on FTP servers rather than the Web, which means that this system is hardly used today.

architecture – The design of a computer, hardware, software, or network. Often used in terms of compatibility, meaning that a computer that has IBM-*compatible* architecture will run with hardware designed for IBM-type computers.

archival back-up – 1. A program that backs up only the files that have changed since the last back-up; it saves both time and storage space.
2. A backed-up file that will be stored for a long time. These files are often stored in compressed form to save space.

archive – 1. (verb) The act of backing up files for future reference.
2. (noun) The file that contains compressed stored files. Specialized computers and web sites may also contain archives.
SEE: FEATURE BOX

archive site – A computer or web site that is dedicated to file storage, which makes such files available for download. Also called an *FTP site*. The files can be accessed and downloaded through e-mail or *anonymous FTP*.

ARCnet – **See:** **A**ttached **R**esource **C**omputer **N**etwork

areal density – The amount of data that can be stored on one square inch of hard drive. Usually expressed in billions of bits per square inch. Hard drives with higher areal densities can store more information than those with lower areal densities.

argument – In programming, there are commands and arguments, e.g. in the phrase "goto file X" the command is "goto" and the argument tells the program where to go, i.e. file X.

Arithmetic Logic Unit (ALU) – Part of a computer's central processing unit that performs arithmetic operations such as adding, subtracting, and either/or options, which form the basis of most operations within the machine.

.arj – *File extension* used for archive files created with the ARJ compression program.

ARP – **See:** **A**ddress **R**esolution **P**rotocol

ARPANet – **See:** **A**dvanced **R**esearch **P**rojects **A**gency **Net**work

array – An ordered list or table of data used within database and spreadsheet programs. Each piece of data (element) within the array has a numbered location.

arrow keys – Arrow keys are used for moving the cursor in the indicated direction. They have a wider range of uses if combined with keys such as ctrl and alt.

---

archive

Most applications on computers have archive facilities, which enable you to store old data in a compressed format and recall it for later use.

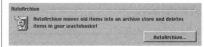

This autoarchive from Outlook Express enables the user to store old e-mails as a backup and to delete unwanted items from the wastebasket.

article – 1. A news or e-zine story. 2. A submission to a Usenet discussion group, which can be sent by e-mail.

artificial intelligence (AI) – The branch of computer science engaged in the quest to build computers that can make decisions similar to those made by the human brain. One example is the IBM super-computer Deep Blue that challenged world chess champion Gary Kasparov to a chess game and defeated him.

ascender – In typography, refers to the portion of a lowercase letter that extends above the main body (x-height) of the letter. The letters "b," "d," and "f" all have ascenders, whereas "a" does not.

SEE ALSO: DESCENDER

ASCII – **A**merican **S**tandard **C**ode for **I**nformation **I**nterchange. Numerical coding system representing keyboard characters with numbers, e.g. A=65, a=97. The computer translates this into a 7-digit binary number such as 0101010. The first 128 numbers are standardized; the remaining 128 (the extended character set) are assigned to symbols and foreign letters. These are subject to some variation.

ASCII art – Designs drawn using only ASCII characters, found in text-based formats lacking more complicated graphic images; e.g. *emoticons*.

ASCII file – A file comprising data in ASCII characters and containing no formating instructions such as line breaks or bold text. Many programs provide an option allowing files to be saved as ASCII files. This can be useful for document transfer if programs prove to be incompatible, but formating instructions are likely to be lost.

ASF – **See:** **A**dvanced **S**treaming **F**ormat

.asf – A file extension that indicates the file has been created using *Advanced Streaming format.*

ASIC – **See:** **A**pplication **S**pecific **I**ntegrated **C**ircuit

Ask Jeeves! – A popular *search engine* that uses an imaginary butler – Jeeves – as a non-threatening way to search the Web.
GO TO: www.ask.com

.asp – A *file extension* that indicates that the file is generated by the system called *Active Server Page* and will contain *hypertext links*.

ASP – 1. **See:** **A**ctive **S**erver **P**age 2. **See:** **A**pplication **S**ervice **P**rovider

Aspect Ratio – The ratio of width to height. It is used in graphics so that an image that has a ratio of 2:1 is twice as wide as it is high.

assembler – A program that converts word-based *assembly language* into numerical *machine language*.

assembly language – Programming language that uses word-type commands to give precise instructions to the computer. The assembler then translates this into numerical codes (*machine language*) that the computer can translate into operations. Mostly used for systems software such as device drivers.
SEE ALSO: ASSEMBLER

assign – To provide a document with a name or password.
SEE ALSO: INTERNET ASSIGNED NUMBERS AUTHORITY

associate – Some *applications* have specific *file extensions* saved automatically as part of the document name; e.g. .doc is the file extension for Microsoft Word files. This associates the file with the program called Word so that when the file is opened the operating system automatically opens Word with the file.

Association for Computing Machinery (ACM) – An American trade association that attracts information technologists from both academia and industry.

asterisk – The * or star key. It commonly indicates a footnote. In e-mail, it is sometimes used emphatically as a substitute for italics.

Asymmetric Cryptography – A type of cryptography in which each user has two keys: a public key and a private key. Text is encrypted using the recipient's public key and decrypted using his private key. The advantage is that no one but the owner has access to the private key.

Asymmetric Digital Subscriber Line (ADSL) – High-speed transmission using a conventional, but upgraded, telephone line enabling simultaneous network connection and telephone use. It is asymmetric in that it can receive larger quantities of data than it can transmit (typically up to 9 Mbps and 640Kbps, respectively). Since it also provides an always-on service, there is no need to dial-up the server.

asynchronous – Communication between two devices that does not rely on a timed interval between the transmission of data. A telephone conversation is asynchronous in that either person can speak at any time. Abbreviated to ASYNC.
SEE ALSO: SYNCHRONOUS

Asynchronous Transfer Mode (ATM) – A very fast method of sending data via the Internet. It makes *real time video conferencing* possible.

AT – **A**dvance **T**echnology. Originally referred to IBM's Advanced Technology personal computer but now refers to any compatible computer using a 16-bit or 32-bit processor.

AT Attachment (ATA) – A specification for a hard drive in which the controller is part of the drive. The controller is the link that enables communication between the computer and other devices such as the CD-ROM drive. In some systems, the controller is found on the *motherboard*.

AT Attachment Packet Interface (ATAPI) – A type of electronic driver or interface used to connect CD-ROMs and other devices with the AT computer.

AT command set – The commands used to control a modem designed by Hayes Corporation. These have become industry standard and are used by all Hayes-compatible modems.

Athlon – The trademarked name of a series of powerful processors from AMD.
Go to: www.amd.com

ATL – See: **A**ctive **T**emplate **L**ibrary

ATM – See: **A**synchronous **T**ransfer **M**ode

at sign – See: @

Attached Resource Computer (ARC) – A computer attached to the *Attached Resource Computer Network*.

Attached Resource Computer Network (ARCnet) – A type of *local area network* (LAN) introduced in the 1960s that can connect up to 255 computers in a building. In this type of network, the computers cannot all send messages at the same time; they have to wait until it is their turn to hold the *token* that passes from computer to computer.
SEE ALSO: TOKEN RING

attachment – A file linked to and sent with an e-mail message. Attachments are usually added simply by clicking the e-mail program's attach button. A dialog box usually opens, allowing the user to choose the file to attach. Once clicked, the file becomes linked to the e-mail message. Warning: Beware of attachments from unknown senders since this is a common method of transmitting viruses.
SEE: FEATURE BOX

attachment

Attachments on e-mails are indicated by a paperclip icon next to the e-mail in the inbox within Microsoft Outlook.

The attached Word document appears as an icon at the end of the e-mail message text.

attack – This is when someone tries to violate computer security systems.

attributes – Used in *HTML* to provide information about the qualities of a command. In the command <BODY text = "blue">, the "blue" indicates the attribute of the body text.

ATX – A standard specification for a *motherboard* originally developed by Intel. It is suitable for multimedia PCs.

.au – A *file extension* format to indicate that the file was generated for the AU sound format.

auction – A type of online shopping web site where it is possible to bid for items for sale. The highest bid is displayed along with the object for sale and bidding continues until a specified date and time. Popular with antiques sites, it is also possible to bid for a range of items from computers to holidays. Users have to register with the site to be eligible to bid.
SEE ALSO: EBAY

audio – Sound production is an integral part of a *multimedia* computer system. Audio files can be downloaded from the Internet and decoded from *digital* to *analog* format via the sound card and played through attached speakers. Most Windows sound files have the file *extension* .wav.

audio Cards – **See: s**ound card

Audio Interchange File Format (AIFF) – A popular format for storing and playing sound. Originally developed by Apple Computers, it can now be used on PCs too. AIFF files generally end with a .AIF or .IEF

audio streaming – This is when sound is played immediately, as it is downloading from the Internet, rather than being stored in file form first. Streaming requires a fast computer and connection.

audioconferencing – This is a type of teleconferencing in real time that uses sound communication.

audiographic teleconferencing – Similar to *audioconferencing,* but the voice connection is supplemented by an electronic whiteboard.

audit trail – Information about the use of a computer can be ascertained from the system log. This can help determine whether there have been breaches in security or can provide information relating to client or employee use.

auditor – Independent company that monitors and tracks the use of *banner ads* on the Internet.

AUP – **See: A**cceptable **U**se **P**olicy

authentication – Verification of identity by means such as *passwords* and *digital signatures*; e.g. when entering a password to gain access to an *ISP*.

authenticator – A service that checks web site *digital signatures.* This is to guard against fake sites masquerading as those of genuine companies. This process happens automatically when visiting a secure site and is an important tool in preventing fraud, particularly on sites that accept credit card payments.

author – 1. (verb) To create a document or program.
2. (noun) The person who writes multimedia software programs.

Authoring software – A software program that can be used for creating multimedia and interactive pages, including features such as video and audio clips and animation. It is generally simpler to use than programming languages.
SEE ALSO: AUTHORING TOOL

Authoring tool – A collection of *tools* that help the user to link objects to create multimedia applications. They are similar to programing tools but are simpler to use. Used by non-programmers.

authorization – After a site has asked for authentication, it checks the password or digital signature. If it receives the correct information in response, it grants access to the site.
SEE: FEATURE BOX

Authorware – See: Authoring tool

Auto-answer modem – A modem that accepts telephone calls and automatically establishes a connection.

auto-bot – An automatic function that has been set up by the user, such as the regular monitoring of share prices.

Autobyetel – A leading online seller of automobiles.
GO TO: www.autobytel.com

AutoCAD – A Computer-aided Design (CAD) program for mechanical engineering produced by Autodesk Inc.

Autoexec.bat – Short for Automatically Executing Batch File. A DOS file that runs when the computer is started up and tells the system which programs to run, as well as loading the mouse driver and a number of other essential drivers, and configuring the serial ports, and others.

authorization

Two entries are usually required in a password authorization box: name and password. For Internet access a domain name is also required.

Enter Password	
User Name:	nnnbbvv
Domain Name:	mkkjjnn
Password:	●●●●●●

| OK | Cancel | Change Password... |

A typical authorization dialog box with the user's password hidden for security purposes.

Automatic baud rate detection –
When a signal is sent to the computer, this automatic process enables it to determine its speed and code type. This makes it possible to receive different types of data without delay.

Automatically executed batch file –
See: Autoexec.bat

autonomous agent – **See:** agent

auto-redial – A function within a modem that enables the modem to continue attempting to establish a connection after a failed attempt.

autoreply – A function within e-mail programs that automatically sends a message to anyone who mails the user. This is a useful way of sending people a customized message or informing them that their e-mail is not being ignored, but that the user is out of the office.

autosave – Some programs save data to the disk every few minutes, without being given a command. This can be set up in *Preferences,* and the user can specify how frequently the work is to be saved.

autosizing – The ability of a monitor to enlarge or reduce an image to fit the space available while retaining the *aspect ratio* of the image.

Autotrace – A program that converts *bitmap* to *vector* graphics.

AUX – Short for **Aux**iliary device. Printers, scanners, and modems are auxiliary devices. They perform a specific function but are not part of the essential workings of a computer. They are connected to the computer by the auxiliary ports.

auxiliary storage – Storage that is external to the hard drive; e.g. disk or tape.

availability – The amount of time a network or a connection is running. For example, if a connection were available for only 45 minutes within a 60-minute period, availability would be 75 per cent.

Avatar – A graphic image representing the participant in a three-dimensional game or chat room. The form the avatar takes is chosen by the user, and is often a cartoon-type character or an animal.
SEE ALSO: MUD

AVI file – **A**udio **V**ideo **I**nterleaved is a Microsoft multimedia *file format* similar to *QuickTime.* It enables audio and video material to be downloaded from a web site and played on the computer.

awk – A programming language for *UNIX* and *DOS.*

AWT – **A**bstract **W**indows **T**oolkit. It is used to create *Java* applications using small images or *icons.* It is very flexible since it will work in conjunction with Windows, Macintosh, and UNIX.

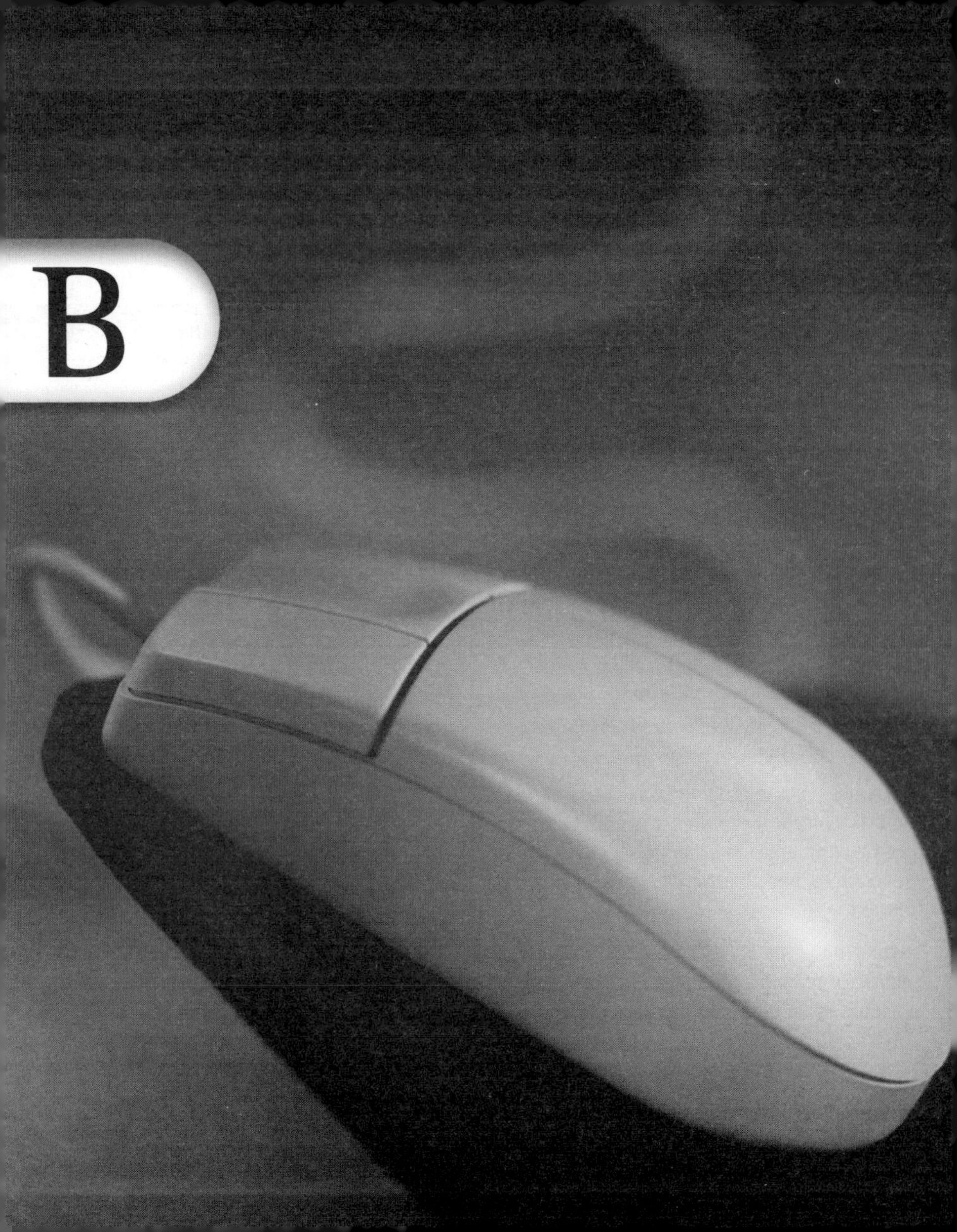
B

b2b - **B**usiness to **b**usiness. Online business and business commerce.

b2c - **B**usiness to **c**onsumer. This is used in electronic commerce for transactions from the business to the customer; for instance, e-shopping.

Babbage, Charles - Born 1791 in Devon, England, died 1871. Acknowledged as the "Father of Computing" for his contributions to the basic design of the computer.

BABT - **B**ritish **A**pproval **B**oard For **T**elecommunications. BABT is a UK-based international company that provides a comprehensive suite of compliance and certification services to help suppliers bring radio and telecommunications terminal equipment to the market. It also helps e-mail operators ensure that their billing systems are accurate.

Baby AT - This style of computer *motherboard,* used up to 1998, is now largely defunct.

back - To return to a previous *web page.*

back button - The back button, available on nearly all web *browsers,* enables you to return to a previous *web page.*
SEE: FEATURE BOX

back door - This provides a means of access to a program, online service or entire computer system. Sometimes known only by the original *programmer,* and intended

for servicing purposes, this "trap door" has the potential for more sinister uses.

back end - A *programming* term that can describe any *software* performing the final stage in a process, or a task not apparent to the user.

back up - Describes the process of making a copy of a *file* or *program* and storing it in a special *archive* directory or on a *CD-ROM, floppy disk, tape,* or other storage device. The aim is to prevent data from being lost or corrupted due to hardware or software problems.

backbone - This provides one of the main connections or pathways that make up the body of the global Internet, carrying high volumes of Internet traffic at high speed over huge distances.

---

back button

This is the *back* button for Microsoft Explorer. When you click this button, the browser returns you to the web page that you were viewing immediately before the current one.

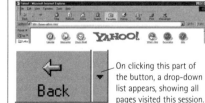

On clicking this part of the button, a drop-down list appears, showing all pages visited this session.

backbone site – A type of web site that processes a large amount of the Internet traffic carried along the *backbone*.
SEE ALSO: INTERNET BACKBONE

background – 1. The area of the screen display that is not covered by characters and graphics.
2. A program run "behind the scenes" so that you can do something else while it is running. E.g. Printing in the background.
SEE ALSO: FOREGROUND

backlit – This describes the "lit from behind" effect used by most *LCD* (liquid crystal display) screens.

backplane – A *circuit board* containing sockets into which other circuit boards can be plugged.

backslash – The backslash character "\" used to separate *directory* names, *components,* and *file* names in Windows. Either a forwardslash or backslash can be used in URLs. Unix uses a forward slash.

backspace – To go back one space, deleting the preceding character.

backspace key – This *keyboard* key causes the *cursor* to move backward one character space, deleting the preceding character.

backtracking – 1. The process of retracing your steps; e.g. to use a web browser to see web pages you have previously visited.
SEE ALSO: BACK BUTTON

2. This is an *algorithmic* way of solving a series of problems. The first problem must be solved before the others can be tackled based on its solution. Backtracking ends when there are no more solutions to the first problem.

backup copy – 1. Files that have been copied for reference or security. The most efficient and cost-effective procedures, hardware, and software for storing backup copies of data (and then restoring them when necessary) have been a computer industry preoccupation since the first computer crashed and data was lost.
2. To copy over files for safekeeping.

backward compatible – This refers to something being compatible with earlier models or versions of the same product. In other words, if a new version of a *program* or computer is said to be backward compatible, it means it can use software, files, and data created with an older version of the same program or model.

bacteria – This type of *computer virus* contains programs that carry out memory intensive operations within the operating system. The bacteria replicate as they work, so that eventually the computer is overwhelmed with them, and either crashes or becomes very slow. Bacteria are also sometimes called *rabbits*.

bad sector – A part of a *disk* that cannot be used, probably because it is flawed.

bak file – A *file* with a BAK extension. The bak extension indicates that the file is one that has been automatically backed up.
SEE ALSO: BACK UP

balance – 1. The matching of computer *tools* to jobs so that the structure of the computer system matches both the structure of the organization and the functions of the work.
2. In sound systems, balance refers to the relationship of the output of the left and right speakers.

balloon help – Pop-up displays that resemble small cartoon speech bubbles. These appear on screen if you leave the *cursor* over a *button* without *clicking* it in certain programs. Also called "tooltips."
SEE: FEATURE BOX

bandwidth – The information-carrying volume of a cable, signal (or even a person) over time. At higher bandwidths more data is transmitted at faster speed. *Congestion* and slow rates of response are often caused by high demands on the bandwidth.

bandwidth junkie – A bandwidth user who is determined to get the fastest connections over the Internet using the latest technology.

bang – Refers to the exclamation point (!), especially as used in *chat room* postings.

bang address – An *e-mail address* that takes the form of john@dk.server.net,

where John is the username, dk is the site name, and server.net is the domain name. This is used by some *Internet Service Providers* to provide a single account with multiple users.

Bank Internet Payment System – This *protocol* is used for sending secure payment instructions to banks over the Internet. It uses XML (*Extensible Markup Language*), and is overseen by The Financial Services Technology Consortium (FSTC).

banner – The web page banner is typically a long narrow box containing a *hyperlink* to another *web site*. Banners are most commonly used for advertising.

---

balloon help

An example of balloon help from the Apple system. It asks the user a question. The user can choose to have further help or tips, or to close the window and proceed without help.

What would you like to do?

The Office Assistant cannot currently answer your questions. Run Setup again to make sure all the necessary Help files are correctly installed.

● ¦See a complete list of help topics¦

| ● Tips | ● Options | ● Close |

banner ad – This kind of advertisement, usually rectangular, is used on many kinds of commercial web sites. It can commonly act as a single click transfer to the site belonging to the banner ad sponsors and/or creator. Most banner ads contain graphics, which can be annoying for the user as they may take time to download.
SEE: FEATURE BOX

bar code – A code represented by sets of parallel bars of varying thickness, that are read optically by transverse scanning. Businesses use a bar code as a universal product code (UPC) on retail items. It can also be used to control videodisc playback.

bar graph – A kind of graph in which data is shown in horizontal or vertical bands.

bare metal – A new or stripped computer that has no *operating system*. Sometimes it is necessary to go back to bare metal to deal with *hardware* glitches.

barf mail – (slang) E-mail that has been *bounced* by the delivery system. Often the message has been sent along a number of different pathways and has blocks of pathway *codes* at the head of the message. Barf is US slang for vomit.

Barney page – (slang) A *web page* that has been developed in response to a trend or incident. The reference is to the Barney doll, which led upon release to a huge number of bandwagon web sites.

base – The minimum specifications on which a system or *program* can run. Games may state minimum 16Mb Ram, 5mb free hard drive in order to run effectively.

base address – Data stored at a fixed, numerical address in the computer's hard drive. Also known as absolute address.

base memory – In IBM-type PCs this refers to the first 640Mb of memory that is available for standard *DOS* programs. Also called *conventional memory*.
SEE ALSO: EXTENDED MEMORY, UPPER MEMORY

banner ad

This shows a typical banner advertisement, appearing at the top of a web page. Clicking on this ad will usually take you to the site for the relevant company or organization.

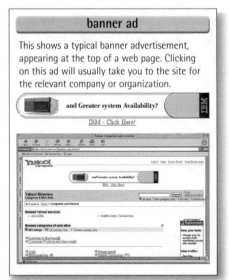

baseband transmission – This is one method of transmitting *digital* information over short distances, often in local *e-mails*. The signal is carried by a single cable taking the complete *bandwidth* to transmit.
SEE ALSO: BROADBAND

baseline – 1. In typography, it is the imaginary line on which characters sit.
SEE ALSO: X-HEIGHT
2. A version of a piece of software that has been made public as opposed to one that has yet to be released.

BASIC – **B**eginner's **A**ll-Purpose **S**ymbolic **I**nstruction **C**ode (BASIC) was developed by John Kemeney and Thomas Kurtz in the mid 1960s. One of the earliest and simplest high-level computer *programming languages,* it is still widely used. There are many different versions; e.g. Microsoft's Visual Basic.
SEE: FEATURE BOX

basic rate interface – This version of *Integrated Services Digital Network* (ISDN) owes its popularity to its use of standard telephone jacks.

bastion host – One way to protect a *secure e mail* from attack is to placc a bastion computer inbetween the e-mail and the Internet. That way any unwanted transmissions have to negotiate their way through the bastion's security systems before reaching the e-mail.
SEE ALSO: FIREWALL

batch – The method of grouping together several *files* into a single batch. Batched files are are often *compressed* for simultaneous transmission.

batch file – This is usually an ASCII text file (in other words, a plain text file) that contains a series of DOS commands and program names. These commands and programs are launched sequentially when the batch file is launched. Batch files have the .bat extension; e.g. the AUTOEXEC.BAT file contains all the necessary configuration and set-up commands for an IBM-compatible computer, and it automatically runs when the computer is started up.

BASIC

This screen shows the user the first window of the QBasic Interpreter created by Microsoft. The user needs to press the escape key in order to hide the dialog box and start programming. There are many tutorials on the Internet, which can help to teach BASIC programming.
GO TO: www.basicusers.net

batch processing – When a number of similar tasks are collected and processed together. This is often done so that jobs that use the computer for a long time can be done when the computer is no longer needed for more urgent tasks; e.g. in an office, printing of documents may be done in the evening.

bat file – **See:** batch file

battery pack – The power unit on a *laptop* computer. A user may have two battery packs, one in use and the other recharging or charged and ready for use.

baud – The unit of measurement (technically one "line-state change" per second) for the speed at which data is transferred over the Internet. Bits per second (bps) is now more common usage. The higher the baud rate the faster the connection.

baud barf – (slang) When random letters and numbers appear on the monitor due to a fault in transmission. (Barf is US slang for vomit.)

baud rate – **See:** baud

baudy language – Using large numbers of acronyms and emoticons in *e-mail* and *chat rooms*.

bay – Bays are slots on a computer's housing *floppy* disk or *CD-ROM* drives. Also called drive bay.

bayonet mechanism – The coupling mechanism found in the BNC connector. This is a plug and socket connection found in many communications devices
SEE ALSO: COAXIAL CABLE

B B C i   BBCi – The British Broadcasting
Corporation's vast and ever-expanding web site is one of the most visited in the world; it covers a very broad range of the corporation's vast number of activities and offers much by way of information and links to other sites. Large areas are devoted to BBC News, Television, Radio, Weather, Sports, and localized information, as well as the opportunity for users to communicate with each other and the BBC.
GO TO: www.bbc.co.uk

bbs – **See:** Bulletin Board System

bcc – Blind carbon copy. In *e-mail* correspondence a message can be sent simultaneously to a number of people other than the principal recipient. Those people in receipt of a bcc will be unable to see the names and addresses of other persons receiving this message; just their own and the sender's address. In this way the principal recipient will not know that any other people have been copied into the same message.
SEE ALSO: CC

bcd – **See:** Binary-Coded Decimal

b-channel – See: **B**earer Channel

bean – See: JavaBean

bearer channel – In *Integrated Services Digital Network (ISDN)* cabling, there are two types of wires, one of which is called the bearer channel. This is used as the main channel for transmitting data. The other wire (the D-channel) is used for sending control information.

 Beenz.com – An online "e-cash" currency venture that issued virtual "beenz" to consumers, which they were then able to trade for specific goods on the Internet. Go to: www.beenzboard.com

beep code – This is the audio signal emitted by a computer to announce the result of a short diagnostic test that the computer performs when it is being booted up. This is also called *Power-On-Self-Test* or *POST*.

Bell Standards – A set of *modem* standards created by AT&T. The standards describe the speed of the modems in *bits per second*, whether the machine has both originate and answer capabilities, the type of transmission, and line specifications.

bells and whistles – (slang) Extra features beyond basic functionality. Usually refers to features that will be added later.
SEE ALSO: VAPORWARE

below the fold – An area of a *web page* not visible on screen at any given time. This reference is to broadsheet newspapers when part of the story was obscured on the other side of the fold of the paper.

benchmark – A specific test with numerical results that allows hardware or software to be compared. E.g. TPC-C is a common database performance test.

benchmarking – Using *benchmarks* to compare the performance of one system or program with that of another.

BEOS – A personal computer *operating system* designed for the *multimedia applications* of the future, requiring fast handling of streaming video, games, etc.

Beowulf – When several smaller computers are linked to provide the computing power of one large supercomputer, these are referred to as "Beowulf clusters." Beowulf was the hero of an Anglo-Saxon poem.

Beowulf Project – The first Beowulf system developed by a contractor to NASA in the mid 1990s.
Go to: www.beowulf.org

Berkeley Internet Name Domain (BIND) – A *domain name server* that records the physical addresses and *domain names* of computers using the Internet. Although generally surpassed, it was once the most widely used DNS server software server.

Berners-Lee, Tim – British scientist credited with the invention of *Hyper Text Mark-up Language* and hence the creation of the World Wide Web, writing the first web browser-editor and server in 1990.

Bernoulli box – A removable *floppy disk drive* for personal computers. Named after the Swiss mathematician Daniel Bernoulli (1700–1782), who described the airfoil principle: that pressure in a fluid decreases with the rate of flow. This has been applied to the design of transportable disk drives.

best-effort service – This describes an Internet service that makes no guarantees regarding speed of transmission, or even that data will be delivered in part or in full.

beta bugs – Problems found in the *beta testing* phase of *software* development.

beta testing – This term describes the secondary market testing of software. The software is tested in a real-life situation by a small group of people so that problems and comments are addressed before general release.
SEE ALSO: ALPHA TESTING

beta version – An early version of software not yet sold on general release. Beta versions are prone to *beta bugs*.
SEE ALSO: BETA TESTING

beyond the banner – An Internet term that refers to types of advertising other than *banner ads*.

Bezier curve – A graphic element consisting of two anchor points and vector values, rather than a *bitmap*.
SEE: FEATURE BOX
SEE ALSO: VECTOR

Bezos, Jeff – Jeff Bezos is the founder and CEO of *Amazon*, the online bookseller.

BFT – See: **B**inary **F**ile **T**ransfer

BGP – See: **B**order **G**ateway **P**rotocol

bible – In computer terms, this is usually considered to be the most authoritative book for an operating system, programming language, or application.

bid – To place a bid in an online *auction*.

Bezier curve

A Bezier curve (named after the French mathematician Pierre Bezier) is a curved line frequently used in computer graphics.

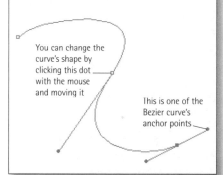

You can change the curve's shape by clicking this dot with the mouse and moving it

This is one of the Bezier curve's anchor points

bid shielding – This describes a system of deceptive bidding that is used to preserve a low *bid* in an online auction. Bid shielding takes three people to operate. The first places a low bid and the other two place higher bids and keep bidding with the intention of eliminating all other legitimate parties. At the last minute, the two higher bidders drop out, leaving the low bid to win. Auction sites try to monitor and reject such activities.
SEE ALSO: AUCTION

bidirectional – This refers to a capability to transmit signals in both directions. It is a term that is frequently used to describe a standard enhanced *parallel port*, which supports bidirectional communication between the PC and devices such as a printer or scanner.

Biff – (verb) To acknowledge the arrival of an *e-mail*.

Big Blue – (slang) A nickname for *IBM*, referring to the blue and white logo on its early mainframes and still on its corporate advertising. Not to confused with Deep Blue, the computer that beat chess champion Garry Kasparov in a televised game.
SEE ALSO: ARTIFICIAL INTELLIGENCE

Big Endian – This is a *programming* detail for the order of bytes (8bits) within "words" (16bits) in a computer instruction. Big endian has the most significant byte first. *Little endian* has least significant byte first.

binary – This numerical system has a base of two, i.e. it uses only the digits 0 and 1. This is the basis of all computer operations. The binary digits are translated into charged and non-charged states, which are easy for the computer to recognize and for which electronic circuitry can be easily developed.

binary-coded decimal – A *binary* number system in which each digit in decimal notation is represented by four digits in binary notation. Hence the number one is represented by 0001 and multiple sets of four-digit groupings are used to represent larger numbers, In this way, ten is represented by 0001 0000.

binary digit – **See:** bit

binary file – A binary file contains data stored in *binary format*.

binary file transfer – By this method, a *binary file* is sent from one location to another. The data must be transferred byte by byte into characters before transmission, then transferred on arrival back into binary.

binary format – A non-text file that has its data reduced to *binary* coding, e.g. sound files. The computer can read this format, but it is unintelligible to people.

binary large object – A *database field* that holds any unstructured binary information, including images, audio, and video; shortened to BLOB.

binary newsgroup – This kind of Internet newsgroup is designed to let computer users post graphics on the Internet. Since most newsgroups only handle text, graphics *files* are converted to text-based *UU-encoded* format, which most *browsers* have built into their system. These files can then be downloaded and converted to their original format for storing on disk. These newsgroups belong to the alt.binaries category.

binary number – This is a number stored in *binary* form. One byte (8 bits) can express the values 0 to 255; while two contiguous bytes (16 bits) express values from 0 to 65,535.

---

binary tree

This shows a binary tree: a data structure that clearly resembles the structure that is usually applied to a family tree. There are two "children" for each single "parent."

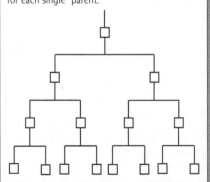

---

binary tree – This is a data structure resembling a family tree. Each node contains one "parent" and a maximum of two "children."
SEE: FEATURE BOX

bind – To link together two *program files* to facilitate an operation; e.g. there are bindings between an *e-mail* and the modem. These can be seen in the Windows e-mail control panel where the TCP/IP is also bound to the dial-up adapter for Internet connection via modem.

BIND – See: Berkeley Internet Name Domain

binder – As part of the *Microsoft* Office Suite, the binder allows documents to be viewed, opened, saved, e-mailed, and printed as a group.

BINHEX – Short for **BIN**ary **HEX**adecimal. This provides a method for converting non-text files (non-ASCII) such as spreadsheets and graphics into *ASCII* for transmission via a modem. Some *e-mail programs* are only capable of working with ASCII. Files that have been converted into BinHex will have the HQX extension.

biometrics – Describes the biological identification of a person, which includes eyes, voice, handprints, fingerprints, and the use of written signatures. Biometrics is a more secure form of *authentication* than using passwords.

BIOS – **B**asic **I**nput **O**utput **S**ystem. These are the instructions that automatically run when the computer is booted-up. The system is stored on a *chip* and is held in the *ROM* (read only memory). It runs the basic functions of the computer, e.g. managing the drivers and the keyboard.

bis – Bis means twice in Latin and encore in French and is generally used for the second version of something. Similarly, ter is third.

B-ISDN – **See: B**roadband and **ISDN**

BIST – **B**uilt-**I**n **S**elf-**T**est. This is an automatic self-testing procedure that is performed by the computer on booting-up.

bisync – **See:** bisynchronous transmission

bisynchronous transmission – This kind of communication requires that both devices - the sending device and the receiving device - should transmit in timed or synchronized intevals.
SEE ALSO: ASYNCHRONOUS, SYNCHRONOUS

bit – A single digit in *binary* numeration. A bit will either be 0 or 1. Information is stored in the computer in multiples of eight bits, which are referred to as one *byte*.
SEE ALSO: BINARY NUMBER

bit bucket – This is the imaginary location where all missing data (such as lost *e-mail)* ends up.
SEE ALSO: E-MAIL NEVER NEVERLAND

bit depth – A *coding* system that uses numerical values to represent something in terms of bits. Most frequently used to refer to the number of bits required to hold a *pixel*. The bit depth determines the number of colors that can be displayed on the monitor where High color is referred to as 16-bits and True color as 24 or 32 bits.
SEE ALSO: COLOR DEPTH

bit error rate – The average number of *bits* that are transmitted in error.

bite – **See:** byte

bitmap – A bitmap is an image made up of thousands of *pixels* (dots), each with its own position and qualities such as color and brightness stored in the bitmap file.
SEE: FEATURE BOX

---

bitmap

This image, when seen on a web site, is a bitmap. If you look at it closely enough, you will see the differently shaded dots or pixels that combine to make up the whole picture.

---

bitmapped font – A font consisting of rows and columns of *pixels* is called a bitmapped font. Such fonts are very simple to use but come in fixed sizes. Increasing the size of a bitmapped font results in seeing the individual dots and jagged edges of the type.
SEE ALSO: TRUETYPE FONTS, which are drawn mathematically.

bitmapped graphics – These kinds of graphics are images that are drawn by using bitmaps. For example, the *Microsoft Paint* program that is found in *Microsoft Windows* creates bitmap images. This is a very easy graphic format for computers to manage, so it is popular with Internet applications. *Files* storing bitmap images usually have *.bmp, .gif, .jpeg,* or *.tiff file extensions*.
SEE ALSO: VECTOR GRAPHICS

Bitnet – Similar to the Internet, Bitnet was developed in the 1980s to connect academics' computers for the exchange of *e-mail*. Although it has been upgraded and has links with the Internet, it is now generally superseded.

bit-rate – The speed at which a *modem* or any similar device functions. The bit rate is most commonly measured in bits per second (bps); this refers to the number of individual bits that are processed in any one second by the computer's processor.

bitstorm – This occurs at certain times when there is a high volume of transmission on the Internet causing a slowing down in communications.

bit-stuffing – The process of adding *bits* to a transmitted message. It can be useful, for instance, to break up a string of *data* bits that could be misunderstood as *control codes*.

bitwise – Operator *programming* commands or statements that work with individual *bits* rather than in *bytes*.

Bix – An online *database* of computer information containing hardware, software, and help with computer-based problems. Originally an off-shoot of Byte Magazine.

biz – Biz is the name of one of the Internet *newsgroup* top-level categories (or hierarchies). Biz is the place for postings for business news (particularly computer industry-related). Other top newsgroup hierarchies include alt, soc, sci, and rec.

black box – Any hardware or software to be treated as an opaque component.

black hat – (slang) A *hacker* who breaks into a computer system with the intention of causing damage or stealing information.
SEE ALSO: WHITE HAT

black hole – An imaginary location that sucks in lost e-mails and files.
SEE ALSO: EMAIL NEVER NEVERLAND

Black Screen of Death – A *Windows 95* error that causes the screen to turn black and the computer to lock up. The only solution is to reboot.
SEE ALSO: BLUE SCREEN OF DEATH

black widow – Usually a Java Applet that is embedded in a web page and performs unwanted, high memory tasks on the computer, compromising its performance.

blackout – A complete loss of power to the computer.
SEE ALSO: BOZO LIST

blank character – The single space blank character is formed by hitting the space bar on the keyboard.

blatherer – Someone who sends long, detailed, and rambling messages, *e-mails,* or contributions to a *chat room.*

bleed – In printing, this refers to printing to the very edge of the paper. It cannot be achieved on many printers since they leave a white border at the edges of the page.

bleeding edge – It is said to be bleeding edge when a company launches a device or *software* release which is at the leading edge of technology, and its success could make or break the company.

blendo – A page on which there are far too many features and distractions, such as flashing graphics, ad banners, video, and sound clips.

blind carbon copy – See: Bcc

b-list – See: Bozo List

bloatware – (slang) This generally refers to computer *software* that is very sluggish and slow to run or that takes up too much memory because it has too many functions or capabilities.

BLOB – See: Binary Large Object

block – 1. To *select* a piece of text or graphic image in order to perform an operation such as cut and paste, spell-check, shrink, or enlarge on that text or image. 2. A combination of files or data that is transmitted or processed as a single unit. 3. To sit idle while waiting for something.
SEE: FEATURE BOX

---

block

This shows an area of blocked text in a larger area of text. The blocked area can now be copied, deleted, formatted, or moved – depending on the program being used.

Lorem ipsum dolor sit amet, consectetuer adipiscing elit, sed diam nonummy nibh euismod tincidunt ut laoreet dolore magna aliquam erat volutpat. Ut wisi enim ad minim veniam, quis nostrud exerci tation ullamcorper suscipit lobortis nisl ut aliquip ex ea commodo consequat. Duis autem vel eum iriure dolor in hendrerit in vulputate velit esse molestie consequat, vel illum dolore eu feugiat nulla facilisis at. Lorem ipsum dolor sit amet, consectetuer adipisc

block move – To move a *selected* piece of text or image.

block protect – To fix together all the elements within a *block* so that the items cannot be manipulated separately.

blocker – **See:** filter

blocking software – *Software* that prevents a user from gaining access to certain web sites; e.g. this may be used to limit the risk of seeing sites featuring adult material. Most blocking software works by recognizing provided keywords and blocking those sites that contain the words.

---

body

The boxes at the top of the screen display the sender, recipient, and the subject line of the e-mail. The bulk text displayed in the remainder of the e-mail is referred to as the body text.

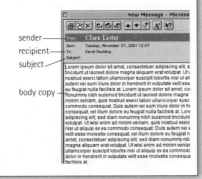

sender
recipient
subject

body copy

---

blow away – To remove *directories* and/or *files* from the computer's *memory*, usually by accident.

Blue Screen of Death – 1. A Windows NT error that causes the screen to turn blue and the computer to lock up. The only solution is to reboot.
2. A Windows 95 crash where the *error message* is displayed in DOS characters on a blue background.
SEE ALSO: BLACK SCREEN OF DEATH

Bluemountain.com – A web site offering *e-greeting* cards for all occasions. The cards used to be free, but, due to overwhelming popularity for e-greeting cards, the site has started charging users for the privilege of sending them.
GO TO: www.bluemountain.com

Blue Mountain™

Bluetooth – A technology from the Bluetooth Special Interest Group that enables wireless connections in a *personal area network* (PAN). It allows the user to link their mobile phone, handheld computer, and other handheld devices - as well as providing Internet access - all without wires. It works by using radio waves. Bluetooth users can also exchange information with each other.
GO TO: www.bluetooth.com

.bmp – The *file extension* to indicate that the data, usually a graphic object, is in *bitmap* format.

board – A *sound card* or *graphics card* consists of circuitry fitted onto a *printed circuit* board.

boat anchor – (slang) 1. Hardware that has creased to function.
2. A person who takes up space but contributes nothing.

Bob – A general name for technical support personnel (a female may be called "Bobette"). It orginated at Demon Internet, where all such interactive staff are called Bob or Bobette.

Bobo the Web Monkey – An uncomplimentary term for an incompetent web designer.

body – 1. In e-mail, this is the main message in the text excluding any information such as sender, recipient address, server details, attachments, etc.
2. In HTML, this refers to main part of the text and is enclosed in a *tag* <BODY Text=green> to indicate that the main text is green.
SEE: FEATURE BOX

bogus – (slang) Something that does not work, is useless, or makes false claims.

boilerplate – A printing term to mean *template* or *style sheet*.

bold (boldface) – Heavy typeface is activated by pressing the B button on the *formatting toolbar*.
SEE: FEATURE BOX

bomb – (slang) When the computer crashes. Also called *ABEND*.

bookmark – 1. A function within a browser to note the *Uniform Resource Locator* (URL) of web sites to which the user intends to return. The user is then directed to that site immediately upon clicking the name in the bookmark. It works in the same way as physical bookmarks by keeping the user's place. The term bookmark is used by Netscape Navigator and is synonymous with *favorites* on Internet Explorer.
2. A trendy term for "I will make a note of that."

---

bold (boldface)

The letter A on the left is in bold, in contrast to the letter on the right. Most word-processing software enables the user to mark text as boldface. In Microsoft Word, the boldface option can be found in the format menu, or by pressing the B button on the toolbar.

bookramping – When an author or publisher writes favorable book reviews about their own work and sends them into an online bookseller for posting on the site.

Boolean – This term refers to a logical process that is used for a set of refining options that are usually applied when using a *search engine*. It is more regularly referred to as Boolean logic when applied to search engines for the Web. Boolean logic is based on mathematical principles developed by the nineteenth century English mathemetician *George Boole*.
SEE: FEATURE BOX

Boolean search – This describes the kind of search when the processes of Boolean algebra are applied to the refinement of a search on the Internet. By using AND, OR, and NOT the user can be more specific about what he or she does and does not want to find information about. For example, legs AND arms NOT furniture will produce information on arms AND legs but NOT chairs.

Boole, George – The nineteenth century British mathematician and logistician who created a branch of mathematics known as symbolic logic or Boolean algebra.

Boolean

Rather than relying on plain language searches, Boolean logic allows more advanced (and better targeted) searches. Simple queries are joined by "AND," "OR," and "NOT." To the right are shown the rules, or truth tables, for Boolean AND, OR, and NOT. This is graphically represented below using electronic switches.

IN	OUT
0	0
1	0
0	0
1	1

OR		
IN	IN	OUT
0	0	0
0	1	1
1	0	1
1	1	1

NOT	
IN	OUT
0	1
1	0

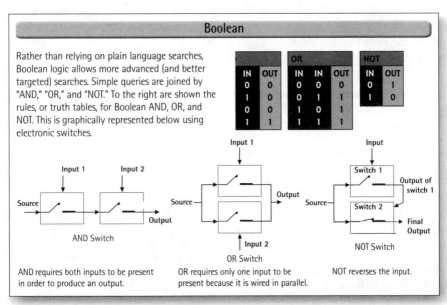

AND requires both inputs to be present in order to produce an output.

OR requires only one input to be present because it is wired in parallel.

NOT reverses the input.

boot – To switch on a computer. The system then automatically runs checks and loads the basic *operating system* to enable it to function in conjunction with the monitor, keyboard, printer, scanner, and all *peripheral devices*.
SEE ALSO: BIOS, AUTOEXEC.BAT, BOOT UP

boot diskette/floppy – A *floppy disk* that contains the *operating system* to load into the computer at start-up. It is most commonly used in association with *laptop* computers, many of which are configured to look for a bootable floppy in the A-drive at start-up.

boot virus – This is a *virus* that infects a computer when the computer is booted-up and may make it impossible for the user to start the computer.

boot up – To load and start the computer's *operating system*. This comes from the expression "to pull oneself up by one's bootstraps," and is often abbreviated simply to *boot*.

bootable disk – This disk contains the *boot-up* information that enables the computer to load the *operating system* on start-up. On most PCs, it is the hard drive that has sectors within it for storing booting-up information. Some *laptops* require a *boot disk/floppy*.

bootleg software – Describes illegally copied software.

bootstrap protocol – An Internet *protocol* used by a computer without its own disks for loading an *operating system* using e-mail from a distant computer.

border gateway protocol – This Internet *protocol* is used to find a route between the Internet and a smaller *subnet* such as an educational or government e-mail.

Borland – Borland is a leading technology provider and software developer. It was founded in 1983. Its headquarters are in California, and it has operations throughout the world.
GO TO: www.borland.com

Borland®

bot – (slang) This is a utility *program* that performs a routine task similar to and often indistinguishable from an *agent*. Bots are used by *search engines* as a means of finding information on the Internet. Bots follow the links found in *web pages*; they then report back in list form. Bot is derived from the term robot.

bottleneck – A bottleneck is a point in a process that causes the system to slow down or stop. For example, if an *ISP* runs Internet access at 56 Kbps but the user's *modem* only works at a maximum of 14.4 Kbps, then the slow modem could be said to be creating a bottleneck.

bounce – When an *e-mail* is returned to the sender, it is said to have bounced. Usually all or most of the original e-mail message is returned with the notification. A message usually provides the reason for the bounce, e.g. address not known, unable to find server.

bounding box – This box is used in graphics to limit the size and shape of the image that it contains. It usually consists of dotted or flashing lines when the object is *selected*. The box can be stretched, shrunk, or re-shaped as desired. The lines disappear once the object is deselected.
SEE: FEATURE BOX

---

bounding box

This bounding box contains two geometric shapes: a black circle and a dark rectangle, either of which can be resized. The enclosing box can be resized as necessary to contain the resized shapes.

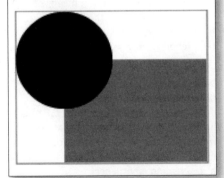

---

box – 1. This can describe a defined area, usually a rectangle, into which a text message or a discrete object of some kind can be placed.
2. A computer.

boxed processor – A computer.

Bozo filter – A filter run within an *e-mail* or *newsgroup program* that removes messages from specified people whose messages you do not wish to receive. These messages are either deleted or placed in a "Bozo folder."

Bozo list – People whose messages are removed by the *Bozo filter*. Also called the *kill file.*

bps – **B**its **p**er **s**econd. The number of *bits* transmitted per second.
SEE ALSO: BIT RATE

Bps – **B**ytes **p**er **s**econd. The number of *bytes* transmitted per second.

br – **See:** linebreak

braces – Braces is a term commonly applied to curly *brackets* {} that are found on the standard *keyboard*. Larger braces, of the kind that are used to link together two or more lines, are available on the drawing autoshape menu.

brackets – There are three bracket (or parentheses) types on a standard computer keyboard: rounded brackets ( ), square brackets [ ], and curly brackets or *braces* {}.

branding - The process of creating and making the public aware of a brand name or even the entire corporate identity.

break key - The break key on a computer keyboard can be used to stop some programs or applications when depressed with the Control key (ctrl). Also try Escape (esc) or ctrl-C.

breakpoint - 1. This is the place where an error occurs or where a process can suddenly stop.
2. De-bugging tools allow insertion of breakpoints in a program to stop and inspect at that point.

breath-of-life packet - An *ethernet data packet* that contains the boot-up information; sent out from a working computer to rescue a computer on *e-mail* that has crashed.

bricks-and-mortar - This phrase is frequently used to refer to the kind of organization that has a physical as well as a virtual presence.

bridge - A term for a hardware device that connects dissimilar networks. E.g. A bridge might connect a serial device to a USB port, or connect an ethernet to a token ring network.

briefcase - A handy desktop folder in which users can keep files such as text files, images, and DTP or Web documents for quick and easy access.

briefcase utility - This utility provides a quick way to compare, copy, and update *files* between a *laptop* computer and a main desktop *computer*, providing they are linked by a cable.

bring to front - When manipulating two graphic objects, this command enables one graphic to overlap the other - to bring it in front of the other. In *Word*, this is found on the drawing toolbar, draw option, order.

broadband - A transmission channel that can carry a large number of *signals* in a variety of formats simultaneously. A broadband connection improves the quality of sound and video particularly for multimedia transmissions.
SEE ALSO: BASEBAND TRANSMISSION

broadcast - When an *e-mail* or other kind of *data* is sent to a number of people on a mailing list simultaneously.
SEE ALSO: MULTI-CASTING, SPAM

broadcasting - The Web can be used to broadcast information, radio, sound, and audio-visual material regardless of the limitations of geography.
SEE ALSO: WEBCAST

brochureware - A non-existent product that is actively marketed.

broken hyperlink - This describes a kind of failed *hyperlink* owing either to the server being down or the page no longer being available.

broken pipe – This describes a failed *download* usually owing to an e-mail failure or overload. It originally referred to a *Netscape Navigator* failure, but now is used more generally.

brouter – A device that performs bridging or routing functions, depending on which is the best option for the transmission.
SEE ALSO: BRIDGE, ROUTE

brownout – A reduction in *AC* power that can cause damage to computer equipment.
SEE ALSO: BLACKOUT

browse – 1. To surf the Internet.
2. To look through *folders* to find the desired file.

---

bullet

Bullet points are useful tools for writing.
- They can be used to separate each point.
- This makes the list very clear.
- You can format your bullet points so that they appear as circles, squares, or even numbers.

Bullets are an extremely easy effect to create on the Web, as the following example shows when placed within the HTML code for a web page.

```
<UL>
    <LI>This is line one
    <LI>This is line two
    <LI>This is line three
</UL>
```

---

browser – An application for viewing and navigating the *World Wide Web*. The most commonly used are *Microsoft Internet Explorer* and *Netscape Navigator.*

browser compatibility – Not all web pages support all *browsers*, neither do web pages always look the same when viewed with different browsers. If an interactive web site fails to work, it is worth trying to operate it within a different browser.

browser wars – This refers to the battle between Microsoft *Internet Explorer* and *Netscape Navigator* for clients and supremacy of the web.

browserless web – The communication over the *World Wide Web* between *programs* rather than between people using *browsers*. It is anticipated that many of these will be automatic program-to-program applications such as ordering and fulfillment operations.

buddy lists – Such lists are a function within direct messaging systems such as *AOL* Instant Messenger. The user compiles a list of friends and can arrange to be notified when one of the users on that list is *logged on* to the system.

buffer – An area of *memory* used for holding *data* temporarily. The buffer can hold data being sent to a printer or being sent from a high-speed device to a low-speed device.

buffer overflow – When more *data* is transferred to the *buffer* than the buffer can handle.

bug – A *programming* error in a computer *program* that causes it to malfunction.
SEE ALSO: DEBUGGING

build – To construct a computer or device.

built-in function – A function that comes as part of a hardware device.

bulk – Often refers to e-mail, usually unsolicited e-mail, that is sent to a large number of people.
SEE ALSO: BROADCAST, SPAM

bullet – A large dot • often used for setting off each item in a list.
SEE: FEATURE BOX

bullet clicker – A derisory term for an inexperienced web user who clicks on *bullets* that are not responsive.

bulletin board system – A web site that displays messages sent on a topic or product. Similar to but simpler to run than a *newsgroup*, they are often run by companies to support their products or run on specialist subjects. Some support mailing facilities that enable users to e-mail one another. Others are run by computer user groups providing information and offering downloads of free *software*.
SEE: FEATURE BOX

bundled software – *Software* that comes free with the purchase of a new computer or other device.

burn – The process of writing *data* onto a *recordable CD-ROM*.

burn rate – The rate at which a new company is spending its capital while waiting to generate profits. The term is often seen in discussions about new Internet companies.

bus – Set of wires known as conductors connecting the functional components of a computer. Local buses connect items within the *CPU*; data buses carry data between the processor, memory, and the hard drive; address buses carry the memory address of data carried on the data bus; while other buses connect to peripheral devices and the memory. The term is used since buses travel various routes and have conductors.

---

bulletin board system

Bulletin board systems enable each participant to see the whole thread of a conversation, and to respond to any person in that thread.

↳Microwaves	Anonymous 02 Nov 01	REPLY
↳Microwaves	Anonymous 07 Nov 01	REPLY
↳microwaves	Anonymous 02 Nov 01	REPLY

This example from a specialist bulletin board shows a discussion in progress on microwaves.
Click on the underlined text to read the message and the reply button to reply to that message.

bus mouse – A type of *mouse* that is plugged into a computer's *expansion board* rather than into the more usual *serial port*.

bus network – A straightforward way of connecting computers and other devices on a *network* that is using a single transmission *pathway*.

bus speed – The speed at which *data* travels along a *bus*. Bus size and speed are independent – the size is the number of conductors, the speed is the clock frequency.

business to business – See: b2b

business to consumer – See: b2c

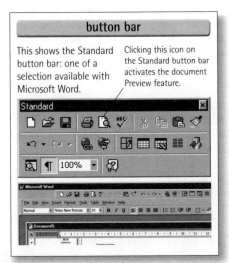

button bar

This shows the Standard button bar: one of a selection available with Microsoft Word.

Clicking this icon on the Standard button bar activates the document Preview feature.

business web transaction processing – This phrase describes a method by which businesses are able to interact, coordinate their services, and maintain integrity over the Web.
SEE ALSO: ON-LINE TRANSACTION PROCESSING

button – A small clickable *icon* or square on the computer screen that is used as a *shortcut* for a command.

button bar – A button bar is a shortcut *toolbar* that consists of a number of clickable *buttons* that reduce the need to use menu options.
SEE: FEATURE BOX

BWTP – See: **B**usiness **W**eb **T**ransaction **P**rocessing

by hand – A repetitive and simple operation that should be performed by the computer, but which an individual has to do manually.

byte – The amount of *memory* space used to store one character, which is usually 8 bits.
SEE ALSO: BIT, MEGABYTE

bzzzt! wrong – A term often used in *newsgroups* to indicate that a participant has given wrong or misleading information. It originated as a spoof on the kind of TV and radio quiz programs in which a contestant buzzes and then is told by the host that they are wrong.

C – Probably the single most-used computer programming language. Also refers to the C-drive (or hard drive) of the PC.

C++ – Important programming language developed by Bell systems. It is increasingly used to develop *Internet applications*, primarily via *Active X* technology. Popular with PC users since it takes up a relatively small amount of *memory*.
SEE ALSO: JAVA

CA – See: **C**ertificate **A**uthority

cable configurator – A helpful *program* obtained via the Internet or at most online cable retailers. It enables you to get the right cables in the right places for your PC.

cable modem – A *modem* that connects the home to a cable provided by a cable TV company. Much faster than using a normal phone line (e.g. 100 kbytes/sec vs. 5.6 kbytes/sec of standard 56k modem).
SEE ALSO: KBIT

cache – (pronounced "cash") 1. An area of *memory* or a *file* in a computer that is used to speed up the storing of data, text, graphics, or programs that are accessed by users over and over again. There are memory and disk caches in every computer that store repetitive instruction, execution, and data retrieval in a single area, and so lower the number of connections that might be required to retrieve the data.

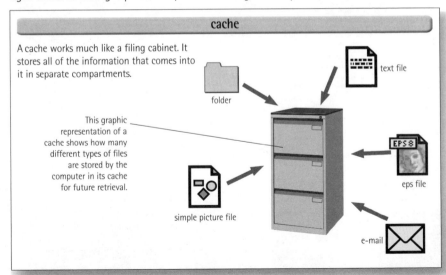

cache

A cache works much like a filing cabinet. It stores all of the information that comes into it in separate compartments.

folder

text file

This graphic representation of a cache shows how many different types of files are stored by the computer in its cache for future retrieval.

simple picture file

eps file

e-mail

Memory (or CPU) cache is memory that is dedicated to increasing the efficiency and operating speed of the computer. Disk cache is a portion of the main memory (*RAM*) that is set aside for programs to store frequently used instructions. It is faster than the main memory with instructions and data being transferred to the cache in blocks.

2. Browser or Internet caches are dedicated Internet areas found in a web *browser* (usually in a separate folder on the disk) and hold a user's favorite web pages. The cache stores the series of instructions and processes for accessing a frequently hit site and minimizes the number of slow and repetitive connections that otherwise might be required to retrieve the data.
SEE: FEATURE BOX

cache hit - What happens when data is found in the *cache* (e.g. a request for a web page in the browser cache) and does not require retrieval from a slower storage area on the hard drive.

cache memory - See: cache

cache miss - What happens when data is not found in the *cache*. E.g. When a web page is requested that is not currently held in the browser cache, it has to be retrieved from the Internet using a slower connection.

caching policy - The guidelines that are chosen to determine which items are to be stored in a cache and for how long.

CAD - See: **C**omputer **A**ided **D**esign

calculator - A program on a computer that simulates the workings of the normal handheld version. Simple math calculations can be performed without having to leave the applications you are already using. It can be operated by the numeric keys or via the mouse and is located in the Accessories menu in PCs or the Apple menu in Apple Macs. Some computers come with more scientific-based calculators offering graphing solutions.
SEE: FEATURE BOX

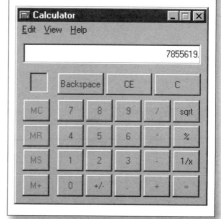

calculator

A desk accessory that works like a four-function pocket calculator. You can copy and paste calculation results into your documents using the Edit command shown onscreen.

calendar – A program in which you can record events and appointments on an electronic diary. You can get automatic entries for regular events or be made aware of upcoming events. Some *web sites* offer online organizers.
SEE: FEATURE BOX

calibration – 1. Adjustment of a *program* or *tool* such as a *joystick* to enable accurate responses.
2. Process that ensures consistency of color for viewing the monitor screen, for scanning and for printing.

call back – The redialing of a network user's phone number to verify the user's validity to access a network; used as a security check.

call detail reporting – The reporting and storage of information concerning the connections made by users of a telephone *e-mail* or *local area network*.

CAM – See: **C**omputer **A**ided **M**anufacturing

camcorder – A popular term for a video camera, a corruption of the words camera and recorder.

Campus Wide Information Service (CWIS) – A computerized information service used by universities and colleges to keep students and staff up to date with what's going on. Often linked to a *web site*.

cancel – 1. To stop a requested operation or action, often prompted by a program dialog box, or achieved by using a *keyboard shortcut*.
2. To send a command deleting one's own message to a newsgroup, perhaps because it is out of date or contains errors.

cancelbot – (from cancel and robot) An automatic *program* that regularly goes through *newsgroups* canceling excessively large, unsuitable, inappropriate, or *spam* e-mails.
SEE ALSO: BOT

---

calendar

Computer calendars can alert you with sound to forthcoming appointments and can be viewed on a daily, weekly, or monthly format. Names, addresses, phone numbers, and tasks can also be attached to the relevant appointments.

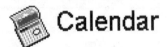

cancelbunny - (slang) Name given to users who delete *postings* to *newsgroups*. They may do this because of copyright infringement, pornographic content, or just because they do not agree with it. Other cancelbunnies may be on the lookout for *spam* in newsgroups and will use a *cancelbot* to delete any postings they consider to be spam. Such a user may sometimes be referred to as a cancelmoose or cancelpoodle.

cancelmoose - **See:** cancelbunny

cancelpoodle - **See:** cancelbunny

CAP - **See: C**ompetitive **A**ccess **P**rovider

CAPI - 1. **See: C**omputer **A**ssisted **P**ersonal **I**nterviewing
2. **See: C**ommon ISDN **A**pplication **P**rogramming **I**nterface

caps - Short for capitals.

Caps Lock - A button on the keyboard that converts lower case letters to CAPITAL letters.

capture - 1. To store data or images that appear on a web page or e-mail and to save and download them on the computer. Browser software includes the facility to capture and download specific text or images from the Internet.
2. To cause a picture or graphic to be saved as a bitmapped image whether using an Apple Mac or a PC with Windows.

carbon copy - Often shortened on-screen to Cc, carbon copy is a copy of an *e-mail* sent to other designated receivers besides the main receiver of the e-mail.
SEE ALSO: BCC

card - 1. A page of data or information.
2. **See:** expansion board

careware - *Software* bought by means of a gift to charity rather than by payment to the author or the owner.
SEE ALSO: SHAREWARE

carpal tunnel syndrome - A form of Repetitive Strain Injury (RSI) produced by repeating the same small hand, wrist, and finger movements many times when using a keyboard and mouse. Stretch the hands frequently and take a break from typing to help avoid this syndrome.

carriage return (CR) - A code that moves the *cursor* to the beginning of the next line.

carrier - 1. A signal that can be used to carry another signal over a transmission line. E.g. A modem transmits data through a telephone line by sending a continuous tone as a carrier (this is audible if you pick up the Internet phone line with a hand receiver). Variations in the frequency and pitch of the carrier tone enable encoding of the data.
2. An alternative name for a phone connection to a network.

carrier service provider – A company offering telephone and data communications within a country, or from country to country.

Carrier Sense Multiple Access/Collision Detection (CSMA/CD) – A type of *protocol* whereby computers on a network trying to transmit or access data from a single channel at the same time (called a collision) do so only when the line is clear. Should a collision occur, it is detected and the data is withdrawn, to be re-transmitted at a later, random time.

cart – Short for *shopping cart* and seen on any web site where purchases are made.

---

cascading windows

In Microsoft Windows, when the windows on screen are cascaded as shown below, the user can see the *title bar* of every window for ease of navigation around the screen.

---

cartridge – A removable storage item such as a disc or tape, it sometimes refers to a type of *hard disk* that you can remove.

cascade – A series of messages that reply to an original message that has been sent to a *Bulletin Board* system.

cascading style sheet – More commonly known as CSS, cascading style sheets are used as a template for pages in *HTML*. They form part of version 4 of *HTML* and enable the web designer to define a standard visual identity for pages that have a similar or same use.

cascading windows – A series of open *windows* that overlap one another with the title bar staying visible.
SEE: FEATURE BOX

CASE – **See:** **C**omputer **A**ided **S**oftware **E**ngineering

case – Letters on the keyboard can be represented in upper case (CAPITAL letters), or lower case (small letters). Keyboard access to and navigation of the Internet, is very *case-sensitive* (and often breaks standard English usage in its use of capital and lower case letters).

case-sensitive – The ability for programs to tell upper case from lower case words (and instructions). E.g. A correct *password* may depend on the case it is typed in: "password" (lower case) may get you in but "PASSWORD" (upper case) may not.

Castanet – Software developed by Marimba Inc. that enables administrators to install and update *applications* and *data* across an entire *network* of computers.

catalog – A list or directory of contents.

catatonic – A system or computer that does not respond to any keyboard or mouse *commands*. A serious failure.

Category 5 cable – Cabling that consists of four twisted pairs of copper wire terminated by connectors. It supports relatively high-speed frequencies.

cathode ray tube (CRT) – Conventional PC monitors have CRTs stored in their deep back end to create images on *screen*.
SEE ALSO: FLAT PANEL DISPLAY

CBT – See: **C**omputer **B**ased **T**raining

Cc – See: **C**arbon **c**opy

CCITT See: Consultative **C**ommittee For **I**nternational **T**elephone And **T**elegraph

CD – See: **C**ompact **D**isc

CD burner – (slang) A device or *drive* that allows the user to record data on a *CD-R*.

CD-E See: **C**ompact **D**isc - **E**rasable

CD-I – See: **C**ompact **D**isc - **I**nteractive

CDPD – See: **C**ellular **D**igital **P**acket **D**ata

CD-R – See: **C**ompact **D**isc - **R**ecordable

CD rack – Stack or shelf for storing *CDs*.

CD rewriter – A device or *drive* that allows the user to record data on a *CD-R*.

CD-ROM – **C**ompact **D**isk-**R**ead **O**nly **M**emory. Like an audio compact disc, but one that stores computer data. They can be read by the computer, but not recorded on.

CD-RW – See: **C**ompact **D**isk - **R**ewriteable

Celeron – A brand name for a line of *Intel microprocessors*, designed for low-cost PCs.

cell – 1. In a *spreadsheet*, a cell is a box in which you can enter a single piece of data or text; with individual cells identified by a column letter and a row number E.g. F15 specifies the cell in column F and row 15.
SEE: FEATURE BOX
2. In *mobile* or *cellular* telephone systems, a cell is a geographic area or region.
3. In communications, a cell is a fixed amount (sometimes referred to as a *packet*) of data.

cell

Spreadsheets such as Microsoft Excel work on a grid pattern of columns and rows. Data is inputted in linear form into individual cells and can be converted into graphs and charts.

cell relay – A technology based on transmitting data in relatively small, fixed-size *cells*, or *packets*. Live audio and video feeds can be carried reliably this way.

cellular – A communications system especially used by *mobile* phone companies that divides a geographic region into sections, called *cells*. The cellular system makes the most use out of a limited number of transmission frequencies.

Cellular Digital Packet Data – A form of wireless technology, using a special type of modem, that allows the transmission of data over unused parts of the telephone network.

cellular modem – A type of modem that allows access to the Internet using a *mobile* or *cellular* telephone.

cellular telephone – A mobile or portable phone that uses a *cellular* network.

censorship – A policy of *content* or information control. The Internet is relatively free of organized censorship, though some countries block pornographic or religious sites as a matter of policy, and there are many organizations that monitor its content. Individuals can block *Internet content* they deem unsuitable (e.g. for their children) from being accessed accidentally or deliberately on to their computer by using *censorware*.

censorware – An uncomplimentary term used for software that may be used to block *Internet content*.

Center For Democracy And Technology – A non-profit-making organization that stands up for privacy, individual rights, and free speech on the Internet.

centered – To place text or pictures in the middle of a line or page. Sometimes referred to as centering.

centi – A prefix meaning 1/100 as in centimeter.

central processing unit (CPU) – The main hardware device of a *computer* – its "brain" – stored on a single chip called a *microprocessor*. Most of the computing calculations, as well as the execution of all program instructions and controls, take place within this minute element of a computer.

Centrex – **CENT**Ralised **EX**change, a service offered by some telecommunications companies, allocates a section of a public telephone switch to dedicated use by a single organization.

CERN – **See:** **C**onseil **E**uropeen pour le **R**echerche **N**ucleaire

CERT – **See:** **C**omputer **E**mergency **R**esponse **T**eam

CERTCC – **See:** **C**omputer **E**mergency **R**esponse **T**eam **C**oordination **C**enter

certificate authority – An established or reputable authority that is able to guarantee or issue a *digital certificate* to authenticate a user's identity or some data associated with that user.

CFML – **See: C**old **F**usion **M**arkup **L**anguage

chain letter – E-mail promising free vacations, or warning of new (but actually fake) computer viruses, or offering get-rich-quick schemes based on pyramid selling. Typically a chain letter e-mail asks for a sum of money to be sent to the first name on the list and asks the recipient to remove this name and add their own at the bottom of the list. Theoretically the recipient can make a large amount of money just by sending a small amount of money and reposting. This never happens, since most recipients do not bother with chain letters and do not send money - quite correctly. The only result of hoax, fake, or time-wasting chain letters is that e-mail systems get clogged up with an overload of e-mails.

chain list – 1. A list of data with each piece of data providing an address for the next consecutive item on the list.
2. **See:** Linked list

Challenge Handshake Authentication Protocol – A type of *protocol* that is used when connecting to an *Internet Service Provider*. It provides a high degree of security against unauthorized intrusion.

challenge–response – A security check technique by which the user of a network or web site is asked a question to which the computer knows the answer, such as the maiden name of the user's mother. If the wrong answer is given, access is denied.

channel – 1. A section of a web site, or a directory of selected *links* or resources on a *portal* site. E.g. An *ISP* such as *AOL* can have many subject specific channels from Art to Sports.
2. Can refer to direct communications between two computers (an alternative for transmission line).
3. In sales and marketing, the medium by which a seller communicates with and sells products to consumers, such as via TV or magazines. The Internet was considered a new sales channel on its inception.

channel bank – The channel bank is essential to all digital communications. It combines a group of channels (up to 24) into a higher bit-rate channel for digital transmission and converts analog signals into digital.

channel bonding – The technique of combining two telephone lines into a single channel, effectively doubling the data transfer speed. There are modems that can support channel bonding.

channel definition format – A file that contains information about other files being downloaded.

channel hopping – To go rapidly from one channel to another.

Channel Service Unit/Data Service Unit (CSU/DSU) – Two devices packaged in a single type of high-powered modem: the CSU performs protective and diagnostic work for a telecommunications line; the DSU connects a terminal to a digital line.

CHAP – See: **C**hallenge **H**andshake **A**uthentication **P**rotocol

character – A symbol from a writing system. In computing it can be one byte or any single symbol or picture.

character recognition – See: **O**ptical **C**haracter **R**ecognition

character set – A list of characters recognized by both *hardware* and *software*. Each character is represented by a number.
SEE ALSO: **ASCII**

character string – The storage space allocated to a series of characters.

characters per inch (CPI) – The number of characters that can fit into 1 inch.

characters per second (CPS) – The number of characters that can be transmitted or downloaded in one second.

charityware – A type of software in which new users are directed to pay a charity instead of paying the author.
SEE ALSO: CAREWARE, SHAREWARE

chassis – The framework (usually metal) that houses the computer's circuitry.

chat – Communicating with other users of the Internet, usually in *real time*.
SEE ALSO: CHAT ROOM

chat bot – An annoying virus that renders *chat rooms* unusable, usually by covering the screen with text.

---

chat room

Chat rooms are probably the most popular forums on the Internet. The "room" is actually a *channel,* but the word makes it sound more user-friendly. Users enter text in real time by using the keyboard, and the entered text appears on other users' monitors. However, there is a great deal of concern about safety, especially about older people preying on younger ones. The key is to be wary and not to give out your e-mail address. Assume people will pretend to be someone they are not when chatting. Keep your online life separate from your real life and do not arrange to meet someone person to person that you have only met online.

Go TO: www.chatdanger.com

CHATDANGER
.COM
ppl online may not b who they say they r

chat client – The software that the user of a chat room needs to participate in the conversations that occur in a *chat room*.

chat history – A transcript of a chat session.

chat room – A virtual place (not really a room but a channel) where online conversation or chat takes place.
SEE: FEATURE BOX

chat site – A web site that holds an online chat facility, often on one subject or a limited range of subjects.

chatiquette – **See:** netiquette

chatterbots – A computer program that is capable of communicating with humans. The ultimate goal is to create a program that interacts in a way indistinguishable from that of humans, giving the illusion of intelligence.

chatter's block – When you cannot think of anything to say in a chat room. Usually caused by too much chat room usage.

check box – A small onscreen box that can be accessed to turn an option on or off. A small cross or tick in the corner of the box indicates the option has been selected.
SEE: FEATURE BOX

checkout page – The web page that sums up the transactions on an online shopping page. Also includes details about delivery and packaging.

checksum – A simple program to check that there has been no alteration or corruption of data sent through a network. E.g. It checks for errors by applying a numeric formula to each transmitted message and comparing the sent and received formula.

Chernobyl packet – Named after the Russian nuclear accident at Chernobyl, this *packet* of data causes a network to malfunction badly. Such error-filled packets are mostly caused by a hardware error.

chip – A complete electronic circuit built on a slice of semiconducting material, usually a silicon crystal barely a few millimeters square. Yet it can hold millions of electronic components and is otherwise known as an *Integrated Circuit*.

chipset – A number of *chips* designed to perform one or more related functions.

---

check box

A highlighted tick or cross in a box indicates which options you have selected for software use. A brief explanation of the option available is given next to each interactive box.

General options

abc ☑ Always suggest replacements for misspelled words
☑ Always check spelling before sending
☐ Ignore words in UPPERCASE
☐ Ignore words with numbers
☑ Ignore original message text in reply or forward

---

choke – A device that restricts the free flow of data between networks; its main use is to prevent unauthorized intrusion.

choke packet – *Packets* of data that maintain the flow of data in a network by detecting where congestion occurs.

choke point – A point through which all data traffic in a *network* flows. This point can be vulnerable to hackers and potential hardware failure.

choose – To pick an option or issue a command by clicking on a specific icon. Choosing usually refers to an action as opposed to selecting, which means to highlight.

chooser – Part of the Apple Macintosh system, it allows you to select a printer or network or any other peripheral.

churn – Turnover of customers and users (gaining or losing customer loyalty) on an online service. Churn is used by online retailers and marketing companies.

churning – A computer that takes a long time to complete a task is said to be churning.

CICS – **C**ustomer **I**nformation **C**ontrol **S**ystem is a program commonly used in customer transaction applications, e.g. hotel reservation and billing systems.

CIDR – See: **C**lassless **I**nter-**D**omain **R**outing

CIF – See: **C**ommon **I**ntermediate **F**ormat

cipher – A code for disguising normal or plain text for use in *encrypted* messages.

cipher text – The text that has been created when a message has undergone the process of *encryption*. It can only be read by someone who has the key or decoder.

circuit – A link between electronic components that performs a specific function. It is also known as a *Transmission Line*.

circuit board – A board made of insulating material that holds electrical components, which when joined together form a *circuit*.

Computers have one or more circuit boards. Each board is a thin plastic plate on which chips and other electronic connectors are placed. The motherboard (or system board or mainboard) and expansion boards are the key categories of circuit boards. They are also called cards.

circuit breaker – A safety device that cuts electrical supply if conditions are dangerous or abnormal.

circuit switched cellular – A type of wireless technology that allows the user of a *cellular phone* to connect to a network.

CIS – **See:** **C**ompuserve **I**nformation **S**ervice

CISCO SYSTEMS **Cisco Systems, Inc** – Founded in San Jose, California in 1984, by a group of computer scientists, Cisco is a worldwide leader in developing Internet and network technology. It has over 37,000 employees. **Go to:** www.cisco.com

CIX – **See:** **C**ommercial **I**nternet e**X**change

class – A term frequently used to define software and hardware. Each class describes what it can do or how it acts or how much data it can hold.

Class A IP – **See:** **I**nternet **P**rotocol

Class B IP – **See:** **I**nternet **P**rotocol

Class C IP – **See:** **I**nternet **P**rotocol

Classless Inter-Domain Routing (CIDR) – A way of dealing with the problem of the Internet running out of addresses or *URLs*. Smaller chunks of space are allocated to organizations that require one address. **See also: Internet Protocol**

clear – Alternative word for erase.

ClearType – A Microsoft product that is part of its Reader program and enables a user to read electronic books or magazines. ClearType is designed to make on-screen reading more natural.

CLEC – **C**ompetitive **L**ocal **E**xchange **C**arrier. Any US-based telephone company that competes with an existing local telephone service by providing networking and switching.

click – The action of placing a mouse cursor over some text or a graphic and pressing down one of the switches found at the top of the mouse. The switch can be pressed down continuously or double-clicked in quick succession to achieve a desired action, depending on the application and command.

clickable image – An image or *hyperlink* on a web page that responds or starts an action when clicked on by the user.

clicks-and-mortar – A type of retailer that offers customers access to its wares both online and physically through its stores. E.g. A supermarket chain where customers tend to purchase bulk items on-line (because they are of predictable quality and delivered to the home), while buying fresh produce or clothes in-store (because they are perishable or prone to variations).

clickstream – A trail left by a user of a *browser* navigating the *Internet*. The trail is identified as a log of mouse *clicks* that can record visitor actions on a web site and from one web site to another. This can be used to inform the site owners and their advertisers and marketers as to whether their strategies are successful.

clickthrough – The effectiveness of Web advertisements is often measured by their clickthrough rate; i.e. how often people who see a *banner ad* actually click on it.

client – A program or a computer that requests a service from a *server*.

client/server architecture – The *client* is an application that runs on a PC, which relies on a *server* to perform some of its operations. E.g. The services that *AOL* provides to its customers where functions are performed on the server computer rather than on the customer's PC. Also known as *network architecture*.

clip art – An electronic picture or graphic that can be downloaded in varying formats on to a web page or document.
Go to: www.clipart.com, which is a directory of the many clip art libraries that exist today.

clipboard – A common file where data is stored temporarily before being copied to another location. Occurs mainly when applying the cut and paste commands.
See also: Cut

clipper chip – A controversial piece of hardware that *encrypts* and *decrypts* signals sent over a network by a "back door" access. You have to register an extra key with the US Government, which they can use to decrypt your data.

clipping – See: **d**rag and **d**rop

cloaking – The process of hiding web pages from visitors. E.g. A web site may send one page to a search engine for indexing purposes, while sending another, more highly designed page to the end user. Sometimes known as *stealth*.

clone – Computer software or hardware that functions exactly like another better-known product. Often used to describe PCs that are not the well-known brand names like IBM but perform the same range of functions and are cheaper.

close – To save a file and remove the program from the screen, but not to *quit* entirely from the desktop.

cloud – In telecommunications, a cloud refers to a space on a circuit that exists between the end points of a transmission. Also known as network cloud.

cluster – A group of sectors on a disk or hard drive treated as a unit for saving space.

CMYK (cyan, magenta, yellow, black) – A color system associated with printing where all colors are built up on a combination of the primary printing colors: cyan, magenta, yellow, and black. Often referred to as the four color system.
See also: RGB monitor

CNET.com – One of the leading online suppliers and customer advisers on computer hardware and software.
Go to: www.cnet.com

coaster – (slang) A *CD-ROM* that is unusable due to a failed attempt at writing to writeable or re-writeable CD-ROMs, or is unwanted (e.g. unsolicited from ISP companies seeking new users). The name refers to use of these redundant CDs as hot beverage mats or coasters.

coaxial cable – Standard cable used in communications, which is insulated by an outer shield to prevent it from picking up electrical and radio frequency interference.

COBOL – **See: C**ommon **B**usiness **O**riented **L**anguage

cobweb – (slang) A web site that has not been updated for some time.

code – 1. To write a series of instructions for a *software program*. This information is encrypted (coded) in machine language or programming language (eg. *ASCII*).
2. Can be used as an alternative to *data*, which is the material that *code* operates on.

codec – Short for coder-decoder. An electronic device that codes and decodes *analog* to *digital* signals (e.g. video signals).

code page – This stores the different codes for interpreting the different *keyboard* layouts used by different languages and countries. Usually English language keyboards are QWERTY standard, whereas the French use AZERTY. In Windows these can be changed via the Control Panel keyboard properties option.

Code Red Worm – A *worm*-type *computer virus* that spreads via *HTTP* traffic, and forces unsuspecting web servers to launch denial-of-service attacks on web sites.

COLD – **See: C**omputer **O**utput to **L**aser **D**isk

cold boot – Starting up the computer from power off. Also known as cold start.

Cold Fusion Mark-up Language – An extension of the HTML developed by the Allaire Corporation, which has since merged with Macromedia.
Go to: www.macromedia.com

collate – A function on a *word-processor* that instructs the printer to print the entire document several times with ordered pages. This is instead of printing each page several times, which leaves the user to compile the final document.

collision – When two *signals* are sent across the same channel and collide and cause an error in transmission.

collapsed view – To condense a computer document so that only the main headings are visible. Similarly, to view the computer's files showing only the main directories or folders. The opposite of expanded view.

co-locate – To site Internet server computers in an environment secure from system failures and natural disasters.

colon – The ":" character on the keyboard (normally the Shift version of the ";" (semicolon)) key used in web addresses after the prefix "*http:*".

color depth – The number of colors a single *pixel* can hold. This determines the number of colors that can be displayed on the monitor where High color is referred to as 16-bits, and True color as 24 or 32 bits. Images with a high color depth can be slow to transfer over the Internet.

color monitor – Computer monitors can be color or black and white, although the latter are now rare. Also known as displays, they come in varying sizes from 15in to 22in (though the VIS, the diagonal **v**isible **i**mage **s**ize, is smaller), and can have color depths expressed in millions of *pixels*.

color printer – Printers that can produce images in color. These are needed to download most web site graphics or images. Ink jet printers are the most common for home use; these produce tiny dots in four colors, which combine to print a huge variety of colors. More expensive laser color printers are for office use.

column – 1. A function of word-processing, to write in narrow columns, such as those found in newspapers, rather than across the width of the page.
2. A number of cells down a spreadsheet (as opposed to rows).
SEE ALSO: CELL

COM – Abbreviation referring to a *Com port* (Communications Port).

.com – A top-level domain name used by companies. New companies that have made (and lost) millions of dollars providing dedicated web site services are also referred to as *dotcom* companies.

Com port – The usual term for a communications port. A serial port or socket on a personal computer usually combined with a number, e.g. COM 1. These are located at the back of the computer housing and are used for connecting printers, scanners, and other *peripherals*.

comic-strip orientation – Placing of images so they are aligned side by side at the top, as in a comic strip.

command – An instruction given to a computer, by way of a keyboard, mouse, voice command, or other method.

Command key – A key marked with a cloverleaf symbol (and Apple logo) on Apple *Macintosh* Computer keyboards. It is used like the shift key on a PC; pressing in conjunction with one or more other keys to give shortcut commands to the computer or to alter the meaning of other keys.
SEE ALSO: KEYBOARD

command line – 1. A type of program that works by written command, e.g. *MS-DOS*.
2. The space on a screen where a command is required.

command prompt – The *MS-DOS prompt* C:/> that appears on the screen awaiting a command.

comment – Information in a program that can be added for extra reference or documentation. It has no effect on the functioning of the program.

Commerce XML (CXML) – Commerce XML is a standard *protocol* for the online exchange of business information in a common format.

commerce server – A *server* that supports *e-commerce* such as an *online* shop, including the management of secure credit card transactions and functioning of the *cart* or other selection tools.

Commerce Services Provider (CSP) – Similar to an *Internet Service Provider*, a CSP provides the facilities necessary to carry out e-commerce. These include the facilities provided by a *commerce server, web design,* and maintenance.

CommerceNet – A non-profit-making trade association for *e-commerce* companies. It endeavors to set standards for existing and emerging technologies.

Commercial Internet exchange (CIX) – A US-based trade association for Internet Service Providers.

committed – To finalize a transaction on the Internet.

Common Business Oriented Language – A programming language used in business data processing.

Common Intermediate Format (CIF) – In *videoconferencing* the standardized format is based on a *frame rate* of 30 fps.

Common Internet File System – A proposed Internet standard that lets programs make requests for files and services from remote computers.

Common ISDN Application Programming Interface – An *API* standard used to access *ISDN* (digital telephone) equipment that allows it to adjust to differences in the hardware being used.

Common Object Request Broker Architecture (CORBA) – Architecture that enables bits of a *program*, called *objects*, to communicate with one another even if they were created in a different *programming language,* or are running on a different *operating system*. CORBA was developed by the Object Management Group (OMG), an industry consortium seeking standardization.

Common User Access – A set of guidelines for standardizing how computer programs *interface* (communicate) with the user. Developed by IBM, the standards deal with menu appearance and the use of keystrokes, as well as other conventions, programming, and communications.

Communications Port – **See: C**om Port

communications protocol – Hardware and software rules and vocabulary for transmission between two computers or devices; e.g the *TCP/IP protocol*.

Communicator – **See:** Netscape Communicator

communities – A group of Internet users who share a common interest.

compact disc (CD) – Widely used in the music and computing industries, a compact disc is a polycarbonate disc with one or more metal layers capable of storing digital information. The data on CDs is stored in microscopic grooves and read by an infrared laser beam that scans the revolving discs. One CD holds 75 minutes of recorded music (the original developers' aim apparently being to absorb at least the whole of Beethoven's *5th Symphony*) or store 680 *megabytes* of computer data. This storage facility and cheap price have made computer CDs an industry standard.

compact disc-erasable (CD-E) – A type of *CD* that can be re-used, the information saved and erased as needed.
SEE ALSO: COMPACT DISC-RECORDABLE, COMPACT DISC-RECORDABLE DRIVE AND CD REWRITER

compact disc-interactive (Cd-I) – A rarely used system invented by Philips and Sony for storing video, audio, and information on compact disc.

compact disc-recordable (Cd-R) – A type of CD that can be re-used, the information saved and erased as needed.
SEE ALSO: COMPACT DISC-ERASABLE, COMPACT DISC-RECORDABLE DRIVE, CD REWRITER

compact disc-recordable drive – With the appropriate software, a disk drive that can create CD-ROMs and audio CDs.

Compactflash (CF) – A *flash memory* format invented by SanDisk Corporation, widely used for handheld digital devices.

COMPAQ Compaq - A leading global provider of enterprise technology and solutions. Compaq designs and manufactures hardware and software, and is best known for its own-brand PCs and recently, for its handheld PC, the iPAQ™.
GO TO: www.compaq.com

compatible – Connected hardware, such as a computer and printer (and the relevant software), that function together satisfactorily are said to be compatible.

competitive access provider – A company that competes with local telephone companies to provide lines for *Internet* access.

compiler – A computer program that translates a high-level programming language such as Java into machine language. This generated machine language program can then be executed by the computer.

component – An element within a system; a component can refer to either hardware or software.

composite video – A video signal that is comprised of several different signals, e.g. one for color and one for brightness.

compositing – Another word for *typesetting*.

compound document – A document containing data from more than one program. E.g. Text from a word-processor, combined with an image from a paint program plus video clips.

compress – To make a file more compact through a re-encoding process. Compressed files save storage space and are faster to transmit. E.g. *PK-ZIP*

compressed file – A file that has undergone compression.

compression – To reduce the number of bytes in a file in order to reduce download times or storage requirements. This is particularly useful for downloading software, graphics, video, and music files. Compression works by removing

unnecessary information, spacing and by the use of coding tricks. Because all compression software uses different tricks, the file must be decompressed using the same program. The type of compression is indicated in the file extension. WinZip with the extension .zip is the most common for PCs, and StuffIt, with the extension .sit is popular with Macintosh users; both are available as *shareware*.
SEE ALSO: DECOMPRESSION, LOSSLESS COMPRESSION, LOSSY COMPRESSION, STUFFIT, WINZIP

Compuserve – Founded in 1969 as a computer time-sharing service, Ohio-based CompuServe was a leading pioneer of the US online service industry. In 1979, it became the first service to offer electronic mail capabilities and technical support to personal computer users. In 1980, CompuServe was the first online service to offer real-time chat online. It now provides Internet access available only to subscribers who dial up to the central computer. In addition, Compuserve supplies a huge variety of discussion forums, databases, and information such as share prices, news, and weather.
GO TO: www.compuserve.com

computer – A machine that has the ability to store, retrieve, and process data. The components that combine to make the computer, e.g. *monitor, CPU, circuit boards*, and wires are called *hardware*. *Programs* that instruct the computer are referred to as *software*. A unique feature of computers is that they can store their own instructions and so perform many functions without the need for keying in new instructions each time.

Computer Aided Design (CAD) – A highly flexible *graphics* program that enables designers and engineers to develop drawings or products in three dimensions, view from any angle, and zoom in and out.

Computer Aided Manufacturing – A type of computer, *program,* or *application* that enables automated manufacturing; e.g. robots in an automobile factory.

Computer Aided Software Engineering – Software that enables programmers to automate and simplify the development process for programs.

computer architecture – See: architecture

Computer Assisted Personal Interviewing – A *program* using a computer-based questionnaire that can form part of a job interview. The interviewer can customize the survey to make it company- and job-specific.

Computer Based Training – An interactive way to learn a subject using computers as the principal medium.

Computer Emergency Response Team (CERT) – An organization that aims to provide help and expertise when a major security incident or virus affects the Internet. CERT has a broad scope to research into computer security and the coordination of teams when a worldwide incident occurs. Go to: www.cert.org

Computer Emergency Response Team Coordination Center (CERT/CC) – The control center of CERT.

computer literacy – To have the basic computer skills to be able to operate *hardware* and *software*.

Computer Output To Laser Disk (COLD) – A system for archiving data to optical disks in a compressed but retrievable format. Useful for keeping records and reports since one million paper pages can be stored on a single five and a quarter inch optical disk.

Computer Professionals For Social Responsibility (CPSR) – Society of computer scientists who look at the impact of computer technology on everyday lives. As concerned citizens, they direct public attention to the choices on the applications of computing and their impact on society. Go to: www.cpsr.org

computer science – The academic discipline dedicated to understanding and developing computer technology.

computer security – 1. The protection of files and data on a computer.
2. The prevention of infection from computer viruses.
3. The maintenance of personal or network privacy within a computer.
<small>See also: security</small>

computer system – A term used to include not just the *Central Processing Unit* (CPU), but also *peripheral* devices such as monitor, speakers, printer, scanner.
<small>See also: bundle</small>

computer virus – An uninvited and unwanted program that infects a computer by attaching itself to another program, propagating itself when that program is executed. A virus can enter the computer through files downloaded over the Internet, or by the use of floppy disks or software that are infected with viruses. A virus that invades a computer pretending to be a friendly e-mail or software offer is called a *Trojan*. Viruses can be sinister and result in serious harm to the computer such as wiping files and damaging the operating system. Prank or hoax viruses may display a rude image on screen or simply waste time.
<small>See: feature box</small>

computer virus

A computer virus will have been written by a computer user somewhere in the world. There are many potential ways for viruses to get from one machine to another - floppy disk, a zip disk, or a borrowed piece of software. Other viruses can be downloaded from the Internet, or a private bulletin board. The representation below shows how a virus can spread by e-mail.

The creator of the virus designs the virus and then e-mails it by attaching it to an e-mail.

The e-mails are received and unwittingly opened - this then transfers the virus to the computer.

The virus then attaches itself to all the addresses in the user's address book and e-mails the virus to them. The virus spreads very quickly and begins to take effect globally.

concatenation – To join a number of files or objects to make a new file or object.

conferencing – Short for *teleconferencing* in which participants are connected by telephone lines and use voice and fax communications.

Config.Sys – A file found in the *root directory* of *DOS* and *OS/2* systems that is used to load drivers and recognize and run the peripheral devices software.

configuration – The settings on a hardware device or software program. These can be setup and customized to suit the user or environment in which the computer functions.

configure – To alter software or hardware functioning by changing or customizing the settings.

congestion – When the Internet is very busy, transmissions may become slow, interrupted or cease altogether due to the volume of traffic. This is particularly obvious if listening to radio transmissions or watching video. Congestion may also occur at certain peak times when there are too many users for a particular *ISP* to handle.
SEE ALSO: TRAFFIC

connectionless – Technology that uses no physical wires to connect computers together, or to the Internet.
SEE ALSO: WIRELESS COMMUNICATION

connectivity – 1. The state of being online or having an active link to a network.
2. Two or more devices or applications that can work together.

connector – The device (e.g. a cable) that connects two computers or devices together.

Conseil Européen Pour Le Recherche Nucléaire (CERN) – A European research company where demand for the transfer of information from its employees led to the invention of *HTML* and *HTTP* by Tim *Berners-Lee.* This led to the creation of the World Wide Web and the Internet.

console – The keyboard and monitor attached to a computer to enable access.

console game – A game that requires the use of a keyboard and monitor.

constant – A fixed value in a program. This could be a date, price, or error message.

constant angular velocity – A way to access data from rotating disks. The disk rotates at a constant speed regardless of which area of the disk is being accessed.

Consultative Committee For International Telephone And Telegraph (Comité Consultatif International Téléphonique Et Télégraphique) – A body that aims to standardize international *telecommunications.* It was renamed *International Telecommunications Union* or *ITU.*

consumables – Any consumer goods, *hardware* or *software*, that can be purchased to enhance the function of a computer. This can range from digital cameras to ink cartridges, modems, and web creation toolsets – such as you might see in a computer supply catalog.

contact manager – Software that keeps notes on people and related information in a computer or electronic organizer. A useful tool for those who regularly encounter a large number of clients and want to recall personal details, business requirements, and previous contact records.

content – The information found on a *web site*. Highly regarded pages are content rich, that is, full of information, well-organized and make good use of *hyperlinks*.

content-free – A web page or other communication that says nothing.

content provider – A site that contains information that needs constant updating. This can include news, travel, industrial, and online e-commerce sites.

content rating system – A system used for *rating* the contents of a web site, most commonly used to filter out sites that contain adult material. The most commonly used standard is the Platform for Internet Content Selection that is used in connection with Blocking Software to allow or refuse access to a web site.

context-sensitive help – A program that can provide dedicated help features depending on what function you are working in when you hit the key. E.g. A context-sensitive key will give you editing help if you press it while in the function of editing and so on.

contextual commerce – Advertorial text found on *e-zines* and *web sites*. The copy reads like editorial comment but is really intended to generate online sales interest.

contiguous – In data processing, a sequence without "holes." E.g. 1-2-3-4-5 is contiguous, but 1-2-4-5 is not. Two data buffers are contiguous if the starting address of one is one greater than the ending address of the other.

contrast – The difference between the light and dark areas on a computer screen.

control box – Generally used for "window decorations," e.g. items put there by the window manager to allow you to control the *window*.

Control key – The key marked Ctrl or Ctl on the computer *keyboard.*

control key combinations – The *control key* used in combination with another or more keys pressed simultaneously to give shortcut instructions to the computer (rather than by using the mouse and pull-down menu). E.g Ctrl + P is used in some programs to print the file.

control menu – The window that is used to minimize, maximize, and restore a document window. In Microsoft Windows this can be viewed using the ALT-hyphen key combination.

control panel – A window on a PC used to adjust settings for the basic functions of Windows operating systems, such as display options, mouse speed, and so on. In Apple Macs the control panel is located under the Apple icon menu and includes simple functional options for keyboard use, screen appearance, Internet access, and so on.
SEE: FEATURE BOX

---

control panel

Windows Control Panel reveals a grid of computer components, some hardware, some software. E.g. The RealPlayer icon, which plays both audio and video content, can be launched here externally from the browser window.

---

conventional memory – In IBM-type PCs this refers to the first 640Mb of memory that is available for standard *DOS programs*. Also referred to as *Base Memory*.

conversation view – An option on Microsoft network's *bulletin board* that allows the user to see the first part of a *thread* to assess whether it is of interest. The thread can be *expanded* if the user wants to view all the contributions.

conversion – The translation of one program into another; e.g. to convert a Word file into HTML format.

conversion rate – The rate at which users interact from seeing an ad on the Web to making a purchase or registering for something. It is used in combination with the *click* rate to determine the effectiveness of advertising.

cookie – Data that is stored in a file on a user's computer accessing a *browser*. It is initially deposited there by a *server* and can be used to store information such as the user's preferences or passwords. Cookies provide a way for *dotcom* companies to monitor *traffic* and to profile who is visiting their sites, so that they can tailor their content the next time that visitor hits the site (in theory to provide a better service). Cookies are also used to store individuals' *shopping cart* content and can be located (and deleted if desired) via the Windows file, then to Temporary Internet Files.

Cooltalk – Software within *Netscape Navigator* that enables Internet telephone connections over long distance calls, which are charged at local rates. The software supports *audioconferencing* and *chat* tools.

Copernic – A *meta-search* program that allows the user to search on two *search engines* simultaneously. The results are merged and purged so that the final list does not show repeated entries. Copernic was developed by Copernic.com, a US technology company producing tools for efficient access to and management of the overwhelming quantity of information available on the Internet and intranets. It can be downloaded from the Web.
Go to: www.copernic.com

co-processor – A secondary computer processor that operates on a separate circuit inside the computer and speeds it up by boosting the *Central Processing Unit*. Many co-processors have specific functions such as handling math, graphics, and networking functions.

copy – 1. To make a duplicate of a disk, document, or file. An essential function. 2. The function of duplicating selected text or objects using the cut/copy/paste feature and commands available in most text-based and word-processing programs. 3. Desktop publishing and word processing term to describe text in a document.
See: feature box

copyleft – (slang) Copyleft is a licensing system that guarantees that uncopyrighted software remains free for the public to share and improve. This is because although *freeware* is technically free, it can nevertheless be taken, altered, and then launched as proprietary software with copyright restrictions. A play on the word *copyright,* which gives software companies and individuals exclusive legal rights to produce and sell their software (effectively limiting the option of freeware).
See also: gnu, open source movement

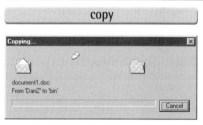

The copy function in Windows allows the user to copy files downloaded from the Internet or sent via floppy disk.

A pictorial folder and arrow, as well as shaded-in scale, indicates when the copying task is being processed and when it is complete.

copy protection – Methods used by software manufacturers to stop people from making unauthorized copies of software. This can be done using serial numbers or a hardware key that is inserted into the back of the computer.

copycat – Web sites or pages that are made to look like another web site or page. These usually imitate high-quality sites and are used for illegal or dubious purposes.

copyright – The licensing system that makes it illegal to use or copy a program without first having purchased the program or gained the publisher's authority to do so.

CORBA – See: Common **O**bject **R**equest **B**roker **A**rchitecture

cordless – See: wireless communications

---

counter

Displaying the number of hits for a particular web site is achieved by a counter script that converts the number of visitors into a graphic display, usually on the home page. This counter shows 27,497 current visitors.

---

core – 1. The memory of a computer. 2. The file produced as a result of a program crashing.

core page – An alternative web site design that uses core pages in place of homepages. These summarize the principal functions of the site and provide key links.

Corel – A Canadian software company. It produces the popular CorelDraw and Corel Ventura programs.
Go to: www.corel.com

corrupted – A term used to describe a damaged file or drive that the computer is unable to read. The damage may have occurred by accident, software or hardware failure, or a virus.

cost per action – The cost to the advertiser of displaying a *banner ad* once.

cost per thousand impressions (CPM) – The cost to the advertiser of displaying a *banner ad* one thousand times.

Coulomb – A unit of electrical charge that is equal to 6.26 x 10 to the18th degree electrons.

counter – The on-screen indicator that shows on a web site how many times that site has been visited.
See: feature box

country codes – The code on an address that indicates the country of origin of a web site or e-mail. Sometimes called a country *domain* name. The code is generally the first two letters of the full country name, e.g: .au = Australia, .ca = Canada, .uk = United Kingdom.

coupons – A money-off coupon found on a web site. The coupon can be printed off the computer, which is then redeemable in designated stores.

Courier – A common type or font that is built-in to most computers and printers as one of the *default* fonts. It looks like the letters have been typed by a conventional typewriter. Although Courier is clear to read, it can print out somewhat thinly.
SEE: FEATURE BOX

courseware – Software designed for computer-based training.

CPI – See: **C**haracters **P**er **I**nch

CPM – See: **c**ost **p**er **t**housand **i**mpressions

CPS – See: **C**haracters **P**er **S**econd

CPSR – See: **C**omputer **P**rofessionals For **S**ocial **R**esponsibility

CPU – See: **C**entral **P**rocessing **U**nit

CR – See: **C**arriage **R**eturn

crack – The act of breaking into a secure computer system, usually a network (carried out by a *cracker*).

cracker – Those who break and enter into a secure computer system, such as a network, without permission and usually with the intent of criminal or dubious activity. The term was introduced by *hackers* who considered themselves law-abiding individuals with a high level of computer proficiency who used unauthorized entry for specifically non-criminal activity. Using cracker in their view helps to make the distinction.

cradle – Device to hold another device, e.g. palm pilot, and connect it to a PC.

crapplet – (slang) A *Java Applet* that is full of errors, has no value, and is memory heavy and badly written.

crash – A complete failure of the computer system or network. Can be caused by software or hardware failure. The only way out is to *boot-up* the computer.

Courier

The Courier font mimics the slightly old-fashioned type produced by a classic 1960s typewriter. It is a clear type with no ambiguity for misinterpreting lower case or upper case characters. It is also a fixed-pitch font whereby all characters have an identical width.

```
This text is
written in
Courier font.
```

crawler – A program that trawls the Web to provide search engines with information, page cancelations and updates, new entries, etc. Also known as *spider*.

CRC – See: **C**yclical **R**edundancy **C**heck

 Creative Technology (Ltd) – A leading manufacturer in PC entertainment products. It was founded in Singapore in 1981. Best noted for its *Sound Blaster,* a leading brand of sound audio. It also produces a version for PCs and notebooks. **Go to:** www.creative.com

creeping featurism – (slang) The tendency to load more features onto systems, making them more complicated and compromising design aesthetics.

crippleware – Software that performs only a limited number of functions. This is often distributed as *freeware* in a trial offer aimed at enticing users to purchase the full version when they get fed up with the limitations of the *demo* version.
See also: demo, freeware

CRLF – **C**arriage **R**eturn/**L**ine **F**eed. A pair of character codes that tells a printer or terminal to return to the beginning of the line. Windows uses both CR and LF end-of-line characters (they are ASCII decimal 13 10, hex 0D 0A). In Apple Macs, only the CR is used to indicate the end of a line in a text file; in UNIX it is the LF.

crop – To select a part of a picture and manipulate it separately. Paint, graphics, and desktop publishing programs have a crop tool that allows the user to draw a rectangle around part of an image and then to cut and paste this selection.

cross–platform – The ability of software or hardware to work on any *platform*, e.g. to crossover from Windows to Macintosh operating systems and vice versa.

crossposting – To send a single message to several newsgroups or message boards (as opposed to posting separate copies of it in different newsgroups). It ensures that all responses made in any newsgroups will be crossposted to all of them. Overuse of this more economical messaging system is considered bad form by many users.

CRT – See: **C**athode **R**ay **T**ube

crunch mode – (slang) A method using an *algorithm* that is highly efficient in processing large amounts of data. E.g. If a file is said to be crunched, it has been *compressed* by such a process.

cryptography – The study and application of secret codes and encoding – which is of ever increasing relevance to Internet, e-commerce, and web site security.
See also: encryption

C/SC – Capitals, Small Capitals.

CSMA/CD – **See:** **C**arrier **S**ense **M**ultiple **A**ccess/**C**ollision **D**etection

CSP – **See:** **C**ommerce **S**ervices **P**rovider

CSS – **See:** **C**ascading **S**tyle **S**heet

Csu/Dsu – **C**hannel **S**ervice **U**nit/**D**ata **S**ervice **U**nit. A hardware device that converts digital data as used on a local area network (*LAN*) into a form acceptable on a wide-area network (*WAN*); e.g. from a digital line to an *ISP* where both the user and the ISP have a CSU/DSU.

CTI – **C**omputer **T**elephony **I**ntegration. The integration of computer and telephone technology.

Ctrl – Abbreviation on the keyboard and in menu for *Control*.

Ctrl-Alt-Del – A *keyboard shortcut* to close an active program. In Windows this brings up a dialog box inviting you to start the task manager or to shut down.

CTS – **C**lear **t**o **s**end. An indication from a wire in the serial port to the modem that it is ready to receive data.

CU seeME A free *videoconferencing* application for use over the Internet that enables users to communicate using voice, white board, and video functions. It was developed by Cornell University (which gives the prefix CU).

CUA – **See:** **C**ommon **U**ser **A**ccess

Cube – **See:** Apple Power Mac G4

cursor – A cursor is the position indicator on a computer display screen. On Apple Macs, the cursor can be a flashing line, arrow, special item tool, or hand depending on the function being used.

In Microsoft Windows, the cursor icon is a hand (left) to indicate an object, and an hourglass (right) to show a request is currently being processed.

customize – To change the specification of *software* or *hardware* to suit a user's requirements or tastes.

cut – To delete. Cut and paste is the method used to move text or objects from one position to another or from one document to another.
SEE: FEATURE BOX

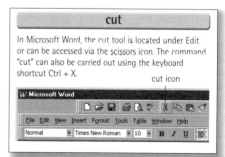

cut

In Microsoft Word, the cut tool is located under Edit or can be accessed via the scissors icon. The command "cut" can also be carried out using the keyboard shortcut Ctrl + X.

cut icon

CWIS - **C**ampus **W**ide **I**nformation **S**ystem. An information retrieval system using Telnet that predates the Web.

CXML - See: Commerce XML

cyan - The blue color that is used in four-color printing.
SEE ALSO: CMYK

cyber - Used as a prefix to words to show that the function is the virtual computer-based form of this activity; e.g. cybercash is a form of virtual cash used on the Web.
SEE ALSO: CYBERSPACE

cyberbunny - A person who is ignorant of computer technology but not afraid to tell others what to do using *newsgroups* and *bulletin boards*.

cybercafé - A place where the public can go to access the Internet. They tend to be in highly accessed pedestrian areas and generally offer café or other social facilities, too. A highly popular service for travelers.

cybercash - A form of virtual cash used on the Web.

cyberchondriac - Someone who is convinced their hardware or software is persistently malfunctioning even when the fault lies with their use of poor commands or loading instructions.

cybercide - The death or end of an *avatar* in an online game.

cybercitizen - A computer user who accesses the Internet.

cybernetics - The study of the regulating mechanisms of the human brain, which is extended to studying the mechanisms of machines, such as computers.

Cyberpatrol - A popular blocking program to restrict access to Internet sites that contain adult material.
GO TO: www.cyberpatrol.com

cyberphobia - A fear of computers.

cyberpork - (slang) Funding given to Internet systems developers by the US government.

cyberprise - A cyberprise is a Web-enabled enterprise. The word combines the ideas of cyberspace and enterprise so well that a company named Wall Data has trademarked it. Wall Data's Cyberprise™ products, which include a web server, a database manager for web pages, and a web page publisher, are aimed at allowing an enterprise to quickly get new and existing information on their public web site or on an intranet or extranet.

cyberrhea - Verbal diarrhea when used in postings to newsgroup or on e-mails (as the name suggests).

cybersexism - Male-dominated traits intruding into newsgroups and web sites.

Cybersitter 2000 – An Internet filter program that provides sophisticated content recognition. E.g. It allows parents the option of keeping undesirable material, such as pornography, away from children. Go to: www.cybersitter.com

CYBERsitter™
For a Family Friendly Internet

cyberspace – A term first introduced by the author William Gibson to describe a virtual world linked by computers.
SEE ALSO: VIRTUAL REALITY

cybersquatting – Registering an Internet *domain name* for the purpose of reselling it for a profit. E.g wallstreet.com was bought for $70 and sold for $1 million. Famous people often have to pay heavily to prevent their names being maligned by association with dubious sites. Companies, however have won important legal battles to win back their domain names against people who cybersquat.

cyberwoozling – A term employed in the security services for the process of monitoring a person's use of the Internet.

cyborg – A word derived from combining cybernetics and organism. It is used to describe the dependence of humans on technology. It has come to mean anyone who relies on computers for their work.

cybrarian – Someone who makes a living by researching information on the Internet.

Cyclical Redundancy Check (CRC) – A method of checking data for errors during transmission.

cypherpunks – Individuals who rely heavily on *encryption* to maintain privacy and who oppose any form of regulation on encryption systems.

Cyrillic – The alphabet used in Eastern Europe and Russia.

cyrix – A low-cost *microprocessor* for use in personal computers.

DAC, D/A Converter – See: **D**igital-to-**A**nalog **C**onverter

daemon – A type of UNIX process that runs continuously in the background, waiting for some event to occur. The programs that handle e-mail are often referred to as daemons. Windows calls similar programs system agents and services. The word comes from the Greek, meaning "an attendant power or spirit."

daisy-chain – To daisy-chain is to link together several computers or devices, such as hard disk drives, in sequence.

dancing baloney – Describes a series of animated images and other moving objects that can add interest to a web site.

dark fiber – A fiber-optic cable that is not carrying a signal. It is called a lit fiber when a signal is being carried.

DARPA – Formerly ARPA.
See also: Defense Advanced Research Projects Agency

dash – The - on the keyboard often used to substitute a space on a *URL.*

DAT – See: **D**igital **A**udio **T**ape

data – Information that is put into a computer. The computer must first translate the data into *binary* code, then carry out the operation and translate the data back into the original form.
See also: data entry

data bits – These are digital bits that contain information, as opposed to bits used for processing.

 data cable – PCs use data cables to link the monitor to the hard drive, as well as to link *peripheral devices.* All cables are cased in rubber or plastic cases for insulation.

data carrier – 1. A medium that can hold machine readable data; e.g. tapes, disks, compact discs, and DVDs.
2. A carrier frequency for the transmission of data.

data center – The department where the main computer systems of an operation are located. It often contains data entry and flow controls, a data library, and other related features.

data communication – The movement of data from one computer to another. Data communication can include binary encoded text, voice, graphics, and video.

data communications equipment – This is typically a device that manages a session on a network; e.g. such equipment might include a modem that also converts and manages transmission signals.

data compression – See: compression

data conversion – Changing data from one file format to another.

data encryption – See: encryption

Data Encryption Standard – A form
of encryption that was developed by the
United States National Security Agency
using a 56-bit key. The Data Encryption
Standard is a very fast and popular system
with security software that enables the
users to have a newly generated key
produced for each session, or to use a
secret key repeatedly. This Standard is
commonly abbreviated to DES.

data entry – The act of inputting
information into a computer. Data entry
is often found in job descriptions to mean
the typing of data into a database.
SEE ALSO: DATA MINING

data integrity – Preventing the
accidental deletion or the corruption
of data in a database of any kind.

data library – A kind of directory held
on a server that contains files that are
available for downloading.

data mining – The process of trawling
through databases looking for certain data
patterns and matches. Data mining is used
in market research, economics, police work,
and science.

data packet – **See:** packet

data processing – The processing of
information by computers. It is abbreviated
to DP.

data rate – **See:** Baud

data recovery – The restoration of data
that has been lost owing to hardware
or software failure or power loss. Backed-
up files may be simply recovered, whereas
other files may require the use of other
special retrieval programs such as
Norton Utilities.

data source name – The identification
name used for data accessed through a
web page that is used with a database.

data terminal equipment (DTE) – The
equipment source or destination of signals
on the network. Usually this is a modem
on a computer.

data terminal ready – This signal is sent
from communications software such as a
web browser to the modem. It indicates
that the program is waiting to activate the
modem. The modem goes into Terminal
Ready mode when this signal is received.

data traffic – The number of TCP/IP
packets traveling across a network.

data vaulting – When data is sent to a
different location in a computer for
backing up.
SEE ALSO: BACK UP

data virus – A computer virus that is
targeted at files that contain data. Program
files are at risk because their start-up files
are attacked in this way, preventing the
program from functioning properly, or
even at all.

data warehousing – This term describes a huge database within a large organization that is used for the processing of data, responding to queries, and the very rapid making of summaries.

database – An organized body of data. It may also be used to mean database management software.

database administrator – The person responsible for the administration and functioning of a database or series of databases. Often abbreviated to DA.

database front-end – An interface that enables database programs to communicate with other applications.

database management software – Software for managing the storage and retrieval of data by organizing it into fields, records, and files. The software also controls access to the database over a network and maintains the security of the database.

database server – A computer in a local area network (LAN) that hosts a database.

datagram – See: packet

dating – A way of meeting people over the Internet. Dating web sites try to ensure that the participants are genuine, but a cautious approach is recommended.

daughterboard/daughtercard – These refer to small printed circuit boards that plug into a *motherboard*.

dB – See: **D**ecibel

DB – See: **D**atabase

DBA – See: **D**atabase **A**dministrator

DCC – See: **D**irect **C**able **C**onnection.

DCE – See: **D**ata **C**ommunications **E**quipment

DCOM – See: **D**istributed **C**ommon **O**bject **M**odel

DDC – See: **D**isplay **D**ata **C**hannel

DDS – See: **D**igital **D**ata **S**torage

dd-mm-yy – Stands for **D**ay**D**ay **M**onth**M**onth **Y**ear**Y**ear.

dead – Describes a computer that has crashed, or, more generally, devices or software features that are non-functional. SEE ALSO: CRASH

dead link – A dead link is a URL that no longer points to the web site that it was intended to reach, possibly because the destination document has been moved or deleted. A number of dead links on a web site makes its use frustrating and indicates poor maintenance. SEE ALSO: COBWEB

dead start – See: cold boot

dead tree edition – (slang) An online document, such as a web page or e-mail, that is printed on paper, i.e. wood from dead trees.

deadlock – When two or more processes are waiting for each other to carry out a function before proceeding. E.g. A server is waiting for input from a modem, which is waiting for a signal from the server.

debug – To fix problems concerning hardware or software.

debugger – Software that debugs a program by stopping at breakpoints and displaying various programming points. In this way it is able to assist the programmer to find and solve the problem.

DEC – See: **D**igital **E**quipment **C**orporation

deca- – Prefix meaning ten, taken from Greek. It often begins technical words.

deci- – This prefix meaning tenth is taken from Latin. Hence, decimal is the numeric system based on tens and decibel is one-tenth of a bel.

decibel – Measurement of loudness named after Alexander Graham Bell. A decibel is one tenth of a bel with audible sounds ranging from about 20 to 100 dB.

decimal number – Decimal numbers are expressed in base 10. The number system 8 in everyday usage. Computers work in base 2 or binary numbers.

decoder – A decoder is hardware or software that translates a signal or data back to its "uncoded" or original form.
SEE ALSO: CODE

decompression – To restore a compressed file to its original format.
SEE ALSO: COMPRESSION

decryption – The process of decoding encrypted data.
SEE ALSO: ENCRYPTION

dedicated – Describes a device that has a single function.

dedicated line – A telecommunications line that provides a direct, permanent connection from one computer to the Internet. Contrast with a dial-up connection that is used for Internet access on an ad-hoc basis.

dedicated server – A service that is used by one organization for one purpose only.

deep link – This kind of hyperlink can only be accessed after repeated clicking on a number of higher level hyperlinks. The results of a search using a search engine or web directory may provide lists of deep links to web sites, because such search software is likely to index all the pages on the web, not just home pages.
SEE ALSO: SHALLOW LINK, DEEP WEB

deep web – 1. Content on the Web that is not found in search engine results, because it is located within databases.
SEE ALSO: SURFACE WEB
2. Content on web pages that is password-protected and consequently available only to members or subscribers.

de facto standard – Unofficial standard or protocol that is still widely accepted.

default – An instruction that a computer assumes, unless instructed otherwise, e.g. a program might adopt Arial font as its default until a user selects an alternative.

default browser – The web browser that the computer uses when opening a web page. Alternative browsers may be selected by changing the computer's settings.

default directory – The disk directory in which the computer will work by default, performing such operations such as saving files unless instructed otherwise.

default drive – The disk drive that the computer uses if no other drive is specified. Usually the C or hard drive.

Defense Advanced Research Projects Agency (DARPA) – The US agency that began as ARPA, and funded initial experiments in the use of computers linked by telephone lines that later evolved into the Internet and attendant technologies.

definition – This describes the amount of detail that is displayed on a monitor or on printed material.
SEE ALSO: PIXEL, RESOLUTION

deflate – To compress a file.

defrag – This term is usually used as an abbreviation for the phrase to defragment a disk.

defragger – The program that enables the hard disk to be defragmented. Also called an "optimizer program." On Windows systems this is called Disk Defragmenter and is found in the System Tools sub-menu of the Accessories menu.

defragment – Areas of any hard disk are generally made up from many pieces of fragmented files. The defragmentation of a hard disk improves its efficiency and so improves the speed of performance for all your programs. When you decide to run a defragmentation program, such as the Disk Defragmenter supplied with *Microsoft Windows*, it attempts to put these pieces back together again. This process is highly recommended for improving disk efficiency, but the longer you leave it before carrying out this defragmentation process, the slower it will perform.

degauss – To demagnetize. Both color monitors and the read/write heads in disk drives need to be degaussed occasionally to prevent the build up of magnetic fields. Many monitors are capable of degaussing themselves automatically when they are turned on.

degree of freedom – This describes the amount of motion available in a virtual reality or robotics system. 3DOF allows three degrees of freedom; horizontal, vertical, and depth. 6DOF adds in pitch, yaw, and roll.

deja.com – Now called Deja.com, DejaNews was one of the first search engines. It was primarily dedicated to accessing newsgroups. It is still considered to be one of the best.
Go to: www.deja.com

Deja News – See: Deja.com

Del (Delete) – A DOS command meaning to delete a file.

Delete Key – A keyboard key that moves the cursor to the left, deleting the character to the left of the cursor. Also called the backspace key.
SEE ALSO: BACKSPACE KEY

Delimiters – Delimiters are those symbols that are generally used for separating one field of data or one part of a program from another part. Commas are the delimiters that are usually employed for separating data fields, while brackets or Return commands are those delimiters that are used in some programs.

delivery failure – 1. Delivery failure is the term that is commonly used for describing the failure of an e-mail message or of some other kind of data file to reach its intended destination.
2. (slang) This term is also regularly used to describe any message, computer based or verbal, that has failed to get through to its recipient (in terms of being understood).

delivery status notification – Delivery status notification is a kind of message that reports the result of an attempt to deliver an e-mail message. This notification status arrives as a MIME formatted message that can be read both by people and by computers. The versions of the messages for computers are designed to enable databases and subscriber lists to be updated automatically in any circumstances when delivery might fail.

Dell Computer – Michael Dell formed Dell in 1984. Dell Corporation is now one of the world's leading computer manufacturers and retailers, primarily dealing in home computing. At the beginning of the 21st century, the company had established a reputation for quality and value.
SEE: FEATURE BOX

delurk – To become an active participant in a newsgroup or a chat area having previously been observing or lurking. It is very common for new visitors to newsgroups and chat areas to spend some time lurking to learn about the common kinds of discussion topics before deciding to delurk and so become a participant.

demibold – A font weight in which the characters are in between regular text and bold. Abbreviated to demi.

demilitarized zone (DMZ) - The area between a trusted internal network and the external world of the Internet. It is a security measure employed in situations that use two firewalls with a space in between. Most ISPs use a DMZ for their Web and e-mail authentication servers.

demo - **See:** demo software

demo software - Demo software is a version of an application that has been released by the manufacturer with the intention of raising awareness and interest in a new program. Demo versions of programs are usually early versions of the software that might contain bugs and flaws. They may contain only a sample selection of the features that will end up being offered in the final version of the product, and will usually be free of charge. Sometimes demo versions will be full-featured but work only for a limited period of time, ceasing to function after a period of thirty days, for example. Demo software is often available for download from the manufacturer's web site.

Demon - The British company Demon was founded in 1992 and has long proven to be one of the UK's most experienced and successful *Internet Service Providers* with a very large customer base. It was purchased in 1998 by Thus (the name for Scottish Telecom).

denial-of-service attack (DOS attack) - This describes the situation when a network is inundated with requests so that regular traffic is either slowed or halted. This may be the result of a computer virus attacking all the computers in a network so that these "zombies" all generate bogus messages simultaneously.

denizen - A pejorative term for a person who frequently uses the Internet.

density - The number of bits or tracks stored on a recording surface, a chip, or other electronic component.
SEE ALSO: DOUBLE DENSITY DISK

Dell computer

This shows one of Dell's typical home business computers, the Dell Precision Workstation 340. These sorts of high-memory computers are designed for web-design or graphics-based work either at home or in the office.

DES – See: **D**ata **E**ncryption **S**tandard

descender – In typography, the part of a character that descends below the baseline, i.e. lowercase "g", "j", and "y" have descenders; "a" and "e" do not.
SEE ALSO: ASCENDER, X-HEIGHT

deselect – To deselect means to cancel a selected area or object. In terms of computer software, it usually refers to the process of canceling the selection of a pre-selected area of text or object. Usually a selected area appears highlighted on the screen. This area can be deselected simply by clicking the mouse pointer outside the selected area.

---

desktop

This shows a simple PC Windows desktop, with the Start button at the bottom left-hand side of the screen. The clock and the calculator accessories windows are open on the desktop.

---

desk accessory (DA) – A small program that is similar to an item on a real office desktop; e.g. a clock, calculator, calendar, and message pad. Windows desk accessories are in the Accessories menu. Macintosh desktop accessories can be placed in the Apple menu.

deskjet – Deskjet is the name Hewlett Packard uses for its printer range.
SEE ALSO: HEWLETT PACKARD

desktop – The whole monitor screen is in effect a graphical interface that represents an office desktop. The icons on the screen resemble objects that would be found on a real desktop, such as a clock, calculator, and files.
SEE: FEATURE BOX

desktop publishing – Describes the use of a computer to produce camera-ready copy for printing. Desktop publishing uses word-processing, page layout, graphics, scanning, and printer facilities to create such items as newsletters, advertising materials, and information leaflets. Two popular programs are QuarkXPress and Adobe PageMaker. Abbreviated to DTP.

destination – The location to which a file or highlighted object is moved or copied.

develop – To write software.

developer – A person who designs and writes software. Synonymous with software engineer and systems programmer.

device – 1. Hardware that forms part of the computer. It can be a small component such as a transistor, a disk drive, or a peripheral device such as a scanner. 2. In semiconductors it is a functional electronic circuit.

device bay – **See:** bay

device driver – **See:** driver

device independent bitmap – Bitmapped graphic files that can be used with many different monitors and printers. E.g. TIFF (Tagged Image File Format).

Device Manager – The Device Manager provides operating system information and enables you to make changes in advanced settings for Microsoft Windows. From the Device Manager you can also make changes to the settings for peripheral devices such as printer, monitor, and keyboard. To access the Device Manager in Microsoft Windows, right-click the My Computer icon and then click the Device Manager tab in the System Properties dialog box that appears.

DHCP Dynamic Host Configuration Protocol – A communications protocol that allows a client to request, and be assigned, an IP Address from a server.

DHTML – **See:** Dynamic **HTML**

diagnostics – On PCs these test to ensure that hardware components are working.

dialog box – Any pop-up message box requesting input from the user. This may be a warning or a request for action. Sometimes the box may simply provide information. Dialog boxes usually demand a response from the user who is asked to click an OK, Yes or No, or Cancel button. It is a generic term not just restricted to Windows nor confined to the system.
SEE: FEATURE BOX

dial-up access – A telephone line that provides temporary Internet access. Usually the line is shared with an ordinary phone line on domestic PCs.

dial-up account – This is a kind of Internet account that requires the user to dial into the Internet Service Provider (ISP) each time a connection is needed. Alternatives to a dial-up account include always-open lines such as ADSL lines.

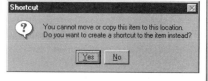

dialog box

This is a typical system dialog box in that it offers the user a simple choice: yes or no. A third choice (cancel) is also commonly offered. Until this yes or no choice (relating to the creation of a shortcut) is made, action is frozen.

> **Shortcut**   ☒
>
> ❓ You cannot move or copy this item to this location. Do you want to create a shortcut to the item instead?
>
> [Yes]   No

dial-up connection - A connection to an ISP or another computer that is accessed through a telephone line. E.g. This may enable the user to make a connection between a home-based PC and an office based computer or network.

dial-up networking - A function of the Windows operating system that manages a dial-up connection by dialing the number and making the connection.

diary site - A web site that allows the user to make an online diary. These diaries can be kept private or can go public.

digerati - People who have contributed to the growth of the computer and Internet age. The foremost of these is Bill Gates.

digest - 1. Postings to a newsgroup or message board that are grouped together and sometimes edited for interest by a moderator. The digest may then be posted on another newsgroup, message board, or on a web page.
2. A mailing list option that sends one large message instead of many small ones.

digicash - **See:** e-cash

digital - Modern computing is based on the digital system, which relies on the positive and negative electric states that correspond to the 0 and 1 in the binary number system. This contrasts with a continuously variable analog signal.
SEE ALSO: BINARY, BIT, BYTE

digital audio - Sound saved in binary format such as .wav or .au files. These are played on programs such as Realplayer. Near-CD quality sound can be achieved using the MP3 file format and are played on programs such as WinAmp.

digital audio tape (DAT) - A magnetic tape originally designed for audio, used now as back-up tapes for computers. They store about 12GB on one tape.

digital camera - A camera that stores the

images in digital format that can be downloaded directly by the PC. The images can then be manipulated and either printed or used as an image in a document or web page.

digital cash - **See:** e-cash

digital certificate - This is a form of Internet security used in e-business and for the safe transfer of information and money online. The certificate verifies identity by means of a digital signature. The certificate authority, usually a trusted company such as Verisign, provides a unique set of numbers, which are encrypted and sent and then decrypted by the receiver.

digital effects - Sounds and animations that have been created digitally, e.g. synthetic sounds and transitions such as fades and dissolves between video frames.

digital envelope – An encrypted message for transmission over a network. Sometimes the term is used to describe inserting data into a frame, or packet, for transmission.

Digital Equipment Corporation (DEC) – A computer and software company that makes high performance minicomputers and workstations and also developed the Alpha processor.

digital film – A flash memory card that is used to store digital images from a digital camera. These are transferred to the computer using a cable or by directly inserting the film module into a drive attached to the computer. Some cameras offer both methods of transfer.

digital imaging – Using digitized images such as bitmap images. These can be manipulated to create visual effects.

digital library – A library of electronic texts. These texts may be specific or more general such as those found on some university web sites.

Digital Millennium Copyright Act (DMCA) – A bill passed by the US government that accepts online copyright provisions agreed to by the World Intellectual Property Organization (WIPO).

digital monitor – A monitor that shows a fixed number of colors or shades of gray. Usually older monitors.
SEE ALSO: ANALOG MONITOR

digital pen – This describes a kind of pen connected to a wire or wireless that is used in conjunction with a graphics tablet or display screen.

digital signal processing (DSP) – A method of enhancing the digital form of analog signals such as voice or music using the computer.

digital signature – This signature refers to the unique set of numbers issued by a certificate authority that act like a passport confirming identity on digital certificate authority.

Digital Signature Standard (DSS) – A standard introduced by the US government for digital signatures and used by Federal information systems.

digital simultaneous voice and data (DSVD) – DSVD refers to a means of sending compressed digitized voice and data signals simultaneously over an ordinary telephone line.

digital subscriber line (DSL) – A telecommunications line that transmits data at high speeds using the existing phone network.
SEE ALSO: ADSL, ISDN

Digital Subscriber Line Access Multiplexer (DSLAM) – Used by the phone company to link customers' DSL connections to a high-speed asynchronous transfer mode line. Abbreviated to DSLAM.

digital surround – See: DTS

digital versatile disk (DVD) – An optical disk that can store up to 17 gigabytes of data on one disk. This capacity makes it a popular format for video, music, and movie storage. DVD is expected to replace the CD-ROM. DVD a few years ago was an abbreviation for Digital Video Disc - a medium that did not really take off.

digital video express – A new DVD-ROM format developed by several leading film companies for the rental market. You can only watch the film in a specified timescale; once the time has elapsed you cannot access the movie, which means you need to return it to the rental store.

digital video interface (DVI) – A standard that prescribes how video material is compressed and stored on a DVD.

---

dingbats

Dingbats is a font made up of special characters, some of which are seen below. They include geometrical shapes such as circles and squares (in outline and as blocked-in shapes) as well as symbols representing infinity.

---

digital wallet – A function offered by browsers for financial transactions.

digital watermark – A security feature in which invisible digital watermarks are embedded in files to track files that are copied and used without the consent of the developer.

digital whiteboard – The use of the computer screen as a type of blackboard where several users are able to write or draw on the screen. It is used in some conferencing systems.

digital-to-analog Converter (DAC) – An electronic circuit that converts data from digital (binary) to analog form. For example, sound stored digitally on a hard drive is converted into sound waves and broadcast through the speakers.

digitize – To translate a signal or data into digital (binary) format.
SEE ALSO: DIGITAL

digitizer tablet – See: graphics tablet

digizine – An electronic magazine stored on a CD-ROM.
SEE ALSO: E-ZINE

DIMM – **D**ual **I**nline **M**emory **M**odule. A way of increasing memory by adding DIMM expansion cards that contain high-capacity RAM chips. These are inserted into sockets found on the motherboard.

DIN connector – See: PS/2

dingbats – A font comprising special characters, such as geometrical characters, and symbols, such as hearts, smilies, little flowers, and graphical bullets. Wingdings is one popular dingbat font.
SEE: FEATURE BOX

diode – An electronic device that relies on current flow in only one direction. Used to convert AC to DC current.
SEE ALSO: ALTERNATING CURRENT, DIRECT CURRENT

dip switch dual inline package switch – A set of tiny switches that are used to configure a device. Sometimes it is necessary to alter the alignment of these switches for the device to run.

dir – This is a common DOS command that lists all the files in a specified directory; e.g. dir c:/games will list all the directories and any files within the games directory on the computer's C-drive.

Direcpc – A two-way, broadband, Internet access service via satellite for large and small businesses and consumers. Direcpc offers always-on, high-speed service using a small satellite dish and a small indoor unit delivering the Internet to your PC.
GO TO: www.hns.com or www.direcway.com

Direct3D – An application from Microsoft that allows programmers to manipulate and develop three-dimensional objects. Microsoft's Direct3D is part of the larger DirectX standard.
SEE ALSO: DIRECTX

direct access – A type of memory that allows data to be retrieved immediately. Some types of memory, such as tape, need to be wound to the point where the data is in order to access that data. It is synonymous with Random Access Memory.

direct cable connection – This describes the situation when computers are cabled together for data transfer. Direct cable connection is a feature of Microsoft Windows 95/98 and all later versions. Direct cable connection is commonly abbreviated to DCC.

direct connect modem – Most modems connect to the telephone line directly. Older modems used an acoustic coupler.

direct connection – This describes the situation when a computer is permanently connected to the Internet. A direct connection is usually maintained over a leased line.

direct current (DC) – Direct current is an electric current that flows in one direction only.
SEE ALSO: ALTERNATING CURRENT

Director 8 Shockwave – A program from Macromedia that enables designers and authors to develop sophisticated graphics and create three-dimensional images for web sites and multimedia productions.

Go to: www.macromedia.com

directory – Directories allow you to group files on a computer disk. They are sometimes called folders. Each holds a table of contents that briefly identifies the files and other directories (sub-directories). This table includes the name of the creator, the date and time of creation, and the size of file. There is no relationship between the files in a directory and their physical placement on the disk drive.

See: feature box

---

directory

This shows the directory (here named screen shots). The directory's five objects are listed by name, along with details about their size, type, and modification dates.

Name	Size	Type	Modified
accessories	3,073KB	Clipboard Clip	18/10/01 12:12
as	3,073KB	Clipboard Clip	18/10/01 12:12
as2	3,073KB	Clipboard Clip	18/10/01 12:13
Doc3.mcw	3KB	MCW File	18/10/01 12:28
Doc4	43KB	Microsoft Word Doc...	18/10/01 12:36

screen shots
File Edit View Help

---

directory on the Internet – A search site that organizes web sites by subject or category. *Yahoo!* is a popular directory site that searches its directories to produce a list of suggested web sites and a brief description of site content. This term also describes sites that contain online versions of reference directories such as the Yellow Pages.

directory service – A database of names, information and machine addresses of users and resources on a network. When a username is requested, it finds all the information it has on the user, which could include a full name, company, telephone number, as well as e-mail address.

See also: naming service

Directory Service Markup Language (DSML) – A markup language that is used to share directory information.

DirectX – Developed by Microsoft, this simplifies for developers the problem of writing programs that need to be used on a variety of different types of hardware. It does this by creating a type of layer that converts the programmer's instructions into the commands needed by the specific pieces of hardware. This DirectX standard includes Microsoft's Direct3D.

See also: Direct3D

dirty connection – This describes a slow Internet connection that is often caused by network congestion.

disassembler – A program that converts machine language back into assembly language.

disc – **See:** disk

disclaimer – To notify the user that the originator of a web site has no legal responsibility for ideas or opinions or offers made on the site. Often these disclaimers are automatically posted on contributions to newsgroups.

discrete speech – Recognition of words pronounced individually - one at a time. Used in speech recognition.

discussion board – **See:** discussion group

discussion group – A feature on a web site that allows visitors to leave a message, which is then shown to other visitors who in turn can post a contribution.

discussion thread – A sequence of postings in response to a single message on a message board or forum.

disintermediation – To remove the middleman. Disintermediation has enabled many e-businesses to cut overheads and reduce prices compared to their bricks-and-mortar competitors.

disk – A device used to store and retrieve data. These include hard disks, floppy disks, and compact discs (CD).

disk cache – **See:** cache

disk compression – **See:** compression

disk dancer – A person who takes advantage of the free Internet access time offered on promotional disks, then cancels when the free time ends, and moves onto another similar offer.

disk drive – A device that spins, reads, and writes disks. On a PC this may be the hard drive or the CD-ROM drive or the drive for floppy disks.

disk farm – (slang) The place where a large number of disks are connected to one computer.

disk operating system (DOS) – A PC operating system developed by Microsoft and the first with widespread use. It is the underlying operating system for Windows and is accessed in order to complete operations such as changing the batch files and formatting the disks.

disk optimizer – A *defragger*.

diskette – Synonymous with floppy disk.

diskless workstation – A workstation that uses the network computer to store, process, and retrieve data.

display – Another word for the computer screen or monitor.

display data channel (DDC) – The communications line between the display adapter and monitor.

Display Properties – A *Microsoft Windows* dialog box found when opening the Display Control Panel. From the Display Properties dialog box the user is able to make a choices from a wide range of options for changing the appearance of the *Windows* desktop. It also enables the user to make many alterations to the color on the monitor, the use of screen saver, the use of icons, and so on.

display space – The area within the screen available for displaying images.

distance learning – This describes higher education classes that can be taken from home: usually via the Internet. The learner completes assignments on the computer, which are checked by a tutor at the college or university that is running the course.

distribute – 1. To use multiple computers in one organization rather than a single centralized networked system. Files may also be distributed over the network rather than stored centrally. The most extreme distributed system is the World Wide Web.
2. To use multiple computers often via the Internet to address a particular problem. E.g. The SETI (Search for Extraterrestrial Intelligence) project, which uses home computers to contribute to the search for extraterrestrial life.

distro – (slang) To distribute.

dithering – Giving an illusion of depth and density of color by varying the dot pattern. When a specified color cannot be produced, the program attempts to approximate it by choosing from the range of available pixels. Newspaper photographs are commonly produced in this way.
SEE ALSO: DPI

DIVX – See: **Di**gital **V**ideo **Ex**press

DLL – See: **D**ynamic **L**ink **L**ibrary

DMCA – See: **D**igital **M**illennium **C**opyright **A**ct

DMZ – See: **De**militarized **Z**one

DNS – See: **D**omain **N**ame **S**erver

DNS Entry – See: **D**omain **N**ame **S**ystem or **S**ervice

DNS Parking – One entry in the Domain Name System.

document.doc

.doc – A file extension indicating that the document was created in Microsoft Word. Because of its universality, this has become a standard for e-mail attachments. When opened, a .doc file may alter in appearance from the original page layout due to the receiving computer having a different *default* font and page set-up.

dock – To connect a laptop computer into a docking station to provide it with the same resources as a desktop computer. These resources commonly include full size keyboard, printer, audio speakers, and networking facilities.

docking station – Describes the housing into which a laptop computer sits to provide it with the same resources as a desktop PC.

document – In computing, this refers to a word-processing file.
SEE ALSO: .DOC

document imaging – Describes storage of images of documents that may or may not have been generated by a computer. These documents are generally scanned and saved as bitmapped graphics files complete with manual annotations and signatures.

Document Object Model (DOM) – This is the specification laid down by the *World Wide Web Consortium*, which defines how browsers represent and manipulate objects on a web page. This enables such features as hyperlinks and rollovers to work regardless of the browser.

documentation manuals – Refers to books, paperwork, or online instructions that accompany new software.

documents – **See:** My Documents

DOF – **See:** Degree of Freedom

dogpile – A situation when a large number of participants in an Internet newsgroup respond to a contribution with hostility. Used as a verb, the participants dogpile the contributor.

 **Dolby Digital** – A standard for high-quality digital audio. It is used mainly for the sound portion of videos and movies. It is also known as surround sound.
Go to: www.dolbydigital.com

DOM – **See:** Document Object Model

domain – On the Internet, computers are grouped by name into hierarchical domains. So ".com" and ".uk" are examples of top-level domains. ".co" is a 2nd level domain, and "dk" (as in the publishing company of this book) is a 3rd level domain. Naming at each level is controlled by the level above, so for www.dk.com, "www" is a 4th level within "dk."
SEE: APPENDIX 3 for a list of domain suffixes.

domain dipping – The process of typing anything in a web browser's address box between www. and .com just to see what comes up.

domain name – The name that identifies one or more web sites using their Internet Protocol (IP) addresses (e.g. dk.com). www is a sub-domain name.

domain name hoarding – The process of buying up domain names in order to sell them for profit.

domain name server – The server that holds an up-to-date list of domain names.

domain name system (DNS) – A database system that responds to an entered name, e.g. "dk.com," by looking it up in the Domain Name Server and translating it to an IP address, which is then used to route the message. "Reverse DNS" converts from an IP address to a domain name. Choosing the right domain name is one of the most important things when setting up a web site. You can find out which names are available and under which domain by visiting a web registration site such as www.netnames.com. They will give you a price, or you can visit one of the many domain name auctions that are held at sites such as www.ebay.com

SEE ALSO: BERKELEY INTERNET DOMAIN NAME

domain poaching – Registering a domain name that may be someone else's name or company, either to profit from it or produce a satirical or fan site. Some recent court cases have given the name back to the original celebrity or company.

domain squatting – Occurs when somebody finds a domain name they like and registers it. They then do nothing with it hoping that someone will pay more money for it. Also known as cyber squatting.

domain trafficking – Selling domain names that have already been registered.

domainism – Prejudging someone on the basis of how cool or uncool his or her e-mail address is.

dongle – A piece of hardware that plugs into a computer port to prevent the illegal use and copying of software. It works by generating a code, without which the software will not function.

DOS – See: **D**isk **O**perating **S**ystem

DOS Attack – See: **D**enial **O**f **S**ervice Attack

dot – A period or decimal point. This is common on the Internet since it is an integral part of domain names.

dot address – See: host address

dot gov – (slang) This is an expression used in chat areas when meaning a government official. It is taken from the .gov tag on government domain name sites.

dot matrix printer – An impact printer that works when tightly packed pins hit an ink ribbon printing out tiny dots. These are arranged to form letters on a page.

dot net – (slang) This is a top level Internet domain that is frequently applied to Internet Service Providers or to services that are communications-related. It comes from the abbreviation for network.

dot pitch – The distance between two dots of the same color on a color monitor. The smaller the distances between dots, the sharper the image.
SEE ALSO: DPI

dotcom – (slang) An e-business.

dotcomify – To turn an existing company or phrase into one with an Internet presence by the addition of a .com.

double buffering – A way of speeding up computer operations. The data in one buffer is being processed while data is being read into the second buffer. This aids efficiency in streaming media, sound, and video applications. When the transfer of the data between buffers is through a hardware circuit, it is faster than when managed by software.

double click – To click the mouse button twice in quick succession. This function is used to open programs, and files and to activate features on web pages.
SEE ALSO: LEFT CLICK, RIGHT CLICK

double density disk – These are types of floppy disks that contain twice as much storage space as that available on single density disks. Single-density disks are rare these days. A double-density 3.5" floppy disk contains 720k DOS, 800k.

double-sided sisk – A double-sided disk is a floppy disk that can be written to on both sides.

down – A term that is frequently applied to any computer system or Internet connection that is not working owing to hardware or software problems.

download – The process by which files or data are transferred from one computer to another via the Internet. To download is to take files from the Internet, whereas to upload is to send files by means of the Internet.
SEE: FEATURE BOX

download

This File Download box shows the beginning of the downloading progress via the Internet. The file is held on the FTP site called ftp.hp.com.

After clicking the OK button in the box above, the file called sj166en.exe is transferred across the Internet from the remote site to this user's own computer.

download manager – A program that manages the transfer of data on the Internet from one computer to another. It checks for transmission errors, repeating the operation if necessary.

download site – A web site containing an assortment of software programs and data files for transfer. These are often associated with freeware and shareware but can also be dedicated to specialist information that is available to share.

dpi

Dots per inch (dpi) provides a measure of the resolution of printers, scanners, and monitors. Close examination of this image will reveal the dots that go to make up the picture.

This image was captured and saved at 72 dpi. Close examination will show the use of 72 dots over one inch.

downstream – The direction in which downloaded information passes from a remote computer toward your own computer. In other words, when you download any file, it will pass downstream. (The opposite applies for the direction in which uploaded information will pass.) Telephone line modems have the same speed downstream or upstream (though some services "throttle" to allow higher speeds in one direction than the other).

Downtime – The period (or the length of time) that a computer or an Internet service is going to be unavailable owing to repair or perhaps owing to system failure or to any other kind of techical problem that will remove it from service. In the case of network maintenance, it is possible for downtime to be announced in advance.

downward compatibility – **See:** backward compatible

DP – **See:** **D**ata **P**rocessing

dpi – **D**ots **p**er **i**nch. This measurement is used as an indication for the resolution of printers, scanners, and monitors. Sharper images are formed by high-resolution equipment.
SEE: FEATURE BOX

Dr. Watson – In Windows, Dr. Watson comes into play when something goes wrong. It stops the program where the

error occurs, takes some diagnostic statistics, and then records them in a text file. It doesn't tell you what's wrong, but it may just stop a serious problem.
SEE ALSO: VIRUS PROTECTION SOFTWARE

draft – A printing mode that provides a quick low-resolution copy and images that are used for proofing.

drag – To move an object around on the computer screen.
SEE ALSO: DRAG-AND-DROP

drag-and-drop – To reposition an object on the computer screen using the mouse. Drag-and-drop usually works like this. Leftclick once with the mouse pointer on the object to highlight it. Click the object again, keeping the mouse button depressed, and drag the object to the point to which you wish to move it. At that point release the mouse button and the object is thus moved. This technique can be used to move objects from one folder to another as well as between drives. With minor variations it can be used to move blocks of text and images within documents as well as between documents. Variations will exist, however, depending on the application or program used and the system preferences set up on the computer.
SEE: FEATURE BOX

DRAM – **See: D**ynamic **R**andom-**A**ccess **M**emory

Dreamweaver – Macromedia's Dreamweaver is widely considered to be one of the leading web site building programs available today.
GO TO: www.dreamweaver.com

Dreamweaver Ultradev – An advanced form of Macromedia Dreamweaver, especially good for web sites that need to use databases.

drag-and-drop

To move the "screen shots" folder across the screen, the user needs to click on the folder to highlight it.

The user needs to hold down the mouse button, at which point a mouse pointer will appear (the arrow and plus sign). The folder is then ready to be dragged across the screen. When the user is ready to place the folder, they will simply release the mouse button.

drive – The part of the computer that spins the hard disk, floppy disk, or CD-ROM or runs the tapes. Conventionally, certain letters in a computer system are allocated to the different disk drives. For example, the main drive in a computer is usually called the C drive and the floppy disk drives are called the A and B drives.

drive bay – The area in the computer case where the floppy drive, CD-ROM drive, or hard drive is positioned.

driver – A type of software that enables the computer's operating system to recognize and function with a broad range of devices such as mouse, printer, scanner. All peripherals and cards (such as video cards) must have the correct driver installed in order to run correctly. When you are updating your hardware, new drivers will be required to run the new device.

---

drop cap

In this block of text, the letter G is a drop cap. It occupies three lines, dropping down below the depth of the first line in the paragraph. Drop caps are useful graphical features for the start of books or chapters.

Gorem ipsum dolor sit amet, consectetuer adipiscing elit, sed diam nonummy nibh euismod tincidunt ut laoreet dolore magna aliquam erat volutpat. Ut wisi enim ad minim veniam, quis nostrud exerci tation ullamcorper suscipit lobortis nisl ut aliquip ex ea commodo consequat. Duis autem vel eum iriure dolor in hendrerit in vulputate velit esse molestie consequat, vel illum dolore eu feugiat nulla facilisis at.

---

drop cap – In typography, a drop cap is a very large initial capital letter that descends below the line of type. A drop cap may be very elaborate and take up several lines. Text will automatically wrap around it. A drop cap is sometimes found as the first letter of a chapter opening or may be employed as a graphic device in newsletters and journals.
SEE: FEATURE BOX

drop-down menu – This kind of menu reveals a range of options when the user clicks on a choice button. The most commonly used drop-down menus are found on the standard toolbar for most operating systems and common applications, appearing under such menus as File, Edit, and View.
SEE: FEATURE BOX

dropout – A damaged bit on a disk or the loss of signal during a transmission of data.

DSL – See: Digital Subscriber Line

DSLAM – See: Digital Subscriber Line Access Multiplexer

DSML – See: Directory Service Markup Language

DSP – See: Digital Signal Processing.

DSS – See: Digital Signature Standard

DSVD – See: Digital Simultaneous Voice and Data

DTE – **See:** **D**ata **T**erminal **E**quipment

DTMF – **See:** **D**ual-**T**one **M**ulti-**F**requency

DTS Digital Surround – A home theater audio system developed by Digital Theater Systems Inc.

Dual Boot – When there is a choice of two operating systems to use when starting the computer.

Dual Home Gateway – A security system that ensures that all data transferred between a computer or network and the Internet passes through a *firewall* to prevent unauthorized access.

dual-tone multi-frequency – The tones that are heard on a push-button telephone.

dumb terminal – A screen and keyboard based system that has no processing power. It is connected to a central computer and can be used for simple processing.

dump – (verb) To transfer a large amount of data, usually as a back-up process.

duplex – The ability of a device to transmit and receive information simultaneously.

dustbuster – An e-mail that is sent to an address that has not been used for some time for the purpose of establishing whether or not the address is still active. E-mail addresses are frequently changed, and this is one good way of confirming addresses in the user's *address book*.

dutch auction – A domain name auction where the price starts high and is lowered until a buyer is found.

DVD – **See:** **D**igital **V**ersatile **D**isc

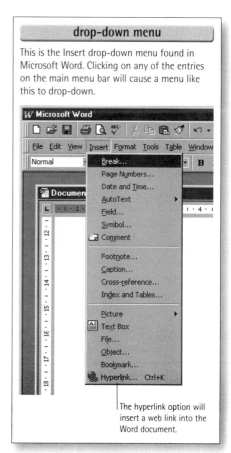

drop-down menu

This is the Insert drop-down menu found in Microsoft Word. Clicking on any of the entries on the main menu bar will cause a menu like this to drop-down.

The hyperlink option will insert a web link into the Word document.

DVD-Ram – This is a rewriteable compact disc that provides 2.6 gigabytes per side of the disc.

DVD-ROM – This is a type of compact disc that holds a minimum of 4.7 gigabytes. This is enough for a full-length movie. This kind of disc is not rewriteable, but it is flexible in that it can support CD-ROM.

DVD+RW – A rewriteable kind of compact disc that can provide three gigabytes on each side of the disc.

DVD-Video – A video format that uses an optical disc for displaying full-length digital movies and supporting programs.

DVI – See: **D**igital **V**ideo **I**nterface

dweeb – (slang) 1. A dweeb is someone considered to be very well informed about computer technology.
2. A derogatory term for someone inept.

dynamic – This term indicates that the program is running.

dynamic content – Web site content that is regularly changed and updated. Some pages and sections are updated frequently throughout the day; e.g. news and money market sites.

dynamic HTML (DHTML) – This describes the combination of HTML, JavaScript (or other scripting language), and cascading style sheets. Taken together these various elements can enable web designers to create many effective web site effects such as rollovers. DHTML works in conjunction with the Document Object Model.

dynamic link library (DLL) – A collection of small programs in Microsoft Windows that can be called upon when a larger program has need of them. It is a means of separating components so that they can be shared by many programs. E.g. Most programs need to be able to pop up a dialog box – the code to do this is in a DLL so that all programs can use it, and it looks the same in every case – and if you update it, all programs get the new version automatically. A very powerful concept.

dynamic random–access memory (DRAM) – Computer memory on a chip that requires a refresh signal to be sent to it regularly. These chips are popular because they are inexpensive for the amount of memory provided.

dynamic rotation – The ability to change the advert on an ad banner, which means that the visitor to the site sees different advertisements in the same space. Often used in conjunction with an ad server. Users may find themselves to be the target of adverts that have been selected as being of special interest to them.

dynamic web page – A web page containing dynamic content such as animated GIFs, video clips, and rollovers.

E – A hexadecimal (base 16) figure equivalent to 14. The *hex* system is a way of representing binary code in a computer.

e- – Prefix meaning electronic; e- refers to any procedure undertaken online, e.g. e-mail, e-commerce. It is popular with corporate marketing departments that want to show their customers and competitors that they have an online strategy.

E-1 – The European version of the *T-1* leased line. It transmits data at approximately 2 *megabites* per second.

e2e – Used in chat rooms to mean e-mail to e-mail or an e-mail dialog.

EA – See: **E**lectronic **A**rts

easter egg – A hidden extra on a web site or program designed to catch a user's interest. It could be an extra skill level in a game or a special offer on a commerce site.

---

e-book

In September 2001, Penguin publishers launched the epenguin imprint, selling e-books on the Penguin web site. They were initially published using Microsoft Reader and Adobe Acrobat eBook Reader software.

---

easy steps – A reference to learning a program or task in small stages.

EAX – See: **E**nvironmental **A**udio

Eb – See: **E**xabyte

e-banking – See: online banking

ebay – One of the leading online auction sites, it was formed in 1995 and has some 30 million users throughout the world. It has a simple mission - to help practically anyone trade practically anything on earth.
Go to: www.ebay.com

eBay effect – A large rise in the price of a company's stock as a result of an announcement that it is to start working in online auctions (as in *ebay*.com).

EBCDIC – See: **E**xtended **B**inary-**C**oded **D**ecimal **I**nterchange **C**ode

e-beam – An electron beam - a stream of electrons, or electricity, that is directed toward a receiver. Some makes of high-tech printers use e-beams to create images.

e-billing – Paying bills either by *e-mail* or via sites with secure connections.

e-book – Short for **e**lectronic book. The e-book is stored on a web site and can be downloaded in a digitized format so that it can be read on an electronic device such as a handheld PC or a specific e-book reader.

The e-book has been much heralded as the replacement for the book, but it has yet to take off. E-books have several advantages over conventional books, such as the ability to search for specific phrases or text; but there is no device as truly portable as a book. Nevertheless, some believe that the future of bookselling and publishing is in e-books, and not in the physical object.
SEE: FEATURE BOX

e-book virus – A hoax *computer virus*. It comes via an e-mail called "An e-book for you" and offers a set of false instructions.

EBPP – **See:** **E**lectronic **B**ill **P**resentment and **P**ayment

e-business – 1. A business that derives at least part of its income by Internet trading. 2. A business that carries out some of its activities using Internet technology.
SEE ALSO: E–COMMERCE

EC – **See:** **e**-**c**ommerce

e-card – An electronic greetings card or postcard downloaded from a web site.
SEE ALSO: E-GREETING
SEE: FEATURE BOX

e-cash – 1. One of the means of carrying out payments online in electronic businesses, such as online shopping.
2. The DigiCash online payment system.

e-catalog – A catalog of goods for sale on a web site.

ECC Memory – **See:** **E**rror-**C**orrecting **C**ode **M**emory

e-centives – A marketing term used by online retailers when referring to customer incentives offered from their web sites.

echo – A reflected wave of a signal on a telephone line. This may cause errors and interference on the line.

Echo return – **See:** Packet Internet Gopher (PING)

e-cinema – Where movies are shot on normal film, then converted into digital format for editing and then converted back into film for later distribution.

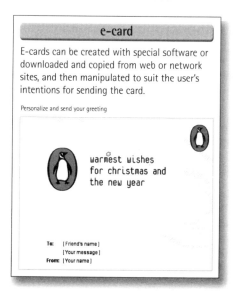

e-card

E-cards can be created with special software or downloaded and copied from web or network sites, and then manipulated to suit the user's intentions for sending the card.

Personalize and send your greeting

warmest wishes
for christmas and
the new year

To: [Friend's name]
        [Your message]
From: [Your name]

Eckerk, John Wallace – (1902-1971)
An American computer pioneer who
worked on new techniques for tabulating
information, he was driven by theories on
the application of computers on his first
love – astronomy.

e-classifieds – Classified advertisements
found on web sites. Some sites are dedicated
to them. Other more general *e-zines* and
e-journals also carry classified
advertisements.

ECML – See: Electronic Commerce
Modeling Language

e-commerce – Commercial activities
carried out via the Internet. E-commerce
includes online shopping, share services,
database management, communications
businesses, and publishing. Since the late
1990s there has been a huge expansion of
e-commerce due to the rapid expansion of
Internet access, which made such business
activities viable.

EcoNet – A network devoted to
environmental issues.
Go to: www.econet.org

Economic Slow Down in US – The title of
a hoax *computer virus*. It encourages the
receiver to send lots of useless e-mails.

e-content – Information that can be
transmitted over the Internet. The term
usually refers to more subjective matter
rather than pure data.

e-cruiting – Recruitment using the Internet.
This is a growing medium for job seekers
and human resource managers. There are
numerous specialist web sites that have
become increasingly popular due to their
wide geographical coverage.

ECP – See: Extended Capabilities Port

ECP – Excessively Cross-Posted ad. An
advertisement that is given wide exposure
on a number of web sites.

ECPA – See: Electronic Communications
Privacy Act

EDI – See: Electronic Data Interchange

edit – To modify documents. Text can be
edited within a *word processing* program.
Web sites can be edited by modifying *HTML*
files, and *programs* can be edited by changing
the original text files in which the program
is written.

editor – 1. The person who *edits* files, web
sites, or programs.
2. A program written to modify files in
general - different editors can manage
different file types (e.g. programming, text).

EDLIN – A *MS-DOS utility* program that
enables the user to make changes to a file
at line level.

e-doctor – A computer engineer who
specializes in fixing *computer viruses*.

e-dress – An *e-mail* or *URL address*.

EDS - Electronic Data Systems. Founded in 1962, EDS is a leading global information technology (IT) services company. It is known for using the latest technology to solve business problems.
Go to: www.eds.com

.edu - A suffix attached to a web site that indicates a *domain* that has educational status – .edu may be associated with a school, college, or university.

education - Using the Internet for learning has become one of its primary uses, as companies made whole libraries of reference available. Educational publishers supply online resources in addition to conventional books and other tools, not as a replacement. There has been a revolution in web-based learning in schools, especially primary but also in secondary, college, and remote learning. There has been much debate about the availability of free information as online providers have now started to charge for what was previously free. *Copyright* laws relating to educational information have also been put under great scrutiny and pressure.

edutainment - Web sites or programs that are both educational and entertaining.

EFF - **See:** **E**lectronic **F**rontier **F**oundation

e-filing - US term derived from filing tax returns. It applies where they can be filled out online, saving time and postage.

e-form - To execute a transaction online, a form often has to be filled in on the computer and filed via a web site. E-forms are supplied over the Internet as a way of ensuring that the information necessary for an *e-commerce* transaction is provided. An e-form will not be accepted into the system until all the necessary *fields*, e.g. full name, address, and so on are completed.

e-flu - A hoax *computer virus*. It offers up the premise that while the computer is unharmed the user is likely to be made ill, and they are recommended to take certain actions to recover. All lies.

EGA - **See:** **E**nhanced **G**raphics **A**dapter

e-games - A generic term used for all electronic games, especially those that can be played online.

Egg - A successful online only bank, based in the UK.
Go to: www.egg.com

egosurfing - To search the Web for references to oneself (only the good ones).

e-greeting - An electronic greeting (like an *e-card*) that is originated on and sent over the Internet. Features of the cards include *multimedia* such as *animated gif* files and music. Many can be downloaded from dedicated web sites and sent free of charge. Popular sites include www.bluemountain.com and www.e-greetings.com.

EIA – See: Electronics Industry Association

Eigenface algorithm – In *face recognition* software, the Eigenface algorithm maps the characteristics of each face with amazing accuracy so that photographs and masks cannot fool it.
SEE ALSO: ALGORITHM

Eight-bit system – An old system or a small, low cost *CPU* that can process eight-bit words.

EJ – A presenter on *radio* programs accessed via the Internet.

e-journal – A journal that is published on the Internet or is available in electronic form. These are usually of academic or specialist interest. They are also called online journals.
SEE ALSO: E-ZINE

elancer – A freelance employee who works mainly using the Internet.

e-learning – An umbrella term used to cover all forms of online *education*.

electroluminescent display (ELD) – A type of *monitor* screen that uses luminescence (emitting light), which comes from the electrical excitation of phosphor on a thin film.

Electromagnetic Compatibility (EMC) – Where there is the use of components in electronic systems that do not electrically interfere with each other.

electromagnetic field (EMF) – A field of force in the form of waves that have both an electronic and a magnetic component. Examples include radio waves, light waves, and x-rays. Computer *monitors* emit low-level electromagnetic radiation, which has led to fears of long-term health implications.

Electromagnetic Interference (EMI) – Electrical disturbances in a system, which can be attributed to natural phenomena, other electromechanical devices, or high-frequency waves from chips and other electronic devices.

Electronic Arts – The largest independent developer and publisher of interactive entertainment software for PCs and advanced entertainment systems.
GO TO: www.ea.com

Electronic Bill Presentment And Payment (EBPP) – An online system of presenting bills and receiving payment.

electronic commerce – See: e-commerce

Electronic Commerce Modeling Language (ECML) – A standard format for *e-commerce* containing client information, including financial and shipping details. ECML is used for purchases made online. It includes methods of sharing information so that the client does not have to supply the same information repeatedly to several commerce sites.

Electronic Communications Privacy Act (ECPA) – A US privacy law that prohibits phone tapping, interception of e-mail, and other similar invasions of privacy.

Electronic Data Interchange (EDI) – A standard method of *converting* data transmitted over the Internet into a format that can be read by the destination computer. Also called *Electronic Document Interchange*.

Electronic Data Systems – See: EDS

Electronic Document Interchange – See: Electronic Data Interchange

Electronic Frontier Foundation (EFF) – A non-profit civil liberties organization that aims to protect privacy, free expression, access to public resources, and data online. Go To: www.eff.org

electronic library – A web site that allows users to download the complete text of books. These are usually classic texts and/or those out of *copyright*.
SEE ALSO: E-BOOK

electronic mail – See: e-mail

electronic mall – A web site that contains links to a number of different *e-tailers*.

Electronic Messaging Association – Organization founded in 1983 devoted to promoting e-mail, voice mail, fax, EDI, and other messaging technologies.
Go To: www.ema.org

Electronic Music Management System (EMMS) – The IBM system for distributing music to the Internet. Its rival, *MP3*, however, has faster download times.

electronic publishing – Documents designed to be viewed on the computer often distributed via the Internet. The text may be augmented by graphics, sound and video clips, animation, and hyperlinks. Electronically published documents may also be distributed on a CD-ROM or a floppy disk.
SEE ALSO: E-BOOK, E-JOURNAL

electronic signature – The electronic equivalent of a hand-written signature created by a program that binds a signature, or other mark, to a document. The software can then detect the alteration of an electronically signed file any time in the future. An electronic signature may be used as *authentication* in the form of a *digital certificate*. In the US, an electronic signature has the same legal authority as a hand-written signature.
SEE ALSO: SIGNATURE

Electronics Industry Association (EIA) – A trade association that has devised Recommended Standards (RS) for hardware and interfaces.

elegant program – A complimentary term for a large, complex program that can be easily understood, maintained, and extended, and is no larger than it has to be.

element – 1. A *tag* in *HTML*. An individual code that specifies how each part of a web page is to be displayed. It includes text, backgrounds, images, and hyperlinks.
2. A single part of a compound document, e.g. a chart or drawing. These elements can be manipulated using the programs with which they were initially created.

elevator bar – The box, often with an inset grid) set in the right-hand vertical area of a document window (resembling an elevator in a shaft). As the elevator is dragged up and down by application of the mouse, the position of the document on the screen is moved. Also called a *thumb*.
SEE: FEATURE BOX

---

elevator bar

A type of scroll bar, the shaded band that runs along the right-hand side of a document window, allows you to move vertically through a document via a mouse or scroll key.

The elevator bar includes a scroll box, which you can click onto and drag upward or downward to find a specific area of the document you require.

Scroll arrows also enable you to navigate up and down the document by simply clicking on the arrow with the mouse in the vertical direction you wish to move.

---

elevator statement – Used to describe the time between floors in an elevator. Specifically used when putting over an *e-business* idea to a busy venture capitalist.

ELF emission – See: **E**xtremely **L**ow **F**requency

ELIZA effect – An interaction with a computer that gives the impression that the user is dealing with a real person. Named after a 1960s computer program that displayed human-like responses.
SEE ALSO: RESPONSE BOT, ARTIFICIAL INTELLIGENCE

E-link – See: link

Eliot – Software developed at the University of Helsinki that animates an *algorithm* written in the programming language *C*.

ellipsis – A three-dot symbol used in on-screen menus to convey that there is another *dialog box* to follow. E.g. The Format menu will show the option "Font...". When the cursor is clicked on the word, the Font dialog box is revealed.

e-loan – A money loan arranged on the Internet.

em dash – A long *dash* equivalent in space to the letter "M."
SEE ALSO: EN DASH

EMA – See: **E**lectronic **M**essaging **A**ssociation

e-mail – Electronic mail. Text messages are sent between computers via the Internet using a mail service provider (usually the *Internet Service Provider)* or between users logged into a network. Software for e-mail services is provided by the *browser,* although specialist software such as *Eudora* can also be used. E-mail enables simple messages to be sent directly, while more complex documents may be sent in their original formatted style as *attachments* (possibly *compressed* to speed up transmission). E-mail provides almost instantaneous communication worldwide and is economical because messages are transmitted for the cost of a local phone call.

SEE: FEATURE BOX

e-mail

The following tips will help you to make the most of e-mail and prevent huge quantities of mail from sitting in your mailbox.

1. Compose and read your e-mail off-line, especially if you are charged for your connection time by the minute.

2. Once written, place your e-mails in a queue for mailing, then upload all the messages together.

3. Create folders that enable you to organize your e-mails as you would paper mail, maybe using file names such as in-tray, urgent, and pending.

4. Use a filtering system to send mail to different mailboxes depending on type. This helps separate out junk e-mail.

5. Acknowledge receipt of e-mails by sending a short message to the sender within a few days.

6. Immediately delete e-mails that are unwanted.

7. Do not allow a build up of e-mails to be stored in your *mailbox*.

8. Transfer addresses of new correspondents into your address book.

9. Only give your address to people and organizations you trust.

10. When sites wish you to register with an e-mail address and you do not want to, make one up or have a free e-mail address that you use specifically for this purpose.

11. When using *Usenet*, use a disguised address. Most *ISPs* allow you to have more than one address; use one of these solely for Usenet since it is used by spammers and mailing list creators. You can then track and delete those you do not wish to receive.

12. Avoid putting your main personal address on a web page.

13. Do not register software; or, if you must, then use one of the alternatives suggested above.

14. When *configuring* your *browser*, do not specify your address when asked. This will prevent anyone sending *cookies* to your browser from being able to discover your e-mail address. However, you will have to use an alternative browser for your e-mail; e.g. if using Internet Explorer, then use *Outlook* for mail.

e-mail address – A unique *address* that contains three key elements: a *username* followed by the @ symbol and immediately by the *domain name* (without any breaks). e.g Jsmith@dk.com, where J. Smith is the recipient located on the dk domain.

E-mail attachment – **See:** attachment

e-mail client – A PC application (e.g. Outlook, Eudora, Netscape) that reads e-mail from a local file (where the server leaves it) and connects to the server to send e-mail.

embed

The butterfly was created as a graphic file in a graphics program, such as Adobe Photoshop. It has then been embedded into a word document, containing a body of text.

e-mail conventions – **See:** netiquette

e-mail filtering – Software that can reject junk and unwanted e-mails by recognizing a sender's name, address, or by identification of keywords in the header or body text of the message.

e-mail flooding – Sending large numbers of e-mails often with data heavy attachments with the purpose of disrupting the efficiency of the network.

e-mail forwarding – A service that forwards e-mails from several e-mail addresses to one *mailbox* (often via an *ISP*).

e-mail never neverland – The ultimate destination for undelivered e-mails.

e-mail Russian roulette – Office game where rude e-mails (e.g. to the boss) are written, then the send button is pressed. The hope is a spell-checker may stop it.

e-mail security – *Security* methods used including *encryption* and *digital certificates* to prevent e-mail interception.

e-mail server – Software designed to receive e-mails and send them on to their destination. Some are also able to detect and weed out *spam* e-mails.

e-mail shorthand – *Acronyms* used specifically to reduce the amount of typing necessary for sending routine messages on e-mails e.g. BFN for **B**y **F**or **N**ow. **See: Appendix 1** for a fuller list.

e-mail tennis – Dialog where a message is read and replied to as soon as it is received, which in turn is read and responded to by the original sender in real time. If the message stream is left in place, this is called an e-mail volley.

embed – To mix objects from several compatible programs into one document. For example, an image manipulated in one program may be placed within a word-processed newsletter.
SEE: FEATURE BOX

embedded command – A *command* written within text or lines of code.

embedded font – A *Microsoft* feature that *embeds* a *font* into a web page.

embedded hyperlink – A *hyperlink* that is incorporated into a line of text. Often these are used to define a keyword or to provide detailed information about the topic.

embedded media – A multimedia feature incorporated into a web page or document.

embedded object – An object, such as a graphic, that has been created by one application and placed in a document created by another application.

EMC – 1. **See:** Electro-magnetic Compatibility
2. A world leader in data management and storage systems.
GO TO: www.emc.com

EMF – **See:** electromagnetic field

EMI – **See:** Electro-magnetic Interference

emotags – The use of mock *HTML tags* in *chat room* or *newsgroup* discussions to express feeling or emotion. E.g <LOUD LAUGH>Great joke!</LOUD LAUGH>.

emoticon – Using text to create *icons* to show an emotion. They are also called *smileys*. They are a popular way of communicating emotion in e-mails and text messages.
SEE: FEATURE BOX
SEE: APPENDIX 2 for a list of emoticons.

---

emoticon

Keyed-in characters that, viewed sideways, resemble facial features and are used to express shorthand emotions in e-mails and chat rooms. E.g. :-) Look sideways to see a happy face.

:-)	smiling
:-D	laughing
;-)	winking
:-(	unhappy

EMP - See: Excessive Mass Posting Ad

Emperor virus - A *virus* that is sent via an e-mail and which overwrites data on the hard drive and may delete the memory settings while the user is reading the e-mail message.

EMS - Expanded Memory Specification. A way of expanding *DOS RAM* from one megabyte to 32 megabytes.

emulator - Hardware or software that is designed to perform as the piece of hardware or software that it is imitating. E.g. A printer may emulate another printer in order to use its driver, or software on *Macintosh* systems that can enable these computers to run *Windows* programs and play PC CD-ROM games that are normally not made available in Mac format. However, emulators often lack crucial functions. *Terminal emulators* enable computer connections with different kinds of networks.

en dash - A short *dash* equivalent in space to the letter "N."
SEE ALSO: EM DASH
SEE: FEATURE BOX

enabled - To have a program or function ready and available for use. E.g. On Windows menus options only those features written in black are enabled.

e-nally retentive - (slang) A person said to be very particular about syntax and grammar when composing e-mails.

Encarta - A leading online (and CD-ROM) encyclopedia and reference tool developed by Microsoft. It offers everything from family reference and homework help to news information and adult education and training.
GO TO: http://encarta.msn.com

encrypt - (verb) To put data (e.g. credit card details) into a code so that only someone with the *key* can translate it.
SEE ALSO: ENCRYPTION, KEY ESCROW, KEY FILE

encrypted viruses - A type of virus in which the virus code encrypts the body of the virus in order to evade detection by antivirus software.

---

en dash and em dash

Punctuation marks similar to a hyphen but both the en-dash and em-dash are longer. *DTP* convention uses an en-dash to link numbers (e.g. 2002-03) and denote a span.

An en dash –

The em-dash (the longer of the two dashes) is used to join sentences – such as this one – and show that words enclosed between them are to be read as if in parentheses.

An em dash —

encryption – A highly effective method of making data and files e-mailed over the Internet secure. Encryption is used to send and receive sensitive material such as credit card numbers and personal details. Encrypted data is also known as *cipher text*. To use it, the receiver must have access to a secret key or password to then *decrypt* the data. In addition, computers may check another computer's *digital signature* to ensure that the receiving computer is trusted. Another similar process, *authentication* may be used to verify the source of any information that is transmitted.

SEE ALSO: DECRYPTION
SEE: FEATURE BOX

encyclopedia site – An online reference tool such as *Encarta* or Encyclopedia Britannica.
GO TO: www.refdesk.com or www.xrefer.co.uk

end – To finish an action.

endian – **See:** big endian, little endian

End key – The keyboard key that is used either by itself or in combination with other keys to move the cursor to the next word, to the line end, to the bottom of the screen, or to the end of the document.

end-of-file mark (EOF) – The _ symbol, which is used to indicate the end of a file or document.

end-of-line mark (EOL) – The ¶ symbol used to indicate the end of a line when codes are visible.

end system – Computing system that lies behind a web page. E.g. A stock control system used by an online retailer.

end tag – An *HTML tag* that cancels a command. Where <BODY> is the command tag, </BODY> is the end tag.

end user – The person who will ultimately visit a web site, perform a transaction on the Internet, or use an Internet application or product.

End User License Agreement (EULA) – A license that states the conditions under which software may be used.

---

encryption

There are two main forms of encryption:

1. Symmetric key: where both the transmitting and receiving computer have the same secret key or code.

2. Public key: where a private key or code is used by the transmitting computer, while the public key is used by all the computers with which the first computer might communicate. One such system is called Pretty Good Privacy. Since public key systems take a lot of computing power to work, most systems use a combination of the two.

---

e-newsletter – A newsletter that is produced and read online. These are common in business environments where they are published on the network. Charities and clubs are also increasingly producing their newsletters online (but may still produce a paper newsletter).

energy Star – US guidelines to promote energy-efficient computers. Approved computers display the Energy Star logo. Such monitors will automatically transfer to low power if the machine has not been used for a specified number of minutes.

engine – A software feature that performs a specific function, usually one that requires a significant amount of processing. On the Internet, the most commonly used are *search engines,* which are found as an integral part of many sites as well as specialist sites such as *Yahoo!*

enhance – To improve a version of software or hardware by making it more powerful or having it perform more functions than a standard version. E.g. Enhanced CDs are music CDs that have additional video clips (of the artist performing the song), and interactive lyric sheets of the songs and graphics.

enhanced graphics adapter (EGA) – A graphics adapter card that improved on the older CGA (Color Graphics Adapter.)

enhanced keyboard – The most common type of *keyboard* found on modern computers with 101 keys.

enhanced parallel port (EPP) – A parallel port that is able to support several devices in a *daisy-chain network.*

enter key – The key on a numeric keypad that, when pressed, enters data and orders the calculation. On some keyboards the *return* key is also called the enter key. When pressed, this key enters the new line command.

entreprenerd – A entrepreneur who has made his money with a high-technology or Internet business.

enterprise network – A network for large businesses, which consists of several local area networks (*LANs*). These tend to have a variety of databases, workstations, and systems, all of which need to be coordinated, integrated, and managed centrally. These may be used to carry out e-*business* functions.

entity – The item about which information is recorded in a database; e.g. information on a person, a retailer, or stock item.

envelope – A number of *bits* that is packaged and treated as a single item. May also be used when a number of data *packets* are combined and treated as one.

environment – 1. A *configuration* of hardware or software that is used in programming. The environment can limit which functions a computer is able to perform. E.g. A computer designed for a database or accounting environment may not be able to perform word processing or connect to the Internet.
2. The type of operation that the computer is working in, e.g. a business environment, an academic environment.
3. A reference to a specific area and the conditions that affect it; e.g. the light is poor in the desktop environment.

environmental audio – A term applied when the complete audio set up of a hi-fi, PC, and/or television takes account of aspects such as room size, furniture, acoustic properties, and echo in order to achieve the optimum audio experience.
SEE ALSO: ENVIRONMENT

EOL – See: end-of-line-mark

EOM – See: end of message

e-paper – 1. Short for electronic paper, this is technology where electric current and special ink combine to change words on a type of paper to simulate the turning of a page.
2. A term for several forms of commercially available specialized printer paper.
3. New technology from Xerox PARC in which the paper effectively acts as a digital screen.

EPROM – See: Erasable Programmable Read-Only Memory

.eps – A file extension meaning that the file is written in Encapsulated *Postscript* format. Such files usually contain *bitmapped graphics* and are used in conjunction with desktop publishing programs such as *QuarkXpress* and PageMaker. Eps files can be converted into *pdf,* files which take up little *memory* and are ideal for e-mailing as graphic and pictorial attachments.

EPSON **Epson** – A leading global manufacturer of high-quality printers and imaging products. GO TO: www.epson.com

The Epson Stylus C60.

A typical Epson inkjet printer with special driver enhancements for sharper Internet printing, capable of printing 10 color pages per minute.

e-purse – See: e-wallet

EQ – Shorthand for **eq**ual to.

equation – Arithmetic expressions commonly used in programming to contain *variables* and ensure specific actions occur. E.g. x-y=z where z is the *variable*.

eradicate – To wipe out a virus from a computer, network, or the Internet. If up-to-date virus protection software is used by a sufficient number of users, any virus can be wiped out, but so far no major viruses have completely disappeared.

erase – 1. To remove data from memory. 2. A tool (mimicking a real eraser) in a graphics program that removes a line or mark leaving the background color intact.

Erasable Programmable Read–Only Memory (EPROM) – A reusable memory (*ROM*) chip. The data once written becomes available as *read only* but can be erased by exposure to ultraviolet light.
SEE ALSO: **PROM**

ergonomics – A term derived from the Greek meaning the study of work. Ergonomics looks at the efficiency of working environments with regard to productivity, ease of use, health, and safety.

Erlang – A unit of *traffic* use that is used to specify the total capacity of a telephone system.

eRoom – A commercial company that enables the use of the Internet as a place for other companies to collaborate online. GO TO: www.eroom.com

errata – A note or *patch* containing a correction to a previously published text or program.

error – A computing mistake that is often due to malfunctioning software or a problem with the transmission of data. Usually accompanied by an on-screen *error message*.

Error–Correcting Code Memory – A type of memory that automatically corrects errors as they occur.

Error Checking And Correcting (ECC) – A system for detecting and correcting errors in either transmitted or stored data.

error message – A warning on the monitor given by the computer. This is usually displayed in a dialog box that gives the user information about a problem with processing, printing, or with the modem or Internet connection. The error is often described along with a coded number. Pressing the *enter* key or clicking on a displayed "okay" option normally removes the message.
SEE ALSO: SIMPLE MAIL TRANSFER PROTOCOL
SEE: FEATURE BOX

error rate – Measuring the effectiveness of a system or communications channel by the number of errors occurring.

error trapping – Many programs have a built-in capacity to recognize and deal with errors, particularly transmission errors.

ES – See: **E**xpert **S**ystem

Esc – Abbreviation for **esc**ape key.

escape key – This key performs different functions in different programs. E.g. In some programs it cancels an action, in others it takes the user back to the previous insertion point, while in other programs it has no function at all.

escape sequence – A sequence of special character codes that allows *modem* commands to be transmitted along with the data.

ESD – **E**lectronic **S**oftware **D**istribution. A means of distributing new software, as well as upgrades, via a network, which avoids having to install the software on each machine separately.

error message

Here is a list of the most common error message codes associated with e-mail:

211 Will accompany a system status message.

214 A help message follows.

220 Service ready.

221 Service closing.

250 Requested action taken and completed.

251 The recipient is not local to the server, but it will accept and forward the message.

252 The recipient cannot be verified, but the server accepts the message and attempts delivery.

354 Start message input and end with <CRLF>.<CRLF>. This indicates that the server is ready to accept the message.

404 A common message meaning that the requested page cannot be found or accessed.

421 The service is not available and the connection will be closed.

450 The requested command failed because the user's mailbox was unavailable.

451 The command has been aborted due to a server error.

452 The command has been aborted because the server has insufficient system storage.

500 The server could not recognize the command due to a syntax error.

501 A syntax error was encountered.

502 This command is not implemented.

503 The server has encountered a bad sequence of commands.

504 A command parameter is not implemented.

550 The requested command failed because the user's mailbox was unavailable.

551 The recipient is not local to the server. The server then gives a forward address to try.

552 The action was aborted due to exceeded storage allocation.

553 The command was aborted because the mailbox name is invalid.

554 The transaction failed.

e-services – **See:** online services

e-signature – **See: e**lectronic signature

e-speak – An *interface* for *online services* from *Hewlett-Packard* that allows different online applications to interact over the Internet.

Escrow – The safe-keeping of a product that two or more parties have an interest in buying or selling. The Escrow service acts as an intermediary during a commercial transaction, temporarily taking care of an item until the vendor and the buyer agree the transaction should proceed. This is becoming common especially on *auction* sites and *domain name* registration.

e-tail – Electronic retailing that uses Internet technologies.

e-tailer – A company that sells goods over the Internet. Many e-tailers exist purely on the Internet without having any *bricks-and-mortar* outlets.

e-text – A text document that is generated and stored in electronic form.

ethernet – A popular *local area network* (*LAN*) system. It provides connections and support for linking computers to a network or to *peripheral* devices such as printers or scanners. It supports communications at a nominal speed of 10 megabits per second. Ethernet was developed in the late 1970s by Xerox Corporation, Intel, and DEC.

ethernet address – A 48-bit *address* that identifies an individual computer on an ethernet. Also called a *MAC address*.

e-trade – Electronic trading via the Internet.

e-tutor – 1. An online study guide or how-to text showing the user how to use a program or perform a particular task within the program.
2. An on-line tutor assigned to advise a student on an online study program.

eudora – A popular type of *e-mail* application, it is especially good for managing large numbers of e-mails since it allows a degree of control. The application works on both PCs and Macs.
Go to: www.eudora.com

EUDORA

EULA – **See: E**nd-**U**ser **L**icence **A**greement

Eurozone – Those European countries that have adopted the Euro as their currency from January 1, 2002. Companies in those countries will be trading online using Euros.

even parity – A way of transmitting data that contains a simple formula for checking accuracy. Each complete character (including its *envelope*) has an even number of bits in it. This is for asynchronous serial lines; when configuring you must set the number of start and stop bits and the parity in addition to the line speed.

events listing – A reference to sites that list upcoming events such as sports competitions, concerts, anniversaries, and festivals. For a good example,
Go to: www.whatsonwhen.com

Everton – An online resource aimed at helping people research their family tree.
Go to: www.everton.com

evil emperor – A derogatory term used to describe the leader of a big corporation.

evil empire – A derogatory term used to describe big companies such as Microsoft.

Evil the cat virus – The title of a hoax *computer virus*. It encourages the receiver to send lots of useless e-mails.

e-wallet – A facility that provides the user with options on how to pay for an e-commerce transaction. It is sometimes called an e-purse.

exa- – 1. The prefix for quintillion (10^18). 2. The prefix for 2^60.
2^60 = 1,152,921,504,606,846,976

exabyte – An exabyte is 1000 *petabytes*, technically equal to 1024.

Exabyte – A leading supplier of tape storage solutions for networks and servers.
Go to: www.exabyte.com

Excel – A leading spreadsheet and analysis program from *Microsoft*.
Go to: www.microsoft.com/office/excel/

excessive mass posting – An unsolicited message that is mailed to a list. These are highly unpopular with users of the Internet whose mailboxes are clogged up with unimportant messages.
SEE ALSO: SPAM

excessive multiple posting – See: excessive mass posting

Excite – One of the first *search engines*. Excite ceased operating in 2001, after the collapse of the American broadband company, Excite@Home.

exe file – A *file extension* that indicates that the file will run in both *DOS* and *Windows* programs.

executable file – See: exe file

executable content – A program within a web page that performs a specific operation such as running a video clip or processing data.

execute – To *run* a computer program or a computer command.

exit – To quit the program or function that the computer is currently running either via the keyboard or mouse.

expanded memory – Extra *RAM* (Random Access Memory) added to a computer's memory.

expanding folders – To click on a folder to reveal the list of contents.

expansion – 1. To increase the computer's *memory* or to add on extra *devices*.
2. To *decompress* data, so as to revert it back to its original format.

expansion board – Another word for an *expansion card*.

expansion bus – Wires that carry the signals between the computer's main processor and other devices; e.g. video card and disk drives.
SEE ALSO: BUS

expansion card – A *printed circuit board* that is plugged into the computer's *expansion slot* to add new features; e.g. a video card or disk drive.

expansion slot – A socket located on the *motherboard* that is designed to hold an *expansion card* and connect it to the *expansion bus*.

 **Expedia** – One of the world's leading travel agents in a highly competitive market. It is owned by Microsoft and combines the latest technology and online booking with good service and reliability.
GO TO: www.expedia.com

expert system – A computer that is programmed to perform limited problem-solving functions. E.g. A medical system may make a diagnosis from the user's symptoms, history, and other data.

A weather system is another example of an expert system. Such systems are limited by the quality of the initial programming and the level of detail provided by the user.

Expert System (ES) – An *Artificial Intelligence* system that uses a knowledge base of human expertise for its problem solving.

expire – To delete a *newsgroup* or *Usenet* posting after it has been stored for a specified length of time.

expireware – Software that is limited to function only until a specified date or to be available only to a certain number of users.

exit page – The web page that is displayed when the user exits from the site. This may be via an *exit tunnel*. An exit page may thank the user for visiting the site, inform the visitor of future site developments, or may ask the user to sign up to the site's mailing list.

exit tunnel – When a user is taken through a number of web pages in order to exit a site. These perform similar functions to an *exit page*.

Explorer, Internet – **See:** Internet Explorer

export – To send a file from one location to another. This often involves converting a file from one program format to another.
SEE ALSO: IMPORT

Extended Binary Coded Decimal Interchange Code (EBCDIC) – The *IBM* alternative to *ASCII*. It was the standard used in many IBM machines but is now largely replaced by ASCII.

extended capabilities port (ECP) – A high-speed *enhanced parallel port* produced by *Microsoft*.

excessive crossposting. – Sending the same message to many *newsgroups*, regardless of whether or not the subject of the message is of interest.

SEE ALSO: CROSSPOSTING, SPAMMING

Extensible Hypertext Markup Language (XHTML) – An updated version of *Hypertext Markup Language (HTML)*. It incorporates the flexibility of *Extensible Mark-up Language,* which can be adapted and used for many purposes. This program may be used extensively in future development of web page design.

Extensible Markup Language (XML) – A new markup language designed for writing web pages. *HTML* has limitations that cause problems for many applications (e.g. form filling and product catalogs) and XML has been developed to overcome such problems. XML enables programmers to customize *tags* so the commands are tailored to their particular needs. The three main advantages of XML are:
1. Commerce sites become more flexible and easier to write.

2. Search engines are able to search on a particular meaning of a word.
3. Mathematical formulas, chemical symbols, and musical notation can be handled as easily as text.

Extensible User-interface Language (XUL) – Developed by *Netscape* and *Mozilla,* this language is a way to exchange data that describes a program's user *interface.* In the past, there have been many problems developing programs that can perform uniformly across different operating platforms such as *Windows* and *Macintosh.*

extension – 1. The letters that sit after the dot in a file name. This identifies the format that the file was written in, and prescribes how it is to be opened and used. E.g. *exe* indicates a executable file or a Windows program file and *wav* indicates a sound file. On the Internet, the browser will encounter a large number of file extensions, which it will have to recognize in order to be able to run multimedia web pages successfully.
2. In Macintosh systems, drivers and some functions are located in the extensions folder, which, in turn, is found in the Systems folder.

SEE: APPENDIX 5 for a list of file extensions.

external modem – A modem located outside the computer. It is plugged into a serial port.

external viewer – A program that is launched or used by a *browser* for presenting graphics, audio, video, and other multimedia found on the Internet.

extranet – When two or more *intranets* are connected. E.g. When two or more company intranets combine to share resources and communicate together.

Extremely Low Frequency Emission – Electromagnetic frequencies below three kilohertz. Long exposure to radiation from computer screens has given rise to unconfirmed health concerns. *MPR II* guidelines suggest acceptable limits within which monitors must function.

SEE ALSO: ELECTROMAGNET FIELD

eyeballs – (slang) The people viewing a web site.

eye candy – (slang) An attractive web page that makes good use of visual features.

Eyestorm – A British online art store, whose web site is acknowledged as being one of the best in terms of design.
GO TO: www.eyestorm.co.uk

eye trash – (slang) Overuse of *banner ads*, continuous *animations*, and unnecessary *video clips*. These make a web site appear too busy and distract from the content of the site.

e-zine – An online magazine. Sometimes abbreviated to *zine*. There is a huge range of e-zines on the Internet covering the same range of material as newsstand paper magazines. However, the reduced costs of producing and distributing e-zines has led to the development of e-zines on more eclectic topics.
SEE: FEATURE BOX
SEE ALSO: E-JOURNAL

e-zine

Vogue's web site offers dynamic access to the publication, e.g. sounds and hyperlinks, and a search function to select articles.
GO TO: WWW.VOGUE.CO.UK

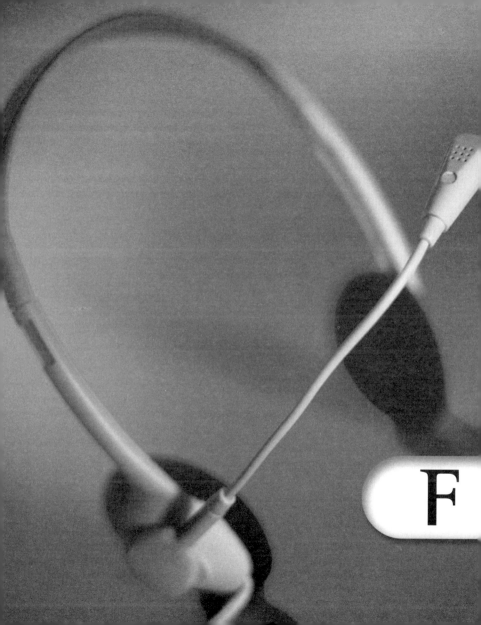

F

F – In hexadecimal numbering, this is equivalent to 15.

F1 – Keyboard key usually pressed to get help.

F10 – Used with the Alt key in Windows, the F10 key will contract or expand the window. Pressing F10 and Shift together brings up the editing box, as though the mouse had been right-clicked.

F11 – Pressing the F11 key on a keyboard in *Internet Explorer* expands the window to a full screen. Pressing Alt+F11 brings up the Visual Basic editing window for the program currently in use.

F12 – The F12 function key has a wide range of uses, from opening and saving files to debugging, depending on the program being used.

F2 – The F2 function key is mainly used for editing cells in spreadsheets.

F3 – The F3 function key is associated with the Find facility in Windows.

F4 – The F4 function key brings up a history of sites visited in Internet Explorer. Pressing Alt+F4 closes the current window.

F5 – The F5 function key usually opens the Go To facility.

F6 – Pressing the F6 function key with the Ctrl key in Windows opens the next window if two or more are open.

F7 – The F7 function key opens the spell checker in *Word*, but is used to save a document in *WordPerfect*.

F8 – The F8 function key has a wide range of uses: from editing and using macros to helping reboot computers.

F9 – The F9 function key has a very wide range of uses depending on the program being used.

F connector – This is a two-wire (one for signal and one for ground), coaxial cable connector. It is commonly used to connect antennas, TVs and VCRs.

F keys – **See:** function keys

face change character – This control character changes the size or type of font in a selected area of text. It is also known as font change or FC.

face recognition – The ability to recognize people by their facial characteristics: an emerging technology based mostly on the *Eigenface algorithm*. Its main advantage is that people can be sure of secure access to their computer and other equipment by looking into a web camera.

face time – Talking to someone *face-to-face* rather than sending them an e-mail.

facemail – A face-to-face conversation.

face-to-face – An interaction in the flesh, i.e. not online. Also used as an acronym F2F.

facilitated chat – This describes a discussion controlled by a chat-room host who assists the progress of the debate and keeps the contributions on subject. Often when a guest is featured on-site, the host controls the discussion, ensuring that a fair selection of people can contribute and ask questions.

facsimile – **See:** fax

factor – A number by which another number is multiplied or divided.

fail soft – This is used to describe failing with the minimum amount of destruction to equipment and software. Fail soft mainly occurs as a commonsense approach to resetting hardware, such as disk drives, when power fails.

failover – A backup operation that automatically switches to another standby database or network if the primary system fails or is shut down.

failure – A term used to describe the situation if a computer, network, or device is unable to perform its intended function.

fair use – A highly complex and vague set of rules governing the use of copyrighted material published on the Internet. The Conference on Fair Use (ConFU) has set out its findings on its web site, the last word on the Web.
Go to:
www.uspto.gov/web/offices/dcom/olia/confu/

fake user interface – This describes adverts appearing on the Web as web pages. They are really there to trick people into clicking on the false buttons, leading them to the advertisers' sites.

fall back – This occurs when two modems experience interference on transmitting data to each other. Data transfer is slowed down until data can be transferred correctly. When conditions improve it is speeded up to the usual transmission speed if possible.

fall forward – **See:** fall back

fall over – One term for a system failure.

false drops – The results of a *search* where criteria are met but the information is irrelevant to the enquiry. E.g. A search for information on Charles "Turnip" Townshend finds information on growing turnips rather than biographical notes on Charles Townshend. A *Boolean* search might help refine the results.

fan – An electrical cooling device inside the computer that circulates air to prevent overheating. Generally there are two fans: one attached to the processor, the other attached to the case.

fan in – Multiple signals directed into one single receiver.
SEE ALSO: FAN OUT

fan out – One signal directed into a number of receivers.

FAQ - See: Frequently **A**sked **Q**uestions

FAQ archive - Many sites keep a record of their most *frequently asked questions*. This FAQ archive is often available for new users.

Farad - In electronics, this unit measures the storage capacity of a capacitor - an electric circuit element that is used to store electric charge temporarily.

fasgrolia - This describes the use of acronyms and abbreviations in chat rooms and e-mails. It is short for **Fas**t **Gro**wing **L**anguage of **I**nitialisms and **A**cronyms.

Fast Ethernet - A version of *Ethernet* that can run at speeds of up to 100 *Mbps*.

fast infector - A *computer virus* that is copied into memory where it infects other programs when they are executed.

favorites

A list of favorite web addresses can be accessed from Internet Explorer's Favorites menu, or by clicking the Favorites button.

favorites button

fast packet switching - A system of transmitting short *packets* of data over networks at high speed.
SEE ALSO: ASYNCHRONOUS TRANSFER MODE which is one form of fast packet switching.

FastCGI - This is a more secure method of programming commercial site interactions with web servers.

FAT - See: File **A**llocation **T**able

fat application - The program that takes up the most memory, i.e. the fattest.

fat client - A computer that houses most of the application software within its own memory. When it is online it requires only a *thin server* to provide it with a small amount of processing power. The advantage of this is that the client computer controls the functioning of the computer and handles all the data, giving the user maximum control over the system.
SEE ALSO: FAT SERVER, THIN CLIENT

fat server - A server which does most or all of the processing, allowing the client computer to use its processing power online. This procedure enables the server to update its software without the need to download files to its clients. Most *Internet Service Providers* provide this kind of service to home users who are generally regarded as *thin clients.*
SEE ALSO: FAT CLIENT, THIN SERVER

fatal error – An error occurring when a computer grinds to a halt owing to hardware problems or *bugs* in the program. Generally the application crashes and must be restarted. It is not usually necessary to reboot with a fatal error – you only need to reboot on serious system errors.

fault management – A system of checking and repeated testing for errors in a system to prevent recurrence.

fault tolerance – This describes when a computer is able to function despite an unexpected fault in the system. This is usually achieved by duplicating vital system components.

favicon – A favorite icon. In Internet Explorer, favorite web links can be added to the links bar as icons. Links can then be dragged from the links bar to the address bar. This is a quick and fun way of accessing favorite sites fast.

favorites – The *Internet Explorer* term for *bookmark*.
SEE: FEATURE BOX

fax – Short for facsimile, a document sent electronically using a fax machine or fax program on a computer.

fax facilities – Software that enables computer-generated *fax* (facsimile) copies of a document to be sent via a *fax modem*. A scanner is used to send hand-written copies..

fax modem – A *modem* designed to handle *fax* transmissions. To send a fax, select the fax modem as the printer for the document, then type in the destination's telephone number. Fax modems may also be able to perform *dial-up access*.

FC – See: Face Change character

Fcc – Forward carbon copy. Synonymous with *cc*.

FCC – See: Federal Communications Commission

FCS – Acronym for First Customer Shipment (the date when software is formally released).

FDD – See: Floppy Disk Drive

FDDI – See: Fiber Distributed Data Interface

FDisk – A *DOS* and *Windows* utility that is used to partition a hard disk. This is necessary before high-level formatting.

FDM – Frequency Division Multiplexing.

FE – See: Fatal Error

feathering – A term used in computer graphics to describe the process of blurring the edge of an image to produce the effect of blending the image into the background.

feature – A beneficial property or attribute of a program or piece of hardware.

feature creep – The continual adding of new functions and benefits to systems and programs while they are in the process of being programmed and developed. This can consequently add considerable cost to the project's original budget.

feature key – The *Macintosh* key showing a cloverleaf. Also called the *Command Key*.

FedCIRC – See: **Fed**eral Computer Incident Response Capability

Federal Communications Commission (FCC) – U.S. government agency regulating communications. Also sets interstate and international communications' standards.

Federal Computer Incident Response Capability (FedCIRC) – US organization that provides security services to federal civilian agencies.
Go to: www.fedcirc.gov

FEDI – See: **F**inancial **EDI**

---

field

These boxes, encountered in forms on web sites, are known as fields. A collection of fields of this kind usually makes up a person's record.

Name	
Ext no	
E-mail	
Location	

---

feedback – 1. Response to a system's output. Internet site developers elicit feedback from visitors to the site or users of the site to monitor its functionality and tailor services to the client's needs.
2. In communications, it is the interference caused by the unintentional return of signals; e.g. the high pitched noise in microphone feedback.

feedback form – This electronic form on many web sites is used for encouraging users to give the web producer *feedback*.

feeware – Feeware, as opposed to *freeware*, is sold as commercial software.

Feliz.Trojan – A *Trojan* that seems to just send an ugly picture and some jolly messages, but is really a *computer virus* that renders some crucial *Microsoft Windows* files inoperable.

female connector – The socket into which a *male connector* (or plug) is plugged.

femtosecond – One quadrillionth of a second.

ferret – This program can search through selected files, databases, or search engine indexes for specific information.
See also: search

ferric – See: ferrous

ferric oxide – An oxidation of iron with the chemical formula Fe_2O_3, used in the coating of magnetic disks and tapes.

ferrous – Containing or relating to iron. The difference between ferrous and ferric is the number of valence electrons they contain; i.e. electrons that can bond with other chemicals. A ferrous molecule contains two and ferric contains three. Iron is vital to any technology using magnetism.

Fiber Distributed Data Interface (FDDI) – A standard that connects two local area networks using a fiber optic cable, enabling high speed transmission at 100Mbps.

fiber optics – Technology using pulses of laser light to transmit data in digital format using cables made from thin glass or silica fibers. Fiber optic cables can transmit huge amounts of data per second over long distances with very little signal loss.

Fibonacci numbers – Discovered by Leonardo Fibonacci in the 13th century, this is a series of whole numbers in which each number is the sum of the two preceding ones: 1, 1, 2, 3, 5, 8, 13, etc. It is used for speeding up binary searches by dividing them into the two lower numbers; e.g. 13 items are divided into 5 and 8 items; 8 items are divided into 5 and 3.

Fiddy – A colloquial term for *Fiber Distributed Data Interface*.

FidoNet – International network of PC hobbyists with e-mail, discussion groups, and free downloads. Its weekly e-newsletter is called Fidonews.

field – An area in a *database*; e.g. an information form filled out online. Each entry is called a record and the lines requesting name, street name, city, and age are the fields.
SEE: FEATURE BOX

FIFO – First-in-first-out. A storage system which deals with data in the order received.

fifth generation computers – The advanced generation of computers currently under development. These will make greater use of *artificial intelligence*.

fifth generation system – This system is foreseen to feature the ultimate in new technology, storing vast amounts of data, handling it at massive speed with outstanding multimedia functions.

figs – A common abbreviation of the word figures; for example, "this option is shown in figs. 8 and 9."

file – Data stored together as bytes under one *filename*. This could be a word processed document, a database, or a sound clip. The file is then stored on the hard or floppy disk.

file allocation table (FAT) – The data file found on a disk that records information about the filenames, size, and storage location of the files on that disk. FAT is the *filesystem* used by DOS and still in use in Windows. FAT32 is an extended version, and NTFS is a newer Windows *filesystem*.

file attachment – A file that a user sends to another user with an e-mail message.

file attribute – A type of file access classification allowing a file to be retrieved or erased. For example, read/write, read only, archive, hidden are all file attributes.

file compression – **See:** compression

file extension – **See:** extension

---

filter

The Microsoft Outlook e-mail filtering system enables the user to forward, delete, or reply to incoming e-mails automatically.

This inbox assistant already has one rule set up: it will delete all e-mails with the subject: ILOVEYOU, because they contain a virus.

You can set up your own rules in the edit rule box. It will ask you for information, such as the sender of the e-mails you want to filter, and to which folder you would like them to be filtered.

---

file find – A *utility* program that searches directories for matching file names.

file format – The way in which data on a file is stored. Every program handles data in a way that is specific to that program. Try to open a file in a different program and the data usually becomes unreadable. For example, *Word* files cannot be opened directly into *WordPerfect*. To overcome this, use the import function of the program to convert the file or use a standard format that allows data to be transferred between formats.
SEE ALSO: DATA CONVERSION, EXTENSION
SEE: APPENDIX 5 for file extensions.

file handle – Used to access the file throughout a session, a file handle is a temporary reference assigned by the operating system to an opened file.

file infecting viruses – These *computer viruses* infect executable programs; they then try to replicate and spread by infecting other host programs. Some destroy programs by overwriting some of the original code. Others are designed to reformat the hard drive or perform other malicious actions. Often, these viruses can be removed from the infected file.

file infector – A *computer virus* sent or downloaded via a file. It attaches itself to, or even replaces an existing program.
SEE ALSO: FILE INFECTING VIRUSES

file manager – *Windows* software that enables copying, deletion, and renaming of files and directories.

file properties – *Windows software* providing information about files such as author, creation date, contents, etc.

file recovery program – This software restores files that have been damaged or lost due to system failure or human error.

file server – A large capacity computer, e.g. a *web server*, that can be accessed by client computers. In a business environment it can be a central store for files to be accessed by a number of employees.
SEE ALSO: FAT SERVER

File Transfer Protocol (FTP) – Method of *downloading* and *uploading* files between a server and a client over the Internet. FTP uses the *TCP/IP protocol*.
SEE ALSO: ANONYMOUS FTP

filename – The chosen name for a file. Some systems allow arbitrary filenames, with or without extensions, and the filename *extension* can be as long as you like. Others are restrictive in usage.

filename extension – **See:** extension

filesystem – The method of storing data on a disk in files and directories (or folders). There are many different ways of doing this. CD-ROMs are commonly in the HSFS filesystem format, also known as ISO9660.

fill – The process of coloring a contained area in a graphic image or field in a chart.

fill out form – A commonly encountered electronic representation of a paper form on which the user can enter personal details online. Fill out forms often occur on web pages to enable visitors to sign up for an online service or newsletter.

film – **See:** digital film

filter – 1. A process of screening out selected data that is based on specified criteria. On the Internet a filter is often used for screening out unwanted or unsuitable e-mails or preventing the delivery of certain types of web page.
SEE: FEATURE BOX
2. A facility used for changing data. For example, an export filter changes files from one format to another.

filterware – Software designed to *filter* data.

Financial EDI – Highly secure **e**lectronic **d**ata **i**nterchange (EDI) specifically designed for the finance and banking industry.

find – A *filter* that finds files specified by name.

finder – A *filesystem* utility in *Macintosh* software that controls the desktop and enables the user to find, copy, and generally manage files.

finger – An Internet program used to find out information about another user. In order to find out such information the person being "fingered" must have registered a personal profile on the system and the user must have the full *domain address* of the person targeted. Through this method personal details such as phone numbers may be found, as well as information about whether or not the person is logged onto the network.

finger of death – 1. Removal from a network for unsuitable behavior.
2. A *wizard* (FOD) in a *MUD* that removes a player whose behavior is unacceptable.

finger trouble – A condition of continually mistyping words or showing ineptitude at the keyboard.

fingerprint – The electronic traces left when surfing the Internet. The term is sometimes used to describe the differing styles and techniques of well-known computer *hackers*.

fire off – To send. Usually someone is described as firing off a quick e-mail without really thinking about the content or consequences.
SEE ALSO: FLAME

firefighter – In a newsgroup, the term firefighter is generally used to describe someone who attempts to to defuse a *flaming* argument.

firewall – An Internet security system that sits between the server and the client's system. It prevents unauthorized persons gaining access to a closed system. The firewall can be sophisticated filtering software that prevents unknown users from sending material into the system, and/or a hardware device that protects sensitive material on the system.
SEE ALSO: BASTION HOST, DEMILITARIZED ZONE, FIREWALL ROUTER, PACKET FILTER

firewall router – Usually a dedicated computer that *filters* packets of data before they enter a system. If a packet passes the filtering checks, then it is sent on to the system; if the packet fails the filtering checks, then it is either rejected, or it is sent to a *proxy server*. At the proxy server stage, the packet is examined prior to entry onto the main system.

firewall server – A server that acts as a *firewall* to provide a secure system.

FireWire – A high-speed data transfer mechanism developed by Apple and Texas instruments. It enables computers to connect with up to 63 digital devices and can transfer data at up to 400Mbps.
SEE ALSO: UNIVERSAL SERIAL BUS, INFRA-RED

fireworks mode – A reference to the large numbers of characters produced by a computer when it is in the process of failing or crashing.

.firm – A proposed new *domain name* meaning a business site.

firmware – Essential software that is stored in the *ROM* or *PROM*. It is more permanent than software that is stored on the hard disk but is easier to change than hardware.

First Amendment – As part of the US constitution, the First Amendment guarantees freedom of speech, religion, assembly and of the press. It is often brought out in the debate over how much censorship there should be on the World Wide Web.

first–generation computer – One of the earliest computers built in the 1940s and 1950s.

first–generation web sites – These earliest of web sites were basic in design, comprising text and a few static images.

fish food – Incentives placed on web sites to attract visitors; e.g. competitions.

FIX – **F**ederal **I**nternet **E**xchange. A connection point between the Internet and North American government internets.

fixed disk – A non-removable *hard disk*. Such disks can only be replaced when the computer is non-operational.

flag – A transmitted code that identifies the control codes, distinguishing them from the data.

flaky – A reference to an unreliable system, program, or computer.

flame – (slang) 1. A term used commonly in *newsgroups*, *e-mails* or *bulletin boards*, describing an angry or inflammatory message often containing some kind of personal attack. Flaming is considered to be bad *netiquette*.
2. A nasty *computer virus* that displays flames on screen and overwrites the *MBR* when the virus is activated by a date change.

flame bait – (slang) A newsgroup posting that intentionally provokes a *flame war*.

flame off/on – When a user of a *newsgroup* indicates a piece of a message that is considered a *flame*. The message begins with the words flame on and ends with the words flame off.

flame war – (slang) When a number of contributors to a *newsgroup* or forum send provocative and inflammatory messages to each other, often initiated by a *troll*. These interactions tend to become very abusive and take time to die down. They sometimes require the intervention of a *firefighter*.
SEE ALSO: FLAME

flaming – (slang) Posting angry or inflammatory messages to a *newsgroup*.
SEE ALSO: FLAME

flapping router – A *router* which uploads data from a number of different sources.

Flash – A widely available animation program developed by Macromedia Ltd. With the correct *plug-ins*, it allows for advanced web site graphics and animation.
Go to: www.macromedia.com

flash crowd – Where a large number of users visit a site, and then quickly leave. This often happens to news web sites posting a particular item of interest.

flash memory – A small printed *circuit board* used for storing a large amount of data. Flash memory is widely used in laptops and personal digital assistants.

flatbed scanner – This *scanner's* scanning head moves beneath the flat piece of glass on which the document is placed.

flat file – A file from which all formatting has been removed.

flat panel display – A thin screen usually associated with laptops and *LCDs*. Most *cathode ray tubes* now have flat screens. Flat-panel displays are much lighter than CRTs but generally have lower resolution.

flat screen – **See:** flat-panel display

flat shading – In graphics, this technique for shading 3D objects uses a one-tone shaded surface to simulate lighting.

flavor – (slang) Used to indicate a type or kind of something; what flavor modem do you use?

flavorful – Describes software that programmers believe to be classy, and full of interest and variation.

flicker – Light distortions on a screen.

flip horizontal – In graphics and drawing programs, to turn a selected image by 180° on the horizontal axis.

flip vertical – In graphics and drawing programs, to turn a selected image by 180° on the vertical axis.

floating – An element that has no fixed location on the computer screen; e.g. Windows toolbars and dialog boxes that can be moved or customized by the user.

floating point operation (FLOP) – A standard measurement that is used when comparing the processing speeds of different *microprocessors.*

floating toolbar – A *toolbar* that can be moved around the screen using a mouse.

flood – 1. A large amount of text dumped onto a discussion; this is considered bad netiquette and can result in a *denial of service attack.*
2. A method of sending *packets*: the router sends a duplicate packet along every available channel to ensure the shortest route is taken. Once a packet arrives at its destination, all the remaining packets are discarded, causing much network traffic. This is only justifiable in certain operations.

floodgater – A person sending an unacceptable number of e-mail messages, many of which have no new content or are off subject, to someone they have approached through a newsgroup or chat room.

flooze – The value of a gift certificate. A certain amount of flooze is purchased by the giver and spent by the recipient. Participating e-tailers will accept flooze in payment for goods and services.

FLOP – See: **flo**ating **p**oint operation

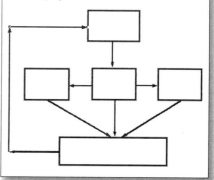

floppy disk – A removable, portable storage device also called a *diskette*. The data is stored in the form of magnetic signals on a thin disk protected by a plastic case. The small 3.5 inch floppy disks have become the standard and most computers have a drive dedicated to them. These disks store 1.44Mb of data while the older 5.25 inch disk stores 1.2Mb.

floppy disk drive – The *disk drive* dedicated to the floppy disk. In most systems this is the A drive.

floptical disk – A type of high density floppy disk that uses *optical* technology.

flow – The data transmission stream.

flow chart – A form of diagram often used in computing to show networks and systems and how data flows across them. **SEE: FEATURE BOX**

flow control – The management of transmissions between *devices*, between a computer and modem. Usually moderates between high and low speed devices to ensure that the receiving device is ready to accept data before it is sent.

flu – (slang) A bad computer virus.

flush – To empty the contents of a memory buffer onto disk.

flush left – To *align* text on the left margin of the page. **SEE ALSO: FLUSH RIGHT**

---

flow chart

This shows a typical example of a flow chart: a graphical representation frequently used in computing to represent a sequence of functions within a program.

flush right – To *align* text on the right margin of the page.

flying mouse – A *mouse* that can be removed from the desk and used as a three-dimensional pointer.

flyover – Used to describe *buttons* that alter when the mouse passes over them or *links* that register the URL of the link address in the status line when the mouse passes over them.
SEE ALSO: JAVA

flyspeck 3 – This is ironic jargon for text on a web page that is so small that it may not be easily read. The term is derived from a pretend font and a pretend typesize.

FM – See: frequency modulation

FM synthesis – See: frequency modulation

fnord – This term is used in e-mail and newsgroups to indicate when the message has passed the bounds of reality and entered those of surreal mind-play.

FoC – Free of charge

focus – 1. The process of sharpening the edges on an image.
2. The part of a *dialog box* or window receiving input from a mouse or keyboard.
3. A point of concentration.

FOD – See: finger of death

fogging – In computer graphics, this means to create the illusion of seeing an image through a fog.
SEE ALSO: ALPHA BLENDING

fold – The part of the document that can be seen without scrolling. The area that is visible depends on the *resolution*: the higher the resolution, the larger the area that can be viewed. It is important to take the need for scrolling into account when designing any web page. Derives from the "fold" of broadsheet newspapers.

folder – 1. In Windows, a folder is a container (sometimes called a directory) of files or other folders that helps to organize files within the system.
2. On the Internet, a folder is a container for storing e-mail messages.
SEE: FEATURE BOX

follow me service – The merging of telephone and Internet services now enables phone companies to divert calls and fax messages to an e-mail account from where they can be accessed and displayed on-screen.

---

folder

This shows the default icon for a file folder used in Microsoft Windows. The Apple Mac uses a similar kind of folder icon by default. A folder contains files and may hold more folders.

Folder

follow-up posting – A newsgroup message made in response to a previous posting. It often contains a copy of the message to which it is providing the follow-up.
SEE ALSO: THREAD

.fon – This *filename extension* is used for *font* files.

font – A set of letter and number characters in a particular style and size. Times New Roman is the most commonly used font. As there are a limited number of fonts available on browsers, web designers are limited in their choice of fonts.
SEE: FEATURE BOX
SEE ALSO: TYPEFACE/SIZE

font cartridge – A small device that can be plugged into a printer to extend the number of available fonts.

fontology – The study of *fonts* and the creation of new fonts.

foo – (slang) Commonly chosen temporary name (like 'John Smith'). E.g. Send this e-mail to foo@dk.com

fool file – This is a non-existent file for bad things. The term might be used in discussion of a particularly poor program; for example, "it should be dumped in the fool file."

foot – This term is frequently used to describe the bottom of the page.

footer – Describes information that appears at the bottom of every page in a document, often containing the author's name or the document's version number.
SEE ALSO: HEADER

foot'n'mouth virus – A hoax *computer virus*, claiming that should the receiver get any e-mails from farms, they shouldn't open them in case they get infected. It should be treated as nonsense and ignored.

footnote – A note placed at the bottom of the page which provides an explanation or reference. This is usually accompanied by a superscript number corresponding with one in the body of the text.

---

font

This feature box shows some basic textual examples using seven different fonts. A font is one set of letter and number characters in a particular style and size.

There are many different fonts
RotisSemiSans 11pt

There are many different fonts
Times 11pt

There are many different fonts
Impact 11pt

There are many different fonts
Courier 11pt

There are many different fonts
Lucida Handwriting 11pt

---

footprint – The amount of space taken up by an object. For example, flat screen displays have a smaller footprint than conventional monitors.

.for – A *filename extension* used in the *FORTRAN* programming language.

force quit – This command will force the user to leave the program that is currently in operation.

forced page break – An automatic page break that is determined by the software, not by the user.

foreground – This term describes the program or document that the user is currently using. The current document or activity is said to be in the foreground while other programs and processes are said to be working in the background.
SEE ALSO: ACTIVE DESKTOP

forward button

The Forward button is found in Microsoft Internet Explorer's web browser button bar.

form – An interactive area within a web page that requires the user to provide information by typing text into *fields*, for example, or by selecting options from a *drop-down menu*. Older versions of browsers were unable to support forms.

format – The organization of text, margins, font, etc. in a document.

formatting – All disks need to be formatted into sectors that are readable by the *operating system* in operation. *Floppy disks* can be bought preformatted or these disks can be formatted in *DOS*. Reformatting a disk will result in the loss of all data on the disk.

FORTRAN – An abbreviation for "**for**mula **tran**slator," Fortran is one of the oldest high level programming languages. John Backus designed it for *IBM* in the late 1950s and it is still widely used today, especially in scientific circles.

FortuneCity – A site offering complete Web hosting service.
GO TO: www.fortunecity.com

fortune cookie – A wise or witty message that is posted daily to greet network users.

forum – Similar to a *chat room* but whereas chat room discussions tend to be removed frequently, forum discussions remain posted for a longer time. Forums tend to be linked to a web site and to be focused on a specialist topic. Often forums are based on *Bulletin Board Systems.*

forward – To send an e-mail message that you have received to a third party, possibly as an attachment to your own message.

forward button – Web browser toolbar button that advances the browsing session by one page. To use this forward option, the user needs to have viewed several web pages and then used the *back button.*
SEE: FEATURE BOX

forward compatible – Developers use this term when claiming compatibility between a current program and future versions.

forward slash – The forward slash, or slash, character. In Internet addresses, it separates the segments of the path e.g. www.dk./publications/children/fiction.html
SEE ALSO: BACKSLASH

four color system – The color system that is used in 4-color printing.
SEE ALSO: CMYK

four zero four – Internet term of abuse for someone who is not very bright. It refers to *error message* 404: file not found.

four zero four compliant – This refers to a web site that no longer exists. The *browser* will search for this nonexistent site and will display the *error message* 404.

fourth generation computers – Microcomputers that use large scale integration are described as fourth-generation computers.

fourth generation web site – A web site that contains the latest developments in multimedia technology.

FPS – See: **f**rames **p**er **s**econd

FPX file – The *file extension* for FlashPix, a *bitmapped graphics* file format. The FPX file format can store files in a number of different resolutions but only the resolution that is required for the current stream will be transmitted, reducing download time.

FQDN – See: **F**ully-**Q**ualified **D**omain **N**ame

fractal – A method of *compression* used for color images. It is a particularly good method for natural images such as plants and skies. Fractal images are based on the mathematical geometry of irregular shapes.

frag – (slang) 1.Common abbreviation for *fragment.*
2. To kill another player's avatar in a multiuser game.
SEE ALSO: MUD

fragment – A piece of a *packet.* A packet is sometimes split during transmission, then reassembled on delivery.

fragmentation – Breaking a file into fragments for more efficient storage in free disk space. When the file is later accessed, the fragments are reassembled for viewing.

SEE ALSO: DEFRAGMENTATION

frame – 1. A bordered area on web pages that acts as an independent window.
2. Bordered area surrounding an image.
3. A single image taken from an animation, video, or film.
4. A complete scan of a monitor screen. Each frame is made up of horizontal and vertical scan lines containing pixels. The higher the number of scan lines the better the *resolution.*
5. A *packet* of data sent in frame relay technology.

frame grabber – This stand-alone device or function within a video graphics card is used for capturing *analog* TV signals and for *digitizing* a single frame, turning it into a *bitmapped image.* Frame grabbers can also accept input from a video cable, camcorder, or VCR.

frame rate – The rate at which *frames* are displayed in film or video, measured in frames per second (fps).

frame relay – A method of sending data *packets* over *wide area networks.* Packets of variable length are transmitted at high speeds over digital lines.

FrameMaker® 6.0 – An advanced desktop and multi-channel publishing program from Adobe.
GO TO:
www.adobe.com/products/framemaker

frames per second (fps) – A measurement of computer and display performance. The number of times the screen is refreshed per second (*refresh rate*) is measured in frames per second.

Free Agent – A program that enables the user to collect information from newsgroups and news information sources from around the world to a specific set of requirements.
GO TO: www.forteinc.com

free Internet service – An *Internet Service Provider* supplying users with free Internet access. The service is usually funded by advertising which users cannot *filter* from the display.

free money virus – This hoax computer virus comes in the form of an e-mail message warning people not to open another e-mail with the title "free money."

free software – Software that is free of charge. This software has no licensing fees nor any restrictions on use, i.e. it can be modified, copied, and distributed freely. Contrast with *freeware* where the developer retains the copyright. It is also called freely available software.

free space - Available space on a *hard drive* which can be used for loading programs or data. A new program usually indicates the amount of free space required for the installation.

free space optics (FSO) - Transmission of optical signals using infrared lasers. This very fast mode of transmission does not require a government license since it does not use the spectrum.

free text search - **See:** full text search

free web page - Web sites that offer web pages free of charge to a group of users or to the general public.

SEE ALSO: FREE INTERNET SERVICE

free-form text - Simple text generated by a word processor or text editor.

 FreeHand9 - FreeHand is a drawing program, ideal for creating logos, line drawings, and other graphic images.
Go TO: www.macromedia.com

freehand tool - If using the conference *whiteboard*, the freehand tool allows the user to draw without any constraint.

freemail - Free web-based *e-mail,* usually supported by advertising revenue. Most freemail can be sent and retrieved through any browser, so freemail can be read on any Internet-linked computer world-wide. It has the advantage of not being tied to an

Internet Service Provider, so users can change ISP without changing e-mail addresses. *Hotmail* is probably the most popular example.

Freenet - A type of *network* that offers free access to members of a local community through bodies such as community centers or public libraries.

Freeserve - The largest *Internet Service Provider* based in the UK.
Go TO: www.freeserve.co.uk

freeware - Software available for public use free of charge, but copyright remains with the producer or author. The copyright holder has the distribution rights and can decide to sell those rights in the future. Contrast with *free software* that has no restrictions on use and can be copied, modified, and distributed by anyone.

freeze - The situation when the pointer and cursor on the computer screen, along with everything else on the display, stops and will not respond to any commands. When the computer freezes in this way, the only solution is to restart the computer and hope that the problem will be resolved by this action. Usually the user cannot restart the computer by pressing any keys.

freeze date – A program that lengthens the lives of shareware and similar programs with a time limit set for their use.

freeze-frame video – Video transmission in which the *frames* are changed once every couple of seconds, rather than the 30 *frames per second* rate as in *full-motion video.*

frequency – The number of times a complete waveform (oscillation) repeats per second. Sound waves and electrical current frequencies are both measured in cycles per second (Hertz).
SEE ALSO: WAVES

frequency division multiplexing – The situation where several different data streams are transmitted along the same *channel* using different *frequencies.*

frequency modulation – This is a method of blending data onto a carrier *signal* by varying the *frequency* of the wave. For example, radio uses frequency modulation (or FM, as it is usually known) to mix the audio signal with the FM carrier signal. In communications, the modem *modulates* data into an audible format in order to transmit that information over the telephone cables. The receiving modem demodulates the signal to return the data to its original format.

frequency shift keying – **See:** frequency modulation

Frequently Asked Questions (FAQs) – Many web sites post a list of the most commonly asked questions to provide information about the site. This is particularly helpful to *newbies* who find it useful to check the FAQs before mailing a question or phoning the helpline.

fried – A computer or device damaged by a surge of electrical current.

friendly name – A common name for a component with a highly technical name.

friends and family virus – A computer virus that spreads by sending itself to all the people named in a person's e-mail address book.

frisbee – (slang) A CD-ROM.

fritterware – Programs overburdened with unnecessary *functions* and capabilities. The term comes from the amount of time users need to fritter away trying to come to grips with the software.

.frm – A *filename extension* used for *form* files, such as order forms.

Frodo.Frodo – A destructive computer virus that triggers on September 22 (the birthday of Frodo and Bilbo Baggins, characters in J.R.R. Tolkien's *Lord of the Rings*). This virus attempts to plant a *Trojan* in boot sectors and the *MBR* in the PC causing the system to crash, mainly because it doesn't actually work properly.

front end – 1. The part of a computer system that the user sees and where data is input. Usually the *graphical user interface*. 2. A simple program that the user operates which fronts a more complicated operation; or a computer that the user operates but which interacts with a larger computer in the *background*.

FrontPage – A leading web site creation program from *Microsoft*.
Go to: www.microsoft.com/frontpage
See also: web design

FrontPage Express – A derivative of Microsoft *FrontPage*, this program enables the user to create and edit web pages using graphic images and without needing to know *HTML*. Frontpage Express does not have some of the more complex features of the full *FrontPage* program.

fry the screen – To post a *flame* message.

FSO – See: free space optics

FTP – See: File Transfer Protocol

FTP Server – A File Transfer Protocol server is one that stores collections of downloadable files, made available to a certain number of users.

FTP site – A computer system on the Internet whose primary purpose is to download and/or upload files.
See also: file transfer protocol, anonymous FTP

FUI – Form-based user interface. A program used on web pages which provides the user with a *form* to fill. Once completed and posted, the details are processed and the results are fed back on another form. A travel site may use FUI for flight inquiries or a medical program may use it for diagnostic purposes.

full duplex –Full duplex is the transmission of data along the same channel in both directions simultaneously.

full-motion video (FMV) – Video transmission where the frames change at the rate of 30 *frames per second.* The minimum rate that provides the brain with the illusion of smooth movement is 24 frames per second. Digitized video stored on a CD-ROM or computer can be run at varying frame rates.

full-text search – A type of *search* that checks all the words in the text of a document rather than simply checking against keywords or a summary. Most web search engines perform full text searches, which can be useful, but they can lead to many irrelevant results or *false drops.*

fully qualified domain name (FQDN) – This is the complete name for a computer on the Internet system, containing both its *hostname* as well as its *domain name*. An example of a fully qualified domain name is www.dk.com.

function – A routine that a program can perform, e.g. one function a browser can perform is to retrieve e-mail.

function keys – A set of keyboard keys identified as *F1*, *F2*, etc. These keys are used as computer commands and perform different functions in different programs. Also called F keys.

functional specification – The technical blueprint for a system.

funneling – Directing a web user to a page with a special offer, such as free software, in order to redirect them to an e-commerce site.

furrfu – (slang) A word used to put over indignation or disgust.

future proof – A system that will not become obsolete. Obsolescence is a major problem for purchasers of computer systems as the technology is immediately superceded by a more advanced version.

fuzzy logic – A logical technique for dealing with problems with more than one answer. Digital computers work on a simple on/off, yes/no or *binary* basis but fuzzy logic introduces degrees of variance in between. It was originally conceived as a tool to aid computerized handwriting recognition, but is now important in the development of *artificial intelligence* and *expert system* technologies.
SEE ALSO: FUZZY SEARCH

fuzzy search – A *search* which returns not only exact matches but close ones too. This is useful if the correct spelling is not known, or the query is general. It is also used by some spellcheckers.

FWP – See: free web pages

G3 - See: Apple computer

G4 - See: Apple computer

gain - 1. To obtain (e.g. to gain access to a file).
2. To increase or get larger (e.g. to gain signal strength).

Galileo - A benchmark that tests a computer's In/Out performance using a controlled transmission. Later this was renamed IOmeter.

gallium arsenide - An alloy used as the base material for *microprocessors*. It is made up of gallium and arsenic compound (GaAs). It conducts many times faster than *silicon* and is used in high-frequency applications such as mobile phones, DVD players, and fiber optics.

game console - A computer specifically designed to play games, often supplied with cartridges or CD-ROMs pre-loaded with games configured for that console.

game port - A computer interface designed to connect a games console, paddle, or joystick to the computer.

gamepad - A handheld device used to control characters or graphics in a computer game.

gamepaddle - See: gamepad

gamer - An enthusiastic game player or anyone who regularly plays online games.

games - Electronic entertainment ranging from card games to "shoot 'em up" games. Games can be bought for *games consoles* and PCs, or downloaded from the Internet.

games clubs - May be formed around a group of like-minded individuals who play one type of game or use a particular type of games console.

games forum - A discussion group in which gaming is the primary topic. Many games web sites have their own *forums* and *message boards*.

games network - A network of personal computers linked in such a way that the users can play games with each other.

gaming - A general term referring to the playing of games both on a PC and over the World Wide Web. It is also applied to gambling over the Internet.

gamma - The term used to describe the difference between the color of the pixels requested on a screen and the actual color. There are voltage differences on PC *monitors* and *cathode ray tubes,* which means that the colors need a correction factor applied to get the color needed.

gamma correction - The factor applied to pixel intensity.

gamut - A whole range or scale (e.g. to browse through a whole gamut of car rental sites before selecting the best deal).

gap – A reference to the space between blocks of data on magnetic tape.

gapless – A magnetic tape that is recorded in a continuous stream without *gaps*.

garbage – 1. Invalid or inaccurate data.
2. Unwanted files or information.
3. Interference or static.

garbage collection – The removal of unwanted files or data.

gardening site – A web site specializing in horticulture. Many sites have sprung up offering information on plants and gardening. Some have very popular chat rooms with lots of advice available. The source may be a national gardening society, local gardening club, garden book or magazine publisher, or enthusiast.

GAS – A shortened name for *gallium arsenide*, also GaAs.

gas-plasma display – A display screen that consists of gas sandwiched between two layers of glass that are covered with grid conductors. These glow on contact with electricity.

gate – A type of electronic switch usually prefaced by a function that describes what sort of gate it is.

Gates, Bill – Founder of the world's largest computer software company, Microsoft, and one of the world's richest men.
Go to: www.microsoft.com/billgates

Gates's Law – "The speed of software halves every 18 months." *Gates's* ironic observation, which plays on *Moore's Law*. It is a comment on the ever increasing size of software packages that in turn demand ever more sophisticated hardware.

gateway – 1. A combination of hardware and software that links two different types of networks.
2. A computer that acts as a link between networks, converting, and re-routing.

🔲 **Gateway** – Founded on a farm in Iowa, by Tom Waitt in 1985, Gateway is one of the largest manufacturers of PCs and associated computer products.
Go to: www.gateway.com

gateway host – A *router* that acts as an entry point into, and exit point out of, a *network*.

gather – To retrieve information from a wide range of sources.

Gaussian blur – A kind of filter that uses a mathematical formula to create the effect of looking through an out-of-focus lens. Named after the German astronomer and mathematician Karl Friedrich Gauss.

GB – See: Gigabyte

Gbit – See: Gigabit

Gbps – See: Gigabits per second

G–byte – Another term for **g***igabyte*.

GCR – **See:** **G**ray **C**omponent **R**eplacement

GDI – **See:** **G**raphical **D**evice **I**nterface

GDM – **See:** **G**lobal **D**OS **M**emory

Geac – The Geac Computer Corporation Limited, founded in 1971, is Canada's largest software company. It provides a wide range of software for the catering and human resources industries in particular.
Go to: www.geac.com

geek – Someone who knows a great deal about computers and software, but whose enthusiastic interest may imply exclusion from normal society.

Geekonics – Describing how geeks speak. A compound word formed from *geek* and phonics.
See also: geekspeek

geekosphere – A web site devoted to geek culture, heavy in content on subjects such as science fiction, trivia, games, and "in" jokes that only *geeks* understand.

geekspeek – A reference to the specialized language, containing many *acronyms* and buzzwords, used by people in the computer and technology industries. Variously called Computer English, computer sounds, nerdspeak, and geekonics.

gender – A reference to cable sockets that have male and female connectors.

gender changer – A cable connector that corrects mismatches between a plug and a socket (e.g. if there is a male socket and plug). Also called a gender mender.

General Electric Company – One of the world's largest and most successful companies, it manufactures everything from aircraft engines to specialized electrical equipment.
Go to: www.ge.com

general failure – A serious fault leading to one or all applications or hardware failing at once.

General failure reading drive x – A DOS *error* message. It commonly means that an unformatted floppy disk is being used, or it appears when the user is trying to read a high-density disk in a low-density drive. The full message reads: General failure reading drive X Abort, Retry, Fail?

General Packet Radio Service (GPRS) – A standard for *wireless applications* that will allow mobile phone connections of up to 150 *kilobits per second*. Compares favorably to current mobile systems of up to 9.6 kps. Its introduction will mean vastly improved mobile Internet connection.

general protection fault (GPF) – A condition in a computer that causes a Windows application to crash. The most common cause is one application trying to use memory assigned to another application.

generation – 1. The production of data, applicable to the output of programs. 2. A family of computers or programs produced at a specific time, e.g. *fifth generation computers.*

generation X – People who were born between 1967 and 1976. "Generation Y" refers to people who were born 1977-1984, and the so-called "baby boomers" are people born 1937-1956. The term refers to the advancement of technology and its effect on each generation: so generation X was the first to embrace technology, while generation Y is the one where technology is a part of life. Most baby boomers remember the introduction of color television.

generation Y – **See:** generation X

generator – A program that can be used to produce other programs.

generic – Relating to or descriptive of an entire group or class of software or hardware, usually from one manufacturer.

genetic programming – Computer programming that uses the "survival of the fittest" principle to constantly improve the functions within a program.

Genie – A UK-based *Internet Service Provider* specializing in *WAP* technology.
Go to: www.genie.co.uk

genlock – Abbreviation for generator lock. In video it is a device that can process two signals at the same time (e.g. combine video graphics with a signal from a video camera).

Genrat.785 – A *file infector computer virus* that attaches itself to the computer's memory and then replicates itself over and over again.

genuine – Something that is truthful, real, or correct. Authentication is crucial in *encrypted* systems.

Geocities – The largest *home page* community on the Web. Geocities allows you to build your own site, which they will then host for you.
Go to: www.geocities.com

Geographic Information System (GIS) - An information system that deals with spatial information and its attributes (e.g. map making, tracking, and exploration).

geographical domain – The two-letter top-level domain assigned to every country except the US. E.g. uk indicates that the site originates in the United Kingdom, cn indicates China, br Brazil, etc.
See: appendix 3 for a full list.
See also: country codes

Geoport – A *serial port* for Apple *Macintosh* computers that provides the interface between a telephone line and the computer.

geostationary - A reference to a satellite that is always a uniform distance from the earth and that travels at the same speed as the earth rotates, so staying above the same geographical point.

Get - 1. An *FTP* command to copy a file from a remote computer onto the downloading computer.
2. In programming, a request for the next file or record in an input file.

Get a life! - Used in newsgroups to indicate that a participant is taking an obscure or technical issue too seriously. The phrase originally came from the US TV program "Saturday Night Live."

Get More Money - A famous hoax computer virus that was named after the title of the e-mail with which it came.

ghost - 1. The postings of a participant who is no longer online, in a *chat room*.
2. A faint image that appears as a shadow to the original image.
3. A button or menu option that is not available and appears gray in color.
4. A secondary signal that arrives in advance of, or after, the primary signal.

ghost site - A web site that has not been updated but can still be seen on the Web.

ghosting - To copy the entire hard disk or operating system from one computer onto another so that the duplicate functions exactly the same way as the original.

ghosting server - A server that contains programs ready to be copied onto other PCs. Generally these contain the operating system and a selected set of applications.

gib - To destroy something completely. The word comes from the game *Quake*. Also spelled jib.

gibberish - Useless or unreadable information and text.

GID file - Windows help files ending with .gid extension.

GIF - **See:** **G**raphics **I**nterchange **F**ormat

GIF animation - A simple animation tool that uses *Graphics Interchange Format*, making it suitable for web page use.

gift certificate - Like a conventional gift certificate, electronic versions can be purchased and spent at participating *e-tailers*. The gift is e-mailed along with an *e-greeting*.
SEE ALSO: FLOOZE

giga- - One billion; abbreviated to "G." In computers refers to the precise value 1,073,741,824.

gigabit - A measurement used to judge the transmission speed of a network. One gigabit is 10 to the 9 bits, i.e. 1,000,000,000.

gigabits per second (Gbps) - The number of *gigabits transmitted* over a *network* per second.

gigabyte (GB) – A measurement used in reference to memory. A gigabyte is 1.073,741,824 bytes.

gigaFLOPS – A measurement used when assessing microprocessor speeds.
SEE ALSO: FLOATING POINT OPERATION (FLOP)

gigahertz (GHz) – In transmission, 10 to the 9 Hz. High-speed radio applications are transmitted in the gigahertz range.

gigapixel – A specific number of *pixels*, actually 1.073,741,824.

GIMP – GNU Image Manipulation Program. A sophisticated paint and image editing program for *UNIX* and for *X Window*. It enables high-quality image manipulation and editing tools.

GIS – **See:** Geographic Information System

GKS – **See:** Graphical Kernel System

glare guard – An attachable/detachable extra screen placed in front of the computer screen that reduces glare and is recommended to ease eyestrain.

glass house – An environmentally controlled room that contains mainframe computers. Most large businesses use Little Glass Houses, which hold their network hardware within their building.

GlidePad – **See:** mousepad

glitch – A problem or *bug* in software or hardware that hinders operation.

G.Lite – A version of *ADSL*, which allows for high-speed "always on" digital communications over standard phone lines. It connects to the Internet via the G.Lite modem and is available on a subscription service basis.

global – A word meaning worldwide, but can also refer to an entire file, database, volume, program, market, customer base, network, or system.

Global DOS Memory – The first megabyte of memory that DOS supports. It consists of conventional memory (0–640K), the *UMA* (640–1,024K), and the HMA (1,024–1,088K).

Global Internet eXchange(GIX) – A *routing* exchange that connects networks worldwide to the Internet.

global new economy – Worldwide Internet commerce, i.e. commerce that respects no political boundaries.
SEE ALSO: E-COMMERCE

Global Positioning System (GPS) – A system of satellites that use triangulation to identify Earth locations through a receiving unit.

global variable – In programming, a variable that is used throughout a program.

global village – Highly used term for the world interconnected via the Internet.

Globally Unique Identifier (GUID) – A number embedded in *Microsoft Windows 98 operating system* that could be used to monitor a user's online usage and related activities.

glossary – A list of words and their meaning. Often found on specialist web sites to give the user an understanding of any technical or specialist words used within the *content* of the site.

glue – Software that provides some conversion, translation, or facility that enables one device or system to work with another.

glyph – Characters or symbols that can be printed by the computer.

Gnu – Shorthand for "Gnu's not UNIX." It is a group of organizations devoted to producing public domain software that is compatible with *UNIX* (but is not the same). The only proviso in its usage is that users cannot restrict its use to others or restrict its redistribution.
Go to: www.gnu.org

Gnutella – One of the first Internet file sharing programs (along with *Napster*) that anyone can download, modify, and send on. By downloading the program you can gain access to files held by other Gnutella users, which can include software and music files. The main difference to Napster is that gnutella is not centralized, which makes it

very difficult to stop the illegal copying of music.
Go to: www.gnutella.co.uk

go bosh – Cyberspeak for "Go **B**ig **O**r **S**tay **H**ome." Usually this phrase refers to e-commerce sites, meaning that if they do not invest enough resources into the site, they will doubtless fail against their competitors.

go button – The browser *button* that contains a menu of navigation options, e.g. back/forward and refresh. On *Internet Explorer,* it gives an extending list of options while on *Netscape Navigator* the recent history list is offered.

go down – When a system or network fails due to software or hardware problems.

go private – In a *chat room*, to hide a dialog from general view.

Godwin's law – The law that states that the longer the *thread* of a discussion continues in a *newsgroup*, the higher the chance that Hitler or the Nazis will be evoked. Some groups have the rule that when this happens the thread is stopped and the discussion is over.

Godzillagram – An online message that in theory could be broadcast to every Internet-linked computer in the universe.

going public – The first sale of stock in a company to the public. In this way many Internet entrepreneurs attempt to make their fortune. The process usually involves creating a web site, building up its reputation, then at the peak of the hype, going public. This can result in massive profits for the original shareholders.

Gold Editor – An easy-to-use yet powerful web page creation program from *Netscape*. GO TO: www.netscape.com

golden handcuffs – Payments offered to good employees to stay with their company. At the height of the late 1990s Internet boom, golden handcuffs were prevalent since good employees were hard to come by.

good thing – (slang) Computer *geek*speek for something that is undoubtedly wonderful and could not possibly have any sideeffects.

Good Times Virus – A successful hoax *computer virus* alert that appeared in 1994. The message warned the user that the computer would become infected if the words "Good Times" were read with his/her eyeballs. Since the subject line included the words "Good Times," the damage, in effect, was already done. A second e-mail was then sent with the same subject line and if the user opened it, he/she was reprimanded for opening e-mails containing the words "good times."

gooey – Familiar term for *graphical user interface* (GUI).

 **Google** – One of the most popular and user-friendly search engines, renowned for its speed and accuracy. Google call its staff, Googlers, and the company HQ, Googleplex. GO TO: www.google.com

googol – A googol is 10 to the power of 100; otherwise written as 1 followed by 100 zeros.

gonk – (slang) An unbelievable exaggeration of the truth.

Gopher – An Internet document retrieval system, popular with universities. Gopher presents the information from thousands of Gopher servers in a hierarchical list, then when a document is requested will retrieve that document and display it on screen. It pre-dates the World Wide Web but is still in use. Today, most Gopher databases have been converted to web pages.

Gopherspace – A general term for the areas of the Internet served by *gopher*.

gorilla arm – The ache that the user feels in their arm after using a touch-screen for some time. It was one of the main reasons that this technology never became popular. It is also used in a cautionary sense to indicate technologies that work in theory, but need to be tried in practice.

Goto/Go to – 1. In word-processing, the utility in the Edit menu that enables the user to move about the current document. 2. In programming, a command to go to some other part of the program.

Gouraud shading – A technique developed by Henri Gouraud in the early 1970s for *3D graphics*. It splits an image into triangles then computes a shaded surface based on the color and illumination at the corners of every triangle. Gouraud shading does not, however, produce shadows or reflections.

.gov – An Internet *domain* associated with government web sites.

GMT – **See:** **G**reenwich **M**ean **T**ime

GPF – **See:** **G**eneral **P**rotection **F**ault

gppm – **G**raphics **p**ages **p**er **m**inute. A measurement of printing speed for non-text pages.

GPRS – **See:** **G**eneral **P**acket **R**adio **S**ervice

GPS – **See:** **G**lobal **P**ositioning **S**ystem

Grabber – **See:** frame grabber

grabber hand – A hand-shaped screen tool that is used to move objects around and within a window.

graceful degradation – Allowing some parts of a system to function even after a part of it has broken down.

graceful exit – Getting out of a problem situation in a program without having to reboot or turn the computer off.

gradient fill – The gradual change from one shade of a color to another, or of one color to another. This is a popular technique used in producing web pages.
SEE: FEATURE BOX

gradient paint roller – A tool in a drawing or paint program that allows the user to create *gradient fill*.

grandfather file – The third most recent backup of a file, after father and son files.

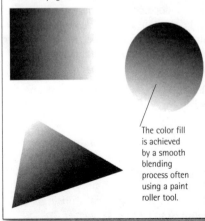

gradient fill

The gradating of colors is a particularly effective tool for web site designers looking for eye-catching backgrounds that will attract users to hit these pages.

The color fill is achieved by a smooth blending process often using a paint roller tool.

granularity – 1. A reference to how adaptable and flexible a system can be. The more features or modules added the more granular it is.
2. The size of memory segments in a virtual memory.

graph – A visual representation of equations or data. Common types are bar, pie, and line graphs, which are features of many spreadsheet and database programs.

graphic anchor – A graphic icon on a web page, which, when clicked, routes the user to another web site that has its *URL* linked to that *anchor*.

graphical browser – A browser that can display images and text. Both *Internet Explorer* and *Netscape Navigator* are graphical browsers.

graphical device interface – A *Windows protocol* for the representation and transmission of graphic objects to devices such as monitors and printers.

Graphical Kernel System – An independent and very adaptable graphics language for 2D, 3D, and bitmapped graphics images.

graphical user interface (GUI) – Computer *commands* generated by clicking on visual *buttons* or *icons*, e.g. drop-down menus. Far easier to navigate than text-based commands. *Apple* Computers were the first with widespread GUI in the 1980s.

graphics – 1. The representation of images on screen and via scanners and printers.
2. A computer program or devise that includes the facility for displaying and manipulating images.

graphics accelerator – An *expansion board* that contains a *chipset* dedicated to graphics. This speeds up the process of drawing lines and images because these operations do not then have to compete with other devices such as keyboard and sound systems to use the main processor. Graphic accelerators make it possible to display 3D images in quick succession at high speeds for applications such as interactive games.

graphics adaptor – **See:** video adaptor

graphics based – The display of text and pictures as graphics images; typically *bitmapped* images (e.g. a document scanned into the computer).

graphics card – A *printed circuit board* that enables the computer to display images.

graphics display system – A *monitor* or other device that can display pictures.

graphics engine – Specialized software that accepts commands from an application and builds images and text that are then directed to the graphics driver and hardware.
SEE ALSO: GRAPHICS LANGUAGE

graphics file format – A file format that handles *graphics*. They are generally either *bitmapped* formats or *vector* formats.

Graphics Interchange Format (GIF) – A compression method used for the display and downloading of *graphics* on the Internet. Highly popular (along with *JPEG*), it uses a limited 256 colors range making it suitable for web sites and graphics programs. It is a powerful format that uses *lossless compression,* which means that it can be transmitted relatively swiftly with no loss of information. It was introduced by *Compuserve* in 1987.

graphics language – High-level language used to create graphics images. It is translated and converted into images by software or specialized hardware.

SEE ALSO: GRAPHICS ENGINE

---

grayscale

The varying shades of gray seen in a manipulated, scanned, or printed image, e.g. this car. Grayscale can range from 0 per cent (e.g white) to 100 per cent (e.g. black).

---

graphics mode – A screen display mode that is able to display graphics.

graphics tablet – A drawing tool used for retouching, image manipulation, illustration, and video editing. The user

draws on the tablet using a digital pen (or puck) either connected to the tablet by a wire or wireless. The user draws on the tablet, and the corresponding image is shown on the monitor and stored as mathematical line segments. Also known as a digitzer tablet.

gray bar land – The hypnotic state of watching a downloaded dialog box or other similar function.

Gray Component Replacement (GCR) – A way of reducing the amount of printing ink. Black is substituted for the amount of gray contained in a color, meaning that black ink is used instead of the three *CMY* inks.

gray hairs – (slang) Someone who has lived long enough to have experience.

gray mail – See: spam

gray market – E-commerce aimed at *over-fifty* year olds.

grayed – Another term for *ghosting*.

grayscale – The use of shades of gray to represent an image.
SEE: FEATURE BOX

grayware – (slang) The human brain.

greater than – The symbol > that identifies the end of an *HMTL tag*.

greeking – 1. The use of random text or marks to show the layout of a page in small scale. E.g. Most programs with a preview mode do not show the actual words used in the document, but replace these with symbols or dots.
2. In printing, the use of nonsense text to illustrate the final layout and design of text. This technique is now used by web designers.
SEE: FEATURE BOX

Green Book Standard – A method of storing software and hardware video, audio, and binary data on compact optical disks.
SEE ALSO: COMPACT DISK–INTERACTIVE

Green_Caterpillar – A *computer virus* that infects one command (.COM) and one executable (.FXF) file on the current drive every time a COPY command is executed. An animated caterpillar that munches text on the screen also appears.

green PC – A PC designed to reduce power consumption through the use of *sleep modes*, which power down non-essential components.

green phosphor – A chemical used for monochrome screens; it displays green characters on a black background.

Greenwich Mean Time – Global standard time. The modern system of timekeeping was developed in Greenwich, England, and the time at Greenwich is used to determine the world's time zones. This is widely used over the Internet and may be different to the actual time in England, which is altered in the summer. May also be called by the more modern term Universal Time or UT.

greetings cards – See: e-greetings

gremlin – Unexplained system fault.

---

greeking

Originally a printing term, greeking has been adopted by web designers to preview how their web pages might look with flowed-in, but not live, text. It is an abstract design function.

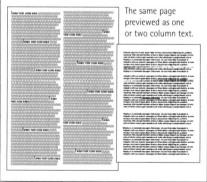

The same page previewed as one or two column text.

grep – **G**lobal **r**egular **e**xpression and **p**rint. A *UNIX* command that searches files for text and outputs matching a pattern.

gribble – Binary data that appears on the screen as scrambled text. Often caused by noise on the line or a malfunction in the modem. Also called *baud barf.*

grid – A matrix of horizontal and vertical *guidelines* used to help with page layout.
SEE: FEATURE BOX

grid snap – A facility within graphics programs that will position a line or drawing object onto a position indicated on a *grid*.

---

grid

Colored guidelines can be called up on-screen to help designers and editors with layouts and text line lengths in DTP applications (e.g. QuarkXpress) but are not visible when printing.

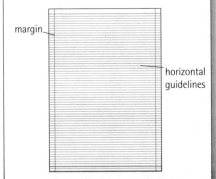

margin

horizontal guidelines

---

grilf – Originally a typo but has become a *newsgroup/Usenet* term for girlfriend.

grim reaper – A program that deletes all files of a certain type on a system. When used as a *computer virus*, it can have devastating effects.

gritch – A complaint. It plays on the word *glitch* and is usually concerned with a bug or similar problem.

grok – To have a thorough and complete understanding of a subject. Derived from Robert Heinlein's classic science fiction novel *Stranger in a Strange Land.*

gronk – To break or malfunction, e.g. computer malfunction.

ground – 1. To regroup and to take stock of a situation.
2. An electrically conductive body (which is not positively or negatively charged). E.g. The earth, or ground, pin in an electrical plug prevents computer cables picking up noise or emitting radio frequency interference.

group – A collection of similar objects. On the Web, a group is a number of users interested in a particular subject.
SEE ALSO: NEWSGROUP

Group 3 protocol – The protocol defined by the *CCITT* for sending *faxes*.

Group 4 protocol – The protocol defined by *CCITT* for sending *faxes* over *ISDN* networks.

Groupware – A program used by a group of people (workgroups) attached to a *local-area network* (LAN). Groupware can be used to run practical organizational functions such as e-mail and diaries, as well as distribute files and newsletters.

GroupWise – Commercially available messaging and groupware software from *Novell* that offers a universal inbox for calendaring, scheduling, task management, document sharing, workflow, and threaded discussions.

grovel – A *hacker* term for painstaking work that gets nowhere. Often used for someone having to go through a program in great detail to look for a *bug* or fault.

GSM – Global System for Mobile Communications. A digital cellular system that enables eight simultaneous calls to be transmitted on the same radio frequency. Used as a standard in Europe and Asia, and available in over 100 countries.

guarantee – A legally binding document that promises that a device will work as promised and that it is of good merchantable quality.

guard band – A section of magnetic tape that splits two channels of recording that have been made on the same tape.

guard bit – A bit within a cell or word that indicates to the computer whether it can be edited or if it is protected.

gubbish – A composite word for rubbish and garbage used to describe text in newsgroups and e-mails.

guest – Someone who logs into a network or service that does not have a user account, but is given a default set of privileges until they officially register with the service. Many web sites allow this as a way of trying out the available service.

guestbook – A simple device for web sites to encourage feedback from visitors. Users give their details and then can type in a message. Subsequent visitors can also read the entries.

GUI – See: Graphical User Interface

GUID – See: Globally Unique Identifier

guideline – A line that can be positioned on screen to aid the accurate positioning of text and objects. The line is not printed with the document.

guiltware – Freeware that requests that the user donate money to a specified charity in lieu of payment.

gulp – A small group of text usually equaling two bytes.

gun – The source of the electron beam within a *cathode ray tube*. Also called an electron gun.

guru – A knowledgeable person in a specialist field such as *e-commerce*.

guru site – A web site compiled by a *guru* on a specialist subject. Comprehensive and usually with an impressive set of *links* and often with commentary and ratings.

gutter – 1. Space between two facing pages on a book or pamphlet, which the text appears to fall into. A gutter is necessary for binding the pages together. 2. More generally used to mean the blank space between columns of text.
SEE: FEATURE BOX

gzip – A data compression program designed to work with *Gnu*. The .gz file extension denotes files condensed using the *zip* algorithm on Unix systems.

---

gutter

Traditionally, the gutter is the far right or far left space of a facing page that is part of the binding process.

There are effectively four gutters in this three column text page.

H

H.323 – A standard that addresses video conferencing over *ISDN* lines, ensuring consistency of delivery and quality.

H.324 – The H.324 *standard* addresses video and audio communications over low *bit rate* connections.

hack – 1. To break into a secure program, site, or application and to modify any of the existing data without authorization. 2. A temporary solution.
SEE ALSO: HACKER

hack attack – The process of modifying a program or web site, sometimes undertaken by several *hackers.*

hack mode – To work seriously and with concentration on the solution of a computer-based problem.

hacker – Someone who *hacks*. Hackers usually possess a high level of computer skills. The word originally meant a person with a great deal of computer knowledge.

hacker humor – The stuff that makes true *hackers* laugh. They like jokes about computer operating systems, parodies of intellectual and scientific concepts, puns and other word games based on grammar and malapropisms, references to the type of humor typified by Monty Python and the Marx brothers, and playing with the themes and characters from well-known science fiction books and films.
SEE ALSO: GEEKOSPHERE

hacker jargon – Terminology used in *hacker* culture, often used to disguise their true motives. Can also apply to computer jargon generally.

hacktools – Utility programs that are used by *hackers* for their "trade"; tools such as network *sniffers* and *spoofers*, and *scanners* that exploit the vulnerability of computers, steal passwords, or send spam.

hairball – (slang) 1. When a store-and-forward network fails to deliver mail regularly but sends a whole batch of messages instead.
2. A large amount of garbled text.

hairline rule – A very thin line, mainly used in page layouts as part of the overall page design.

hakspeak – Shorthand using numbers to replace some of the words. For example, "see you later" is translated to CU L8R. Originally from hacker speak, now popularly used in text messaging.

HAL – See: Hardware Abstraction Layer

Hal – The name of the rogue computer in Stanley Kubrick's film 2001 Space Odyssey. Legend has it that Hal was derived by shifting the letters "IBM" by one letter each up the alphabet.

half duplex – A transmission in a network where information can travel in both directions, although not simultaneously.

half height – Little-used term for the size of the bay into which disk drives fit in a PC. Once full height, drive bays are now all half height.

half-inch tape – Cartridge drives using half-inch (1.27cm) wide magnetic tape. They are used for backup with mainframes.

halftone – A color image that has been converted in a graphics program into a black-and-white image.

This halftone image was produced originally from a color image. So, it is not as sharp as the original.

hand coding – Writing a program in proper programming language, such as HTML, rather than using some of the high-level programming tools available, eg. *WYSIWYG*.

hand-held device – **See:** hand-held PC

hand-held device markup language (HDML) – A markup language used to format content for web-enabled mobile phones. Only phones connected to Openwave's system can use it.
Go to: www.openwave.com

hand-held PC – A computer small enough to hold in the hand. Such PCs have now become highly sophisticated, offering much by way of an organizer, *MP3* player, *e-book reader,* calculator, and games.

handle – 1. (slang) A number used to identify an active file within a program. 2. In programs that use a graphical user interface, a small square that can be dragged to change the shape of an object. 3. (slang) Someone's name or alias.

handler – A program routine that is designed to perform a particular task.

handoff – Transferring an ongoing wireless call from one transmission site to another without disconnecting the call.

handshake – Transferring data between two entities, such as a server and a client, on the Internet. Often a handshake protocol is used in secure transactions.

handwriting recognition – A popular application in *hand-held PCs.* It recognizes characters written by hand, negating the use of a keyboard.

hang – When a piece of software or hardware has stopped working and is probably waiting for an event that will never occur.

happy – This term describes software that is performing well but 100 per cent incorrectly, in a state of ignorance about something it is failing to do.

Happy 99 – A fairly harmless but annoying *Trojan* program that acts like a *virus.* Happy 99 attaches itself to e-mails and is transmitted without the knowledge of the sender. It only activates when the icon happy99.exe is clicked on. Although originated in 1999, it is still around today.
SEE: FEATURE BOX

Happy 99

When the Happy 99 e-mail is received, the user may open the attachment. This produces a firework display with the announcement: Happy New Year 1999!! The virus is then activated. Several cures are available online.
Go to:
http://www.symante
c.com/avcenter/venc
/data/happy99.worm
.html

haptic interface – A kind of interface that provides a means of communicating with a computer using a tactile method. Haptic devices sense some form of movement by finger, hand, head, or body.

hard boot – *Booting* or restarting a system from power off. Often a computer that is jammed must be turned off and on to clear the memory before it can be operated again. Contrast this method with a soft boot where the computer is restarted without needing to turn the power off; e.g. pressing Ctrl+Alt+Delete twice on a computer using Windows (or DOS), a method also called a *warm boot.*

hard card – A piece of equipment containing a hard disk drive, which can be slotted into a systems expansion connector. Easy to install, but it offers limited memory.

hard copy – A physical copy of a document, such as an e-mail that has been printed out.

hard disk – A metal, magnetic disk that can store and retrieve much more data than a floppy disk. Also known as hard disk drive (HDD). Not normally removable.

hard error – A permanent system error.

hard page beak - **See:** forced page break

hard reset – A switch common to nearly all computers, it generates an electrical signal that resets the *CPU.*

hard return – A code used in word processing for the end of a paragraph.

hard–coded – Instructions that are written directly into a program are said to be hard-coded. A user other than the programmer or company that owns the program cannot modify them easily.

hardware – The physical components of a computer.

hardware abstraction layer (HAL) – A complicated component that allows a computer or piece of *hardware* to interact with its *operating system* at a general level (hence abstract) rather than at a specific and detailed level. It provides a common *interface* to the hardware, which allows *programmers* to write *code* that will work on hardware from different vendors.

hardware compatibility list (HCL) – A list of equipment or hardware that shows which pieces of *hardware* and *software* are *compatible* with the hardware listed.

hardware interrupt – An *interrupt* signal that is sent by the hardware rather than by the software.

hardware key – **See:** dongle

hardware reset – **See:** hard reset

hardwired – Describes a physical or permanent connection. Also a synonym for "hard-coded."

hardwired program – A program that has been built into the *hardware* but cannot be removed or changed.

harmonic distortion – In the field of communications, this describes one or more frequencies that are generated as multiples of an original frequency. This is due to faults and irregularities that occur in the transmission line.

Harvard Graphics – A commonly used presentation graphics program for DOS and Windows from the Software Publishing Corporation. It is a competitor of the widely available Microsoft PowerPoint program, which has largely supplanted it in business.
Go to: www.spco.com

Harvest – A popular data retrieval program that allows searchers to use keywords to locate files quickly. Results from the search can display the lines from the files containing the actual search string and full paths to the files.
Go to: http://harvest.cs.colorado.edu/

hash – 1. The symbol #.
2. A number generated for a string of text, technically called the *hash value*. Hash is mainly used for security verification, but also to speed up looking up the string value in a table - the hash value, being a simple numeric, can be compared much more easily than the full value of the list element.
See also: hash code

hash code – The kind of security coding system in which the code numbers for the first three letters are added together, producing a new number that is called the hash code. This hash code can then be used to verify the authenticity of documents and files.

hash mark – **See:** hash

hash table – A list of all file entries listed by their hash code.

hash value – **See:** hash

hashing – The process and production of hash values.

HASP – **See:** Houston Automatic Spooling Program

hat – The name for the ^ character.

---

header

This header box in Microsoft Word is provided for the user to type in information and then opt to view, display, or print it as required.

The header is outlined by *marching ants*

The body text is seen in gray to differentiate it

Hayes compatibility – This language for programming *modems* was developed by Hayes Microcomputer Products. Hayes compatibility has become the industry standard and nearly all modems made today are Hayes compatible.

HCL – **See:** **H**ardware **C**ompatibility **L**ist

HD – **See:** **H**igh **D**ensity **D**iskette

HDML – **See:** **H**and-Held **D**evice **M**arkup **L**anguage

HDSL – **See:** **H**igh bit rate **D**igital **S**ubscriber **L**ine

HDTV – **See:** **H**igh **D**efinition **T**elevision

head – A head is a device that reads *data* from or writes data to a *magnetic disk* or tape. It is sometimes referred to as a *read/write head.*

head crash – A corruption of data caused by a fault in the head, which leads it to hit the spinning *hard drive,* causing damage.

head end – In the communications field, the head end is the originating point in a system. For example, in terms of Internet service provision, the head end describes the service company's computer system and its databases.

head skew – On a compact disc, the head skew is the distance that is offset between tracks; it allows the head to be at the right place to play or read the next track.

header – 1. Text at the top of page in the background - often inserted automatically. SEE: FEATURE BOX
2. Data *packet* sent before transmission to provide information on the destination.
3. List of data at the beginning of a page relating to the rest of the data; e.g. e-mail headers contain information on sender, date, and subject.

head-mounted display – Display or viewfinder mounted directly in front of the eye(s), usually via a helmet or glasses associated with *virtual reality* devices. At best they can give a level of reality unmatched by conventional screens.

headphones – An electrical device that consists of two earphones mounted on a flexible strap passing over the user's head.

headset – A set of headphones with a microphone attached.

heap – 1. A portion of memory that is reserved for data while a program is executing a task.
2. A specialized type of *binary tree*.

heap sort – This is a type of *binary tree* in which a list of data is first sorted into a heap by a heap sort algorithm and is then reorganized rationally.

heartbeat – A signal periodically emitted by software or hardware, often for synchronization purposes, and so that a monitoring program can tell that the signal emitter is still alive.

heatseeker – Someone who will always buy the latest computer update or hardware.

heatsink – A device that conducts heat away from electronic components or hardware to prevent damage.

heatsink fan (HSF) – Part of a *heatsink* unit, the *fan* is one of the principal devices used to cool electronic components; e.g. the *CPU*.

hect- – A prefix meaning 100.

hecta/hecto - See: hect

Hello, World – The nickname for the first software program completed by new programmers as part of their training.

Helloween 1376 – A DOS virus that infects program files with the .com and .exe filename extensions. It loads itself into memory and reproduces by infecting other .com and .exe files as they are opened. Files that are infected will increase by 1376 bytes. On November 1 it displays the following message: Nesedte porad u pocitace a zkuste jednou delat neco rozumneho!!! Poslouchejte HELLOWEEN - nejlepsi metalovou skupinu.
SEE ALSO: COMPUTER VIRUS

help – This function in a program aids the use of that program, usually by calling up an online instruction manual. It is accessed within many Windows-based applications by pressing the F1 key.

help compiler – A program that can translate text and *compiler* instructions into a help system located online.

help desk – A service, run by most companies who deal directly with their customers or with the public, to aid them with any problems that might arise.

help window – Sometimes called the help page or screen, this contains information requested to help with a specific query.

helper applications – Programs that add some functionality or improve performance to another program. For example, the way a *plug-in* improves a *browser*.
SEE ALSO: UPGRADE

Helvetica – A popular family of fonts. The original Helvetica was designed in 1957 by Max Miedinger, a Swiss type designer.
GO TO: www.linotype.com
SEE: FEATURE BOX

hertz – Named after German physicist Herman Hertz, this a unit that is used to measure *frequency*.

heterogeneous network – This kind of network is made up from a disparate collection of computers, programs, or *protocols.*

heuristics – A system that is commonly employed by anti-virus programs. These programs use heuristics to monitor and identify a *computer virus* by the way it works, rather than by looking for a specific file.

Hewlett-Packard (HP) – Widely known for their slogan "invent," Hewlett-Packard was founded in 1939 and is one of the world's leading manufacturers of computers and office and imaging equipment.
GO TO:
www.hp.com

Helvetica

Helvetica is one of the most commonly used fonts in publishing. Designed in the late 1950s, the name is derived from Helvetia, the Latin name for Switzerland. The examples here show Helvetica and Helvetica bold.

Helvetica

ABCDEFGHIJKLMNOPQ...
abcdefghijklmnopqrstuvwxyz
1234567890!@#$%^&*()

Helvetica (bold)

ABCDEFGHIJKLMNOPQ...
abcdefghijklmnopqrstu...
1234567890!@#$%^&*()

Hewlett-Packard Graphics Language (HPGL) - Designed by *Hewlett-Packard* to work with their printers, HPGL is a standard set of commands used to describe specific graphic images.

hex (hexadecimal) - The base-16 number system, consisting of 16 unique symbols: the numbers 0 to 9 and the letters A to F. E.g. The decimal number 13 is represented as D. This system is useful because it can represent every *byte* (8 bits) as two consecutive hexadecimal digits, so is less cumbersome than the *binary* system.

hexadecimal numbers - See: hex

HFC network - See: Hybrid Fiber-Coax network

hibernate - When a computer goes into its standby mode, which saves energy.
SEE ALSO: GREEN PC

hidden attributes - Properties built into files and programs, to which the user cannot gain access to or see.

hidden files - Also called *invisible files* and possessing *hidden attributes;* normally invisible to avoid corruption by users.

Hidenowt - This *computer virus* infects *.com* and *.exe* files; besides targeting the specific file c:\command.com, it does nothing more then replicate.

hierarchical - A pyramid organizational system used to organize files and programs.

hierarchical file system - Pyramid filing system starting at the top with *directories,* then *files,* then *sub-directories.*

hierarchical routing - Describes the situation where a *network* is divided into a number of regions. Each contains details used for routing within the region, but does not contain information on other regions.

HiFD - A kind of high-density *floppy disk* developed by Sony, HiFD can hold some 200 *Mb* of data.

High bit-rate DSL (HDSL) - This form of digital subscriber line allocates *bandwidth* in a symmetrical pattern, aiding efficiency.

high capacity CD-ROM - This is another name for a *DVD*.

high color - This is 32,768 colors (15 bits) or 65,536 colors (16-bit). The 15-bit color uses five bits for each red, green, and blue *pixel*. The 16th bit may be a color, or an overlay bit that selects pixels to display on video, for example.

high definition television (HDTV) - This is a relatively new kind of color television that can produce high-quality pictures on larger screens.

high density disk (HD) - *Disks* can be high density, medium density, and low density according to the amount of data stored. High density means that bits of data are physically held closer together.

high level language – Programming language simple both to learn and to write by the use of easily understood words and commands. The result is translated into the right *machine code* to enable functionality.

high level language application program interface (HLLAPI) – An *Application Program Interface* developed by *IBM* that allows a PC application to work with a *mainframe* computer.

high memory – Area of memory between 64k and 1mb (applied mainly to DOS).

high memory area (HMA) – Memory area available to programs, equivalent to 64k of extended memory above 1mb.

---

highlight

To delete, copy, or move text in a document, it must first be highlighted. This is usually done by holding down the mouse button and dragging from beginning to end of the area for selection.

The highlighted text is given a shaded background.

IN TRO TEXT COES HERE Lorem ipsum dolor sit amet, consectetuer adipiscing elit, sed diam nonummy nibh euismod tincidunt ut laoreet dolore magna aliquam erat volutpat. Ut wisi enim ad minim veniam, quis nostrud exerci tation ullamcorper suscipit lobortis nisl ut aliquip ex ea commodo consequat. Duis autem vel eum iriure dolor in hendrerit in vulputate velit esse molestie consequat, vel illum dolore eu feugiat nulla facilisis at. IN TRO TEXT COES HERE Lorem ipsum dolor sit amet, consectetuer adipiscing elit, sed diam nonummy nibh euismod tincidunt ut laoreet dolore magna aliquam erat volutpat. Ut wisi enim ad minim veniam, quis nostrud exerci tation ullamcorper suscipit lobortis nisl ut aliquip ex ea commodo consequat. Duis autem vel eum iriure dolor in hendrerit in vulputate velit esse molestie consequat, vel illum dolore eu feugiat nulla facilisis at. IN TRO TEXT COES HERE Lorem ipsum dolor sit amet, consectetuer adipiscing elit, sed diam nonummy nibh euismod tincidunt ut laoreet dolore magna aliquam erat volutpat. Ut wisi enim ad minim veniam, quis nostrud exerci tation ullamcorper suscipit lobortis nisl ut aliquip ex ea com-

---

high performance – Very good quality and specification.

high performance computing – A branch of computer science concentrating on the development of supercomputers and related software.

high performance parallel interface (HIPPI) – A device for physically connecting hardware at short distances and for providing high-speed data transfer.

high ping – Describes a slow kind of Internet connection.

high res (resolution) – This usually refers to a large amount of information displayed on a screen, normally by dots per square inch (dpi). The higher the dpi the better the quality. The term, high res, can also be applied to *screen resolution* and to the amount of information per second that is transmitted in a digital audio recording: the *sampling rate*.

highlight – To treat words, numbers, or a set of symbols in such a way that they stand out from the surrounding text.
SEE: FEATURE BOX

High-Speed SDRAM – A type of *Dynamic Random Access Memory* that can work at much higher speeds than the usual types of memory found in PCs. High-Speed SDRAM can work at up to 133 Mhz, although newer, even faster, technology is already in the pipeline.

High-Speed Serial Interface (HSSI) – A *serial interface* with transmission rates up to 52 Mbps.

HIPPI – **See: H**igh **P**erformance **P**arallel **I**nterface

histogram – A bar graph that shows how often something happens. On a computer, a histogram is usually found in a graphics program to show how to manipulate an image. The user slides together the ends of the graph to alter contrast and brightness.

history – A kind of folder or file on the computer that records the actions a user takes during the course of a period of use; e.g. a record of web sites that have been visited. Some applications may keep this kind of history log or a similar record of these actions.

SEE: FEATURE BOX
SEE ALSO: HISTORY FOLDER

history folder – Sometimes referred to as a *cache,* the history folder provides an area of memory where a log is kept of the actions that a user takes during the course of a period of use. This folder can aid efficiency when revisiting web sites through the use of *cookies,* since it minimizes the amount of time required for reconnecting to the site, as it stores all web site addresses.

hit – The action of visiting a web site or web page. The number of hits can be monitored by the web site owner, and used to improve the site by tailor making it to its customers' interests.

SEE ALSO: COUNTER

HLLAPI – **See: H**igh **L**evel **L**anguage **A**pplication **P**rogram **I**nterface

.hlp – In *DOS* an file *extension* for any help file in ASCII text.

HMD – **See: H**ead-**M**ounted **D**isplay

hoax – A deception or practical joke, most commonly played using spoof e-mails. At its most sinister it can be used to get money under false pretenses.

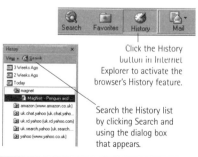

history

The history feature in Internet Explorer enables the user to view all web sites that have been visited, grouped according to pre-specified time periods. In this case, there are folders for Today, 2 Weeks Ago, and 3 Weeks Ago.

Click the History button in Internet Explorer to activate the browser's History feature.

Search the History list by clicking Search and using the dialog box that appears.

holographic storage – This technology records data as holograms. They fill up the entire volume of a small optical cylinder no larger than 1mm by 1cm. There is much debate about the future of this science and the effect it will have on current technology.

holy war – A heated discussion on a newsgroup site where opponents take extreme views.

home – This term is often used as an abbreviation for home page.

home button – Not an actual button but an icon that represents the beginning of a file or a set of basic functions.

---

home page

Clicking this icon in Internet Explorer at any time will return the user to the browser's home page. The default home page is part of the manufacturer's site at www.microsoft.com.

The user can customize the location of the browser's home page at any time.

Use Internet Options from the Tools menu to change the home page.

---

home computer – A computer designed for use in the home. Home computers first started to appear in the late 1970s but have since developed into the sophisticated PCs and Macs that are used today.

home key – A key on the main *keyboard* used to move the cursor to the top of the screen, or file, or to the previous word or beginning of the line.

home page – The first page on a web site. It has two functions, firstly to tell the user what the site is about, and then to keep their interest. Web browsers allow users to set their own home page, which is the page that the browser opens routinely on setup.
SEE: FEATURE BOX

honeypot – 1. A trick program designed to catch *hackers;* it will look interesting and enticing but will contain security software. 2. A web page designed to attract and deter senders of *spam* e-mail. It works by *hanging* any e-mail sent to it.

hook – These instructions used in programming provide breakpoints for future expansion of the program.

hookemware – *Freeware* or *shareware* that contains specific features designed to entice the user into purchasing the more comprehensive version of the program.

hop – A link between two networks.

hop count – The number of times a *packet* of data hops between network nodes. This can happen frequently on the Internet depending on the number of *routers* used to transport the packet.

horizontal – Lying flat. Side to side movement rather than up and down.

Horizontal market software – Software designed to work across industries and homes such as spreadsheets, and word processing and presentation programs. Vertical market software is industry specific.

horizontal rule – A straight line drawn across a page, or the horizontal ruler.
SEE: FEATURE BOX

host – Computer connected to a network; e.g. a PC connected to the Internet.

host adapter – An adapter that connects to a *host computer.*

host address – See: host name

host computer – 1. A computer given a specific task or service in a network. 2. The main controlling computer in a multi-channel and multi-user network. 3. A computer used to write and *debug* software for other computers.

host name – The name given to a computer attached to a network.
SEE ALSO: DOMAIN NAME

host server – See: server

host-based – Operations that function through the *host computer.*

host-based security – Security measures that are undertaken by the *host computer* rather than on the local computer.

hot desking – In this office environment, workers are not given permanent desks or workspaces but can access their work from any computer. A common way of working for consultants and temporary staff.

hot key – Method for activating a command by simultaneously pressing two keys; e.g. in most *Windows* programs pressing the control key and the S key prompts a save; control and end takes the user to the end of the current document.

---

horizontal rule

Microsoft Word allows the user to view the rulers at the top and side of the page. The ruler at the top is the horizontal rule, which allows the user to measure, in order to space their document correctly.

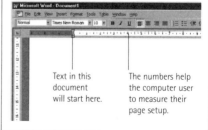

Text in this document will start here.

The numbers help the computer user to measure their page setup.

hot list – A list of top web sites, containing high-quality content and having excellent design. Many web sites have their own hot lists aimed at their clientele.

hot plugging/swapping – To add or remove *plug and play devices* while the computer is operative. The special operating system software detects the device and reconfigures the system automatically.

hot site – A very popular web site.

hot spot – 1. A part of a multimedia web site that, when clicked, generates a link or an activity such as running a video or sound clip.
2. A very popular part or link on a web page. Such areas can cause *choke points*. In many applications, the term hot spot refers to a part of the program that is frequently used.

 **HotBot** – One of the most popular and largest search engines on the web.
Go to: www.hotbot.com

HotDog – A leading web site creation and HTML editing program.
Go to: www.sausagetools.com

  Hotdog Professional and Hotdog Pagewiz: two leading web page creation applications.

hotfix – A code (also known as a patch) that fixes a *bug* in a product.

HotJava – This term covers a set of products developed by Sun Microsystems to utilize *Java* technology. It includes a web browser and a suite of programs designed to make use of the Java graphics.
Go to: www.sun.com

hotlink – An active *hyperlink*.

 **Hotmail** – The world's most used e-mail service, provided by Microsoft. It can be accessed remotely from any browser.
Go to: www.hotmail.com

Hotmail account – A user *account* with the Hotmail service. Hotmail accounts are popular with travelers since they are readily accessed from any computer linked to the World Wide Web. Many people keep a hotmail account or another remote e-mail service as an alternative e-mail address from their work or school address.

HotMetal Pro – This popular Windows-based web authoring program is produced by SoftQuad Inc. The company is also a founding member of the *World Wide Web Consortium*.
Go to: www.softquad.com

HotSync® – HotSync is the trade name for a method of linking a *Palm* hand-held computer to a more substantial one - notebook, desktop, or other computer.

hourglass icon – The shape of the *cursor* on a PC when the computer is carrying out an operation.

hourglass mode – Referring to the Windows hourglass icon, this is the process of waiting for some lengthy event to occur.

Houston Automatic Spooling Program – A mainframe *spooling* program that offers flexible data management, job, and task functions.

HPCC – **See:** high performance computing

HP-compatible – A product that is compatible with Hewlett-Packard's range of products, (e.g. a computer that can use an HP printer).

HPGL – **See:** Hewlett-Packard Graphics Language

.hqx – **See:** BinHex

HR – The command for producing a *horizontal rule* in HTML.

HSB – Shorthand for **h**ue, **s**aturation, **b**rightness, which are qualities of colors produced in a display.

HSDRAM – **See:** high-speed SDRAM

HSF – **See:** **H**eat**s**ink **F**an

HSSI – **See:** **H**igh-**S**peed **S**erial **I**nterface

.html – A filename *extension* that indicates the file has been produced using *Hypertext Markup Language*.

HTML – **See:** **H**ypertext **M**arkup **L**anguage

HTML checker – Useful tool that examines the *HTML* in a particular web page to check its grammatical and syntactical accuracy, and verify that the *browser* can easily display it.

HTML editor – A program that is used for designing web sites. It contains facilities for developing web pages.

HTML form – An interactive online form that displays graphics such as buttons and other icons. These forms are used primarily for gathering information about visitors to a site. Data from them is sent to a server where the form is stored; at this stage there may be a number of automatic actions taken, such as the production and dispatch of an acknowledgment e-mail.

HTML page – A screen's-worth of information displayed on a web site, usually as though it is a virtual page from a book, although it is often much larger. The first page shown is often referred to as the *home page*. Also known as a *web page*.

HTML reference library – A *Microsoft* program that contains information on using HTML, including codes and tools.

HTML template – *HTML* code that provides the structure for a particular page on a web site. It can be copied, edited, and reused time and time again with new details being added or taken away depending on the design.

HTML validation site – A service site that will check the quality of a new or existing site, it typically advises on things such as spelling, grammar, syntax, whether the links work, and how accessible the site is.

HTTP – **See:** **H**ypertext **T**ransfer **P**rotocol

HTTPS – **See:** **H**ypertext **T**ransfer **P**rotocol **S**ecure

hub – 1. A web site that contains *portals* or is linked to portals via *hyperlinks.* 2. A common connection for hardware within a network.

hue – The tint of a color.

h/w – An abbreviation for **h**ard**w**are.

Hybrid Fiber–Coax network – A cable TV network that uses a combination of *optical fibers* and *coaxial cable.*

hyperlink – A synonym for both *link* and *hypertext link.*

hypermedia – Documents that contain links between *multimedia* objects, such as sound, video, and virtual reality. Documents that can be described as hypermedia are non-linear and involve a high level of user/network interactivity in comparison with *hypertext* documents.

hyperspace – This describes the totality of computers linked to the *World Wide Web* and their interconnections. The term is often used to express the condition of being overwhelmed by the vastness of it all in the phrase: lost in hyperspace.

hypertext markup language (HTML)

This example shows the HTML used to create one of Dorling Kindersley's web pages. The code <html> at the top of this example indicates to web browsers that the following text is written in hypertext mark up language. The eventual appearance of </html> will close the web page.

```
<html>
<head>
<LINK rel="stylesheet" href="styles/dkshop.css" type="text/css">
<meta name="description" content="The Dorling Kindersley official website and complete online
store - every DK book available here.">
<meta name="keywords" content="DK, dk, Dorling, Kindersley, Dorling Kindersley, DK books, D-K,
Penguin Group, book, books, read, reading, publishers, publishing, book sellers, book store, shop,
dorlingkindersley, on line, on-line, online, gifts, present, best sellers, bestsellers, arts, crafts,
```

hypertext – Information on a web site and the range of associated interconnections. The interlinking within hypertext forms the *backbone* of the *World Wide Web.*

hypertext link – The *links* between hypertext documents, which together form the *World Wide Web.*

hypertext markup language (HTML) – The language used to develop pages that are placed on the *World Wide Web.* The markup tells the web browser how to display a web page's words and images for the user. Each markup code is referred to as an *element* (but most people call it a *tag*).
SEE: FEATURE BOX
SEE ALSO: HTML REFERENCE LIBRARY
GO TO: www.wdvl.com for an overview of HTML and its uses.

hypertext transfer protocol (HTTP) – An important *protocol* used when a browser is connected to a web server. It governs the transfer of files, both text and multimedia, across the Web. It is based on the idea that files can contain links to other files which, in turn, link to other files. Servers make requests, wait for the response, then process the received file using HTTP .

hypertext transfer protocol client – A *browser* that sends *hypertext transfer protocol* requests to a server machine, either by opening a web page or through the use of *links.*

hypertext transfer protocol secure (HTTPS) – Software that enables the user to engage in a secure transaction, e.g. for buying goods from an online vendor. In Windows, a small padlock icon appears on the toolbar. The site address will begin with https:// in the address line.

hyphen – The dash that is used to break words or that is used in compound words.

hyphenation – The breaking-up of words that extend beyond the right margin by splitting the word into syllables. Most text processing programs use a hyphenation dictionary or a built-in set of rules to determine whether or not a word should be hyphenated. This function can be turned on or off within the text tools options.

hysterical reasons – A play on the phrase historical reasons, hysterical reasons is used when something is done for a really stupid reason or without reason.

Hz – See: Hertz

i – A prefix often used on products to indicate they are *interactive* or connected to the *Internet* in some way. It often gives an element of modernity and trendiness to the product (e.g. *iMac, iMode, iPaq*).

I2 – A fast *network* for government, academia, and research, currently being developed by a consortium of universities, commercial companies, and the US government. It is designed to exchange real-time, multimedia data at high speed. Technological advances should eventually be incorporated into the Internet. I2 uses existing telephone networks.

IAB – **See:** **I**nternet **A**rchitecture **B**oard

IAC – **See:** **I**nternet **A**ccess **C**oalition

IANA – **See:** **I**nternet **A**ssigned **N**umbers **A**uthority

I-bar – The on-screen cursor when it is shaped like an I.

I-beam pointer – **See:** I-bar

IBM (International Business Machines) – The largest computer manufacturer, IBM developed mainframe computers in the 1950s and launched the personal computer in 1981. However, competition from *clones* and *Apple Macs* took away a huge slice of its PC market (now recovered).
Go to: www.ibm.com

IBM compatible – Any personal *computer* that is compatible with the *IBM PC*.

IBM PC – **I**nternational **B**usiness **M**achines **P**ersonal **C**omputer. The *architecture* of this computer forms the basis of most PCs on the market today.

iBook – Stylish *laptop* computer from Apple introduced in July 1999 as the portable version of the *iMac*.
The iBook provides an "AirPort" option, which allows wireless connection via an antenna built into the laptop case.

ICANN – **See:** **I**nternet **C**orporation of **A**ssigned **N**ames and **N**umbers

ICCP – **See:** **I**nstitute for **C**ertification of **C**omputer **P**rofessionals

ice – Content on a web page that is fixed to accommodate an optimum set of browser display criteria, e.g. window size, pixel width resolution, and left hand alignment. Programmers have to decide how flexible to make their pages, but ice pages are inflexible and may not display as intended on all systems. More flexible formats are known as *jello* and *liquid.*

ICE – **See:** **I**nformation and **C**ontent **E**xchange Protocol

ICMP - **See:** Internet Control Message Protocol

ICMP flood - *Denial of service attack* that sends more ICMP *ping packets* than can be handled.

I-Comm - A graphical browser downloadable as *shareware.*

icon - The small pictures used on a *graphical user interface* to identify a command, directory, or file. The user clicks twice on the icon to open the program or file, and files can be moved by *clicking* and *dragging* icons to a desired location.

ICQ - Software developed to support *Instant Messaging.* This informs the user that his contacts or "buddies" are online and allows two or more users to exchange messages in *real-time* in the form of a conversation. Pronounced "I seek you."

ICR - **See:** Intelligent Character Recognition

ICVerify - A program that enables a PC to be used as a credit card terminal.

IDE - **See:** Integrated Device Electronics

identifiers - Methods used to tell a network the *address* of the computer or to identify a user. These include *digital certificates, passwords,* and *pin numbers.*

identity - The network address of a computer or the actual name of a user.

identity hacking - In *chat rooms* and *bulletin board* postings, to use a pseudonym or adopt a false persona.

identity theft - (slang) The theft of personal identification such as *digital certificates, passwords,* and *pin numbers* in order to gain unauthorized entry to a site or system.

ideograph - **See:** ideogram

ideogram - 1. A character or symbol representing an idea or an object without expressing the pronunciation of a particular word for it.
2. A common graphic symbol.

& $ £ @ 3

idiot proof - Something easy or straightforward to use. Many systems and programs are designed to be idiot proof. In working to the lowest common denominator, programmers and system designers can cut down on potential complications and faults.

IDL - **See:** Interface Definition Language

idle character - In data communications, this is a character sent to keep the line synchronized when there is no data being actively transmitted.

idle interrupt - A point of interruption that is generated when a device changes from an operational state to an idle state.

idle time – Describes the time when a computer is operational, but not in use.

IE – **See:** Internet Explorer

IEC power connector – **See:** International Electrotechnical Commission

IETF – **See:** Internet Engineering Task Force

IGC – **See:** Institute for Global Communications

IGP – **See:** Interior Gateway Protocol

IIS – **See:** Internet Information Server

illustration program – Software designed for drawing illustrations and image editing, which are stored as vector graphics; e.g. *Adobe Illustrator, CorelDRAW*, and *Macromedia Freehand*. Fast growing demand for artwork on web pages has made them much sought-after packages.

IJ – **See:** EJ

ILEC – **See:** Incumbent Local Exchange Carrier

illegal operation – A message given in a *dialog box* to explain an operation that is not authorized or understood. In Windows this *error message* indicates that the program has crashed.
SEE ALSO: ABEND

Illustrator® – A graphics software and *image editor* program from *Adobe* that enables the user to produce excellent reproduction of art works on the Internet and other media.
GO TO:
www.adobe.com/products/illustrator/

iMac – A *Macintosh* computer from *Apple* introduced in 1998. It is a low-priced, self-contained, Internet-ready PC aimed at beginners. Against an eye-catching design and built-in features (e.g. iMovies, *iTunes*) and connectivity with digital cameras, DV camcorder, *iPods* and *MP3* player, it lacked some basic features - only the memory could be upgraded and it did not have a floppy disc drive. But the formula proved very successful and by 2001 over 5,000,000 iMacs had been sold.
GO TO: www.apple.com
SEE ALSO: IBOOK

iMac colors - iMac was launched in five distinct colors – grape, strawberry, lime, tangerine, and blueberry. Printers, e.g. Epson, followed suit. It was the first time that color and style had been used to sell computer hardware. It quickly caught on – a computer became a fashion accessory. Later colors (e.g. graphite, snow, and indigo) have been less fun orientated.

image - A picture or *graphic* viewed on screen in a document or web page. Images on the computer are stored as image formats – either *bitmaps* or *vector* graphic files. On the Internet there are many formats for storing graphics, including Interchange Format and *Joint Photographic Experts Group* format.

image editor - A program designed to make changes to computer images. Images can be imported into the program to be cropped, enhanced, or painted. Some programs are stand-alone such as *Illustrator,* while some page layout programs such as Pagemaker and *QuarkXpress* support image editing.

image enhancement – To manipulate an image. This may be to make the image sharper, improve contrast, or add some special effect such as fogging or texture.

image loading – Refers to the speed at which an image from a web page appears on screen. Fast image *loading* is essential to keep the users' interest.

image map – A map in an *HTML* document that has within it *hot spots* or *hyperlinks.* (These are defined in terms of their *x-axis* and *y-axis* coordinates.) The user can click on the hot spots on the image to transfer to a related web page. E.g. On a travel web site, clicking on a dot on a map will bring up another page detailing hotel information in that location.

image preview – A screen view of the whole laid out page, but one that is not *WYSIWYG.* The user can revert back to the original page for editing purposes.

image processing – 1. The analysis of a picture using techniques that cannot be perceived by the human eye, e.g. detailed shade and color identification. Image processing works on bitmapped graphics images that have been scanned or input as a digital image.
SEE ALSO: BITMAP
2. Any manipulation of an image. For example, the use of an *image editor* on scanned or other digital images.

imagesetter – A high-quality device that can produce a high-resolution page. Also called a *typesetter*, the imagesetter produces film or film-based paper which is used to make printing plates.

ImageWriters – Programs designed to write and encode images and graphics.
SEE ALSO: IMAGE EDITOR

imaging – Producing images and storing them in a form recognizable to a computer. This can be through the use of photography, film, video recording, or scanning.
SEE ALSO: IMAGE

IMAP – See: Internet Message Access Protocol

IMDB – See: Internet Movie Data Base

IMG – An *HTML tag* that identifies the location of a graphic image such as a *GIF* or *JPEG* file.

iMode – An information service for mobile phones that provides e-mail and customized web browsing, chat, news, and games. iMode uses a version of HTML called cHTML, as opposed to a WAP phone which uses a different version, WML..

impact printer – A printer where the images of the character hit a ribbon and it transfers the image onto paper.

impedance – The resistance to the flow of current in a circuit.

import – To access a file that was created in one application while operating in another (e.g. if producing a newsletter in PageMaker, the required text might be imported from Word and a picture from Adobe Illustrator).
SEE ALSO: IMPORT FILTER

import filter – A function within a program that *converts* a file into a format that it can read. Some programs require the user to specify the *file format* of the imported file, others select the appropriate import filter automatically.

impression – 1. A single advertisement held on a web page.
2. The number of times an ad is downloaded and seen on a web page.
SEE ALSO: BANNER AD

in-betweening – An animation technique that uses starting and ending images and creates the "in-between" frames. It is also called *tweening.*
SEE ALSO: MORPHING

inbox – Any folder in a *browser* memory that stores e-mails and faxed messages received on the Internet, or over a network. The browser inbox holds both read and unread messages.
SEE ALSO: OUTBOX

incompatible – Hardware and software combinations that conflict (are unable to work together). For example, a newly downloaded operating system may conflict with software already installed on the hard drive.

 INCONTEXT **Incontext Webanalyzer** – A
systems commercial program designed to check web sites for errors such as broken links, missing images, and duplicated files.
GO TO: www.incontext.com

incremental backup – A system of creating duplicate files where only those files that have changed since the last backup are resaved. This method saves both time and memory space.

incumbent local exchange carrier (ILEC) – A technical term, ILEC is used to describe a standard, traditional local telephone company.

indefinite iteration – Repetition of an instruction an endless number of times until a specific condition is met.

indent – To *align* a body of text farther inside of the margin than the surrounding text (normally the left-hand margin). SEE: FEATURE BOX

Indeo – Software developed by *Intel* that is used to record, compress, and decompress computer video. It is used in video conferencing.

index – 1. Directory listings maintained by the operating system or application. Many web pages contain some indexing either on a dedicated web page or on the homepage.

2. Indexes are used by *search engines*. These are lists of *keywords* linked to the *URLs* of documents that contain these specific keywords.

indexed file – A file listing all entries and their addresses in sequence.

index page – The web page within a web site that contains links to different pages on the site.

index spamming – Submitting the same web pages to the index of a *search engine*. This swamping strategy can ensure the web site appears at the top of search results submitted to an inquirer. Another method is to send pages containing a large quantity of descriptive detail to increase the number of retrievals. Also referred to as spamdex.

indexing – 1. The use of indexed materials. 2. The process of building an index.

indicator light – A light on a computer or device to indicate it is on/operational.

indices – The plural form of index. It is used in reference to indices of index lists or directories on web sites.

indirect address – **See:** relative address

inews – A UNIX program used to post Usenet articles.

INF file – A *configuration* file that enables new devices to be correctly installed by *Windows.*

---

indent

Indenting is a good way to make the hierarchy of lists clear and easy to read. This is why it is used especially for new paragraphs and *index* entries (as well as for poetry).

Lorem ipsum dolor sit amet, consectetuer adipiscing elit, sed diam nonummy nibh euismod tincidunt ut laoreet dolore magna aliquam erat volutpat. Ut wisi enim ad minim veniam, quis nostrud exerci tation ullamcorper suscipit lobortis nisl ut aliquip ex ea commodo consequat. Duis autem vel eum iriure dolor in hendrerit in vulputate velit esse molestie consequat, vel illum dolore eu feugiat nulla facilisis at. Lorem ipsum dolor sit amet, consectetuer adipiscing elit, sed diam nonummy nibh euismod tincidunt ut laoreet dolore magna aliquam erat volutpat. Ut wisi enim ad minim veniam, quis nostrud exerci tation ullamcorper suscipit lobortis nisl ut aliquip ex ea commodo consequat. Duis autem vel eum iriure dolor in hendrerit in vulputate velit esse molestie consequat, vel illum dolore eu feugiat nulla facilisis at.

    Lorem ipsum dolor sit amet, consectetuer adipiscing elit, sed diam nonummy nibh euismod tincidunt ut laoreet dolore magna aliquam erat volutpat. Ut wisi enim ad minim veniam, quis nostrud exerci tation ullamcorper suscipit lobortis nisl ut aliquip ex ea commodo consequat. Duis autem vel eum iriure dolor in hendrerit in vulputate velit esse molestie consequat, vel illum dolore eu feugiat nulla facilisis at. Lorem ipsum dolor sit amet, consectetuer adipiscing elit, sed diam nonummy nibh euismod tincidunt ut laoreet dolore magna aliquam erat volutpat. Ut wisi enim ad minim veniam, quis nostrud exerci tation ullamcorper suscipit lobortis nisl ut aliquip ex ea commodo consequat. Duis autem vel eum iriure dolor in hendrerit in vulputate velit esse molestie consequat, vel illum dolore eu feugiat nulla facilisis at.

This middle paragraph of this passage of text has been indented. It now stands out more clearly.

---

inference engine – A set of rules used to deduce goals or results from information received. They are used in artificial intelligence programs and devices.

inference rule – A logical rule used to make inferences and decisions and to derive new facts from facts already known.

Infiniband – S*erver* architecture for an *I/O server* aimed to enable much faster information transfer speeds than are currently available. It will also enable networks to function more efficiently.

.info – New *domain name* from 2000.

Infobahn – The *information superhighway.* The expression is derived from the German word "autobahn," meaning a large highway for vehicles.

infopreneur – An entrepreneur in the electronic information-based industries.

informatics – The science of information processing and transmission.

Information and Content Exchange Protocol (ICE) – A XML protocol intended to simplify information management over a secure network by large businesses. ICE will simplify e-commerce sites, enabling them to automate and reduce online costs.

information engineering (IE) – The generic term for the systems and technologies used to process and handle information within an organization.

information packet – **See:** packet

information service – An Internet service such as America Online, CompuServe, and Prodigy, that provides easy access to a wide range of information.

Information Superhighway – A popular buzzword for the Internet or World Wide Web, especially for those promoting the Internet (and their e-businesses). Its general usage was given a kick start by former US Vice-President Al Gore in 1991 when he introduced new legislation deregulating the Internet.

Information Technology (IT) – The technology of computerized information management.

information warfare – To attack an organization by damaging its business computer systems.

Infoseek.com – A popular *search engine* and information provider, now part of the Disney Corporation.
Go to: http://infoseek.go.com

infospace – The whole Internet, which includes the World Wide Web, all the chat rooms, and newsgroups.

infosurfing – *Web browsing* using text only. This speeds up download times because it eliminates the time taken for graphic, sound, and video files to be downloaded. Web browsers offer users the option to turn off multimedia features.

infra-red – Wireless transmission of data between computer devices and handheld remotes for TV and video equipment. For example, an infra-red mouse has no cables but emits electromagnetic waves (whose frequency range is below that of the visible spectrum, but higher than microwaves) to connect with a PC. Infra-red transmission requires a clear line of sight between transmitter and receiver. It is an emerging *local area network* technology.

infrastructure – The physical networking of computers connected to other computers and to the Internet via cables and telecommunication links. Computers linked to other computers are all part of a network, e.g. a home computer may be linked via a modem to an *Internet Service Provider* (ISP), or through a local area network (LAN). Connection to the ISP makes the home or workplace computer part of the ISP's network. All such networks interconnect to form the Internet infrastructure.
SEE ALSO: BACKBONE

INI file – **INI**tialization file. An information file required to launch a program or operating system.

initialization string – A group of commands that initialize a device, such as a printer.

initialize – To activate the set-up process on a program or device.

inkjet printer – A printer that shoots droplets of ink onto paper. The printer uses black and cyan, magenta, and yellow ink in combinations to create composite colors.

inline graphic – A graphic image that is *embedded* and displayed by the *browser* as part of an *HTML* document. The software to view the image is retrieved along with the document and does not require a separate viewer.

inline image – **See:** inline graphic

inline video – A video clip that is *embedded* and displayed on an *HTML* page by the *browser*. The inline video plays in real time and does not require a separate video player.

inlining – To *embed* a graphic, video clip, or other object in a web page that is accessed without invoking other software.
SEE ALSO: INLINE GRAPHIC, INLINE VIDEO

input – To enter data into a computer via an *input device*.

input device – A device that is used to enter commands or data into a computer; e.g. keyboard, mouse, joystick, modem, or scanner.

input focus – The area within a window that is available for data input via a keyboard or mouse.

insert – To add text or bring an object into a document.
SEE ALSO: EMBED, INPUT

Insert key – A key that is used to switch between *insert mode* and typeover mode. Also referred to as Ins key.

insert mode – When characters are moved along as new text is inserted, in contrast to typeover mode, which overwrites pre-existing text.

insertion point – The point at which an object is inserted into a document, identified where the *curser* is located.

install – Part of the process of loading new hardware or software onto a system. An install program is also called a setup program and carries out processes such as making folders, coping files, and decompressing files so the program or device is ready to run.

InstallShield – Founded in 1987, this Illinois-based company provides training, support, consulting, and software products to technological companies worldwide. Its range of products includes a well-used and effective *install* (and uninstall) program.
GO TO: www.installshield.com

instant messaging – A popular *real-time chat* and e-mail service between two or more people who are online simultaneously. The user writes a list of "buddies" with whom they wish to chat. When any of these people log on the user is informed so they are able to hold a private *interactive* chat session. If the user's friends are not online, then the user can leave an e-mail message. Instant messaging programs include *AOL's* Instant Messenger (AIM), *Microsoft* Network Messenger Service (MSNMS), *ICQ* and *Yahoo!* Messenger. These programs are not compatible; buddies wishing to hold a chat session must all use the same software.
SEE: FEATURE BOX

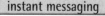

instant messaging

Messenger software allows those logged on to see who is active. They can then type in and receive instant messages with other buddies online (providing they use the same software).

Live "call and response" scrolling page showing who's saying what.

Dedicated area for keying in message.

Institute for Certification of Computer Professionals (ICCP) – Certifies computer professionals on an internationally recognised basis. Certification is awarded on the basis of tests, academic qualifications, and/or job experience. Four levels of certification are awarded: Associate Computer Professional (ACP), Certified Computer Programmer (CCP), Certified Data Processor (CDP), and Certified Systems Professional (CSP).

Institute for Global Communications – An organization that promotes the use of high technology to advance the causes of peace, human rights, and preserving the environment.
SEE ALSO: PEACENET

instruction – A command that tells the computer to perform an operation. An instruction can be in *machine language* or a *programming language.*

instruction cycle – For each *instruction* that a computer is given, the *CPU* must perform a cycle of four steps: fetch the instruction from main memory, decode it, execute it, then store the result.

insulator – A material that does not conduct electricity.

integrated – Refers to a system that consists of several diverse hardware and/or software components.
SEE ALSO: COMPATIBLE/INCOMPATIBLE

integrated circuit – A microelectronic device comprising miniature *transistors* and electronic components placed on a thin rectangle of silicon or sapphire. Such integrated circuits can contain anything from a few, to millions of electronic components. They are fast, efficient, and relatively inexpensive to manufacture.
SEE ALSO: CHIP, SILICON

integrated device electronics (IDE) – Interface for connecting additional hard drives to a computer.

integrated optical chip – A *chip* powered by light instead of an electrical current. Part of an emerging technology, such chips would generate little or no heat, operate faster, and be immune to electrical distortion.

Integrated Services Digital Network (ISDN) – High-speed digital phone-to-phone connection method. This communication service is offered by telephone companies and permits telephone networks to carry data, voice, and other source traffic. Often supplied as two lines (each transmitting at 64 Kps) it can transmit data at speeds of up to 128 Kps. More common that other digital systems, e.g. *cable modem* or *asymmetrical digital subscriber line.*

integration testing – Combining software and/or hardware components to ensure that they are *compatible.*

Intel – The world's largest producers of microprocessors and PC components. In 1971 Federico Faggin, Marcian E. Hoff and Stan Mazor invented the first single chip microprocessor. This revolutionized the integrated circuit – and the PC – making it possible to combine all the thinking parts of a computer into one chip.

Intel microprocessors – The first *microprocessor* was the Intel 4004, made in 1971; the basic design has not changed that much since. Intel also make the *Pentium microprocessors*.

intellectual property (IP) – Creative idea (not necessarily a finished physical product) that is legally the property of an individual or organization and protected by *copyright*.

intelligent agent – An *agent* that uses knowledge that it has acquired to perform a task; e.g. searching through incoming mail and picking out subject-related items.

Intelligent Character Recognition – The ability of scanners and software to read hand-written characters or poor quality type.

intelligent hub – A *hub* in a network that, as well as forwarding signals, provides intelligent functions such as bridging, routing, and switching. Some may perform network management tasks.

intelligent modem – A modem with a programmable command state and an automatic online state for dialing, answering the phone, handshaking, and transmitting and receiving communications. Intelligent modems were introduced by *Hayes* Microcomputer Products and are now industry standard.

intelligent terminal – Network terminal using a central computer for data storage, but having its own processing capability.

interactive – Computer programs that rely on input from the user while they are running. The program halts and waits for a response from the user before continuing. SEE: FEATURE BOX

interactive games – Computer *game* that relies on *interactive* user responses.

---

interactive

Spreadsheets or calendar are examples of interactive software responding to commands, mouse clicks, or other interfacing tools and interacting with other features of that software.

The names and dates have been input by the user, and the program, at a command from the user, can manipulate the data to form a graph.

interactive processing – A program that demands commands from a user in order to operate. (In contrast to batch processing, where instructions are performed without stopping for input.)

interactive session – A computer session involving an exchange of communication between the user and the computer.

interactive television – Television that supports interactive viewer participation. Cable or digital shopping and movies-on-demand channels have this facility.

interactive video (IV) – Video allowing a user to select which part of a program to view, or that allows a user to interact with certain parts of the program.

interactive voice response (IVR) – A telephone answering filter using pre-recorded spoken options. The caller is requested to press phone buttons or give voice responses. Computer helpdesks often channel customers through such systems.

interactive webchat – See: instant messaging

intercharacter spacing – In typography, the space between characters in a word.

interface – The boundary and the means of communication between two systems or devices. The interface between the user and the computer is the keyboard, mouse, and display screen.

Interface Definition Language (IDL) – A complex language used to describe the *interface* to a routine or function. Web IDL allows the automation of all interactions with *HTML* and *XML* documents, allowing the Web to be utilized universally.

interference – Unwanted communication channel noise.

Interior Gateway Protocol (IGP) – An Internet *protocol* used to exchange routing information within an autonomous system. Examples of common Internet IGPs include IGRP, OSPF, and RIP.

interlaced – A method of display which shows the odd lines, then the even lines. It quickly displays objects on the screen but does have a noticeable flicker which makes reading text, in particular, more difficult. Traditional analog TV is an example of interlaced transmission.

interlaced GIF – A type of *GIF* that appears to *download* more quickly as a basic image appears first, but then more detail is downloaded and the image gradually fills out.

interleaved memory – 1. A method of organizing disk drives on alternate tracks to make them more efficient.
2. Data storage where parts of one sequence alternate with parts of another. A retrieved file is reconstructed and audio, images, or text may be stored this way.

intermediate system – A system that relays communications between two end systems.

intermittent error – An *error* that will occur unpredictably.

internal bus – A *bus* connecting components that are located in close proximity, e.g. main memory with the CPU.

internal cache – **See:** cache

internal command – A command, such as copy, dir, and rename, which is executed by the command processor program. An internal command is loaded when the operating system is running.

internal font – A font that is permanently built into the printer on ROM chips. Also known as resident or built-in font. It contrasts with a soft font or font cartridge.

internal interrupt – An interrupt caused by a machine instruction, e.g. requiring input or output.

internal modem – A modem that is located inside the computer (as opposed to an external modem or PC card version). Internal modems are used by computer manufacturers to link and lure new users both to PCs and to the Internet.

International Electrotechnical Commission – An organization that oversees international electrical and electronics standards.

International Organization for Standardization – **See:** ISO

International Phonetic Alphabet – An alphabet designed as a pronunciation guide for all languages. Each sound in human speech is represented with its own symbol. It has application in programming *voice recognition* systems.

International Standard – The standards – including those used in the computer and Internet industry – developed by the International Organization for Standardization (ISO).

International Telecommunications Union (ITU) – United Nations organization overseeing international telecommunications standards and frequency allocation.

International Telecommunications Union-Telecommunication – The newer name for the Consultative Committee For International Telephone and Telegraph.

internationalization – A program that can handle many languages. This generally means extracting all text messages into external files. The program must then be "localized" for each language, e.g. translating the message files.

internaut – A person who navigates the Internet.

internesia – The inability to remember on which website some crucial data was seen.

Internet – The global Internet, connecting thousands of *networks* and millions of computer users worldwide through the *TCP-IP* protocols. Each connecting computer is called a *server* and acts rather like a telephone exchange for computers connected to the network. Individual users subscribe to an *Internet Service Provider,* which provides them with access to their server for the cost of a local phone call. The subscriber is given a unique *address* that enables *e-mail*, files, and documents to be exchanged between connected computers. Access to the Internet also enables access to the vast wealth of information available on web sites on the *World Wide Web.*
SEE ALSO: ARPANET, CERN, TIM BERNERS-LEE, TCP-IP, UNIX

Internet 2 – See: I2

Internet Access Coalition (IAC) – A consortium of major companies whose purpose is to maintain the affordability of Internet access over telephone lines. IAC is also responsible for accelerating the availability of inexpensive digital telephone network connections to the Internet.

Internet account – An account with an *Internet Service Provider* for the provision of Internet access, normally paid on a monthly or annual basis.

Internet appliance – Any electrical appliance (e.g. a TV) that can log in to the Internet. Also includes network computers.

Internet Architecture Board – Body that aims to maintain the openness of the Internet. It provides documentation on subjects related to the development of the Internet and monitors Internet *protocols*. It operates under the auspices of the *Internet Society.*

Internet Assigned Numbers Authority (IANA) – The group that used to delegate authority and maintained a database on IP address allocation and domain-name assignment. It has been replaced by the *Internet Corporation of Assigned Names and Numbers.*

Internet backbone – The high-speed telecommunications network spanning the world from one major metropolitan area to another. The Internet backbone is provided by a group of Internet service providers. It consists of high-speed lines that link up at national access points in major metropolitan areas, and local ISPs that connect to this backbone by way of *routers*.
SEE ALSO: BACKBONE

Internet box – A device that plugs into a telephone jack or network to gain access to the Internet.

Internet café – See: cybercafé

Internet community – The body of users of the Internet. A specific community may consist of contributors to a newsgroup or other specialized group.

Internet Connection Wizard – The facility within *Windows 98* that guides the user through connection to an *Internet Service Provider*. *Wizard* sets up the telephone connections and places shortcut icons on the desktop. It can be downloaded from the Internet.

Internet Content Rating Association – A non-profit making organization that provides a system for rating game software and online content.

Internet Control Message Protocol – A network *protocol* that reports errors and provides information relevant to *IP packet* management.

Internet Corporation of Assigned Names and Numbers (ICANN) – The non-profit corporation with responsibility for IP address allocation, domain-name assignment and management, and root server system. It replaced the *Internet Assigned Numbers Authority*.

Internet dating – The Internet has proved a popular way to extend social contact and organize dating services.

Internet directories – Web sites that provide access to searchable databases that contain e-mail addresses. This includes residential and business addresses and telephone numbers. Other directories provide information on web site (*URL*) addresses for general and specialist interest.

Internet Engineering Task Force (IETF) – Organization responsible for short-term engineering developments on the Internet and defining new standards. IETF works under the auspices of the *Internet Society*.

Internet error message – **See:** error messages

Internet Explorer – Developed by *Microsoft,* IE is the most used web *browser,* allowing PC and Apple Mac users to view web pages. It was launched in the 1990s in response to the success of competitors including *Netscape Navigator.* Its companion e-mail software is called *Outlook Express.*

Internet Favorites – An area of memory where the user can store *URLs (domain names)* for quick retrieval at a later date.

Internet gateway – A system for converting messages between TCP/IP and other protocols. The World Wide Web depends on Internet gateways to link all the various networks together.

Internet history – An area of memory where a log of web sites visited is kept. SEE ALSO: CACHE, HISTORY

Internet Information Server – *Microsoft's* popular web server software. This uses *Hypertext Transfer Protocol* to deliver files via the *World Wide Web.*

Internet Message Access Protocol – Method of accessing e-mail or bulletin board messages on a remote server rather than on a local computer. It holds messages until users log on and retrieve e-mail while enabling e-mail retrieval and the creation, deletion, and renaming of mailboxes. It cannot be used to send e-mail.

Internet Movie Database – A film buff's dream, the Internet Movie Database catalogs, reviews and makes recommendations on virtually every movie ever made.
Go to: www.imdb.com

The Internet Movie Database
Visited by over 8 million movie lovers each month!

Internet Network Information Center (InterNIC) – The group that manages Internet *domain names* and provides relevant help, documentation, training, and registration. It was formerly called NIC.

InterNIC

Internet Open Trading Protocol (IOTP) – A protocol defined by the *IETF* to improve existing systems for e-commerce. It uses *Extensible Markup Language* to improve transaction handling.

Internet Packet EXchange (PX) – A protocol performing equivalent services to Internet Protocol *(IP)*.

Internet Phone – The technology used to send real-time voice conversations over the Internet.

Internet piracy – The illegal copying and reuse of materials found on the Internet including text-based information, graphics, video clips, music, and so on.
SEE ALSO: COPYRIGHT

Internet Protocol (IP) – See: IP

Internet Public Library – An online public library sponsored by University of Michigan School of Information and Library Studies.
Go to: http://ipl.sils.umich.edu/

Internet radio – *Streaming* technology that enables the user to listen to radio broadcasts in real-time on the Internet. It is necessary to use a *multimedia* plug-in such as RealNetworks and Microsoft Network in addition to the browser. Over 4,000 audio broadcasts are now available over the Internet. Traditional-looking Internet radios are becoming available; these devices utilize the computer's Internet connection but have self-contained speakers.

Internet Relay Chat (IRC) – An early Internet chat system accessed through *Telnet*. It provided a world-wide "party line" protocol allowing users to converse in real time. Some IRC channels are dedicated to specialist subject areas while others have a social function.

Internet security - **See:** security

Internet Service Provider (ISP) - A company that provides *Internet* access to individuals and other companies. The user sets up an *account* and this allows their computer to be linked to the company's *server* via telephone lines, which in turn supply a high-speed link to the Internet.
SEE: FEATURE BOX

Internet shortcut - **See:** shortcut, hyperlink

Internet Society - A professional society that oversees the development of the Internet. It has two main branches; the *Internet Architecture Board* and the *Internet Engineering Task Force.*

Internet Talk Radio - An audio news system provided by the National Press Building, in Washington, DC. The files are available by *FTP.*

Internet telephony - Using the computer and the Internet to hold conversations rather than traditional telephones. This technology has huge potential due to the low cost of using this method for long distance or international phone calls. When conversations occur over a Wide Area Network (*WAN*) or private intranet it is called "voice over IP," or "VoIP."

Internet utility - A program for searching the Internet, e.g. *Archie* for *FTP* sites; *Veronica* for *Gopher* sites.

Internet Service Provider

It can be difficult to discern the good from bad among the vast number of ISPs seeking to connect you to the Internet. Consider the following before committing:

1. Price. Select a service whose prices are in line with competitors. If it is very inexpensive, then look carefully as it probably does not provide as many services, e.g. technical support can be very expensive.

2. Phone costs. Make sure the ISP's dial-up number is a local call. Some ISPs include the cost of net access within their package deal.

3. Speed. Your modem will only connect at its top speed if the ISP has the same speed capacity.

4. Users to modem ratio. Generally the lower the better. If your ISP offers a ratio of more than 10 users to one modem, then you will sometimes get the busy signal.

5. Technical support. Be sure the ISP provides inexpensive or free technical support. It is vital.

6. Personal web pages. Some packages allow the user to have personal web pages within the package. Useful if you need one.

7. E-mail addresses. Would it be useful to have several e-mail address at one account?

8. Regional or National ISP. If you travel, then go for a national server who will provide local access numbers wherever you go. Some provide unlimited Internet access, others provide access during certain hours of the day.

Internet video phone – An application for talking over the Internet using both audio and video.

Internet Worm – First serious virus attack on the Internet, and only successful *Unix worm*. It infected the memories of over 6,000 computers in November 1988.

internetwork – A wide area network (*WAN*) that connects smaller networks.

internetworking – To pass between two or more *networks* via a *router* or *gateway*.

InterNIC – **See:** Internet Network Information Center

intranet

DK, the publisher of this dictionary, is part of the larger Penguin Group, which operates a company-wide Intranet site for inter-personnel e-mailing, company web news and global links.

HTML text takes the user straight to other web pages by clicking on the hyperlink.

interoperability – The ability of software and hardware on different machines to work together.
SEE ALSO: COMPATIBILITY

Interpreter – A program translator that works by translating and running the program at the same time.

interpupillary distance – The distance between the eyes. This measurement is used when designing head mounted devices used to create *virtual reality* environments.

interrupt – A temporary suspension of a current process. The suspended process is only resumed after the interrupt has been completed. There are two main types of interrupt:
i. an outside interrupt when an instruction comes from outside the processor, e.g. when the keyboard is touched, diverting the processor's attention.
ii. When the system decides to "pre-empt" one program to run another which requests input or output.

Interrupt request – **See:** interrupt

interstitial – An advert that appears on a separate *browser* window to the one being used. Sometimes called *pop-ups*, they are felt to be one of the more effective forms of advertising on the internet. They often cause complaints because they slow down the loading time of destination pages.

interword spacing – Variable spaces between words that exist to equal out lines.

intranet – A *local area network* set up by a company for its exclusive use. Many intranets function just like the Internet, but are not accessible to anyone outside the company. Some internal networks maintain servers so employees have access to web documents. Certain ranges of *IP addresses* are reserved for use in intranets, e.g. 192.168.0.0. The idea is that servers on the external net will ignore them, and it is easy to test externally for *leakage*.
SEE: FEATURE BOX

intraplanetary Internet – Currently under development to provide probes and astronauts with Internet connections so that they can send large quantities of information to and from space.

intrusion – An unauthorized user on a closed system such as an intranet.

intrusion detection – Software that detects an unauthorized user of a closed system. These work by personnel either spotting unusual activity or patterns on the system, or by tracking unusual data packets.

intrusive testing – A software function test which changes the normal behavior of the program.

invalid – Input to a system which is inappropriate and rejected, e.g. keying in a wrong password for modem or e-mail access.

invalid directory – **See:** error message

invalid page fault – A page fault that produces an error. This is due to one of three reasons: shortage of memory either physically, or through lack of disk space, and possibly a corrupted memory.

invert – In binary code this means the changing of all the ones to zeroes and vice versa.

invisible file – **See:** hidden file

invisible page – A page on a web site that the user of a browser is unable to see because the site does not provide *hyperlinks* to that page. The only way to find the page is usually through the *URL* of the page.

invoke – To activate a program, routine, function or process.

I/O – **See:** input, output

I/O address – Input/Output address. A unique address given to a *peripheral* device for input and output.

I/O device – Input/Output device. Synonymous with *peripheral* device.

Iomega – An American company formed in 1980, Iomega is a world leader in the manufacture of smart, portable storage solutions, including drives and disks.
GO TO: www.iomega.com

IOTP – **See:** Internet Open Trading Protocol

IP – Short for **I**nternet **P**rotocol, IP is part of the *TCP/IP* standard method for transmitting *packets* from a source to a destination. The packets are grouped together by the *Transmission Control Protocol* (TCP). IP deals with address, type-of-service specification, fragmentation and reassembly, and security particulars.

IP address – A numeric address activated into a host computer: the *domain name server* translates a name into an IP address so that other machines can find it.
SEE ALSO: ADDRESS

IP datagram – See: IP packet

IP Multicast – Transmitting data over the Internet or intranet to more than one recipient simultaneously. It can be used to download files to a number of users or for *streaming* audio and video. The data is transmitted in one data stream and split by routers at the end of the path, saving network bandwidth.

IP packet – The basic unit of information transmitted via the Internet. It contains the addresses of its source and destination, the data and transmission details.

IP Security – See: security

IP spoofing – To gain access to a computer system that is only open to users with a registered IP *address*. The spoofer inserts look-alike IP addresses into *packets* in an attempt to fool the system.

IP switching routers – High speed TCP/IP packet *switching*.

iPaq – A popular *hand-held* computer or *personal digital assistant* (PDA) made by *Compaq*.

iPass – A company that is a world leader in *remote access* technology. It enables business employees and travellers to access their e-mail and networks outside the office.
GO TO: www.ipass.com

IPng (Internet Protocol next generation) – A new version of *IP* that allows more computers to join the system and transmits more data.

IPO – **I**nitial **P**ublic **O**ffering. The first time a company offers shares of stock to the public. Web sites that go public are particularly focused by their IPO.

iPod – Lightweight *MP3* player from Apple Computers that can store 1,000 songs downloaded from an iMac by *Firewire* and played with iTunes software. Internet *interoperability* in action.

IPSec – Standards that provide for data authentication, confidentiality, and integrity, and between participating servers.

IPX – See: **I**nternet **P**acket e**X**change.

IR – **I**nfra-red **R**adiation.
SEE ALSO: INFRA-RED

IRC - **See:** Internet Relay Chat

Ircii (irc-two) - An *Internet Relay Chat* program or client that allows connection to the IRC network of choice. Ircii is associated with *Unix* and is text-based without menus or tool bars.

Ircle - An *Internet Relay Chat* program or client that allows connection to the IRC network of choice. Ircle is associated with *Apple* Macintosh.

IS - Information Systems. Synonymous with data processing, other similar terms include management information systems, management information services and *information technology.*

ISA - Industry-Standard Architecture. PCs with a 16-bit *bus* used for *peripherals* such as modems, video displays, and speakers. These PCs have either an 8-bit or 16-bit expansion slot.

ISAPI - Internet Server **API.** A programming interface on Microsoft's web server that integrates applications and the Windows operating system.

ISDN - **See:** Integrated Services Digital Network

ISDN adapter - The device that replaces a modem and connects a computer to an ISDN channel. It can be an external unit or a plug-in adapter card.
SEE ALSO: **ISDN**

ISO - International Organization for Standardization. An International organization that is responsible for a wide range of standards, including those relevant to networking.

ISOC - **See:** Internet Society

isochronous - Something that is equal in time or duration and occurring at regular intervals.

isochronous transmission - A way of transmitting data in which there is always a regular number of intervals between individual characters. *Isochronous* transmission is used for data such as real-time voice and video. Compare with *asynchronous transmission.*

isometric view - A way of drawing a 3D object without perspective. Used in technical drawings. In perspective drawing, parallel lines converge on a vanishing point; in isometric drawing they do not.

isotropic - Having properties that are the same when measured in any direction, e.g. transmission speeds.

ISP - **See:** Internet Service Provider

ISV - Independent Software Vendor. A company that specializes in software development and retail.

IT - Accepted business and retail shorthand for *Information Technology.*

italics – Type that is slanted to the right. It is generally used for emphasis.

italicize – To change text into *italics*.

Itanium – The code name for *Intel's* long awaited *64 bit chip*. It has different *architecture* to *Pentium*, and it runs at speeds of over 1.5-2Ghz. This is considerably faster than the speeds mustered by the latest Pentium chip.
SEE ALSO: MERCED

iteration – 1. Term given to the process of running a series of instructions over and over again until certain preset conditions are met.
2. One repetition of a sequential operation.

It's All In The Subject

There are many shorthand conventions for sending and receiving e-mails (see Appendix 1 for a full list of abbreviated text-speaks). IAITS is a very useful shortcut in which the full short message is given in the subject line and 'IAITS' is left in the dialogue box as an alert.

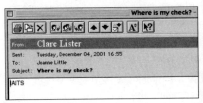

This e-mail shows that the whole message is contained in the subject line; "Where is my check?"

It's All In The Subject (IAITS) – When the entire message of an e-mail is contained in the subject line.
SEE: FEATURE BOX

ITU – See: International Telecommunications Union

iTunes – *Freeware* that can be downloaded from Apple's web site to convert CD songs into *MP3* files, provide fast CD *burning*, *iPod* compatibility, Internet radio access and other features.

ITU-T – See: International Telecommunications Union-Telecommunication

IV – See: interactive video

IVR – See: Interactive Voice Response

iway/i-way – See: Information superhighway.

J Random – Used in chat rooms and newsgroups to represent the average person in the street.

jabber – To chat without obvious purpose in an online chat room, or to send generally pointless information by e-mail, or to post irrelevant messages in newsgroups, or any other online medium.

jack – A connector plug that has one central pin. An audio plug is a typical example of a jack.

jacking in/out – These terms generally refer to the process of connecting to, or disconnecting from, a network. For example, entering a *bulletin board* site, a *virtual reality* simulation, an Internet relay chat network, or even just logging in to or logging out from a computer of any kind. The terms originate from the terminology used in fiction known as cyberpunk science fiction or cyberfiction.

jaggies – Computer graphics that appear as stepped edges rather than smooth curves on diagonal or curved lines. This jagged appearance is a result of drawing diagonal or curved lines out of small squares. It can be rectified by drawing the image in a large format and then reducing it to a small size, thus reducing the pixel size and the effect. Alternatively, *anti-aliasing* techniques can be used, inserting pixels along the jagged edge, which are of an intermediate color

between the background and the image, and so blend in.

JANET – **See:** **J**oint **A**cademic **Net**work

 Java – This is a very flexible programming language that was developed by Sun Microsystems. Its features make it excellent for developing programs for the Internet and it contains a large number of facilities that enable the carrying out of key tasks, thus speeding up programming times enormously. It also enables programs to be embedded within a web page with the development of small programs called *applets*. This means better animation and improved effects on web sites.
Go to: http://java.sun.com

Java applet – A small application written in *Java* language, which is often embedded in an *HTML* document. Java applets can be run by most browsers. They enable such features as animations, interactivity, forms, and database-handling via web pages.

Java chip – A *CPU* chip from *Sun Microsystems* that is designed to run *Java* bytecode. It contains the basis of the *Java Virtual Machine* and is used in a variety of devices from cellphones to desktop and network computers.

Java Development Kit (JDK) – This freely distributed software package is designed to produce and debug *Java* programs.

Java Server Page (JSP) – This is an HTML page with embedded Java features. The HTML generates the page layout and the Java enables the processing and runs the page's dynamic content. It is a useful technology for web pages where the content changes very quickly, such as news and financial pages.

Java servlet – A *Java applet* that runs within a web *server*. Java servlets are increasingly popular, partly because Java applets are persistent. Once activated Java servlets stay in memory fulfilling repeated requests without the need to be loaded on each occasion.

Java Virtual Machine – A simulated computer that runs on a host computer, but behaves as if it is a separate computer. It activates *Java applets* from the host's operating system.

JavaBean – There is a specification that dictates how *Java* objects interact. Any object that conforms to this specification is called a JavaBean. It is similar to an *ActiveX* control. JavaBeans are popular on web pages as they enable interactive features and mouse-click activated objects.

JavaScript – A scripting language used to write small programs that are embedded in *HTML* pages and activated by the browser. JavaScript is not the same as Java. It is easier to learn, but is more limited, and is used to run forms and mouse activated

dynamic features, e.g. activating a video clip at the click of the mouse.

JavaScript tags – The code in *HTML* that activates a *Java* feature. It is written as: <script language="JavaScript">.

JavaSoft – Division of *Sun Microsystems* that works with Java technology.

Jaz drive – A small, removable, cartridge disk drive made by Iomega Corporation.

JDK – See: Java Development Kit

Jello page – A web page in which the content is centered on the page regardless of the window size and resolution of the displaying monitor. Contrast with ice page, which is ranged right.

jewel case – A portable container for a CD or CD-ROM. Sometimes called a jewel box.

Jigsaw – A web server from the *World Wide Web Consortium* that is used to assess new web technologies.

Jini – Pronounced "gee-nee." A technology that has sprung from *Java* that enables devices to be plugged into a network more simply. Devices range from laptops, PDAs, printers and non-computing devices such as fire alarms and televisions. Also, resources and devices on network-linked computers using Jini may be shared more easily. Jini reduces the dependence on operating systems and hopes to reduce the influence of Microsoft Windows.

jitter – A fluctuation in a transmission signal or a flickering display image.

jitterati – These are highly stressed personnel working at the cutting edge of the high-tech industry.

SEE ALSO: DIGERATI

job – A piece of work done on a computer.

Jobs, Steve – The co-founder of *Apple* and the current CEO of Apple and *Pixar*, the animation studios. Apple was launched in1976 with the aim of providing high quality personal computers beginning with the Apple II. Jobs based the company name on his favorite fruit; the logo features an apple with a bite taken out of it – a pun on the computer word "*byte*." He started the company with Steve *Wozniak*, and it has been said that they both sold their most prized possessions to start up the company: Jobs sold his Volkswagen, and Wozniak, a scientific calculator. They subsequently went on to become multi-milionaires. Jobs lives in Silicon Valley.

Joint Academic Network (JANET) – A university-based network run by the United Kingdom Education and Research Networking Association. Since upgrading it has become known as Super-JANET.

Joint Photographic Experts Group (JPEG) – A *bitmapped* format for still images commonly used on web pages. It can handle up to 16.7 million colors and so is useful for high-quality resolution graphics, as well as for graphics with special effects. Its popularity is due in part to its efficiency in compressing images by using *lossy* compression techniques.
SEE ALSO: **MPEG** for the motion picture equivalent of JPEG.

Jolt – An American soft drink that is very high in caffeine and has become popular with students, and in particular, Internet surfers, who want to stay awake at night. It has become a cult drink.

journal – This is a record of messages sent and received, file changes, etc. It is useful when trying to recover previous versions of a file or recover an older version of a damaged file.

joypad – A hand-held device for playing games, popularized by *Playstation*. It is more versatile than a *joystick*.

joystick – A hand-held stick that is used as a directional device in arcade games, video games and some design programs. It usually has push buttons for shooting, or for kicking the ball in soccer games. Almost all games consoles are packaged with a joystick.

JPEG – See: **J**oint **P**hotographic **E**xperts **G**roup

JPEG Optimizer – The compression

program used by bitmapped image files created in *JPEG* format.

.jpg – A bitmap format for high-quality color photographs.
SEE ALSO: JOINT PHOTOGRAPHIC EXPERTS GROUP

JScript – Shorthand for *JavaScript*.

JSP – See: Java Server Page

jukebox – This is a device that holds optical disks and can select and read from them on command. Synonymous with *optical library*.

jump page – 1. A web page containing information that is able to provide a quick and easy starting point for the gathering of data about any particular subject.
2. Used in web advertising and marketing, a jump page is a web page that appears temporarily in order to capture the user's attention. It may use flash animation or other attention-grabbing techniques.
3. A temporary web page used for redirecting the user when the page's address has been changed.

jumper – A simple on/off switch.

junk e-mail – This is the kind of e-mail that is sent to unsolicited recipients and is now prohibited by US federal law. It usually carries an advertisement, and can be offensive, and contain pornographic material. It is also known as *spam*.

junk fax – These are the types of faxes containing unwanted content that are often sent to unsolicited recipients. Junk faxes are subject to the same laws as *junk e-mail* in the US.

justification – In typography, justification refers to the alignment of text on both the left-hand and the right-hand margins.

justified – Text that has been aligned simultaneously on the left-hand and right-hand margins with the last lines of any paragraphs ranged flush left.
SEE ALSO: ALIGN
SEE: FEATURE BOX

JVM – See: Java Virtual Machine

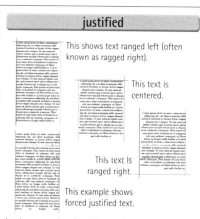

justified

This shows text ranged left (often known as ragged right).

This text is centered.

This text Is ranged right.

This example shows forced justified text.

In the example of justified text above, the final line of the paragraph has been forced justified, creating unnaturally large spaces.

K – (kilobyte) The letter used to denote a storage unit that technically equals 1024 bytes, although in general usage the kilo prefix (as in kilometers or kilograms) refers to 1000.

K56flex – A technology developed by Rockwell International and Lucent Technologies that enables information to be transferred at 56 Kbps through standard telephone lines.
SEE ALSO: **V.90**

Kbps – (**k**ilo**b**its **p**er **s**econd) A measure of data transfer speed – 1000 bits per second. Also seen as Kbs. Modem speeds are measured in Kbps and most new PCs come with 56Kbps modems, capable of receiving data at 56,000 bits per second.

Kbs – See: Kbps

Kbytes/sec – A measure of data transfer speed – 1000 *bytes* per second.

KDE – **K** **D**esktop **E**nvironment is a *GUI* based desktop environment just like Windows. It is freely distributed and is associated with *UNIX* and *Linux*.
GO TO: www.kde.org

Kerberos – A security system that establishes identity at *log on*, and which uses that identity throughout the user session. Developed at the Massachusetts Institute of Technology, it also enables two users to share private data over an open network.

Kermit – A popular *file transfer protocol*, which was developed at Columbia University. It is renowned for its settings that opt for accuracy over speed.

kern – See: kerning

kernel – The core part of the operating system. For example, the single program that is booted.

kerning – A software feature that enables the adjustment of the spacing between letters so that they are printed closer together. This variable pitch helps to make the fonts look more natural.

key – 1. A button on a keyboard that operates a switch that sends data to the user's computer.
2. A password needed to encode and decipher a file.
3. A table of explanation for a chart or graph.

key escrow – A system using a trusted third party to act as an intermediary in a transaction. A key file is entrusted to the third party who will make it available when necessary. It also acts as security against loss.

key field – A field, cell or area of memory used to sort data.

key file – A file containing a key for operations such as encrypted web sites. It usually requires a password to open.

keyboard

Keyboards for PCs come in three designs with differing numbers of keys and variations in the placement of function keys, and Control, Return and Shift keys. Apple keyboards are usually either standard or extended. The extended Apple keyboard has an additional 15 keys. The Command key on either displays an apple logo.

Original PC keyboard displays 84 keys. Special spelt out keys include Cap Lock key, Num Lock key, Alt Lock, Esc, Ctrl, and Scroll Lock key. Shift key is not spelt out.

AT standard PC keyboard also has 84 keys with a narrower space bar and the numeric keypad more clearly separated to the right for typing digits.

AT enhanced PC keyboard has 101 keys with the function buttons running across the top of the pad and extra separate command keys such as "page up."

key frame – Animation drawn by the artist or user rather than by a computer. A sequence of key frames is used to form the basis of the animation or cartoon, with the animation program doing the rest of the work by creating intermediate frames in between the artist's key frames.

key in – To enter data into the computer by typing on the keyboard buttons.

key pal – An Internet pen pal.

keyboard – A device resembling a typewriter that allows the user to input data into a computer using keys. There are three classifications for the *keys* on a keyboard: alphanumeric – these are letters and numbers; punctuation keys – these are the comma, period, apostrophe, semicolon and so on; and special keys for functions and controls. Keyboard layouts can vary but *QWERTY* is the standard English language layout. The name refers to the first six letters on the top left row of letters (Q-W-E-R-T-Y) and a layout arranged to prevent typists in the 1800s from jamming the keys they used the most. The International keyboard is designed for use with a specific language. In Windows the keyboard language can be changed using the Control Panel, Keyboard dialog boxes.

There are many different types of keyboard. The Dvorak keyboard is designed for fast typing, with the most used keys placed in the middle of the keyboard. There are also natural keyboards, which are designed for ease of use and comfort, and cordless keyboards, which connect to the PC via an infra-red port. Another variety is touch-sensitive keyboards, whose keys are pads made of a thin, flat membrane.
SEE: FEATURE BOX

keyboard buffer - See: buffer

keyboard shortcut - A *key* that performs a function that otherwise would involve clicking on several icons or windows using a mouse (e.g. in *Windows*, the key F1 usually acts as a shortcut to the program *help* facility).
SEE: FEATURE BOX

keyboarding - The action of entering data via a keyboard.

keying - To input data via a keyboard.

keystroke - The action of pressing a *key*.

keywords - 1. An index entry identifying a specific word, file or document.
2. A word reserved in a program that has a specific or special meaning.
3. A word used in a query (e.g. when using a *search engine*).

kill - To erase a file, stop an action, or stop a program during operation.

kill file - A file used in *newsgroups* to filter postings by removing unwanted ones.

killer app - (slang) 1. Short for a killer application program that is so successful or useful that it drives a huge demand for manufacturers and programmers to support and interact with it.
2. An application that will drive the competition out of business.

kilo- - A prefix meaning 1000.

kilobaud - 1000 bits per second.

kilobyte - See: K

kilohertz (KHz) - A frequency of 1000 cycles per second.

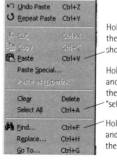

keyboard shortcut

Shortcut keys usually involve holding down the Ctrl or Alt keys with another key. In Microsoft Word, for example, the keyboard shortcuts are displayed alongside the appropriate command.

↶ Undo Paste	Ctrl+Z
↻ Repeat Paste	Ctrl+Y
✂ Cut	Ctrl+X
📋 Copy	Ctrl+C
📋 Paste	Ctrl+V
Paste Special...	
Paste as Hyperlink	
Clear	Delete
Select All	Ctrl+A
🔍 Find...	Ctrl+F
Replace...	Ctrl+H
Go To...	Ctrl+G

Holding down the Ctrl and the V key gives you the shortcut key to "paste."

Holding down the Ctrl and the A key gives you the shortcut key to "select all."

Holding down the Ctrl and the F key gives you the shortcut key to "find."

kiosk – A booth with built-in computer and keyboard, often used in public areas or in stores as an information point.

kluge – Sometimes spelt kludge.
1. Hardware used only for demonstration purposes.
2. A temporary correction to a software fault or error. Actually often a quick and messy "*hack*" to fix an immediate problem.

knockout software – Image manipulation software used to "knock out" parts of a picture or photograph (e.g. cutting out and moving a figure in front of a different background).

knowbot – A program designed to seek information in a system or network, reporting back to the user when the information has been found.

knowledge base system – A program that uses defined knowledge from experts to solve a problem on a particular subject.
SEE ALSO: HEURISTICS

knowledge management – The management of data that has been built up in an organization or system for use in a proactive and constructive way.

Kruegerapp – (slang) From a reference to Freddy Krueger, the murderous character from the horror films series, *Nightmare on Elm Street*. This term applies to a downloaded application that, instead of improving performance, "*kills*" the system.

KVM switch – **K**eyboard **V**ideo **M**ouse switch. A device used to connect one keyboard, mouse, and monitor to two or more computers.

L1 cache – **See:** Level **1** cache

L2 cache – **See:** Level **2** cache

L2TP – **See:** Layer Two Tunneling Protocol

label – 1. An adhesive piece of paper stuck to a disk on which the user can write.
2. The text name given to a disk during the formatting process.

lag – Describes the time in which nothing happens between a command and the action's occurrence.

lamer – (slang) A derogatory name for a person who lacks knowledge about the Internet and *netiquette*.
SEE ALSO: LUSER

LAN – **See:** Local-Area Network

LAN server – **See:** Local-Area Network server

landline – The traditional telephone system using wired lines, as opposed to a wireless service.

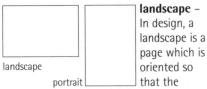

landscape

portrait

landscape – In design, a landscape is a page which is oriented so that the horizontal side will be longer than the vertical side. In the case of the more common *portrait* format the vertical side will be the longer side.

LANE (LAN emulation) – This describes the use of *asynchronous transfer* mode to connect together *ethernet* networks and *Token ring* networks.

language – *Microsoft Windows* supports many different languages and recognizes the different keyboard layouts associated with those languages. Some language options such as Asian and Arabic require the purchase of new fonts.

LAP – Linux Application Platform
SEE ALSO: LINUX

laptop – The name commonly applied to most kinds of portable computer. Laptops are usually equipped with rechargeable batteries that provide for a few hours' operation, along with a mains connection option. Such computers usually weigh in at less than eight pounds (3.5 kg) and have a flat screen LCD monitor. Laptops can usually be attached to a larger monitor, keyboard and peripheral devices, on returning home or to the office.

laser – Light Amplification by Stimulated Emission of Radiation. A thin beam of light generated by the oscillation of atoms or molecules between energy levels. Laser technology is widely used in CD-ROM players, laser printers, and in all kinds of fiber-optics equipment.

laser pointer – A *laser* beam that is emitted from a pen-like pointer, used when giving presentations and lectures to point things out on a distant screen.

laser printer – A variety of printer that uses a *laser* beam to create high resolution print. A black powder, known as toner, is attracted onto a series of tiny dots drawn by the laser beam. The powder is heated, then melts and sets to the paper. Laser printers require toner cartridges as opposed to ink cartridges.. They work in the same way as photocopiers.

LaserJet – A family of laser printers from *Hewlett-Packard* that revolutionized the desktop laser printer market. They all have a large number of built-in fonts, and it is possible to download extra from the computer, or buy cartridges.
GO TO: www.hp.com

Laserwriter – A family of desktop laser printers from *Apple*, introduced in 1985.

lasso – This is a tool available with many kinds of image editing programs that allows the user to select an irregular object on screen. The user drags the mouse around the required area with the mouse button held down; releasing the mouse button will now lasso the selected area. This area can now be dragged to another part of the page, or it can be cut, copied, or deleted.
SEE: FEATURE BOX

last mile – This is a phrase commonly used to describe the telecommunications connection between the computer or telephone and the telephone or cable company. The last mile is usually the slowest and poorest part of the telecommunications network.
SEE ALSO: LOCAL LOOP

lastminute.com – A British online company that specializes in selling holidays. It encourages its customers to be, in its own words: "spontaneous, romantic and sometimes adventurous." This site, like other top online holiday sites, has sections devoted to skiing, flights, hotels, luxury breaks, restaurants, auctions, sport, travel insurance, and more.
GO TO: www.lastminute.com
SEE ALSO: EXPEDIA.COM

lastminute.com

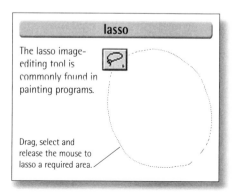

lasso

The lasso image-editing tool is commonly found in painting programs.

Drag, select and release the mouse to lasso a required area.

latency – 1. In memory, the time lag between the beginning of a request for data retrieval and the moment it appears. 2. The time taken for data to travel over the network from its source to its destination. This process should uncover any delays that are occurring on the network.

launch – 1. To open and run a program. 2. To bring a new web site or other product into the marketplace.

LAWN – **L**ocal **A**rea **W**ireless **N**etwork. This is a wireless network technology from O'Neill Communications, Inc. that uses a radio transmitter/receiver.

layer – Some computers are designed to work with layered *architecture*. Each layer is responsible for a different action and is able to draw on the resources of the layer beneath it. Some computers use five layers, others seven.

Layer Two Tunneling Protocol (L2TP) – A standard for enabling data transfer between small *Virtual Private Networks* (VPN) and the Internet or other large network systems.
SEE ALSO: TUNNELING

LCA – **L**otus **C**ommunications **A**rchitecture.
SEE ALSO: LOTUS

LCD – **See:** **L**iquid **C**rystal **D**isplay

LCD monitor – The **L**iquid **C**rystal **D**isplay monitor is used as part of many kinds of laptop computer and the PDA (personal digital assistant).

LCD panel – An LCD panel is a projector that displays computer output on a liquid crystal screen that is placed on top of an overhead projector. It can also be called a *projection panel*.

LDAP – **L**ightweight **D**irectory **A**ccess **P**rotocol. A type of *e-mail address* directory that is increasingly found on browsers and e-mail. It is hoped that this program might eventually create a global White Pages.

lead generation site – A price comparison web site that recommends where to go to find goods at the lowest prices.

---

leading

This feature box shows four examples of leading, with the greatest leading in the last paragraph.

INTRO TEXT GOES HERE Lorem ipsum dolor sit amet, consectetuer adipiscing elit, sed diam nonummy nibh euismod tincidunt ut laoreet dolore magna aliquam erat volutpat. Ut wisi enim ad minim veniam, quis nostrud exerci tation ullamcorper suscipit lobortis nisl ut aliquip ex ea commodo consequat. Duis autem vel eum iriure dolor in hendrerit in vulputate velit esse molestie consequat, vel illum dolore eu feugiat nulla facilisis at. INTRO TEXT GOES HERE Lorem ipsum dolor sit amet, consectetuer adipiscing elit, sed diam nonummy nibh euismod tincidunt ut

INTRO TEXT GOES HERE Lorem ipsum dolor sit amet, consectetuer adipiscing elit, sed diam nonummy nibh euismod tincidunt ut laoreet dolore magna aliquam erat volutpat. Ut wisi enim ad minim veniam, quis nostrud exerci tation ullamcorper suscipit lobortis nisl ut aliquip ex ea commodo consequat. Duis autem vel eum iriure dolor in hendrerit in vulputate velit esse molestie consequat, vel illum dolore

INTRO TEXT GOES HERE Lorem ipsum dolor sit amet, consectetuer adipiscing elit, sed diam nonummy nibh euismod tincidunt ut laoreet dolore magna aliquam erat volutpat. Ut wisi enim ad minim veniam, quis nostrud exerci tation ullamcorper suscipit lobortis nisl ut aliquip ex ea commodo consequat. Duis autem vel eum iriure dolor in hendrerit in vulputate velit esse molestie consequat, vel illum dolore

The greater the leading, the more space between the lines of text.

INTRO TEXT GOES HERE Lorem ipsum dolor sit amet, consectetuer adipiscing elit, sed diam nonummy nibh euismod tincidunt ut laoreet dolore magna aliquam erat volutpat. Ut wisi enim ad minim veniam, quis nostrud exerci tation ullamcorper suscipit lobortis nisl ut aliquip ex ea commodo consequat. Duis autem vel eum iriure dolor in hendrerit in vulputate velit esse molestie consequat, vel illum dolore

leader – A line of dots or dashes, designed to lead the reader's eye across a page, used in menus and lists, etc.

leading – In typography, this is the space between the lines of print.
SEE: FEATURE BOX

leaf - A page on a web site that contains no *links*.

leaf site - A web site dedicated to *newsgroup* postings.

leak – A bug in a program that prevents it from releasing memory. The program uses memory until it crashes because there is no more memory left.

leap frog attack – To gain access to a computer or network using an unauthorized password.

learnware – Educational software.

leased line – A telecommunications line that is used exclusively for a permanent Internet or other network connection. Also called a *dedicated line*. Contrast with a *dial-up* connection which is used for Internet access on an ad hoc basis.

LED – **L**ight-**E**mitting **D**iode. A semiconductor diode that emits light when an electrical current passes through it. Used for computer indicator lights, while Infra-red LEDs are used in remote control devices.

LED printer – **See:** laser printer

left-click – To *click* on the left-hand mouse button to confirm a selected command indicated by the *pointer*, to select text, and to drag objects. The left- is used more frequently than the right-hand mouse button.

left justify – To align text to the left-hand margin leaving the text at the right-hand margin ragged.
SEE ALSO: JUSTIFIED

legacy – An older version of the software that is still supported by newer versions of the software. Legacy is also a term that is used when describing an older way, sometimes even an obsolete way, of carrying out computer-related tasks of many different kinds.

legacy system – A computer system that has been used for a long time.

legend – The text that explains an illustration or photograph. Often legends use a different typeface or font size to distinguish themselves from the main body text.

less than – The < symbol used in *HTML* to indicate the beginning of a *tag*.
SEE ALSO: GREATER THAN

letter bomb – An e-mail with an *attachment* that contains a virus or carries out an illicit or malicious action on the receiving computer.
SEE ALSO: COMPUTER VIRUS

Level 1 cache – A section of high-speed memory within the processor chip that improves data handling. It works in conjunction with the *Level 2 cache* to provide the CPU faster access to important and frequently-used data by bypassing the need to access the main memory.
SEE ALSO: CACHE

Level 2 cache – An L2 cache is a section of high-speed memory within the motherboard, or in some cases within the processor chip. This cache is slower than the *Level 1 cache* but faster than the main memory.
SEE ALSO: CACHE

lexicographic sort – To sort items in alphabetical order.

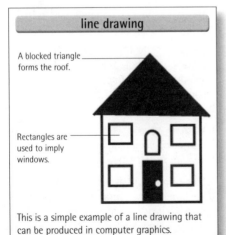

line drawing

A blocked triangle forms the roof.

Rectangles are used to imply windows.

This is a simple example of a line drawing that can be produced in computer graphics.

LF – **See:** line feed

library – 1. Describes a collection of files and/or documents.
2. In programming, a collection of routines available to a programmer.

license – The license is the legal agreement that identifies the *copyright* holder of the product; for example, the software. The license also sets out the conditions of use regarding that product. These conditions may limit the installation of the software to one computer, for example, and state that the copying of the software to another computer is forbidden.

LIFO – **L**ast-**I**n-**F**irst-**O**ut. This acronym is used in the case of a memory routine in which the data stored last will be the data retrieved first.
SEE ALSO: FIFO, LILO

LILO – **L**ast-**I**n-**L**ast-**O**ut. Used for a memory routine in which the data stored last will be retrieved last.
SEE ALSO: FIFO, LIFO

ligature – Two or more type characters that touch; for example, ff, fl, ffi, tt, æ.

light bar – The light bar is the currently *highlighted* menu item.

light client – **See:** thin client

light pen – This light-sensitive pen is used with a touch screen for drawing pictures or selecting menu options.

line – 1. A telecommunications link.
2. Text written on one horizontal row.

line drawing – The simplest images in computer graphics, created by solid lines outlining a shape in black.
SEE: FEATURE BOX

line feed – A printing term for the character code that tells the printer to advance the paper by a single line. Line feed also refers to a button or command that activates line feed.

line spacing – This refers to the space between the lines of text. In normal circumstances this is simply the result of single line spacing, but for easy reading this may be increased to one and a half line spacing or double line spacing. In word processing programs, such as Microsoft Word, this operation is is set up through the menu responsible for formatting paragraphs (in this case, the Paragraph option on the Format menu).
SEE: FEATURE BOX

link – A commonly employed abbreviation for *hyperlink*.

link checking service – A commercial service that checks that the *hyperlinks* on a web page are operative and reports back to the commissioning company.
SEE ALSO: COBWEB

link farm – A web site that provides a large number of *hyperlinks* on a particular

subject area. For example, a health site might provide a list of hyperlinks to various sources of information on diabetes. These sites are different from a more authoritative *guru site*.

link rot – A programming term for a list of items, each of which has a pointer to the next. A Doubly Linked List (DLL) has pointers also to previous elements.

link text – This is a word or phrase on a web page that provides a *link* to another page. Typically, link text is underlined.
SEE ALSO: HYPERTEXT, HYPERLINK

linked list – A list in which every entry has a *hyperlink* to another page.
SEE ALSO: LINK FARM, GURU SITE

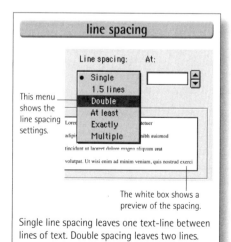

line spacing

Line spacing: At:
• Single
  1.5 lines
  Double
  At least
  Exactly
  Multiple

This menu shows the line spacing settings.

The white box shows a preview of the spacing.

Single line spacing leaves one text-line between lines of text. Double spacing leaves two lines.

Linux (Linus Unix) – A free UNIX-like operating system designed for PC users. Linux may eventually become a popular alternative to Microsoft Windows. The name is commonly pronounced lee-nucks.
Go to: www.linux.com

Linux box – (slang) Refers to a PC using the *Linux* operating system.
See also: box

liquid – A web page that is designed for adapting itself to any size of window

without the use of excessive margins or blank spaces.
See also: ice, jello

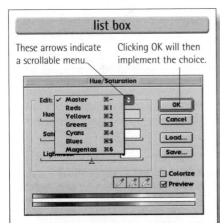

Liquid Audio – A music distribution service from Liquid Audio, Inc.
Go to: www.liquidaudio.com

Liquid Crystal Display (LCD) – A display technology that uses liquid crystals; these are rod-shaped molecules that behave like liquid and bend light.
See also: flat panel display

list – 1. **See:** mailing list
2. An ordered set of items.
3. A command that causes the computer to display a list of items.

list administrator – The person who organizes and maintains a mailing list.

list box – A scrollable area within a dialog box displaying a list of items from which a user can make a selection.
See: feature box

list server – This is a program that handles requests for mailing lists and distributes messages to the list of subscribers. The list server should not be confused with the mail server; which handles e-mail communications.

Listproc® – A *UNIX* automated mailing list server developed and owned by BITNET.

---

list box

These arrows indicate a scrollable menu.

Clicking OK will then implement the choice.

Hue/Saturation

Edit:	✓ Master	⌘~		OK
	Reds	⌘1		Cancel
Hue	Yellows	⌘2		
	Greens	⌘3		Load...
Sat	Cyans	⌘4		Save...
	Blues	⌘5		
Ligh	Magentas	⌘6		

☐ Colorize
☑ Preview

An example of a list box, which gives the user the opportunity to select color for their image.

Listserv® – Mailing list management software from L-Soft international, Inc., Landover, MD, that runs on mainframes, VMS, NT, and various UNIX machines. LISTSERV scans e-mail messages for the words subscribe and unsubscribe to automatically update the list.

Go to: www.lsoft.com
See also: MAILING LIST

lit fiber – A *fiber-optic cable* that is carrying a signal.
See also: DARK FIBER

liteware – This term is used frequently for describing a partial version of a program, especially the kind that is given away, or bundled free with other software. Usually, the aim of liteware is to give the user a limited taste of the software in order to encourage them to purchase the entire program.

little-endian – Within each pair of bytes (often called a "word"), the little-endian is the byte with the lower address and is the less significant. Big endian is the reverse.
See also: BIG-ENDIAN

live – Happening in *real-time* or currently active.

live chat – Live chat is real-time, online, typed conversation. As one user types, the words seem to appear simultaneously on the recipient's monitor. It is found in chat rooms that are accessible via many web sites. For many years multi-user live chat has mainly been carried out via Internet Relay Chat (IRC) sites using dedicated chat software such as mIRC .

live link – Describes a particular kind of active document or image that can be accessed via a *hyperlink*. These are live because they enable users to access e-mail attachments, a database or a web site.

Live3D – Live streaming of 3D video to produce a virtual reality experience. It relies on stereopsis where the depth of vision is created by presenting each eye with a slightly different image. Most technologies require the user to wear special glasses, although emerging technologies aim to ely on the screen alone.

LiveAudio – A *plug-in* that makes sound files immediately accessible, without having to lauch an application to download them.

LiveScript – This was the original name for *JavaScript* when it was first developed as a simple programming language by Netscape.

liveware – This term is sometimes used in reference to real, live human beings.

LMB – An abbreviation often used for left **m**ouse **b**utton.

LNK – Abbreviation for *link*.

load – 1. To copy a program or disk into memory so it can be run.
2. To transfer data onto a disk.
3. The total amount of work that a computer or entire network system is required to undertake.

load time – This describes the amount of time taken for the computer to load a web page and all its features. This load time can be considerably increased on occasions when the relevant network is congested, perhaps by web pages heavy in graphics, video, or audio components.

local – 1. Describes the kind of computer terminal on which the user is working, in contrast with remote.
2. In communication, systems and devices that are accessed directly without a telecommunications line.

log in

Logging in (usually with a password) is needed for most kinds of online activity.

Enter Password

User Name:	joanne
Domain Name:	uk-london
Password:	•••••

[OK]   [Cancel]   [Change Password...]

These activities include accessing a personal and/or network account, the Internet, and e-mail servers.

local area network (LAN) – A network of computers that are physically close to each other and linked by a cable or a wireless transmitter. However, a LAN can be connected to other LANs via telecommunications lines or radio waves. Once linked, a *wide-area network* (WAN) is created. A node in a network is an individual computer usually with its own CPU and the capability to run programs. A node can also access data and share devices, such as printers, anywhere on the LAN. Users can send each other e-mail and conduct chat sessions within the network.
SEE ALSO: ETHERNET, TOKEN RING

local area network server (LAN server) – A computer that manages the communications and data handling on a *local area network*.

local bus – A type of *bus*, which provides a fast data connection between the CPU, memory, and peripherals.

local echo – When transmitting data in *half duplex* mode, every separate character is displayed on the screen immediately upon transmission.

local loop – The local loop is the part of the telecommunications network that links homes and offices to trunk lines. This part of the system often tends to be slow and will usually depend on old-style analog phone lines.
SEE ALSO: LAST MILE

localization – Customizing an operating system so that the graphical user interface is suitable for the country in which it is located. This involves modifying time, units of measurement, keyboard, language, etc.
SEE ALSO: INTERNATIONALIZATION

LocalTalk – A local area network (LAN) protocol that is built into all *Apple* Macintosh Computers.

lock – A mechanism to regulate access to data (e.g. a file, a record within a file, or a data structure in a program).

log – To make a record of an action.

log file – The log file on a computer contains the record of the events that have occurred on a computer or during an Internet session. Web servers can analyze this log to get a better understanding of their customers' browsing habits, and employers may look at the log in order to check up on employees.

log in – To log in means to sign on and gain access to a system, network, or user account. Most web browsers require users to log in and identify themselves by providing an *account* name and *password*. Individual computers on a network also require the user to log in and *log out* at the start and end of their session for security reasons.
SEE: FEATURE BOX

log on – See: log in

log out – This means to sign out when exiting a computer system; usually refers to networks, including the Internet.

logic bomb – This is code hidden within a program or operating system that can trigger a (usually destructive) response when the user performs a specified action. For example, in downloaded software or freeware a logic bomb may trigger a routine that destroys data or corrupts a security system.

logic error – This kind of programming error can cause a program to operate incorrectly in a discrete area, but not prevent it from working.

logical – 1. The way systems and/or data appear to be organized to the user. An individual file logically appears to be one unit whereas in reality it is physically fragmented on the disk.
2. A *Boolean* operation.

logical operator – See: Boolean operator

login/logon – See: log in/out

login name – The name that a user needs to be able to access computer systems (such as a network drive) or their Internet or e-mail account. Many web sites now require users to have a unique log in name and password for access, so the longer one spends as an Internet user, the more log in names (and passwords) one is likely to acquire for different web sites.

login script – A small program that automatically runs a set of instructions (e.g. sending a user name and password) when logging on to a dial-up networking service.

logo – An icon used by a company to identify its goods or services.

long lines – In communications, line or circuits that are designed to handle long distance traffic.

look and feel – This phrase is used to describe the overall style and appearance of a web site. Sometimes the look and feel of a web site may imitate a major company's site with the intention of fooling visitors into thinking they are at one site, when really they are at a competitor's site.

loop – In programming, a series of instructions that will be executed repeatedly by the computer until a certain condition is reached. Each repetition of the process is called an *iteration*.

lossless compression – This is a type of data *compression* where no data is lost. A *GIF* file is an example of an image file that uses lossless compression.

lossy compression – A description of data *compression* that will produce comparatively small compressed files, although some data is lost as part of the compression process. Nevertheless, the loss is not generally considered to compromise

the functioning or intent of the original. The *Joint Photographic Experts Group* (JPEG) file is an example of the kind of image file that uses lossy compression.
SEE ALSO: LOSSLESS COMPRESSION

Lotus – The Lotus Software Group, which is now a subsidiary of *IBM*, achieved success by developing the *Lotus 1-2-3* spreadsheet for the IBM PC. The Group followed this success by producing a number of other applications including Lotus Notes. Some of these programs have gone on to become industry standards.
GO TO: www.lotus.com
SEE ALSO: LOTUS 1-2-3, LOTUS NOTES

Lotus 1-2-3 – The spreadsheet part of the Lotus SmartSuite package. The 1-2-3 name reflects the integrated spreadsheet, database, and graphical components of the software.
SEE ALSO: LOTUS

Lotus Notes – Groupware from *Lotus* that provides a browser, e-mail, data sharing, group discussions, and calendaring and work scheduling.
SEE ALSO: LOTUS 1-2-3

love bug – A *computer virus* that was sent as an e-mail attachment with the file name "I LOVE YOU TEXT.vbs. Recipients of this virus who were using Microsoft Outlook spread the virus to everyone in

their address book, causing six billion dollars worth of damage in May 2000.
SEE: FEATURE BOX

low-level format – Sector identification on a disk. The drive uses this identification to locate sectors which are available for reading and writing.

low memory – Memory locations in the range from 0 to 640Kb.

low ping – A description of a very fast Internet connection.
SEE ALSO: PING

low res/resolution – Low res describes the kind of onscreen images made up from a small number of dots or lines per inch. Low res images will require less memory than *high resolution* images but the result will be noticeable in the poorer display quality. The resolution of images on-screen will also be reflected in the quality of the printed output.
SEE ALSO: DPI, LPI

lowercase – Refers to small letters rather than uppercase (large or capital) letters. Most web addresses are produced with the use of lowercase characters only.

a b c d e f g h i j k l m
n o p q r s t u v w x y z

LPI – Lines per inch.

LPT port – Line Print Terminal port. This is a name used by operating systems for a printer port. Although LPT originally stood for line printer terminal, it is now generally used for indicating any kind of printer.

LSI – Large Scale Integration. A computer chip comprising between 3,000 and 100,000 transistors.

Luhn formula – This mathematical formula is used for the validation of a credit card numbers. It is used in online financial transactions.

luminance – Describes the amount of light or brilliance that is emitted by a pixel or by an area of the display screen. Luminance can also sometimes be referred to as lightness or intensity.

---

love bug

The Love Bug worm first appeared in May 2000, badly clogging up mail servers.

From:	Clare Lister
Sent:	Wednesday, December 05, 2001 9
To:	Joanne Little
Subject:	**open this**

I LOVE YOU TEXT.vbs

This is an example of what the e-mail containing the love bug looked like.

lurk – To join a *newsgroup* without becoming an active participant. Some new users may lurk for a while to assess the discussion and gain the confidence to participate. Other people logged on to the newsgroup are aware of the presence of a silent witness and many tend not to mind, although some prefer the lurking not to go on for too long. Other newsgroups may discourage lurking completely.

lurker – A term given to one who lurks in a newsgroup.
SEE ALSO: LURK

luser – A derogatory word that is generally applied to a *newbie*; i.e. a new computer user, or someone who is utterly confused by computing.

 **Lycos.com** – For some time one of the most popular *search engines* on the web.
GO TO: www.lycos.com

 Lynx – A keyboard-operated (mouse-free) text-only *browser* developed for UNIX workstations. It displays no graphics and cannot operate Java but is very fast.
GO TO: www.lynx.browser.org

M

M – An abbreviation for:
1. The prefix mega-.
2. In electronics and computing, the symbol for 2 to the power of 20 or 1,048,576.
3. A million.
4. The Roman numeral for 1000.

M$ – An uncomplimentary abbreviation for *Microsoft*.

Mac – **See:** Macintosh

MAC address – **See:** **M**edia **A**ccess **C**ontrol

 Mac OS – The *operating system* used by *Apple* computers. The much more flexible *UNIX*-based Mac OS X was introduced in 1999.

Mac TCP – A *transmission control protocol* specific to Apple computers.

MacApp – A reference to any applications specific to Apple computers and operating systems.

machine address – An *address* that is assigned to a storage location in a computer.
See also: absolute address, relative address

machine code – The language that is actually read and understood by the computer. Usually these are instructions written in *binary* code, e.g. the files that make up the operating system on a PC are written in machine code.

machine-dependent – Software that runs on only one type of computer.

machine-independent – Software that runs on many different types of computers.

machine language – The same meaning as *machine code*.

machine-readable – Data in any format that can be input into a computer.

Macintosh – (Mac for short) The name for the highly successful series of computers created by *Apple* in 1984. They were the first PCs to successfully incorporate *GUIs* with drop-down menus and mouse-operated controls. Apple Macs also have their own operating system. Their user-friendly features and eye-catching designs have made them popular with advertising, design, and publishing companies including those working on the Internet.
Go to: www.apple.com
See also: imac

macro – A sequence of simple instructions or keystrokes that are saved as a file so they can be implemented together. Macros are useful for frequently used operations in word processing, spreadsheets, and data handling.

macro virus – A *computer virus* that attaches itself to a macro and causes a sequence of actions to be run automatically. Most macro viruses are spread through e-mails.

Macromedia – A software company, founded in 1992, specializing in multimedia program authoring tools. They are best known for their *Flash* program.

Go to: www.macromedia.com

MAE – **See:** Metropolitan Area Exchange

mag – Abbreviation for magnetic.

magazine style columns – Text formatted in columns. The text flows from the bottom of one column to the top of the next column. Newspapers and magazines use this print style, but it should be used with caution on web pages where different users will see different amounts of the page on display.

Magellan – A disk management program that searches for file names and contents. Its main feature is the file viewer, which lets you look into various data files as if you were using the applications that created them.

magic cookie – An old term for a *cookie*.

magic wand – Some photo-editing programs include this image manipulation tool. It enables a selected area of the image to be copied, moved, rotated, and the colors changed.

magnetic bubble memory – A type of memory found in some portable computers.

magnetic disk – Any disk that relies on the magnetic recording of the data. *Floppy disks* and *hard drives* are both magnetic disks. The disks are made up of concentric rings called *tracks*, which are in turn divided into numbered *sectors*. The disk rotates and a mechanical arm moves a read/write head backward and forward over the disk. Magnetic disks are easily erasable and the memory space can be reused.

magnetic tape – A magnetically coated strip of plastic, or *tape*, on which data can be stored. Often used as a *backup* copy.

magneto-optical (MO) drive – A *drive* for a magneto-optical disk. These are glass or plastic disks that record data using a combination of magnetic and optical technologies.

mail – A system for sending letters and parcels from one place to another. The term is now used to mean electronic as well as conventional mail – as in "you've got mail."
See also: e-mail

mail bombing – E-mailing large numbers of messages to a single address to protest about something the recipient may have allegedly done.
See also: letter bomb

mail box – A file within a browser where incoming mail is stored until it is opened via the *POP3* or *IMAP* protocols.

mail bridge – A *gateway*, either a server or a server and software combination, that delivers e-mail between networks. E.g. A gateway is needed to send an e-mail from a *local area network* to the Internet.
SEE ALSO: BRIDGE

mail client – **See:** e-mail client

mail enabled – Any application that incorporates mail capabilities, e.g. it can send and receive messages.

mail etiquette – **See:** netiquette

mail exploder – Enables a user to send a message to a single address that "explodes" to all the individual mailboxes in the list.

Mail eXchange Record – **See:** MX Record

mail list server – **See:** list server

mail merge – Customized form letters. Such programs merge a letter with a mailing list and other databases. So in a letter written as "Dear A," the software automatically inserts a specified name.
SEE: FEATURE BOX

mail storm – When an unusually large quantity of e-mail messages are sent and/or received. This can happen as a result of an absence from the office or as a result of malicious activity such as a mail-based computer virus.
SEE ALSO: MAIL BOMBING

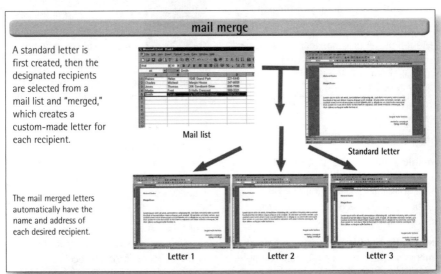

mail merge

A standard letter is first created, then the designated recipients are selected from a mail list and "merged," which creates a custom-made letter for each recipient.

Mail list

Standard letter

The mail merged letters automatically have the name and address of each desired recipient.

Letter 1   **Letter 2**   **Letter 3**

mail thread – A series of e-mails on one topic. These may or may not contain the previous messages.

mail virus – A virus sent as an *attached* file in an e-mail message. When that file is opened, the virus is activated. A good example is the *Melissa* virus.
SEE ALSO: COMPUTER VIRUS

mailbot – A program that automatically sends messages via e-mail.

mailer – A program that delivers e-mail.

mailing list – 1. A list of e-mail recipients who receive regular news and updates from a specific company.
2. A special interest discussion group (but not a newsgroup) using e-mail. Subscribers receive messages on a specific topic written by other participants. They can then e-mail their contributions to those on the list. Messages may be reviewed by a moderator before passing on.

main memory – **See:** memory

mainboard – **See:** motherboard

mainframe – A large (company-based) computer with a huge memory usually kept in a special room and accessible to many users at one time. Now being overtaken by *client server* computing, where the memory capacity of the large machine is shared among small computers that are linked on the organization's network.

Majordomo – A free *mailing list* program, available on the Internet. When e-mail is sent to the Majordomo list, it is sent automatically to everyone on the list. GO TO: www.majordomo.com

male connector – A plug that fits into a *female connector* or socket.

malicious applet – An *applet* downloaded from a web site that runs a malicious operation on the computer such as a *denial of service attack*.

malware – Software that contains a *computer virus* or other malicious feature.

MAN – **See:** Metropolitan Area Network

man-in-the-middle – An attack whereby messages are intercepted and modified by the attacker using wiretapping, while the two parties involved in the message exchange are unaware of the intrusion.

man pages – Short for manual pages. Instructions and information about hardware and software. More commonly downloaded from the Internet than supplied as traditional (book) manuals.

management console – A computer terminal used to monitor and manage a network.

management information base (MIB) – The information needed to manage devices attached to a *TCP-IP* network using the *Simple Network Management Protocol*.

management information system (MIS)
– The *integrated* management of operations, data, and information technology from the various departments within a company.

management service provider – A company that manages information technology for other businesses, (e.g. they may maintain and provide technological support for a network). Increasingly, such services are being provided remotely – with interaction between the management service provider and client taking place on a web site.

many–to–many network – A network where everyone can get in contact with everyone else.

map – 1. A web site map is a page within a web site that simply shows the organization and contents of the web site. 2. Map sites that contain online maps that range from worldwide to local. Some sites specialize in route maps that advise the user on how to drive from one place to another.
SEE: FEATURE BOX

map file – A list of data that is stored in the *memory* or on a disk.

MAPI – **See: M**essaging **A**pplication **P**rogramming **I**nterface

mapping – In e-commerce, to target an audience (e.g. an *e-zine* site may say that it is mapping teenage girls).

mappucino – A *Java applet*, created by IBM, that provides a map showing the various *HTML* pages within a web site. Mapuccino can create a horizontal map view, a vertical map view, a table of contents, and a goldfish view. The maps are all *hyperlinked* so that they can be used as a way of navigating around a site.

marching ants – (slang) In paint, draw, and database programs, a selected object is displayed on the screen surrounded by moving black and white dashes sometimes called "marching ants."

These cells in a spreadsheet are surrounded by marching ants.

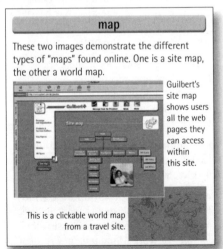

map

These two images demonstrate the different types of "maps" found online. One is a site map, the other a world map.

Guilbert's site map shows users all the web pages they can access within this site.

This is a clickable world map from a travel site.

margin – The blank space between text and the top, bottom, left, and right edges of the page. These can be adjusted by the user to reflect changes in paper size and printing areas.

SEE: FEATURE BOX

marketing – The means by which a company promotes and sells its products or services. The Internet has proven to be a highly effective marketing tool, enabling potentially anyone in the world at any time to view or download immediate information, ask questions, and to compare products. For those companies that had a small market reach, marketing via the Internet has massive potential benefits. There is also scope for one-to-one marketing using e-mail technology to target individual customers.

SEE ALSO: BANNER AD, CLICKSTREAM, COUPONS, FOOTPRINT, HIT, ONLINE TRADING, SPAMDEXING, VIRAL MARKETING

markup language – A text-processing language that provides instructions to the computer for layout, font style, insertion of graphics or video clips, hyperlinks, or other information. The markup language most commonly associated with web page design is *Hypertext Markup Language* (HTML), which has made web page design dynamic and flexible. Other relevant languages include *Extensible Markup Language* and *Standard General Markup Language*.

marquee – 1. A banner that moves across the screen on a web site, usually created using a *Java Applet*. It is used to continually deliver news, share prices, advertisements and so on. Also called a *ticker tape*.
2. A graphic image, usually the program name and logo, shown for a few seconds when a program is launched. Also called a *splash page*.

marquee select – In graphics programs, a way of selecting several items at a time. These are highlighted by an outline of moving dashes, giving the impression of a theater marquee.

martian – Any unexplained event on the Internet or network.

martian mail – Misdirected e-mail.

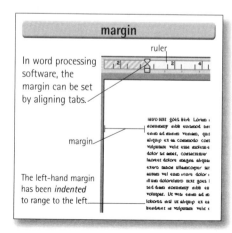

margin

In word processing software, the margin can be set by aligning tabs.

ruler

margin

The left-hand margin has been *indented* to range to the left.

mask – A filter that includes or excludes certain values. E.g. The user can specify the type of data to be included on a form, such as a date, zip, or postal code.

mass individualization – The process of customizing mass-produced products for an individual customer. Used in *e-commerce,* examples include insurance services and holiday packages.

mass storage – Large-capacity backup storage. An external hard disk or magnetic tape may be used to avoid using large chunks of the system memory.

masquerade – To gain entry to a system by pretending to be an authorized user. Often an attacker obtains passwords or exploits a weakness in the security system.

massage – To process information.

master – A computer that manages other computers and/or secondary devices.

master boot record – The information on the first sector of a hard or floppy disk that locates the operating system so that the system can be run.

master document – Used in word-processing programs, such as *Word*, to create and organize large documents from smaller ones, and to create a uniform layout, add cross references, indexes etc.

master page – The template that formats each page in a printed document, adding features such as footers, logos, and borders.

Mathematics Markup Language (MathML) – An *XML* markup language for including mathematical and scientific expressions on web pages.

MathML – **See:** Mathematics Markup Language

matrix – An *array* or organization of data in rows and columns to form a table.

matrix printer – **See:** dot matrix printer

Mauchly, John – The man credited with the creation of the first general purpose computer, ENIAC, produced in collaboration with John Eckert.

maximize – In *Windows*, to enlarge a window to full size. This is done by clicking on the maximize button in the top right-hand corner of the window.
SEE: FEATURE BOX
SEE ALSO: MINIMIZE

---

maximize / minimize

The minimize and maximize buttons are located on the top right-hand corner of the window.
The minimize button is indicated by a short line, and shrinks the window, so that it only shows as a bar on the task bar.

The button to the right of the minimize button maximizes the window across the entire screen width for easy reading.

Maximum Transmission Unit (MTU) – The largest *packet* that can be transmitted in a packet-based network. Computer operating systems provide a default MTU value but sometimes an *Internet Service Provider* (ISP) may advise a client to alter their default value.

MB – Abbreviation for **m**ega*byte*.

MBone – See: **m**ulticast backbone

Mbps – Abbreviation for **m**ega*bits* **p**er **s**econd.

MBps – Abbreviation for **m**ega*bytes* **p**er **s**econd.

MBR – See: **M**aster **B**oot **R**ecord

Mbit – Abbreviation for **m**ega*bit*.

Mbyte – Abbreviation for **m**ega*byte*.

MCAFEE•COM **McAfee VirusScan** – Anti-virus software, the main product of Network Associates. It uses a *Graphical User Interface* and has excellent virus scanners that can be launched or activated automatically. It can also update its virus definition files from the Internet.
Go to: www.nai.com
SEE ALSO: VIRUS PROTECTION SOFTWARE

m-commerce – **M**obile-commerce. Using smart phones and palmtop computers with wireless connections to conduct business over the Web.

MD5 – **M**essage **D**igest 5. A popular security technique that uses a mathematical formula to determine whether or not a message has been tampered with during transmission.
SEE ALSO: MESSAGE DIGEST

MDRAM – **M**ultibank **D**ynamic **R**andom **A**ccess **M**emory. A high-performance memory used in *video adapter cards*. This enables graphics to be displayed at a very fast rate.
SEE ALSO: RANDOM ACCESS MEMORY

MDS – See: **M**essage **D**elivery **S**ervice

Mean time between failures (MTBF) – A means of assessing the reliability of a piece of equipment. The higher the MTBF, the longer the equipment should last.

meat space – (slang) A term that means the real world, as opposed to *cyberspace*.
SEE ALSO: VIRTUAL REALITY

meatware – (slang) Animal systems, as opposed to computer systems. The term is used to compare human biology to a computer system.

media – 1. Plural of *medium*, the means of transmitting signals; e.g. through a telecommunications wire.
2. Anything that stores data, generally used to refer to a floppy disk, zip disk, or CD-ROM.
3. The components of *multimedia*, i.e. sound, graphics, and video.

Media Access Control (MAC) – Controls the means by which connections to the network are shared by several computers (e.g. *ethernet* uses Media Access Control).

media broker – In advertising, an agent that sells advertising space. As access to most web sites is free of charge to the user, advertising revenue is vital to the funding of web sites. People setting up non-commercial sites often go to a media broker to find suitable advertisers.

Media Player – A *Windows utility* program that allows the user to play and control multimedia devices, such as CDs, and to play back multimedia files including Motion Picture Experts Group (MPEGs).
Go to: www.windowsmedia.com

media rich – A site that consists of any combination of graphics, audio, video, and animation. Media rich sites require more storage than ordinary text and are *bandwidth* intensive, requiring longer download times.
See also: MULTIMEDIA

media stream – A video or audio stream that plays in real time.

media type – The media type informs the application that is receiving a message what sort of program is needed to process its content. E.g. A program such as Java is required to process certain graphic transmissions.

MediaCast – A company specializing in broadcasting, especially live and archived music events over the Internet.
Go to: www.mediacast.com

medium – The single form of media.

Medline – US National Library of Medicine's online database. This is a fee-based service providing thousands of articles on medical related topics via the Internet.

meg – (slang) Abbreviation for **meg**abyte.

mega- – A prefix meaning 2 to the power of 20.

megabit – Transmission speed of 1,024 kilobits.

megabyte (Mb) – Data storage for 1,024 kilobytes.

megaflop – A million *floating point operations* a second, a measure of the speed of a processor.

megahertz (MHz) – The measure of frequency, equal to one million cycles per second. This is used to measure the clock speed of a computer.

megapixel image – An image made up of a million or more pixels. Such images have a lot of detail and create very large files.

Melissa – A famous *Word macro virus* that was released onto the Internet in 1999. It sends an e-mail with a list of pornographic web sites to the first 50 names in the user's *Microsoft Outlook* address book. The subject field contains the phrase "an interesting message from" followed by the name of the user so that recipients are duped into thinking it has come from someone they know. The virus then attaches itself to future Word documents sent by e-mail, but only if the user has Microsoft Outlook. In 2000 the "I love you" or Lovebug virus caused billions of dollars of damage by forwarding itself to everyone in a person's e-mail address book simply on opening.
SEE ALSO: COMPUTER VIRUS

meltdown – When a network or site becomes overloaded, slows down, or malfunctions. This can be a result of a serge of users on a site due to a special event, or it can be the result of a *Chernobyl* packet.

membrane keyboard – A keyboard in which the keys are covered by a transparent, plastic case, to protect the components from dust. The keys are pressure-sensitive to enable typing.

meme virus – An idea that is passed on from one generation to another, similar to a gene. A pernicious meme infection parasitizes the computer, which then prioritizes propagating the virus.
SEE ALSO: COMPUTER VIRUS

Memorex – A commercial company specializing in audio-video products, memory storage solutions, and other computer accessories.
GO TO: www.memorex.com

memory – The means of storing data. When talking about computer memory, it refers to the Random Access Memory (RAM). This is used to run the computer's software and holds the parts of the operating system and data that is currently being worked on. RAM only functions when the computer is operating. it is also distinguished from longer term storage memory supplied on external hard disks and diskettes, where the data is recorded magnetically. There are many types of RAM including *SRAM, DRAM,* and also SDRAM.
SEE ALSO: CACHE, EPROM, FLASH MEMORY, MEMORY PAGE, RAM, ROM

memory cache – **See:** cache

memory dump – **See:** dump

memory leak – **See:** leak

memory management unit (MMU) – The component that manages data storage in the RAM chips.

memory map – The location of data and instructions in the memory.

memory page – An operating system's main memory is split into pages for the purpose of management. Pages are doled out to applications as needed.

memory-resident – Data that remains in the random access memory (RAM) after being used, and so is available for further use, and is easily accessed.

Memphis – The code name *Microsoft* used for *Windows 98*.

menu – A list of program options.

menu bar – The line of program command options that is written on a *graphical user interface*. When the words are clicked on they usually generate a drop-down menu providing more command options.
SEE ALSO: TOOLBAR
SEE: FEATURE BOX

menu driven – Programs that are run by choosing options from menus, as opposed to typing in commands.

---

menu bar

W Microsoft Word - Document1

File Edit View Insert Format Tools Table Window Help

Clicking on any of the words on the menu bar, such as File, triggers drop-down menus, which allow the user to manipulate the word document in all sorts of different ways.

---

menuing software – Programs that run applications and other operating system instructions through a menu-based launching system.

Merced – The code name formerly used by *Intel* for its latest generation 64 bit Central Processing Unit architecture. It has since been renamed Itanium.

merchant account – A paperwork agreement between a credit card processor and an e-retailer. The agreement regulates credit card purchases and fund transfers. All e-retailers must have this in order to be able to process credit card transactions.

merchant server – A *server* in a *network* that handles online purchases, fund transfers, and credit card transactions according to the protocols agreed through *merchant accounts*.

merge – To join together two or more items, such as documents or files.
SEE ALSO: MAIL MERGE

merge purge – To merge two or more lists and remove duplicate or unwanted items from the main list.

message – Data sent from one part of a network to another.
SEE ALSO: E-MAIL

message based – A communication interface between two systems that is based on text commands.

message board – Part of a web site where the user can post a message. Postings tend to be organized into subject areas, and conversations called *threads* take place within these areas.
SEE ALSO: BULLETIN BOARDS, NEWSGROUPS, USENET

message box – A small window that opens to alert the user to an error or to inform them that the operation requested is unavailable. Also called a *dialog box*.

message broker – A messaging system for applications that includes a message transport, a rules engine, as well as a formatting engine.
SEE ALSO: MESSAGING MIDDLEWARE

message digest – A mathematical process used to determine whether a message has been tampered with during transmission.
SEE ALSO: MD5

Message Delivery Service (MDS) – In transmission, the facilities used by nodes to communicate with each other. The MDS keeps *duplexed* components synchronized.

message flooding – A *denial of service attack* that sends a huge volume of messages to the computer, which may lead to a *meltdown*.

message handling – The text in an e-mail that describes the route that the message has taken. It is normally only seen when mail is returned as undeliverable.

message header – 1. An e-mail system.
SEE ALSO: MESSAGING SYSTEM
2. The method that is used to transfer data over a network. This includes coding and decoding data.

message of the day – Some web sites provide the user with a piece of information daily. This may be helpful advice or a witty saying.
SEE ALSO: FORTUNE COOKIE

message sink – The part of the *messaging system* that receives messages.

message switching – A switching technique for the transmission of messages from node to node through a network. The message is stored at each node until a forwarding path is available.
SEE ALSO: PACKET SWITCHING, ROUTING, SWITCH

messaging – Any means of transmitting messages over a network, including e-mail, fax, and mobile phone text messaging.

messaging gateway – A computer system that translates one messaging protocol into another.

messaging middleware – The software that handles the communication between applications, allowing them both to send and to receive data. Information sent by one program can be stored in a queue, then forwarded once the receiving program is able to process it.

messaging system – A program that provides an e-mail delivery system. It consists of a client e-mail program, such as Microsoft *Outlook*, and a message transfer agent that sends and receives messages.
SEE ALSO: SMTP PROTOCOL

Messaging Application Programming Interface (MAPI) – A protocol that sets out how messages are transmitted and received. Messages can be sent and received by any two e-mail programs that are MAPI-compliant.
SEE ALSO: API

meta- – A prefix that means about.

meta tag – An HTML tag that provides additional information about a web site. One use is in indexing; a meta tag records which keywords identify the site, and search engines use this information when creating their indices. Meta tags can also be used to create a jump to another web address after a few seconds. This is useful if several domain names are listed for one site, or if the site has moved.

Metacrawler – A search engine that allows the user to select more than one search engine and to search them simultaneously.
GO TO: www.metacrawler.com

metadata – Data about data.

metafile – Files that contain information about other files.

metalanguage – A language used to describe other languages.

metamerism – Describes the quality of colors that appear different under varying light conditions. E.g. A color may change its appearance when seen in natural as opposed to artificial light.

metasearcher – A *search engine* that exploits the strengths of several other search engines and reports their combined findings in answer to a query.
SEE ALSO: COPERNIC, METACRAWLER
SEE: APPENDIX 6

metaverse – (slang) A description of a world that has been generated using *virtual reality* technology.

Metcalf, Robert – The man who, along with his assistant David Boggs, invented and developed the first computer network in 1973, while working for *Xerox*.
SEE ALSO: ETHERNET

Metropolitan Area Exchange (MAE) – Formally Metropolitan Area Ethernet. Major *network access points* (NAPs) where Internet Service Providers can connect.

Metropolitan Area Network (MAN) – A *network* that serves a city or town area, although it is occasionally extended to describe a network connecting several businesses or universities.
SEE ALSO: LOCAL AREA NETWORK, WIDE AREA NETWORK

MFM – Modified Frequency Modulation. The magnetic disk encoding system used by older hard disks and floppy disks.

MHz – **See:** megahertz

MIB – **See:** Management Information Base

mic – **See:** microphone

mic in – The socket, usually at the back of the computer, into which an external microphone can be plugged.

mice – The plural of *mouse*.

Mickey Mouse – **See:** noddy

micro- – 1. A prefix meaning small. 2. A prefix meaning one millionth.

microbrowser – A *browser* used with a wireless hand-held device such as a mobile phone or PDA (personal digital assistant). They have reduced capabilities and smaller files, in order to cope with the limited capacity of the hand-held devices.

Microcom Networking Protocol (MNP) – An error detection system that enables a modem to request that data be re-sent when an error in transmission has occurred.

microcomputer – A small computer, commonly known as personal computer or PC. The central processing unit of a microcomputer consists of a single integrated circuit. All home users use a microcomputer.

micron – A unit of measurement representing one millionth of a meter. It is represented by the symbol _.

micropayment – A payment so small that it is not cost effective to collect payment through the banking system. This has become a problem on the Internet and has lead to the development of several token account-based and alternative payment systems such as e-wallets.

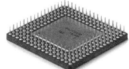

microphone – A device that converts sound waves into electrical signals that are transmitted and reproduced through an amplifier and speaker system. To record and use sound on a computer, the *sound card* must be able to accept and convert electrical signals.

microprocessor – The chip on a computer where most of the calculations and processing takes place. Also called the central processing unit (CPU). Computer memory is separate from this unit.

microsite – A small web site that sits within a larger web site. Often, companies use a small site dedicated to one branch of their business to attract the user to the main company site.

Microsoft

Microsoft – The world's largest software company. It was founded in 1975 by Bill Gates and Paul Allen. They were college students when they wrote the first program interpreter for the Intel 8080 microprocessor. This was BASIC, and it was licensed to Micro Instrumentation and Telemetry Systems to go with its Altair 8800 computer. In 1981, Microsoft's collaboration with IBM brought great commercial success; the combination of Microsoft operating systems and IBM PCs, proving irresistible. When the two companies split in the 1990s, Microsoft focused on the Windows operating system, which has become the standard on PC desktops throughout the world. (Microsoft also offers a number of programming languages and integrated software.) However, Microsoft's aggressive marketing policy, influence over manufacturers, and market dominance eventually led the US Government and 19 states to sue the company for antitrust violations. This was on the grounds that including the Internet Explorer browser free with Windows was killing the market for other commercial browsers such as Netscape Navigator. In June 2000, the court ordered that Microsoft be broken into two companies, but a year later, the appeals court stopped the break-up and sent the case back to the lower court.

Microsoft BASIC – A computer language and interpretation program that translates programs and runs them at the same time. This was one of the first of its kind and its introduction started the ball rolling for Microsoft as a company.
SEE ALSO: **BASIC, MICROSOFT, VISUAL BASIC**

Microsoft Cluster Server (MCS) – A fail-safe system for *Microsoft* operating systems. It works by allowing a second server to take over if the first one fails.

Microsoft Disk Operating System (MS-DOS) – The master control program used and developed by Microsoft. It runs the computer; managing data, tasks, applications, and hardware.

Microsoft Internet Explorer – See: Internet Explorer

Microsoft Network (MSN) – An *Internet Service Provider* that offers many extra information services and channels, such as news, shopping, and financial advice. It has a personalization service so that users can filter the content they receive, and also links to *Hotmail*. It offers a search facility, MSN messenger, a diary service, and much more. Many Microsoft users use www.msn.com as their default *home page*.
GO TO: www.msn.com

 **Microsoft Office** – A software package from Microsoft that provides users with a combination of word-processing, spreadsheets, and presentations programs.
Go to: www.microsoft.com/office

Microsoft Reader – Technology that enables the user to read e-books on a backlit screen for easy reading. It uses *ClearType* display technology.
Go to: www.microsoft.com/reader
See also: e-book

Microsoft Windows – See: Windows

Microsoft Word – The most widely used word-processing application for creating documents and desktop publishing.
Go to: www.microsoft.com/office/word
See also: microsoft office

microspacing – In printing, the positioning of characters by making tiny horizontal and vertical movements. All laser, ink-jet, and some dot matrix printers have this ability.

middleware – The software that operates between the client and the server or between disparate applications. E.g. Programs that encrypt and decrypt data, those that carry out security checks, and programs that convert data that needs to be processed between a PC and a Mac.

MIDI – Musical Instrument Digital Interface. The set of standards that specify how musical instruments, recording systems, and computers interact. MIDI includes hardware, such as electronic instruments, and software. Because music formatted into MIDI is *digitized*, it is downloaded quickly and requires little storage space. Such files are saved using the .mid extension. The MIDI *interface* usually comes as part of the *sound card*.

MIDI Mapper – A program supplied with *Windows* that allows the user to manipulate music stored in the *MIDI* format. This enables the user to redirect musical lines from one instrument to another or alter sound characteristics.

MIDI sequencer – Hardware or software that can be used to create, edit, or play *MIDI* files.

.mil – A suffix for web sites related to the US military.

milli- – A prefix meaning one thousandth.

MIME – See: Multipurpose Internet Mail Extensions

minicomputer – A computer midway in size between a mainframe and a microcomputer, such as the DEC VAX and IBM AS/400. A minicomputer physically occupies a large part of a room but is not as big as a mainframe.

MiniDisc – A small music disc from Sony with variations for data storage available.

minimize – In Microsoft *Windows*, to reduce a window to an *icon*. This is done by clicking on the minimize button, the first of the three small buttons in the top right-hand corner of the window. If a program is minimized, it means that it is running in the background but is not currently active.
SEE ALSO: MAXIMIZE

MIPS – Million Instructions Per Second. A unit used to measure the processor speed.

mIRC – An *Internet Relay Chat* program that provides a graphical interface.

mirror – 1. To create a site on a network that is a duplicate of another site, in order to enable more users to access a busy site. 2. To write data to two or more disks, or other storage devices, as a back-up, in case one copy is lost.

mirror site – A duplicate of a busy archive site that is maintained in order to reduce the load on the source site and to speed up access for all users.

MIS – See: Management Information System

misc – A description of a *newsgroup* area of interest that is not covered by any other category. Short for miscellaneous.

misfeature – (slang) A computer feature that causes problems, often due to technological advances, which the original programmer could not have predicted.

mixed reality – A combination of *virtual reality* and real images.

mixed-signal – A chip that can process a combination of analog and digital data.

M-JPEG – Motion-Joint Photographic Experts Group. A moving image which is made by storing each frame of a moving picture sequence in *JPEG* compression format. The still frame images are then decompressed and rapidly displayed, which creates the illusion of movement on the screen.

MMC – See: MultiMedia Card

MMDS – See: Multichannel Multipoint Distribution Service

MMX – See: Multimedia Extensions

MNP – Microcom Networking Protocol. A family of error detection and data compression standards.

mobile agent – An *agent* that visits many computers in a network.

mobile client – A client that is not in a fixed location.
SEE ALSO: MOBILE COMPUTING

mobile computing – The provision of access to the *World Wide Web* to users who are not at a fixed location. This includes Internet access via mobile or cellular phones, hand-held devices, and laptop access from remote locations.

mobile phone – A wireless phone that receives signals in remote locations. Vastly popular, most mobile phones now have a text messaging facility, and some WAP phones provide for Internet access.
SEE ALSO: CELLULAR PHONE
SEE: APPENDIX 1 for text messaging acronyms.

mobile Internet – Accessing the Internet using a hand-held device such as a mobile or cellular phone.
SEE ALSO: WAP

Mobile IP – Mobile Internet Protocol. A means of forwarding e-mail to users who are at a *remote* location.
SEE ALSO: INTERNET PROTOCOL, MOBILE COMPUTING

mobo – (slang) *Motherboard*.

mockingbird – A means of attack that imitates a system, then intercepts transmissions when users are logging on, thereby obtaining passwords and other restricted information. It is a type of *Trojan* computer virus.

modal dialog box – A modal operation that switches from one mode to another.

mode – The operational state of a device or system. Software and hardware operate in various modes. One example is the safe mode that the Microsoft Windows operating system can switch to after a program has crashed.

modem – Mo**dulator-Dem**odulator. A device that enables a computer to transmit data along a telecommunications line. It converts digital signals to analog audio frequencies and vice versa. Modems are most commonly internal to the computer, although external devices also exist. It is necessary to have a modem to send digital data from the computer over a phone line. The sending modem modulates (changes) the data into an analog signal that is compatible with the phone line, and the receiving modem demodulates (returns) the signal back into digital data to be read by the computer. The earliest modems worked at 300 bps (bits per second), using a method called frequency shift keying. In this method, the originating modem sends a different frequency (tone) for each of the different bits; i.e. it transmits a 1,070 hertz tone for a zero and a 1,270 hertz tone for a 1. At the same time the receiving modem transmits a 2,025 hertz tone for a 0 and a 2,225 hertz tone for a 1. The originating and receiving modems can both use the line simultaneously because they are transmitting at different frequencies. This type of transmission is called a full-duplex operation. It became necessary to introduce faster technologies with the introduction of Internet access: Phase Shift Keying (PSK), and then Quadrature Amplitude Modulation (QAM), with the fastest 56K-bit modems taking this technology to its limits. These modems all test the phone lines as they transmit and send at slower speed if the line is unable to handle transmissions sent at their optimal speed. The latest modems, ADSL, are asymmetric, that is, they transmit data faster in one direction than they do in another. These modems divide the phone line's bandwidth into 249 virtual modems, each of which optimizes its transmission rate. The total of the 249 virtual modems' output is the speed of the transmission.

SEE ALSO: DIGITAL-TO-ANALOG CONVERTER
SEE: FEATURE BOX

modem eliminator – A device that allows two computers to be connected without *modems*.

modem pool – Two or more modems and associated software that are shared by users.
SEE ALSO: REMOTE ACCESS SERVICE

moderator – The person who monitors e-mail submissions in a mailing list, *newsgroup*, or *chat room*. All postings are read and assessed to ensure that the content contains no *spams*, or libelous, or offensive material.

moderated mailing list – A *mailing list* that is screened by a *moderator*.

moderated newsgroup – A *newsgroup* that is supervised by a *moderator*, who screens submissions to ensure that the discussion is focused and spam-free.

modem

When the computer sends information to the modem, it is converted to binary data and sent as sound waves over the phone line. When data is returned, it uses the same process in reverse.

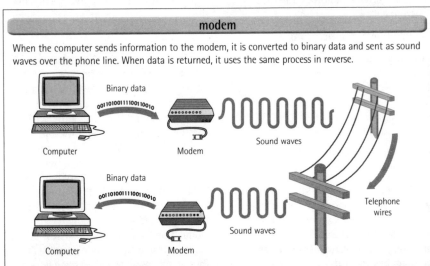

Binary data
001101001111001100010
Computer   Modem   Sound waves

Binary data
001101001111001100010
Computer   Modem   Sound waves

Telephone wires

modifier key – A key on a keyboard that only has a meaning when it is combined with another key, (e.g. Control, Alt, or Shift keys).

modular architecture – A system that consists of smaller sub-systems, which interact with each other.

modulate – In communications, to add a signal to a carrier wave for transmission over a network. The two most popular methods are amplitude modulation (AM), which modulates the height of the carrier wave, and *frequency modulation* (FM), which modulates the frequency of the wave. The receiving modem demodulates the signal in order to return the data to its original format.

module – A self-contained functional unit that is used within a larger system. A software module is a part of a program that performs a particular task. A hardware module can be a packaged unit that physically attaches to a system.

moiré – In graphics, a visible distortion of an image. This can occur for a number of reasons; when half tones are scanned at a resolution inconsistent with the printed resolution, when geometrical patterns are superimposed, or if there is a problem with monitor alignment.

Monitor cable

monitor – A device resembling a television screen that displays the text and graphics generated by a computer. Desktop monitors generally use *cathode ray tubes*, while laptop monitors use *liquid crystal display* technology. Most contemporary monitors work in full color, although black and white monitors (*monochrome*) also exist. Monitors can sometimes be referred to as *displays*. Desktop monitors are attached to the computer with a cable, whereas laptop monitors are part of the computer.

monochrome – Monochrome generally refers to a black and white *monitor*.

MOO – **See:** **M**ud, **O**bject **O**riented

Moof – (slang) When disconnected from the Internet or a chat room for no obvious reason, it is common to blame the Moof monster. Used as a verb: "I got moofed."

Moore's Law – Gordon Moore, the co-founder of *Intel*, states that "The number of transistors on a chip doubles every 18 months." Most experts, including Moore, believe that this will be the case for at least another two decades.
SEE ALSO: PENTIUM

Moria – A Dungeons and Dragons style game named after J.R.R. Tolkien's Mines of Moria in *Lord of the Rings*.
SEE ALSO: **MUD**

morphing – An *animation* technique whereby one image is transformed into another by gradually adding characteristics of the second image onto the first. E.g. A picture of a young person can adopt the characteristics of an older person.

mortuary site – A web site that has not been updated and is consequently no longer of interest. Synonymous with *cobweb site*.

Mosaic – The first World Wide Web *browser* with a *multimedia* capability, developed by the National Center for Supercomputing Applications (NCSA). It has since been overtaken by more advanced browsers, such as *Netscape Navigator* and *Internet Explorer*.

MOTD – See: **M**essage **O**f **T**he **D**ay

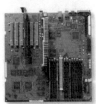

motherboard – A computer's main circuit board consisting of the *central processing unit* (CPU), the *bus*, *memory,* and *expansion* slots. It is usually the green board with soldered circuitry located at the bottom of the computer case.

Motion JPEG – A video format where every frame that makes up the moving image is compressed in *JPEG*.
SEE ALSO: **M-JPEG**

Motion Picture Experts Group (MPEG) – A compression technique for video images. MPEG1 is for Internet Video while MPEG2 is for broadcast video.
GO TO: www.mpeg.org

Motorola – Leading company (founded in 1928) in communications services and products. Best known for its range of small mobile phones, but also very active in the cable and set-top box markets.
GO TO: www.motorola.com

mount – What the client system does to a "shared" folder to make it accessible locally over a network. The server "shares" the folder, and its clients "mount" it.

mouse – A pointing device that is used to move a *cursor* or pointer around on a display screen. Clicking the left button generally activates the object under the cursor, e.g. "pushes" the button, or selects the icon. The button may start an application, or do something else - e.g. pop up the "start" menu.

mouse ahead – To input commands with a mouse so fast that the computer cannot keep up. The computer remembers a few mouse moves ahead and will catch up.

mouse around - Synonymous with *surf*, i.e. to browse the Internet.

mouse mat - See: mousepad

mouse miles - The distance the mouse travels when using the computer. There are programs on the market that track mouse miles.

mouse pointer - The screen symbol that is moved with the mouse. In text-based operations the pointer appears as a *cursor*, but it can change to a paintbrush, an hourglass, an arrow, a hand, or a cross, depending on the application requested.

mouse port - The socket in a computer case used to plug in the mouse.

mouse potato - (slang) The cyberspace version of the couch potato.

mouse-driven - A program that is operated by a mouse, as opposed to keyboard commands.

mouseover event - When a mouse is moved over an object on screen causing the icon to change its appearance or explanatory text to appear. Synonymous with *rollover*.

mousepad - A rubber pad that provides a smooth, flat horizontal surface on which to operate a *mouse*. Also called a mouse mat.

.mov - A file *extension* indicating a QuickTime movie program.

movie file - A full-motion, digital video file, such as an *AVI file*.

moving-bar menu - A bar menu that can be dragged around the display screen for ease of use. E.g. Windows menu bars.
SEE: FEATURE BOX

Mozilla - The code name given by *Netscape* to its Navigator web *browser*. The name is a corruption of the words Mosaic Killer, which refers to *Mosaic*, the web browser that established widespread use of the Internet.

MP3 - Also known as MPEG Layer 3, which is an abbreviation for **M**otion **P**icture **E**xperts **G**roup, Audio Layer 3. A popular digital audio *compression* format that enables users to download near compact disc-quality music over the Internet. MP3 can be played on any multimedia computer with MP3 player software. This software will also record music from audio compact discs and store them on the computer.

---

moving-bar menu

A Microsoft Word menu bar that can be moved around the screen.

W Microsoft Word - Document1

File Edit View Insert Format Tools Table Window Help

You can move the menu bar by left-clicking with the mouse on the left-hand side of the bar. Hold down the button and drag the menu to the preferred position.

The compression technique reduces the audio file size by a factor of 12, to about eight per cent of its original size, with no perceptible loss of quality, by taking out all the frequencies that cannot be heard anyway. This means that files can be downloaded from the Internet, and exchanged comparatively quickly, making it feasible to buy, sell, and promote music directly over the Internet. MP3s also opened up all sorts of questions about bootlegging (illegally copying CDs without copyright permissions) and freedom of the Internet. Portable MP3 players containing a disk drive are beginning to gain in popularity, which will spread the technology beyond Internet-based computers. An MP3 file is created by converting an audio signal from a CD into a wave file, which is in turn encoded into the MP3 format. This is achieved by a process called *ripping* software.

GO TO: www.mp3.com

SEE: FEATURE BOX

SEE ALSO: MP3 PLAYER, NAPSTER

MP3 Player – Software that enables audio files in *MP3* format to be listened to on a computer's speaker system or carried in a portable player.

MP3 utility – The toolkit used for editing, sorting, and working with *MP3*.

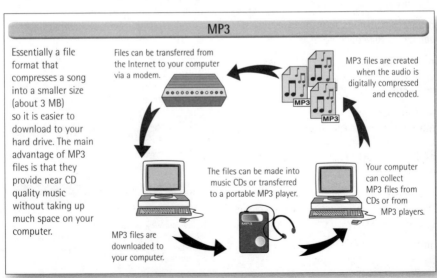

MP3

Essentially a file format that compresses a song into a smaller size (about 3 MB) so it is easier to download to your hard drive. The main advantage of MP3 files is that they provide near CD quality music without taking up much space on your computer.

Files can be transferred from the Internet to your computer via a modem.

MP3 files are created when the audio is digitally compressed and encoded.

The files can be made into music CDs or transferred to a portable MP3 player.

Your computer can collect MP3 files from CDs or from MP3 players.

MP3 files are downloaded to your computer.

MPC – See: **m**ultimedia **PC**

.mpg – *Motion Picture Experts Group* formatted files.

MPEG – See: **M**otion **P**icture **E**xperts **G**roup

MPPP – **M**ulti**L**ink **P**oint-to-**P**oint **P**rotocol. A development of the point-to-point *protocol* that doubles the amount of data transmitted over a channel. It is used for ISDN transmission.
SEE ALSO: CHANNEL BONDING

MPR – **M**ultiservice **R**oute **P**rocessor. A card that carries voice over an *IP* network. It links *Ethernet LANs* using *WANs*.

MPR II – Swedish guidelines that define acceptable levels of electromagnetic radiation, which all computer screens emit.

MR – **M**odem **R**eady.

MRU list – **M**ost **R**ecently **U**sed list. A list of sites visited within the past few days that is kept within the *browser*.
SEE ALSO: HISTORY

MS – Abbreviation for *Microsoft*.

ms (millisecond) – One thousandth of a second.

MSCS – See: **M**icrosoft **C**luster **S**erver

MS-DOS – See: **M**icrosoft **D**isk **O**perating **S**ystem

MSI – See: **M**edium **S**cale **I**ntegration

MSN – See: **M**icrosoft **N**etwork

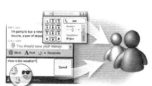

MSN Messenger – A chat and messaging program from *Microsoft* that enables the user to see when friends are online and exchange near instant messages with them.
GO TO: http://messenger.msn.com
SEE ALSO: ICQ

MSP – See: **M**anagement **S**ervice **P**rovider

MSRP – **M**anufacturer's **S**uggested **R**etail **P**rice.

MTU – See: **M**aximum **T**ransmission **U**nit

MUCK – See: **M**ulti-**U**ser **C**hat **K**ingdom

MUD – See: **M**ulti-**U**ser **D**omain/**M**ulti-**U**ser **D**imension/**M**ulti-**U**ser **D**ungeon

Mud, Object Oriented Multi-User Dungeon (MOO) – A virtual reality environment that uses *object-oriented* programming to add dimension. In contrast to this, *MUD*s are just text based games.

MUD client – A program run on a user's PC that enables connection to a *MUD*. It enhances the formatting and visual features. It is also possible to connect to more than one MUD simultaneously.
SEE ALSO: CLIENT

muddie/mudhead – A person who is addicted to *MUD* games.

multicast – Communications sent between multiple selected sites, as opposed to *broadcasting,* which sends data to everyone, e.g. e-mail messages sent to a selected list of people.

Multicast backbone – A group of Internet sites that support *Internet Protocol* multicasting. It is a fast method of transmitting real-time audio and video programs, and for videoconferencing.

Multichannel Multipoint Distribution Service (MMDS) – A wireless broadband communications technology used for accessing the Internet.

MultiFinder – A version of the *Apple* computer Finder that allows more than one program to be put into memory at a time.

multifrequency monitor – A monitor capable of adjusting within a range of refresh frequencies, e.g. 60 -110 Hz.

multi–homed – A computer or device that is connected to two or more networks and/or has two or more network addresses. This is sometimes used to guarantee a service in event of a system failure.

multimedia – The use of a variety of different media. Animation, audio, graphics, music, text, and video are the main types of media used in multimedia systems.

Multimedia applications generate large quantities of data requiring systems to have adequate memory provision. Most web sites now contain multimedia elements, which can make them slow to download. Multimedia programs include interactive games, encyclopedias, and training applications.

MultiMedia Card (MMC) – A small ROM chip card used in mobile/cell phones and PDAs. It weighs less than two grams, with 64MB capacity.

multimedia conferencing – See: videoconferencing

multimedia extensions (MMX) – An Intel *CPU* that enhances multimedia applications without the need for additional sound and video cards.

multimedia kit – All the hardware and software necessary to upgrade a PC into a *multimedia PC.*

Multimedia PC (MPC) – A personal computer equipped with CD, large hard drive, sound, graphics, and video compliant with the standards laid down by the MPC Marketing Council.

multimedia speaker – A term usually applied to a set of speakers designed to work with a PC to provide high-quality sound. The set usually consists of a three piece sub-woofer (covering the bass sound) and satellites for higher frequencies.

multiple search engine – To submit a web site to a single maintained site for indexing. This site then distributes indexing details to a large number of individual *search engines*. This eliminates the need to list a web site on each search engine separately.

multiplatform – Software or hardware that can be used in conjunction with several types of operating systems.

multiplex – Short for multiple access.
1. When two or more signals are combined into a single signal for transmission.
2. To transmit two or more signals simultaneously over a single channel.

multiplexor (mux) – A communications device that combines signals to enable *multiplex* transmission.

multiprocessing – Using two or more linked computers or processors to run more than one operation simultaneously.

multiprogramming – **See:** multitasking

Multipurpose Internet Mail Extensions (MIME) – A method of sending non-text files by e-mail. MIME encodes the files by identifying blocks of data by type; these include plain text, HTML, graphics, audio, or video. These are then transmitted and decoded by the receiving browser, which recognizes the MIME type and will decode it accordingly.
SEE ALSO: **S/MIME, UU**CODE

MultiRead – A specification for *CD-ROM* and CD players that enables them to read discs created by *CD-RW* drives. Developed by *Hewlett-Packard* and Phillips Electronics.

multiscan monitor – A *monitor* that is able to display graphics in more than one resolution.

multisession CD – A compact disk on which data is recorded in more than one session. This is particularly useful for photo CDs where the images are recorded onto the disks on several different occasions. Most current CD-ROM drives have the capacity to operate multisession CDs.

multitasking – Running several programs at once, e.g. Windows operating systems allow the user to switch between programs without having to quit and reload.

multithreading – Processing several transactions or operating different functions within a single program at the same time. Technically, however, this is not the case, any more than it is with *multitasking*, but both provide the appearance of doing several things at once.

multi-user 1. An operation that involves two or more users.
2. A system that can handle multiple users, e.g. Unix, and Win2k.

Multi-User Chat Kingdom (MUCK) – A text-based *MUD* system similar to *MUSH* although it uses different software.

multi-user domain/multi-user dimension/multi-user dungeon (MUD) – *Multi-user, interactive,* three-dimensional games played over the Internet in a chat room environment. Players on these complex graphical games are represented by *avatars* and explore different *virtual reality* environments where they encounter various challenges while interacting with other players.
SEE ALSO: **MOO, MUCK, MUSH**

Multi-User Shared Hallucination (MUSH) – A variant of *MUD* in which the players develop new environments, or create new objects and challenges.
SEE ALSO: **MOO**

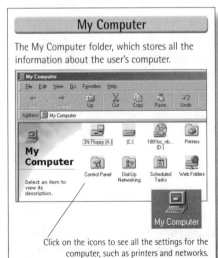

My Computer

The My Computer folder, which stores all the information about the user's computer.

Click on the icons to see all the settings for the computer, such as printers and networks.

Multi-User Simulated Environment (MUSE) – A type of *MUD.*

mumble – A word used in *newsgroups* when a user wishes to keep some information private, e.g. the word mumble may be used in place of a user's name or other identifying feature.

munching – Exploiting loop-holes in a systems security system. Generally used to prove that it is possible to gain access rather than for malicious purposes.

MUNG – To make significant changes to a file or to destroy features within a file either by accident or maliciously. The word is an *acronym* for **M**ash **U**ntil **N**o **G**ood.

munpack – A *UNIX* program that will restore a *compressed MIME* or unencoded file into its original format.

museum – One of the seven new *domain* names adopted in 2000.

MUSE – See: **M**ulti-**U**ser **S**imulated **E**nvironment

MUSH – See: **M**ulti-**U**ser **S**hared **H**allucination

music – Once *MP3* was established, a revolution in downloading music occurred. Web sites such as *Napster* started to use new file sharing technology to swap music for free over the Internet. Copycat sites appeared and many major recording artists and record companies successfully sued to ensure their livelihood. These days users can buy music downloads and get many free samples to try out new bands; a visit to a site like www.mp3.com gives a glimpse into what is available. There are also many specialist sites offering the latest in everything from hip-hop to jazz to nu-metal and classical music. The Web has also become a place where fans can get information on groups, artists, and forthcoming events as well as lyrics and information on learning to play an instrument. It also showcases sites where new bands can perform in the hope of getting a recording contract.

Music_Bug – A virus that lays dormant for four months during which time it infects floppy disks. After four months, Music_Bug activates and plays a random tune when a floppy disk in accessed. Sometimes known as Music Boot.

Music Markup Language – *XML* software for incorporating music into web pages.

MusicMatch Jukebox– A popular MP3 player that allows the user to play and record CDs, organize and store music, watch video, and listen to digital radio. **GO TO:** www.musicmatch.com

mux – Abbreviation for *multiplexor*.

MX Record – **See:** **M**ail e**X**change **R**ecord

My Computer – In Microsoft *Windows*, all the information regarding the individual computer system can be accessed through the My Computer icon. This includes file locations, content, control panels, and peripherals, e.g. the hard drive and printers. **SEE: FEATURE BOX**

My Documents – In Microsoft *Windows*, this folder stores all the user's documents. **SEE: FEATURE BOX**

My Network – An overview of network information in Windows 2000 and Windows ME. In earlier versions it was called *Network Neighborhood*.

My Documents

The Microsoft Office folder that stores all the documents saved by the user.

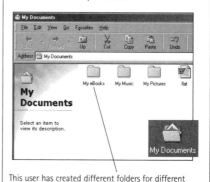

This user has created different folders for different personal files; e-books, music, and pictures.

n/n – (fraction) Refers to a large or indeterminate number of objects.

NAC – See: **n**egative **ac**knowledgement

NADF – See: **N**orth **A**merican **D**irectory **F**orum

nag screen – Window or screen in a *shareware* program reminding the user to register and pay the fee.

nagware – Shareware that on opening and closing displays a *nag screen*.

nailed down – A permanent connection on a telecommunications line; e.g. a leased, private, point-to-point line.

naïve user – (slang) A play on the term *native* meaning inexperienced or stupid user. Pejorative only if used to mean stupid.

NAK – See: negative acknowledgement

.name – One of the seven new domain names introduced in 2000. It denotes a site related to a named person.

name daemon – *UNIX* process translating hostnames into *TCP/IP* Internet addresses.

name mangling – Adding or changing characters in a name.

name resolution – The process of resolving an *IP address* to a name understood by the network. E.g. Using a *domain name server* to locate an individual computer on the Internet.

name server – A *domain name server* on the Internet that provides a *name resolution* service.

named pipes – A means of exchanging data between two entities or processes on the same computer. Named pipes are for IPC (Inter Process Communications), used within the computer, not between computers. Also called a *FIFO* as the first data written is the first read.

namespace – Unique group of names that follow a recognized convention to identify the resources on a network. In a small *LAN* the namespace may be limited to a small set of users. On the Internet the namespace is in the millions and uses a hierarchical structure employing *top level domain* names such as .com, .net, and .org to help identify each site on the system.

naming services – Software used for translating a name into a physical address on a network, acting rather like a telephone directory for the network; e.g. taking a username and finding the exact computer on the network with which it corresponds. Names are assigned for shared resources such as databases, computers, and programs on a widely distributed system such as the Internet. This allows all users of the system to access shared resources and locate resources even if they have moved.
SEE ALSO: DOMAIN NAME SERVER, WINS, DIRECTORY SERVICE

NAND – Not AND. A *Boolean* operation is true if any one of its inputs is false.

nannyware – **See:** net filtering software, parental control.

nano- – A prefix meaning one billion – one thousand million.

nanometer – One billionth of a meter.

nanosecond – One billionth of a second.

nanotechnology – Science that concentrates on building devices at the molecular and atomic level.

NAP – **See:** Network Access Point

NAPLPS – **See:** North American Presentation-Level Protocol Syntax

Napster – Created in 1999 by Shawn Fanning as a means of sharing files through a central file server. It ended up causing a revolution in the music industry, however, as millions used the technology to download, swap, and share *MP3* files of their favorite bands. The music industry eventually sued Napster on behalf of musicians who felt they were being cheated. A membership subscription service is now being planned, which will ensure artists and record companies get paid a percentage for what has been downloaded.
Go to: www.napster.com
See also: MUSIC

narrowband – A kind of transmission channel that will carry only one single signal at any one time. It is capable of transmitting data from 50 bps to 64 Kbps.

narrowcasting – Describes the process by which video is transmitted to a selected audience via the television or World Wide Web; for example, paid-for cable television.

NAS – **See:** Network Attached Storage

nastygram – 1. A malicious e-mail message, or *letterbomb*.
2. A *Daemon* error message.

NAT – **See:** Network Address Translation.

National Center for Supercomputing Applications (NCSA) – The organization that played a key part in the technical development of the Internet and created the Mosaic web browser.
Go to: www.ncsa.uiuc.edu

national characters – Describes characters that do not appear in English, nor in the basic *ASCII* character set; for example, accents, or those characters that vary from one country to another, such as the dollar sign $. These national characters are modified on international keyboards by using the extended ASCII and ANSI character sets.

National Information Infrastructure (NII) – The US government's policy group for managing advanced technology, they were enthusiastic about the Internet from the start and proposed it be made available to rich and poor alike, but that it should be funded by private industry.

National Information Standards Organization (NISO) – A US-based organization that writes standards that are for both traditional and information technology services.

National Research and Education Network (NREN) – A supercomputer network dedicated to High Performance Computing and Communication.

National Science Foundation (NSF) – A US governmental body charged with the fostering and support of American research. It played an important role in the early development of the Internet.
Go to: www.nsf.gov/

National TV Standards Committee (NTSC) – This is a color TV standard developed in the US that broadcasts 30 interlaced frames per second using a composite of red, green, and blue signals. The standard has been adopted by many countries including Canada, Japan, South Korea, and several Central and South American countries.

native – In computer systems, this term means basic or in the original state.

native mode – The normal operating mode of a computer.

natural language – All human languages are natural language; that is, they evolved naturally. Contrasts with the development of those languages that can be described as being logically constructed. Those computer programs that are written to resemble human languages rather than resembling logical languages, are usually referred to as natural languages.

natural language processing – This term is used to describe the comprehension and the generation of natural human languages by a computer. For example, natural language processing is used by the kind of voice responsive filtering systems popular with customer service departments.

natural language query – A query sent to a search engine or database that the user types in English, Spanish, or any other spoken language, as opposed to having to use single words or Boolean operators. *Ask Jeeves* is one search engine that operates by enabling users to submit this kind of natural language query. It operates by asking the user to type in a question.

natural language recognition – Natural language recognition is synonymous with voice recognition.

navigation – To go from one location to another on the World Wide Web using *hypertext links*.

navigation agent – Synonymous with navigation assistant.

navigation assistant– Software that enables the user to navigate the Internet.

navigation bar – (nav bar) Directional buttons or graphic images used on a web site to help the user move around the site. They are usually in a row or column on each web page.

navigation keys – Keys on the keyboard that enable the user to move around a page; namely the page up, page down, and the arrow keys.
SEE: FEATURE BOX

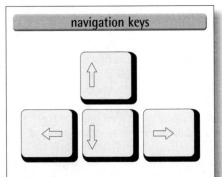

navigation keys

These four arrow keys appear on all computer keyboards. They can be used in most programs for moving the cursor around the screen.

Navigator – **See:** Netscape Navigator

NC – **See: n**etwork **c**omputer

NCSA – **See: N**ational **C**enter for **S**upercomputer **A**pplications

NDS – **N**ovell **D**irectory **S**ervices. A *directory service* from Novell, it contains a database of information about network resources, including networks, users, subgroups, servers, volumes, and printers.
SEE ALSO: NOVELL

near online – **See:** nearline

nearest neighbor – **See:** sampling

nearline – Information or data that is available within a short period of time, but not instantly. Tape and disk libraries are considered nearline devices, because they take a few seconds to retrieve the cartridge before it can be read. Contrast with online which is instantaneous.

neat stuff – Neat stuff can be described as interesting stuff; in other words, extraneous bits and pieces of information retrieved while surfing the Web that are viewed as a bonus rather than a hindrance.

NEBS compliant – **N**etwork **E**quipment **B**uilding **S**ystems compliant. This is a stringent standard for durability, cabling and hardware. It was developed by Bellcore for measuring equipment used in Telco central offices but has since been adopted elsewhere.

 **NEC** – Electronics company involved in development of computers, communication equipment, and software worldwide. Formerly Nippon Electric Co. Ltd.
Go to: www.nec.com

neep – Someone whose only passion in life is computers. Not necessarily a *nerd*.

negative acknowledgement – This phrase means not acknowledged. A communications code meaning the transmitted *package* was not received.

negative image – An image where the color values are inverted so that black becomes white, and blue becomes yellow.

nematic – The chemical stage between a crystal and a liquid which has a threadlike nature, e.g. the liquid crystal used in a *LCD*.

neologism – A newly invented word or term. The Internet and information technology in general is littered with neologisms that often prove daunting to the uninitiated.

nco-Luddite – One who adopts a Luddite philosophy towards the Internet. Luddites were English workers who, in the 1800s, smashed their new (Industrial Revolution) weaving and spinning equipment.

neophiliac – (slang) Someone overexcited at the thought of new technology.

 **NeoPlanet** – A commercial company that produces a web *browser* alternative to Internet Explorer and Netscape. It uses components from Internet Explorer to function. Its main point of difference is that it can be easily customized.
Go to: www.neoplanet.com

nerd – A person interested in technology or other intellectual pursuits who has a limited grasp on social skills and trends. The term has become less derogatory with the advancement of the Internet due to the financial success of nerds in setting up Web-based businesses. The term computer nerd is grudgingly used with some admiration. There is even a Nerd Pride movement which aims to educate children in the positive elements of being a nerd.

nerd rustler – A recruiter who specializes in finding employment for those working with computers.

nerdspeak – Alternative word for *hacker jargon*.

nesting – 1. To embed one object in another object of the same type. Occurs in in programming and applications, e.g. to place one document inside another.
See also: object linking and embedding
2. In formatting, to indent a block of text away from the left margin. This is usually to indicate a quotation or similar material.

.net – A top-level domain name for companies involved in networking or other closely related activities.

net/Net – 1. A network
2. Short for the Internet. It is usually capitalized in text.

NET Act – **N**o **E**lectronic **T**heft Act. This US legislation was passed in December 1997 with the intention of outlawing the unauthorized distribution of software over the Internet.
SEE ALSO: PIRACY

net address – **See:** IP address

net appliance – A device designed for accessing the Web and/or e-mail, e.g., *WAP*/smart phones, palmtops and Internet TV.

net filtering program – Software that aims to filter out sites that are unsuitable for unsupervised children's access.
SEE ALSO: PARENTAL CONTROL

net god – Someone who has been an important and influential person on the Internet for some time. This would include a moderator of a newsgroup or Bill *Gates*. Sometimes written as net.god or called a net.deity.
SEE ALSO: DIGERATI

net personality – A person who is well-known on the Internet

net phone – **See:** Internet phone

net police – A derogatory term for those who seek to moderate or restrict the material available on the Internet. Typically this is used in reference to newsgroup contributors who *flame* messages that do not conform to their own ideas.

net site – **See:** network site

net surfing – **See:** surf

net telephony – The telecommunications network and associated systems that enable the Internet.

Net Toob – A Windows multimedia player that can operate most formats found on the Internet, such as *MPEG*, AVI, and *QuickTime* for Windows.

netaddress – This is a *white pages* directory for Internet addresses. Its main advantage is that one query can be used to search a number of different directory services.

NetBEUI – **NetB**ios **E**xtended **U**ser **I**nterface. This refers to an improved version of *NetBIOS*.

NetBill – A business model that enables computer users to buy and sell intellectual property and information over the Internet.

NetBIOS – **Net**work **B**asic **I**nput/**O**utput **S**ystem. A program created by *IBM* that allows computers to communicate within a *local area network* (LAN).

NetBuddy – A facility that checks those web sites specified by the user in order to see if the site has been updated recently. Sites can be checked by NetBuddy at pre-determined times: every few minutes, daily, monthly, or however often the user requires. When changes occur to the site, the user is informed.

Netburst – Technology used in the *Intel Pentium* 4 chip that enables it to run with a 400Mhz system *bus*.

netcam – **See:** webcam

netcast – **See:** webcast

NetCenter – This is *Netscape Navigator's* web site.

netdead – Someone who is absent from the Net; not a permanent condition.

netfilter – **See:** filter, parental controls, censorware

Netfind – Netfind is the name that is used by *AOL* (America On-Line) for its own search engine.

nethead – (slang) Someone who is addicted to the Internet.

netid – **See:** IP address

netiquette – Network etiquette. Use of proper manners over the Internet. E.g. TYPING IN CAPITALS is considered to be like shouting, while typing everything in lower case can show laziness or a lack of concern.

netizen – A member of the Internet community. Sometimes refers to those who use the Net for political purposes.

netlag – A temporary loss of an Internet service caused by network delays.

net.legend – In Usenet, this refers to someone who is well-known and has made a positive contribution.

Netlib – This is a library of free software, information, and databases, mainly of scientific and mathematical interest. NetLib is run by the University of Tennessee and Oak Ridge National Labs.
Go to: www.netlib.org

NetLoad – A commercially available file transfer system that makes a mirror image of an offline web site on the user's PC, by uploading files to the user's online web site using *FTP*. In this way, sites can be updated without undue time delays or fuss.
Go to: www.netload.au.com

 **Netmanage** – A company that helps businesses transfer their traditional applications into systems accessible via the Internet.
Go to: www.netmanage.com

netmask – A string of 0s and 1s that when applied to an IP address screens out the host part. E.g. 255.255.255.0 means that the top 3 bytes are the network address and the 4th byte is the host address.

NetMeeting – Collaboration and conferencing software from *Microsoft*. It is built into *Internet Explorer* and includes telephone and videophone capability over the Internet, a virtual whiteboard, and also a level of application sharing.
GO TO:
www.microsoft.com/windows/netmeeting
SEE: FEATURE BOX

NetNanny – This is a program that enables the user to filter out certain types of web sites, e.g. those containing unwanted content such as pornography, when searching the Internet.
GO TO: www.netnanny.com

NetMeeting

NetMeeting is provided free with Windows 98 (and later versions of Windows) and with Internet Explorer. It enables users to chat, use video to communicate, collaborate in shared applications, and much more.

This basic screen shows that the user is not currently involved in a call.

NetNews – The *Usenet* news service.

netopath – (slang) The word is a combination of Internet and psychopath. It describes someone who is considered to be indulging in deviant behavior on the Internet.
SEE ALSO: CRACKER, BLACK HAT, AND COMPUTER VIRUS

NetPC – A network computer developed by *Microsoft* and *Intel* that has been designed to work as cost effectively as possible. The NetPC's main functions are as normal but its management functions are performed via a server, and many peripheral functions are inhibited. NetPCs do have a hard disk but this is used as a *cache* to enhance performance. Many large companies use a NetPC system.

Net–savvy – To have considerable knowledge of the Internet, how it works, and how to get the best out of it.

Netscape (Netscape Communications Corporation) – One of the Internet's seminal companies, now owned by *AOL*. James Clark and Marc Andreessen, who, along with Eric Bina, created the *Mosaic* browser at the University of Illinois, founded Netscape in 1994. It produces Internet software and applications.
GO TO: www.netscape.com

Netscape color palette – A suite of 216 colors that is peculiar to Netscape. It is used on both the Windows and Mac versions of the browser.

Netscape Communicator – The suite of browsing and editing applications from *Netscape* that were packaged as a bundle. The Netscape Communicator suite included a web browser, e-mail client, HTML editor, and conferencing software.

Netscape LiveWire – A suite of development programs and tools that is used to produce Netscape-based web sites.

Netscape Messenger – This is the name of the e-mail service that is packaged with the *Netscape Communicator* and offers many integrated functions.

Netscape Navigator – *Netscape's* web browser for Windows and Macintosh. It provides secure transmission over the Internet, and rivals Internet Explorer.

Netscape Netcaster – No longer available, Netcaster was part of the *Netscape Communicator* package. It allowed users to subscribe to many content channels, from news to hobbies and sport. It updated automatically, when online.

Netscape newsgroup – This is the component of *Netscape Communicator* that enables the user to access and use Internet *newsgroups*.

Netscape preferences – A set of instructions that enables the user to personalize the way *Netscape* is set up. Go ᴛᴏ: http://my.netscape.com or go to the toolbar, select Edit, then Preferences and adjust accordingly.

NetShow – A *Microsoft* system that provides audio and video over the Internet without interruption or interference.

netsourcing – This describes the process of outsourcing work that can be carried out over the Web.

netspeak – The language and vocabulary associated with the Internet. The entire content of this book is netspeak.

netsplits – This is the term used when a *server* goes down and disconnects from the Internet. When the server comes back it is called a "netjoin."

netter – Describes someone who uses Usenet regularly.

nettie – Someone who regularly contributes to *newsgroups*.

net-top box – The set-top box used with Internet TV.

NetView – This is a network management system developed by *IBM*.

netwar – Damage caused by corrupting the computers that manage vital services such as power, emergency services, and telecommunications. Usually launched via a virus such as 1999's Explore.zip worm, which caused significant disruption.
Go to: www.infowar.com

NetWare – **See:** Novell NetWare

NetWare certification – Certification for technical competence undertaken by *Novell.* Levels include: CNA (Certified NetWare Administrator), CNE (Certified NetWare Engineer), CNI (Certified NetWare Instructor), and ECNE (Enterprise CNE).

NetWatch – Another product from *Netscape*, this is *Netscape* Navigator's built-in ratings protection feature. NetWatch lets the user control what kind of web pages can be viewed.

network – The term network describes the situation when two or more computers are connected together, and includes the hardware and software used to connect them. There are two main types of network: a *local area network* (LAN), which is comprised of computers linked by cables within a single building; and a *wide area network* (WAN), which is comprised of computers connected together in distant locations via telecommunications lines. Inter-company networks are often WANs. The Internet is the largest WAN.
SEE: FEATURE BOX

network access point (NAP) – Major Internet interconnection points that link together the Internet access providers.
SEE ALSO: NSFNET

network accounting – The monitoring of network usage. It provides details regarding user activity, including number of logons, resources used, databanks accessed, and CPU time.

network adapter – A *card* that plugs into an expansion socket in the computer and transmits data between computers on a network using cables.

---

network

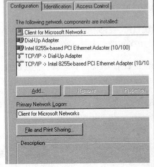

This is the Network Control Panel for the Windows operating system. The configuration tab, shown here, lists the network components that are installed on the user's computer.

The TCP/IP Dial-up Adapter that appears in this list is required for an Internet connection.

network address translation (NAT) - A standard that allows the owner of a *local-area network (LAN)* to use one set of *IP addresses* for internal traffic and another set of addresses for external traffic.

network administrator - A person responsible for the day-to-day management and maintenance of the computers on a network and associated devices. Sometimes called the *systems administrator*.

network architecture - This describes all features that comprise the design of a network, including the hardware, the software, the method of connection, and the protocols used.

network attached storage (NAS) - A type of *server* that is dedicated to file sharing storage only.

network closet - The installation area for network hardware and other network-related paraphernalia.

network computer - 1. Any computer within a network.
2. Computers within a network where management functions are performed centrally via a *server*, and many peripheral functions are inhibited for efficiency. There are many variations of network computer, and many systems available.

network configuration - See: network architecture

network driver - The software that is capable of managing the transmission and the receipt of data over the network.

network effect - The result of increased Internet accessibility and content has been to encourage even more computer users and others to seek Internet access. The same effect was seen with telephones and faxes. The network effect drives compatibility and protocol solutions.

Network File System (NFS) - A *client/server* application that enables network users to access and manipulate shared files stored on computers of differing types.

network management - This term generally describes the smooth administration of a networked system. Network management is the responsibility of the *network administrator*.

network meltdown - In those situations when the network becomes overloaded and the network's performance becomes very slow or grinds to a halt, the likely result is that the system crashes. This phenomenon is called network meltdown.

network news transfer protocol (NNTP) - NNTP is a part of the *Internet Protocol* that manages the posting and retrieval of messages that are sent to a newsgroup. All kinds of newsreader software must abide by the network news transfer protocol.

Network Neighborhood – In Microsoft Windows this folder appears by default, listing the computers, printers, and other resources connected to your *local area network* (LAN), but only if you are connected to a LAN.
SEE: FEATURE BOX

network operating system – A generic term for an operating system that handles computers on a network. The system usually runs on a dedicated server linked to other computers on the network. It manages shared resources, such as databases and printers, and performs security checks. Novell NetWare, Windows for Workgroups, and AppleTalk are all network operating systems.

network printer – A printer shared by computers on a network.

network neighborhood

The network neighbourhood folder will show all the connections in your LAN.

Network Neighborho

This folder contains links to all the computers in your workgroup and on the entire network.

The connections will be shown as small icons in the folder, and might include printer, scanners, shared drives, and any other digital add-ons.

network protocol – The communications protocol adopted by a network.
SEE ALSO: **OSI**

network security – Describes restricted access to files and directories in a network. Authorized users are assigned an ID and password for access either to a limited area of the network or to the entire network.

network service provider (NSP) – A company that provides backbone services such as high-speed phone lines to an *Internet service provider* (ISP).

network site – A site where a number of network services are managed together and considered as a single unit.

network topology – **See:** topology

network weaving – An attack that relies on the use of a third party computer to break through the network's security.

networking – 1. In information technology, the design, configuration, and use of a network.
2. Generally, networking means exploiting connections to increase useful business contacts.

neural networks – Computer operations that mimic the operation of the human brain. Such processes rely on a bank of processors, each of which performs a specialized task.
SEE ALSO: **ARTIFICIAL INTELLIGENCE**

Neuroquila – An infectious boot sector virus. Once a computer is infected, the disk drives can only be seen when the virus is in memory. If you boot the computer from a floppy disk that does not have the virus, the drives are not accessible. About three months after infection, the virus displays the following text: "by Neurobasher Germany '93/Germany -GRIPPED-BY-FEAR-UNTIL-DEATH-US-DO-PART-." The Neuroquila *computer virus* targets the *antivirus* programs ThunderByte and Central Point Anti-Virus, to attempt to prevent them from detecting the virus. It is also known as Havoc or Wedding.

new economy – The terrific rise and influence of information technology companies in the economy. After the dotcom failures in 2000 and 2001, the new economy was viewed with more scepticism.

new media – General term for advances in computer technology since the static black and white text era. It encompasses both *multimedia* and *hypermedia* features, including: special audiovisual effects, such as *GIF*s and animation; interactive graphical user interfaces, virtual reality environments and effects; live Internet broadcasting; streaming video and audio; DVD; CD-ROMs and music CDs; online services; mobile computing; person-to-person visual communication; integration of telecommunications with computer operations; video- and teleconferencing.

new public network – The Internet-enabled telephone network supporting voice, video, and data transmission. Also called the next generation.

newbie – (slang) A newcomer to the Internet: someone unaware of how the system works. Used with a mixture of compassion and exasperation, this is not a derogatory term.

news – Top-level category for newsgroups with discussions focusing on network news.

news posting – An e-mail sent to a newsgroup.

news server – A computer that manages access to a newsgroup. All users connect to the news server to access or post messages to the newsgroup.

news site – A web site dedicated to current affairs. Such sites operate in real time, bringing the latest developments almost instantly.

news ticker – A ticker that feeds news headlines constantly to the user. These can be run across the display regardless of the application in operation.

newsfeed – 1. A news source that provides an *Internet Service Provider* with news updates, which are posted to newsgroups. 2. The transmission of news stories from source to news servers, services, and news broadcasters.

newsfroup – Originally a typographical error, now adopted to mean a newsgroup with bizarre or lunatic content.

newsgroup – A *discussion group* or *forum* with a particular specialization run over the *Usenet* discussion network on the Internet. Members post messages for everyone to read, and other users respond by sending e-mail messages to individuals or to the newsgroup. There are thousands of newsgroups, devoted to subjects ranging from current affairs, and space exploration, to detailed discussions about software and hardware performance. To access a newsgroup, a user must have access to a *newsreader*: software able to post and read newsgroup postings. Newsgroups can be *moderated* or unmoderated. Moderated groups have their postings screened to ensure that postings are relevant. There is a hierarchical structure in newsgroup naming to identify the topic of the newsgroup. Of the thousands of newsgroups in hundreds of categories, the following are the major categories:

- **alt** (alternate)
- **comp** (computers)
- **humanities** (arts and culture)
- **misc** (miscellaneous)
- **news** (news and current events)
- **rec** (recreational)
- **sci** (science)
- **soc** (social)
- **talk** (general discussion)

SEE ALSO: ORGANIZATIONAL HIERARCHY for a full description of how the Usenet network is categorized.

SEE: FEATURE BOX

newsgroup war – A heated debate about the status of a newsgroup: should one be set up, split, or deleted?

newsletter – A regular letter published by an organization to inform interested parties of news, new developments, event listings, and special offers, etc. e-mailed newsletters afford a standard way of disseminating information over the Internet and many sites give the visitor the option to sign up for a newsletter.

---

newsgroup

This example shows nine examples from the tens of thousands of newsgroups available on the Usenet network. These newsgroups were returned after a search for the word "computer."

News groups matching search (computer)

GROUP NAME	TOTAL ARTICLES
alt.binaries.domirion.dads.computer	12
alt.binaries.domirion.moms.computer	7
alt.binaries.hacking.computers	25
02.computertalk.01.amiga-talk	1
alt.ads.forsale.computers	257
alt.bestjobsusa.computer.jobs	1746
alt.business.import-export.computer	87
alt.chess.japanese.computer	5
alt.computer	2007

The column on the right shows the number of articles in each newsgroup at the time of searching.

newsreader – Software necessary for reading or posting contributions to *newsgroups*. The software is often integrated into the *browser* and offered as an *online service*. A newsreader should be able to filter the most relevant postings and provide help in following threads. It should also provide an offline facility for reading postings, and a search facility.

newswatcher – Once a commercial program, the term newswatcher is now used for any program that monitors the online news services for specific stories or topics, relaying them to the user's desktop.

Nexor – A commercial company specializing in the secure transfer of data and communication.
Go to: www.nexor.com

next generation – **See:** new public network

next generation Internet – **See:** Internet 2.

NFS – **See:** network file system

nibble – Half a byte (four bits). It can also be spelled nybble.

NIC – Network Interface Card. A *card* that is installed in a computer so that it can be connected to a network.

NiCad – **Ni**ckel-**cad**mium. The oldest type of battery used in portable computers, now mostly replaced by nickel metal hydride.

nick – (slang) This is an abbreviation for *nickname*, which is used on Internet Relay Chat (*IRC*).

nickname – 1. A codename or playful name used on the *Net*. Internet address books have a *field* for contacts' nicknames and provide the facility to search for people by nickname.
2. All users on Internet Relay Chat have the option to adopt a nickname, and most use this option.

NII – **See:** National Information Infrastructure

NiMH – **Ni**ckel-**M**etal **H**ydride. This is the rechargable battery that is popular for use in many portable computers, cellular phones, and camcorders.

Nintendo – The company that produces arcade-like video games, each with its own *games console*. The consoles can be attached to a modem, and users can play on XBAND, which is an interactive, multiplayer games network.

NNTP – **See:** Network News Transfer Protocol

no wait state memory – A type of memory that is fast enough to meet the demands of the CPU.

noddy – A word derived from the children's story books. It is used to describe a simple program that is written to illustrate a point, particularly for new users or someone learning a new language. Another similar term is mickey mouse.

node – An end point or connection point on a network; e.g. a home computer, a printer, or a router.

noise – This term refers to interference on a telecommunications signal. Common causes for this include power lines, heavy machinery operation, and electromagnetic radiation from other devices, TVs, or radios.

noise reduction – In computer graphics, this is the manipulation of an image to remove unwanted effects from the image.

nom – A proposed new *domain name* that is given to an individual.

Non Disclosure Agreement (NDA) – An agreement signed between two parties who have to disclose confidential information to one other. Signing the NDA prevents this information being passed to other parties.

nondelivery – In e-mail, nondelivery is when a message cannot be delivered to its destination. The message transfer agent generates a nondelivery report, which is delivered as e-mail to the sender.

nondelivery notification service – A service that informs the sender of a nondeliverable e-mail that their message was not delivered to its destination, and gives a reason why.
SEE ALSO: NONDELIVERY

nonillion – Ten to the power of 30 (US and Canada); 10 to the power of 54 (Europe).

non-impact printer – A printer that prints without striking the paper; e.g. inkjet and laser printers.

noninterlaced – A method of display that shows every line of data in one pass over the screen. Such displays do not flicker.
SEE ALSO: INTERLACED

non-linear video – Video that is neither viewed nor edited in a linear sequence. CD-ROMs and LaserDiscs enable the user to go from frame to frame in any order.

non-parity memory – Memory chips without a ninth chip for checking *parity*. These are used to check for system processing or network errors.
SEE ALSO: PARITY CHECKING

non-preemptive multitasking – A *multitasking* situation where one program dominates another. The program running in the background is given processing time only when the dominant foreground program hands over control, e.g. when an instruction is completed.

non-virtual hosting – To host a web site for an individual within the same *domain*

name as that of the hosting service provider. Generally this provides the users with free web space in return for some advertising on the user's web page.
SEE ALSO: VIRTUAL HOSTING

nonvolatile memory – A type of *memory* that saves content when a computer is turned off or loses power; e.g. a floppy disk.

nooksurfer – A person who *surfs* a small specialist area of the Internet.

NOR – Not OR. A *Boolean* operation which is true if none of its inputs are true, and false if any one of its inputs is true.

North American Directory Forum (NADF) – The NADF is a group of organizations that offer directory services in North America.

North American Presentation-Level Protocol Syntax (NAPLPS) – A protocol for videotex and teletext *compression* used for data transmission over narrow bandwidth lines.

Northern Light – This is a search and research engine that accesses full-text documents within well defined categories known as folders.

 Norton AntiVirus – A widely available anti-virus program from Symantec; formerly from Peter Norton Computing.
SEE ALSO: NORTON, PETER

Norton, Peter – Peter Norton is synonymous with computer efficiency; he introduced the concept of fine-tuning a computer to ensure it worked at peak performance. He has written many books on getting the best out of computers and sold his company to Symantec, a leading Internet security company, in 1990.
SEE ALSO: NORTON UTILITIES

 Norton Utilities – A suite of security and efficiency programs developed by Peter Norton and available from Symantec.
GO TO: www.norton.com

NOS – See: Network Operating System

NOT – A *Boolean* operation that performs a logical negation. In a Boolean search you might specify "fly NOT insect" to find sites whose content is related to flight without also listing those interested in flies.
SEE ALSO: AND, OR

notebook – Notebook can describe the kind of portable personal computer about the size of a looseleaf paper notebook, but which contains a flat, hinged LCD screen, and holds a small keyboard. Notebooks of this kind are usually smaller and lighter than laptop computers.

notwork – This term is used to mean an unreliable or faulty network
SEE ALSO: NYETWORK

Novell - Founded as Novell Data Systems in 1981 by Jack Davis and George Canova, Novell is now one of the leading makers of operating systems for networks.
Go to: www.novell.com

Novell NetWare - This is probably the most widely used server *operating system* for PC networks, available from Novell.
Go to: www.novell.com

NOW project - Network Of Workstations. The NOW project is a computing project coordinated by the University of California at Berkeley. Its aim is to discover ways for improving high-speed connections between multiple computers.
SEE ALSO: BEOWULF

NP - Number Portability. The ability to keep your telephone number when you switch to another *Internet Service Provider*.

NREN - See: National Research and Education Network

NRG - (slang) A term used in chat rooms and newsgroups meaning energy.

ns - Nanosecond. A billionth of a second.

NSAPI - Netscape Server API. A server application interface that is used for web-based programs.
SEE ALSO: API

NSF - See: National Science Foundation

NSFNET - National Science Foundation Network. This was an early form of the Internet. NFSNET was a precursor of the modern Internet designed for academic use. It was surpassed in the mid-1990s.
SEE ALSO: NATIONAL SCIENCE FOUNDATION

nslookup - A program that finds an *IP address* from a *hostname*.

NSI - Network Solutions, Inc. Now part of VeriSign Inc., NSI provides network and web site infrastructure services, particularly in secure business transactions.
Go to: www.netsol.com

NSP - See: Network Service Provider

NT - New Technology.

NTP - Network Time Protocol. A method by which clocks on computers can be synchronized with atomic or radio clocks accessed over the Internet.

NTSC - See: National TV Standards Committee

NTSC port - Analog video connection, usually providing input for an analog video source, such as a camcorder or standard VCR.

nuke - To erase permanently.

null modem - The connection of two PCs via their serial ports to exchange files or play games. Also called *modem eliminator*.

number crunching – (slang) Automatic computing of enormous amounts of mathematical calculations.

Number Lock – The key operating the keyboard in numerical entry mode. This is shortened to Num Lock key.

number sign – The # character, also known as *hash*.

numeric keypad – A section of a computer keyboard, located to the right of the typewriter keys, that consists of number keys and arrow keys, which are used to move the cursor.

nut cluster – A group of people who play *MUD* games.

NVRAM – **N**on-**v**olatile **R**andom **A**ccess **M**emory. Permanent memory that does not rely on the power supply.
SEE ALSO: NON-VOLATILE MEMORY, RANDOM ACCESS MEMORY

nyetwork – An unreliable or unworkable network. From the Russian for no, "nyet."
SEE ALSO: NOTWORK

nym – Short for pseudonym – a name adopted by a user to hide their true identity or to create a new Internet persona. There are many legitimate reasons for communicating anonymously; e.g. to reveal something in the public interest, which might cost the user their job. A *remailer* service can also protect identities.

nymrod – Someone who is unable to resist turning words and phrases into *acronyms*.

OA - **O**ffice **A**utomation. An office that is networked through a *LAN,* which allows office functions to be fully integrated. This includes word-processing, data processing, graphics, desktop publishing, and e-mail.

ob - (slang) Short for obligatory.

object - A self-contained chunk of data that has a function. Within the data are instructions for the operations to be performed on it; e.g. a graphic, a file, or a form is an object.

object linking and embedding (OLE) - A feature within *Windows* and certain other software, e.g. *Microsoft Office,* that allows an *object* created in one program to be *linked* or *embedded* into another. To transfer objects the user should use the Special Paste option in the Edit menu.

Object Management Group (OMG) - A group of companies and organizations involved in the set up of the *Common Object Request Broker Architecture* (CORBA). This is technology that helps manipulate objects between various applications on a network.

object request broker (ORB) - Software that enables objects on several *remote* computers to interact with each other using messages. The software directs the messages to their destinations and deals with any subsequent replies.
SEE ALSO: **CORBA**

object request conferencing - Software that manages communication between a client and an *object* on a server.

object-oriented - A computer function or program that is based on discrete *objects.*

object-oriented graphics - Graphical features that are written as mathematical formulae. These include geometric shapes such as circles and lines.
SEE ALSO: VECTOR GRAPHICS

object-oriented programming (OOP) - A program that is written so that its pieces work as discrete, functioning units, which can interact within the program.

object-oriented technology - Software development that uses *objects* as the basis of applications.

oblique stroke - Another term for the *forward slash* "/" character.

obliqueness - In typography, the degree to which type leans, either to the right or left. E.g. *Italic* fonts are slanted. Some programs allow the user to modify the degree of slant.

OC - **O**ptical **C**arrier. The speed of transmissions carried by optical devices.
SEE ALSO: FIBER OPTICS

OCR - See: **O**ptical **C**haracter **R**ecognition

octopus cable - A cable that is spliced into several lines, each of which has a separate connector.

OCX - *Active X* file *extension*. An *object linking and embedding* control that is used for such features as window resizing and scroll bar operation.

octet - 1. The four numbers in an *IP address*, which have eight positions when viewed in binary form. They are split into *net* and *host*: net identifies the network, and host or *node* indicates the particular computer or device.
2. A byte that consists of eight bits.

octothorpe - The # symbol, more commonly called the *hash* mark, number sign, or square sign.

offline

This dial-up connection gives the user the option of working offline, or connecting.

odd header - A *header* or line of text at the top of the page that appears on only odd numbered pages.

odd parity - A simple formula for checking accuracy of trasmitted data. When making a connection to an *Internet Service Provider* or other online service, the system must be set up to accept either odd or *even parity*.
SEE ALSO: PARITY

ODI - **See:** **O**pen **D**ata-link **I**nterface

odor - A technology that hopes to enhance realism on the Internet by introducing odor-making peripherals. One such device is called I-smell, developed by DigiScents. The manufacturer has indexed the chemical structure of thousands of smells. These files can then be embedded in web page content or in e-mails, and are triggered by a mouse click or opening the message. Vapor is then released by the *peripheral device*.

OEM - **See:** **O**riginal **E**quipment **M**anufacturer

off hook (OH) - A light on a *modem* indicating that the modem is switched on and ready to receive data.

off the grid - The time when a user is not connected to the Internet.

off the trolley - A program that is malfunctioning.

off topic – In chat rooms and newsgroups, a response to a question that is inappropriate. Can be abbreviated to OT.

Office, Microsoft – **See:** Microsoft Office

offline – 1. A computer that does not have a live link to a network. Some users prefer to compose e-mails offline, and then go online just to send them.
SEE: FEATURE BOX
2. A printer that is powered up but not ready to receive data input. To prevent printing during an operation, it is possible to turn the printer into offline mode so it cannot accept more data.

offline advertising – Advertising a web site and its URL in conventional media such as newspapers, magazines, radio, and TV.

offline browsing – The ability to copy whole web sites and e-mail them to the home or office computer so that they may be browsed at leisure without using slow or costly telephone lines.

offline reader – A program that downloads e-mail or other material from an online service, to be read offline.

offline world – The real world outside the Internet.

offload – To take work from one computer to process on another.

offset – In word-processing, the distance a document is printed from the left margin.

offset printing – A printer that uses a cylinder known as a blanket to transfer the image onto the paper. The printing is first offset onto the blanket and then to paper, in contrast to most printers which transfer the image directly onto paper.

off-site storage – Files, disks, and tape stored away from the computer's location to provide backup in case of loss.

OH – **See:** Off Hook

OK – This is a very common on-screen *button* that is generated by a program or operating system for the user to click on, in order to confirm an action or command. Often, alongside the OK button is a Cancel button which, if pressed, returns the user to their prior action.

OLE – **See:** Object Linking and Embedding

OLED – **See:** Organic LED

OLTP – **See:** Online Transaction Processing

OM-Express – An *offline* Internet *browser* that automatically dials up and downloads web pages and stores them for *offline* reading. Developed by Open Market, Inc., Cambridge, Massachusetts.

OMG – **See:** Object Management Group

on board – A *chip* or other hardware device that is directly attached to the *motherboard*.

on hook – A telephone line that is able to receive incoming calls.

on-the-fly – A web page that has *dynamic* content.; it changes frequently while the program is running, such as money market reports and news.

one-click buying – To buy goods on the Web by clicking a single button on the web page. The user's name, address, and credit card information is stored on the vendor's server or kept within a *cookie* on the user's computer. This way, the site automatically knows the customer, and the customer's payment details. Many web sites offer this function as a fast way to shop on the Internet.
SEE ALSO: DIGITAL WALLET

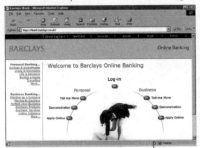

online banking

Customers on most online bank web sites can choose between personal or business banking.

The padlock symbol indicates to the user that the site is secure.

one-way function – **See:** one-way hash function

one-way hash function – In *cryptography*, a way of generating a fixed string of numbers from a text message. It is one-way because of the difficulty in translating the fixed string back into the text message. This technique is used to create *digital signatures*.

Onion, The – An American adult satirical online newspaper, renowned for its humor and spoof news items.
Go to: www.theonion.com

⌀the ONION®

online (on-line)– 1. An active link to any network or the Internet. Contrast with *offline*.
2. Any activity that takes place on the Internet as opposed to the "real" world, e.g. online chat, *online banking*.

online advertising – The use of the Internet to advertise goods and services. Techniques include e-mail messages, *banner ads*, special offers and inducements, sponsored software and, increasingly, the targeted use of Internet-enabled *WAP* phones.

online bank – A bank that offers full banking services via the Internet. Some banks are uniquely e-banks; they have no branch outlets and rely completely on their web site to carry out business. The resulting reduction in overhead is supposedly passed on to the customer in reduced transaction charges.

online banking – A banking service that is accessed via a bank's web site – at any time. Different banks offer customers different services online, but typically users can check accounts, move money between accounts, and pay bills on the Internet.
SEE: FEATURE BOX

online business – **See:** e-business, e-commerce

online chat – **See:** chat

online community – **See:** virtual community

online content provider – An *Internet Service Provider* that also provides *content*. This includes exclusive chat rooms, and information services. *America Online* is probably one of the most successful. More generally, it has come to mean any web site that offers content such as online newspapers and encyclopedia sites.

online coupons – An *online service* that sends discount coupons from e-commerce companies as a purchasing incentive.

online dictionary – A dictionary that is accessed online. Some dictionaries are free, others require a subscription for the service.
GO TO: www.dictionary.com

online gaming community – 1. Those committed to playing computer games online. These include interactive games, role playing games, and more traditional games as well.
2. Those who gamble online.

online help – Software, hardware, and Internet support offered via web pages. Sometimes this comes in the form of a downloadable information manual, *Frequently Asked Questions*, or by providing the opportunity to post a question to customer support services.

online industry – A generic term for the companies which enable online services and commerce.

online loan – A bank loan arranged over the Internet. These often offer favorable terms due to lower overheads.

online penpal – Similar to a regular pen pal - someone with whom a person communicates in letter form, but the relationship is conducted over the Internet via e-mail. Also known as an e-pal.

online profile – Information about a customer held by the *Internet Service Provider* or by a *user* of a *network*.

Online Public Access Catalog (OPEC) – A bibliography of a library collection that is available to the public via the Internet. Most libraries have made their OPEC accessible world-wide.

online service provider – Company supplying exclusive online *content*, often with an exclusive *web browser*, *chat rooms*, and shopping areas.
SEE ALSO: AMERICA ONLINE, MSN, INTERNET SERVICE PROVIDER, ONLINE CONTENT PROVIDER

online services – E-mail, databases, information services, shopping, news, and games, provided by an *Internet Service Provider*, *online service provider,* or *online content provider.* Such services are generally charged by monthly fee.

online stalker – Someone who gains the trust of another person in a chat room with the intent to harass or pursue that person.

online storefront – An e-commerce web site that provides goods for sale. The store is able to handle the financial transaction online, and may or may not have a *bricks-and-mortar* presence.

online trading – The buying and selling of stocks and shares online. More generally referred to as *e-commerce.*

online transaction – A financial operation or business arrangement that is carried out online; e.g. purchasing, stock control, travel services, banking.
SEE ALSO: ONLINE BANKING

online transaction processing – Processing *online transactions* on the computer in real time.

online voting – An election system that relies on *encryption* to allow voters to transmit their secret votes over the Internet. Such systems are currently in use for organizations, but it is expected that national government elections may adopt this facility in the future.

on-screen display (OSD) – The on-screen control panel that is used to adjust contrast, brightness, and horizontal and vertical positioning on computer monitors and TV screens. Normally accessed via the mouse, most computer monitors also have button controls attached to the monitor to allow users to change displays..

ontology – Used to describe a system and its component parts. In metaphysics, the term means the study of the nature of reality.

OOBE – **O**ut **O**f **B**ox **E**xperience. The action of setting up and customizing a new computer or software package.

OOP – See: **O**bject-**O**riented **P**rogramming

open – To access a program or file.
SEE ALSO: RUN

open air – A *wireless LAN protocol.*

open architecture – **See:** open source system.

Open Buying on the Internet (OBI) – A proposed standard to reduce e-commerce costs and to simplify and standardize

procedures. For example, the use of digital certificates to ensure that ordering and payment is secure. Open Buying on the Internet is aimed at business-to-business web sites with high-volume, low-cost-per-item transactions.
SEE ALSO: DIGITAL CERTIFICATE

open collar worker – Someone who uses the Internet and other mobile technologies to work from home.
SEE ALSO: REMOTE COMPUTING

Open Data-link Interface (ODI) – A standard that enables the transfer of text, graphics, and facsimiles between *operating systems*.

open file – A file that the operating system has made accessible to an application for processing.

Open eBook – A specification for electronic book content that allows it to be viewed on various devices, e.g. PC display, Personal Digital Assistant, and e-Book reader.
SEE ALSO: E-BOOK

Open Financial Exchange – A standard for the secure online transfer of financial data. Customers can safely interact with financial institutions to transfer funds, make payments, and download bank and credit card statements.
GO TO: www.ofx.net
SEE ALSO: ONLINE BANKING

Open Group, The – A consortium of some of the world's biggest computer companies; its aim is to promote *interoperability*: to ensure systems from different companies work together for greater efficiency.
GO TO: www.opengroup.org

open network – A network, e.g. the Internet, that is available for public use with few limitations or authentication.

open pipe – A continuous transmission line from sender to receiver. In an open pipe system it is not necessary to break transmitted data into *packets*.

open shortest path first – A system used in *routing* data around a *network*.

Open Source Movement – Influential movement proposing that programming codes for software should be *freeware*. This would provide the opportunity for people (usually *hackers*) to customize software and extend and improve its use for others. This is at odds with the huge corporations (e.g. *Microsoft*) who make their money by keeping their software codes secret and getting consumers to pay for the next (improved) update. This idealist movement is evident in the *Linux* operating system. However, the logical conclusion of this would be to remove all copyright and patent restrictions on software. Also known as the Free Software Movement.
SEE ALSO: BETA VERSIONS, COPYRIGHT, COPYLEFT, SHAREWARE, PATENT

Open Source Software – When the programming codes of software are publicly available so that others (often techies) may develop the software, which in turn is shared with others.
Go to: www.opensource.org
See also: copyleft, Linux, Mozilla

open standards – Hardware and software specifications that are publicly available. This enables components to be replaced or upgraded with those manufactured by a vendor other than the original manufacturer.

Open Systems Interconnection (OSI) – A system for organizing the exchange of data across networks that is based on a seven-layer model.
1. The presentation layer converts data into a format understood by other layers.
2. The application layer deals with e-mail and other applications.
3. The session layer manages the data flow between applications.
4. The transport layer handles communications between computers on a network.
5. The network layer manages the routing of data across the network.
6. The data link layer looks for and fixes transmission errors.
7. The physical layer works on the transmission of data packets at a hardware level.
See also: data communication

Open Trading Protocol (OTP) – An Internet standard aimed to create a consistent experience for consumers, regardless of the hardware and software that they are using, e.g. the transfer and delivery of goods and payment methods.

Open With – A *dialog box* requesting "Open with what application?" appears when a user tries to open a document by double clicking on it, but the document is not linked to any *application*. Some files are associated by their *file extensions* e.g. .doc and .zip, others have to be selected.
See: appendix 5 for file extensions.

opera – Popular web browser known for its reliability, speed and built-in zoom facility.
Go to: www.opera.com

OpenGL – **O**pen **G**raphics **L**ibrary. A 2D and 3D graphics *application program interface*.

operand – The data or object upon which an operation is to be performed.

operating system (OS) – The main control program that manages the essential hardware and peripheral resources of a computer, and provides services to application programs., running disks, memory, keyboard, screen, and CPU. Examples are *MS DOS, Macintosh OS, Windows*, and *UNIX*. The main function of the operating system is to manage the hardware and to mediate between it and the software to allow programs to run on different types of hardware.

operation – An action that, when applied to something (e.g. text, an image, or file) impacts and changes the original or produces a new entity.

operator – 1. Someone who just operates the computer, much like a bus driver. 2. In programming and logic, the code that performs an operation on some entity. *Boolean* operators are the AND, OR, NOT options that refine a search.

optical character recognition (OCR) – Software that can recognize text characters optically. OCR programs take images of scanned text in *bitmap* format and convert it into a form that can be edited with *word-processing* programs.

optical disk – A disk on which data is recorded and read by a laser beam. *CD-ROM*s and videodiscs are optical disks and are not rewritable. There are several forms of rewritable compact disks.
SEE ALSO: COMPACT DISK

optical disk library – **See:** jukebox

optical fiber – **See:** fiber optics

optical library – **See:** jukebox

optical mouse – A now defunct type of mouse that uses a light sensor to bounce off a special reflective mouse pad.
SEE ALSO: INFRA-RED

optical networking – Communications between computers or telecommunication devices which are based on fiber optics. Such systems are more efficient and have a greater capacity than wire-based systems.
SEE ALSO: FIBER OPTICS

optical reader – An input device that can recognize typed text, printed characters, and bar codes. It converts this data into assigned digital codes.

optical recognition – **See:** optical character recognition (OCR)

optical resolution – The resolution at which an optical scanner or camera captures an image. It is measured in *dots per inch* (dpi).

optical scanner – A device that uses light to scan text or pictures, and converts it into *bitmap* format for use by the computer.

optical technology – **See:** fiber optics

optical wireless – **See:** free space optics

optical zoom – To change the focal length of a *digital camera* with the use of lenses. Digital cameras also have digital zoom capabilities controlled by the software.

optimization – The tuning of the computer to run optimally for its intended use. E.g. A database server would be optimized in quite a different fashion than a web server.

optimizer program – *Software* that improves computer system performance.
SEE ALSO: DEFRAGGER

opt-in – To agree to something that is optional, e.g. to allow a web site to use your personal details for marketing purposes.

opt-in e-mail – E-mail that the recipient has chosen to receive from a web site.
SEE ALSO: OPT-IN MAILING LIST

opt-in mailing list – A mailing *list* that requires a member's permission for inclusion. A web site might use such a list for newsletters, advertising, and product and marketing updates.

option – 1. To select. This could be text formatting or making a choice when faced with different possibilities.
2. In software, the choices that enable a user to customize the program.
SEE ALSO: OPTIONS MENU

option buttons – Small circles commonly used for selecting options in an interactive form. The button is selected by clicking on it, which highlights it and deselects all other options. Also called radio buttons.
SEE: FEATURE BOX

Option key – The key on a Macintosh keyboard that activates special characters, such as accents, and a range of commands.

Options menu – The tools that enable the user to customize their computer or software such as browsers. In Windows, options are found in the Tools menu. Some programs call options *Preferences*.
SEE: FEATURE BOX

opt-out – To elect not to participate in a situation which is optional, e.g. users may decide against joining a mailing list.
SEE ALSO: OPT-IN

opt-out mailing list – A mailing list that includes everyone who does not make a positive decision to opt-out. This is a common method of collecting names and addresses for large mailing lists. Details are often less reliable than on opt-in lists.

optoelectronics – Technologies that combine light and electronics.

Oracle – A company whose main commercial activity is in database products.
GO TO: www.oracle.com

---

option buttons

Contents
● White
○ Background Color
○ Transparent

Circular buttons indicate the options available: the option selected (e.g. "white" here) is shown by a dark center circle.

Orange Book – US Government guidelines for secure computing, known as Trusted Computer Security Evaluation Criteria.

OR – One of the key *Boolean search* processes, OR searches on a two-word basis. E.g. Type "tree OR oak" into a search engine, and the resulting search will pull up documents indexed on the words tree or oak.
SEE ALSO: **AND, NOT**

ORB – **See:** **O**bject **R**equest **B**roker

.org – A top-level domain name that, purely by convention, indicates a non-profit making organization.

organic electroluminescent (OEL) – **See:** organic LED

organic LED (OLED) – A thin, film-based, light-emitting process to display bright images with low power demand.

organizational domain – The *top-level domain* that includes .com, .edu, .gov, .int, .mil, .net, and .org.

organizational hierarchy – In *Usenet*, the hierarchy system to categorize postings:
1. comp   computers
2. misc   miscellaneous
3. news   usenet itself
4. rec   recreational, hobbies
5. sci   science and technology
6. soc   social and cultural
7. talk   discussion, debate, and controversial issues

They are mainstream hierarchies. Alternative hierarchies have also been introduced including alt, bionet, bit, biz and k12. A second level of categorization is added after a dot to further refine the indexing. So comp.virus indicates a Usenet group interested in computer viruses.

Organizational Unique Identifier (OUI) – Part of a Mac address identifying the network adapter; registered with the IEEE.
Go TO: www.standards.ieee.org

organizer – Short for a *personal digital assistant* (PDA) or *personal information manager* (PIM). Also refers to any online personal, group, or club organizers.

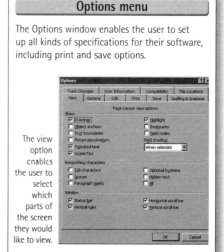

Options menu

The Options window enables the user to set up all kinds of specifications for their software, including print and save options.

The view option enables the user to select which parts of the screen they would like to view.

orientation – The way in which a page is held for printing. *Portrait* (when the paper is tall) is the default orientation; *landscape* refers to the paper held widthwise.

origin server – A web server that holds the original web page. This differentiates the web server from a *cache* server as there is no physical means of telling the two apart. The original server maintains and updates the page.

original equipment manufacturer – The company that manufactures a product.

originator – The person who writes, addresses, and sends a message.

orphan – When the last line of a paragraph appears alone at the top of a page. Most text-based programs set an orphan limit to a minimum of two lines.
SEE ALSO: WIDOW
SEE: FEATURE BOX

---

orphan

suscipit lobortis nisl ut aliquip ex ea commodo consequat.

Duis autem vel eum iriure dolor in hendrerit in vulputate velit esse molestie consequat, vel illum dolore eu feugiat nulla facilisis at. Lorem ipsum dolor sit amet, consectetuer adipiscing elit, sed diam nonummy nibh euismod tincidunt ut laoreet dolore magna aliquam erat volutpat. Ut wisi enim ad minim veniam, quis nostrud exerci tation ullamcorper suscipit lobortis nisl ut aliquip ex ea commodo consequat. Duis autem vel eum iriure dolor in hendrerit in vulputate velit esse molestie consequat, vel illum dolore eu feugiat nulla facilisis at. Lorem ipsum dolor sit amet, consectetuer adipiscing elit, sed diam nonummy nibh euismod tincidunt ut laoreet dolore magna aliquam erat volutpat. Ut wisi enim ad minim veniam, quis

This one-line orphan sits uncomfortably at the top of the page with a column of text hanging below it.

---

orphan link – A link with no corresponding *URL*.

OS – See: **O**perating **S**ystem

OS/2 – *Operating system* from *IBM* that can run OS/2, DOS and Microsoft Windows programs, and supports Presentation Manager graphical user interface.

oscillate – To move between minimum and maximum values. Typically used to describe a wave cycle where an oscillation is one complete cycle in an alternating frequency.

OSD – See: **O**n-**S**creen **D**isplay

OSI – See: **O**pen **S**ystem **I**nterconnection

OSP – See: **O**nline **S**ervice **P**rovider
SEE ALSO: INTERNET SERVICE PROVIDER (ISP)

OSPF – See: **O**pen **S**hortest **P**ath **F**irst

OTP – See: **O**pen **T**rading **P**rotocol

OUI – See: **O**rganizational **U**nique **I**dentifier

out of band – 1. (slang) Communication that is not an e-mail, e.g. *snail* mail. 2. A signal that is operating outside the primary frequency.

out of memory – A system resource warning that informs the user the system's memory is full. Other than increasing the memory capacity of the computer, certain actions can be taken to limit working memory requirements:

1. Keep windows minimized rather than displayed as full screen.
2. Remove data from the clipboard.
3. Turn off the desktop wallpaper in Control Panel.
4. Close non-vital running applications.

out of the box - **See:** OOBE

outboard devices - Devices that are not built into the main unit.
SEE ALSO: OFFBOARD

outbox - A *folder* in a *browser* where e-mail is stored before it is sent.

outdent - A paragraph in which the first line begins at the left margin, and the rest of the lines are indented. Also called a hanging *indent*.

outline - A screen view that shows the hierarchy of headings and organization of a table in text processing, or a graphic outline of an image.

outline font - A type font name that shows basic outlines of the characters.
SEE ALSO: SCALABLE FONT

Lorem ipsum

Microsoft **Windows** Technologies

Outlook **Express** - Microsoft's mail client and personal information account manager. Not to be confused with *Internet Explorer* for web browsing.

output - Anything that is generated by the computer; e.g. an image on the display screen, a printed page, music or radio coming from the speakers, files saved to disk, data transmitted over the Internet.

output area - **See:** buffer

output device - The *peripheral device* through which *output* from the computer is communicated; e.g. a display screen, printer, modem, or speakers.

outside plant - In telecommunications, all the equipment and facilities that link a telephone company to the end user. This includes cables, junction boxes, and so on. Unfortunately, these are all liable to damage from accident, degradation, and adverse weather conditions.

outside the box - Imaginative thinking. To invent a new way of doing something, e.g. the application of Internet technologies to education, trade, international relations.

outsourcing - The use of a specialist contractor to provide services such as computer hardware and software care.

over the wire - The state of being *online*.

overclocking - To modify a computer to run faster than the manufacturer's specifications. The danger is that the *Central Processing Unit* and *motherboard* may not be able to function at increased speeds.

Over-fifties – Otherwise known as *silver surfers*, over-50 year-olds make up the fastest growing group of Internet users. Dedicated web sites for this age group include Internet training schemes, as well as information, articles, and links to major content providers such as *CompuServe*.

overflow error – An *error* resulting from entering more data than can fit into a *register* or *field*. The user is usually informed via a dialog box or the field will be left empty.

overhead – Company costs. This includes the cost of *bricks-and-mortar* and staff. E-businesses have the advantage of hugely reduced overheads.

overlaid windows – The ability to have

---

several windows open (in *Microsoft Windows* systems). The various windows are displayed one on top of the other with the active window (i.e. the window where the processing is taking place) being uppermost.
SEE: FEATURE BOX

overlay – Where text is inserted or overlaid onto a video sequence.

overloading – A *denial of service attack* that is due to part of the system being overloaded with data. E.g. When the user receives an e-mail with so many attachments that the system cannot process other data.

overrun – When data is lost due to the receiving device being unable to accept data at the rate at which it is transmitted.

oversampling – A way to create an accurate *digital* representation of an *analog* signal – technically sampling at more than double the highest sampled frequency. Analog signals are sampled by the computer a number of times per second, then converted into digital code. The more samples that are taken, the closer the digital information will be to the real live sound.
SEE ALSO: SAMPLING

overstrike – To type over a previously typed character.

overstuffing – A way of ensuring that a

---

overlaid windows

In Windows, on a PC, and on Apple Macs, it is possible to have several windows displayed at the same time.

The active window is foremost on the screen.
It is overlaid over a series of other open windows.

web site is picked out by search engines. This is achieved by adding material and key words to increase the chance of the site being highly ranked.

SEE ALSO: SPAMDEXING

oversubscribed – Refers to ISPs that take on more users to a system than can be supported during periods of high *traffic*. In such instances, some users will be denied access to the network. Many ISPs intentionally oversubscribe in the belief that all users will not want to use the network at the same time. An oversubscription rate of eight to one is not uncommon among ISPs. Such rates or ratios are one way of helping a user make a choice between different ISPs.

SEE ALSO: INTERNET SERVICE PROVIDER

Overture – A search site where advertisers send in their summaries and bid for their placement in the results list. When the list of results for a search is displayed, the highest bidding advertiser's summary is located at the top of the list. The amount of money bid for each placement is displayed so that competitors can adjust their bids for a higher position on the list.

GO TO: www.overture.com

overwrite – To write over data that is already stored on a disk.

owner – The person or organization who owns a *mailing list*. It is the list owner's responsibility to manage the list, inform participants that they are included in the list by way of a welcome message, and sort out problems.

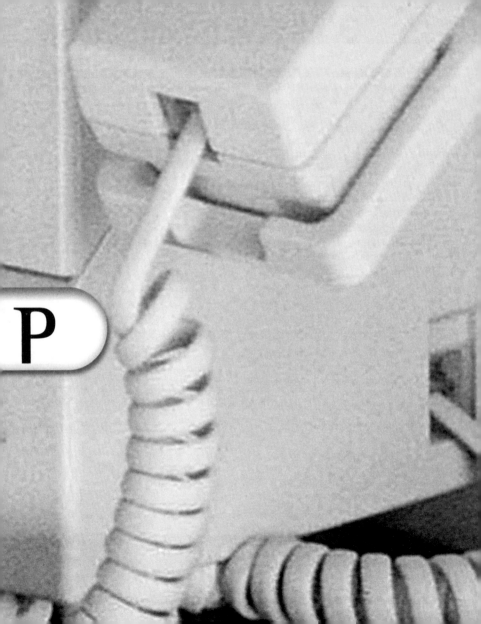

P24T – A down-sized Pentium microprocessor from *Intel*. It is an upgrade for the 486 on *motherboards* that have the correct socket.

P3P – **P**latform for **P**rivacy **P**references is a protocol for sharing private information over the Internet. It allows for transmission of sensitive data such as credit information to a P3P-enabled web site.
SEE ALSO: SECURE

P4 – The term *Intel* use for their *Pentium* 4 chip.
SEE ALSO: MICROPROCESSOR

P6 – The generic code name *Intel* use for the *Pentium Pro*; it includes the Pentium Pro, *Pentium II*, *Pentium III* and *Celeron* microprocessors.

P7 – The code name *Intel* use for the IA-64 Central Processing Unit (CPU) architecture, now officially named *Itanium*.

P JPEG – **See: P**rogressive JPEG

PABX – **See: P**rivate **A**utomatic **B**ranch E**x**change

PAC – **See: p**erceptual **a**udio **c**oding

pack – To compress and store data in a way that can be reversed (*unpacked*).

package – A software package.

Packard Bell NEC – Part of the *NEC* Group and based in the Netherlands, Packard Bell are one of the world's leading computer manufacturers.
GO TO: www.packardbell.com

packed decimal – A method of storage that places two decimal digits into one byte, each digit occupying 4 bits.

packet – Everything that is transmitted over the Internet is divided into blocks of data called packets. These blocks of data are then *routed* over the network using the *TCP/IP* protocols. In addition to the content data, the packets contain the recipient's and the sender's *Internet Protocol address* as well as error-checking information.
SEE ALSO: PACKET CLASSIFICATION

packet assembler/disassembler – This is hardware that enables data from a computer not set up for packet switching to use a packet-switching network. It packs data into discrete packages and then reassembles any packets that arrive.
SEE ALSO: PACKET SWITCHING

packet classification – The identification of *packets* for quality-of-service reasons. The packets can be identified by their source and destination ports, address, and protocol type.
SEE ALSO: PACKET SWITCHING

packet filter – This check ensures that *packets* that pass through a system meet basic criteria to minimize the risk of breaches in security.

Packet Internet Gopher (PING) – A message (echo return) that is sent from one computer to another to test that the receiving destination is online and ready to receive data. Most operating systems verify sound connections before attempting the delivery of any mail.
See also: PACKET

packet loss – The discarding of data *packets* in a network when a piece of hardware or system is overloaded and cannot accept any incoming data.

packet monkey – Generally considered a nuisance, a packet monkey is someone who intentionally inundates a web site or a network with data packets that disrupt or terminate the service.
See also: E-MAIL FLOODING

packet overhead – The continual assembly and disassembly of *packets* during transmission reduces the overall speed of the data transmission, hence contributing to what is known as the packet overhead.

packet radio – This term is used to describe the transmission of *packets* between computers by means such as chat, e-mail, file transfer, and games by amateur radio enthusiasts.

packet sniffer – A program that is generally used with malicious intent to find and read *packets* that meet certain criteria such as those that contain financial details (credit card numbers), passwords, or other secure information. Secure e-mail systems are resistant to packet sniffers.
See also: FIREWALL, SECURE

packet switching – *Packets* from the same message traveling over the Internet do not necessarily have to travel over the same pathways. Once the packages arrive at their destination, they are reassembled.
See also: PACKET ASSEMBLER/DISASSEMBLER, TCP/IP

PacketHound – A commercially available product that aims to help businesses or universities to regulate online traffic that might otherwise slow services down for all users of a *local area network* (LAN). For example, employees or students downloading large music files may disrupt the speed of a system.

packing density – Refers to the number of bits or tracks per inch on the recording surface of a disk or compact disc. It refers also to the number of memory bits on a microprocessor.

PAD – See: **P**acket **A**ssembler/**D**issembler

padded cell – A program that limits the facilities that a user is able to employ on a computer or a network. It is used to restrict access or ensure that new users do not damage a system.
See also: SECURE

padding – Meaningless data that is transmitted to fill unused space, such as blanks or zeros.

paddle – The secret identity given to the participant in an online *auction*.

page – **See:** memory page

page break – A code used to mark the end of a page.

page description language (PDL) – Codes and keywords that describe the kind of text and graphics contained within a document. This enables printers and similar devices to handle the data correctly.

Page Down key – The keyboard key that (in many programs) moves the cursor to the next page.

page fault – An application has a range of virtual memory addresses with which to work. Not all addresses are backed by physical memory. When an application tries to access a page in virtual memory that is not backed up by a physical page, a page fault is generated. This is a normal part of running applications.
SEE ALSO: MEMORY PAGE

page frame – The segment of memory that has the size of a page.

page header – Text that is printed at the top of every page. The header will usually include the page number and the headings above each column in a spreadsheet.

page layout program – Another term for a *desktop publishing* program.

page layout software – Software that is used to create camera-ready copy; i.e. material that is acceptable by commercial printers.

page makeup – The features that constitute a printed page, including the basic layout of page, *headers*, *footers*, *tables*, *graphics*, rules, and borders.

page preview – Used to see how a page under construction will look when printed out or shown on a web site.
SEE: FEATURE BOX

page recognition – A program that recognizes the content of a printed page once it has been scanned into the computer.

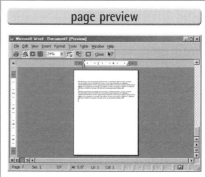

page preview

Most word-processing or desktop publishing programs have a page preview feature to show how the printed page will look.

page requests – This refers to the number of times a web page is requested via web *servers*. The information is used for judging the amount of traffic that has visited a site on the web and can prove particularly useful to advertisers.

page source – The *HTML code* or *source* of a *web page*.

Page Up key – The keyboard key that, in many applications, moves the cursor to the previous page.

page views – 1. How pages of a document or web page are seen on the display. 2. Synonym for *page requests*.

pagejacking – To make a web page resemble the layout of an existing web site

pagination

Paginating means assigning page numbers to each page. These numbers will usually appear at the top or bottom of the page.

run by a prestigious organization or company. The site may also use keywords to get search engines to recommend the web site to visitors searching for the targeted official site, so attracting visitors (especially to porn sites and financial con sites) and lulling them into a sense of security based on the reputation of the site mimicked.

PageMaker – PA widely used desktop publishing program for *Windows* and *Macintosh* from *Adobe*. It is considered the standard in the graphics arts and publishing industry. It is used to create catalogs, magazines, ads, brochures, leaflets, and books.

PageMill® – A web site authoring program from *Adobe*. It offers a visual environment for creating Web pages. A sister program, SiteMill, works with PageMill for managing the web site.

pager – Device for transmitting and receiving text, using wireless technology.

pages per minute (PPM) – The number of pages that can be printed in a minute.

pagination – In printing, the page numbering system. Different schemes can be set up in word-processing and other document handling programs.
SEE: FEATURE BOX

paging – 1. In memory, this describes the transfer of parts of the program's working

memory, that are less needed at that particular time, from RAM into an area of temporary secondary storage.
2. The process of contacting someone by using a *pager*.

pain in the net – This phrase refers to anyone considered to be an annoying *flamer* in a *newsgroup*.

paint – To use a paint program to simulate a paintbrush when using a tablet stylus or a computer mouse.

paint program – Software that enables the user to create freehand drawings and manipulate, cut, paste, and resize a bitmap image. The more sophisticated programs will create graphic effects and allow scanned photographs to be enhanced.
SEE: FEATURE BOX

Paint Shop Pro – A powerful graphics and image-editing program from Jasc Software.
GO TO: www.jasc.com

PAL – See: **P**hase-**A**lternate **L**ine

palette – The range of colors that is made available to the user in a graphics program, or made available to a color printer.

Palm Inc. – This company is one of the leading makers of hand-held computers, electronic organizers and *PDAs*

(*personal digital assistants*). Their first major product, the PalmPilot, was introduced in 1996.
GO TO: www.palm.com

Palm.Liberty.A – Palm.Liberty.A is the first *Trojan* that can infect *hand-held devices* that run the *Palm OS*. It was released as a *patch* for a Palm OS program named Liberty, but it is actually a program that can delete applications.

Palm Organizer – **See:** Palm Pilot

Palm OS® **Palm OS® (Palm Operating System)** – Operating system and platform Palm Inc. use for Palm computers and organizers.

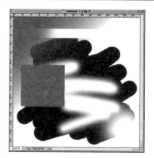

paint program

Simple effects like the filled shapes, and colored brushstrokes, shown here, can be created with most paint programs.

Palm Pilot – The Palm Pilot is a hand-held electronic organizer with a kind of pen interface and handwriting recognition for entering data. It contains an address book, scheduler, and to-do list, and newer versions can download e-mail. It also synchronizes with a PC using *HotSync* software. It is now known just as a "Palm" or sometimes colloquially Palm Organizer.
Go to: www.palm.com

palmtop – A small computer that literally fits in your palm. Compared to full-size computers, they are limited, but they are practical for certain functions such as phone books, schedules and calendars. Palmtops that use a pen for data input are often called *hand-held* computers or *PDAs*. Most do not include disk drives, but most contain PCMCIA slots into which you can insert disk drives, modems, memory cards, and other devices.

PAM - 1. **See:** Pulse Amplitude Modulation
2. **See:** Pluggable Authentication Modules

pan – Short for panorama. As a verb, to pan can mean to make a section of text or an image move continuously across the user's view. For example, to reveal different parts of an image in a slow sweeping movement across a computer screen, or to move an actual movie camera gradually across a scene.

PAN - **See:** Personal Area Network

panacea – A panacea is a mythical antidote or remedy that completely solves a problem.

Panduit – The Panduit Corporation is a leading manufacturer of wiring and communications products.
Go to: www.panduit.com

panel – 1. The flat section of a (computer) casing; e.g. the back panel, which holds all the connecting sockets.
2. A graphic representation of a panel onscreen; e.g. a control panel with its switches and indicators.

panic – The situation when an operating system or program encounters a serious problem, making it unable to run. Panic reactions include displaying error messages, freezing, and automatically rebooting.
See also: crash

Pantone Matching System – Pantone Inc. is a commercial company acknowledged as the world authority on the communication and accuracy of color. Their system ensures consistency of colors; it is considered the international reference for the selection, specification, matching and controlling of ink colors.
Go to: www.pantone.com

PAP - **See:** **p**assword **a**uthentication **p**rotocol

paper feed - The mechanism to feed paper into a printer.

paper mail - **See:** p-mail

paper net - The postal service.

Paper sizes - Although not unique, the ISO standard is one of the most widely used for measuring paper size, appearing in the Page Setup feature of most applications.
SEE: FEATURE BOX

paperless office - A term commonly used when referring to a fully automated office.

paradigm - An example, a model, or a pattern. It is pronounced para-dime.

paradox - A conflicting statement or one that offers an opinion that conflicts with common thinking.

paralanguage - The system that has developed to enhance the emotional quality of Internet communications. This system includes *acronyms, emoticons,* and other iconic and graphical devices that substitute for the visual and verbal clues that contextualize and enhance face to face communications.
SEE: APPENDIX 1 and 2 for a list of acronyms and emoticons.

parallel - Used with regard to the Internet, it means when two or more activities are run simultaneously. Contrast with serial when events happen one after another.

parallel computing/processing - Running together two or more computers or processors to perform a single task.

parallel port - The connection socket on the back of a PC. Parallel ports are used by printers for sending data over eight parallel wires simultaneously. A *serial port* has only one wire so it is eight times slower.
SEE ALSO: PARALLEL

parallel printer - A printer that runs off a *parallel port*.

parallel server - A computer system that is used as a server, which provides simultaneous processing.

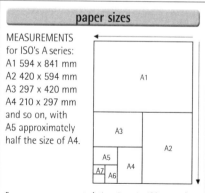

paper sizes

MEASUREMENTS
for ISO's A series:
A1 594 x 841 mm
A2 420 x 594 mm
A3 297 x 420 mm
A4 210 x 297 mm
and so on, with
A5 approximately
half the size of A4.

A1

A3

A2

A5

A4

A7 A6

For some measurements (other than the ISO system) for paper size, see Page Setup in most applications.

parallel transmission – Simultaneous transmission of at least one bit over parallel channels. Contrast with serial transmission in which only one bit is transmitted at a time. Generally parallel transmission uses an eight channel parallel cable.

Parallel Virtual Machine - Program that enables a worldwide network of multiple *UNIX* and *Windows NT* computers to function as one large, parallel machine. All this extra power is used to solve complex scientific, industrial, and medical problems.

parallelism – Parallelism is the overlapping of information during processing, whether it is input, output or both.

parameter – Specific value usually given and used to alter a program or subroutine.

para-site – A controversial practice where a web designer uses frames or *pages* from other web sites within its own site so as not to have to originate them.

parent – The first or main program that is loaded into the memory.

parent/child file – The main file in a database that contains basic information about an item. Child files are created later with more expansive information.

parent directory – The parent *directory* is the disk directory that is one level up from the directory that is being accessed (the current directory).

parent message – The first posting in a *newsgroup* or on a *bulletin board* that generates a response and forms a thread

parental control – Browser or filtering program that rejects web sites not suitable for children. Such programs screen pages by word content, site rating, or by URL. SEE ALSO: CYBER PATROL, NETNANNY

parity – **See:** parity checking

parity bit – An extra *bit* attached to a piece of text, byte, character or word. It is used to detect errors in a transmission.

parity checking –A test for errors in data transmitted or moved within the system. An extra bit (parity *bit*), is added in a *binary* transmission to each *byte*, for checking purposes. The sending and receiving modems agree whether to send in *odd parity*, *even parity*, or no parity. A parity bit is then added and, if the parity does not agree with the agreed mode, an error has clearly occurred. Note that if an even number of bits are wrong, parity checking will not detect the error. No parity assumes that other checking methods are operative and leaves more room in each byte for data.

parity error – Occurs when a character's *parity bit* is incorrect during transmission.

Parity_Boot – This is a *computer virus* that checks hourly whether it has infected a floppy disk. If it has not, this message appears: PARITY CHECK. To clear the virus from memory, the user must shut down the system or use the Reset button.

park – To secure the disk drive heads so that they cannot be moved.

parse – The process of analyzing something in an orderly way.

parsing – To break data up into smaller pieces that can easily be managed. E.g. *Search engines* parse the phrase in a search into component words and use these to carry out *Boolean operations* by using the Boolean options when searching.

partition – In a personal computer, the partition is a division of a hard disk that allows for different operating systems on the same hard disk. The term also refers to the creation of (or the appearance of having) separate hard drives.

Pascal – This high-level programming language was developed by Niklaus Wirth in the late 1960s. It is named after Blaise Pascal, a seventeenth-century French mathematician who constructed one of the first mechanical adding machines. Although influential on future programs, Pascal is commonly used as a teaching language; its relative inflexibility has meant that it is not popular in business. Wirth invented a follow-up language called Modula 2 to bring more features and flexibility.
SEE ALSO: PROGRAMMING

passive attack – A method of attack where the data on a site is read without being changed in any way.

passive matrix display – A type of LCD display used in portable computers which is made up from a matrix of wires.

passphrase – This is a similar concept to the *password*, but consists of a phrase rather than a single word.

password – A secret word that is used by someone to identify themself. Most ISPs and secure web sites require users to enter a password to gain entry to their accounts. To be effective, passwords should not be obvious, such as the user's first name; they should be based on something obscure and hard to guess, and should contain a mixture of case or numbers.

Password Authentication Protocol (PAP) – A method of authenticating *passwords* used by ISPs. The password is sent to the ISP as plain text and is less secure than the *challenge handshake authentication protocol* which serves a similar function.

password constraint – The rules laid down by the site administrator to create *passwords* in an acceptable format with the aim of improving security. Passwords must have at least eight letters or numbers and contain no spaces, or must reject the user's name or e-mail username.

password cracker – A program run by a system administrator to ensure that a user's *password* is not easy to guess or work out.

password fishing – Describes an attempt to trick or con a user into revealing his or her *password*.
See also: HACKER

password hint – A reminder from a web site given to a user who has forgotten their password. It is usually given via an e-mail for security reasons. Password hints can consist of questions such as mother's maiden name or a favorite pet's name.

password protection – To protect a file by requiring users to enter a *password* before that file can be opened.

password sniffer – A program that looks for *passwords* while being transmitted. These are always located in the first section of data transmitted and when captured may allow an attacker to gain access to a closed network.
See also: PASSWORD CRACKER

paste – To insert a piece of text or graphic that has previously been cut or copied from a document and placed in the *clipboard*.

paste bomb – This is a long piece of text that is inserted into a newsgroup posting or into an e-mail message. It is likely to be irrelevant and designed simply to irritate the recipients.

patch – A change to a program that may correct an error or bug or may extend the functioning of a program. Patches are generally quick and easy to download over the Internet and are particularly popular with games enthusiasts.

patch panel – A patch panel is a hardware device containing an assembly of *port* locations used in a network. In a *LAN* or *WAN* this panel is capable of operating as an interconnecting switchboard.

patent – A legal claim to the ownership of a piece of technology so that the inventor is financially rewarded for his investment.
See also: COPYRIGHT

path – 1. Synonymous with *pathname*, i.e. a file's location on disk.
2. The route taken by data over a network or within a computer.

path control – See: pathing

Path not found – An error message in *DOS* that means the user has entered an invalid path name.

path to profitability – An important step in any business, however in the early days of the Internet boom this did not seem to have the priority it should have had. Nowadays having had their fingers burnt Venture capitalists ensure this is a key part of the strategy of any new commercial web site, before investing in it.

pathing – In storage networks, pathing is a method used to address specific needs by changing the way that communication paths are managed and organized. Storage networks are sensitive systems that must avoid crashing and maintain good security so pathing is vital in improved efficiency. Also called *path control*.

pathname – The directory name for a file showing its drive, folders, and sub-folders. For example, the pathname here is for a file called John Smith that is stored on the C drive of a PC: C:/data/work/letter/johnsmith

pattern – Standardized, digitized signal of an audio or visual entity stored in a PC.
SEE ALSO: PATTERN RECOGNITION

pattern recognition – Used in artificial intelligence, computers are programmed to recognize audio and visual patterns which they store in memory and then recall on demand. This is used in voice recognition, handwriting recognition, and in some sophisticated security devices.

payload – The useful data in a *packet*, excluding headers, etc.

pay-per-click – A popular marketing system on the Internet whereby the advertiser pays only when the site visitor *clicks* on its advertisement and then goes to its site. This is unlike just paying a fee for the advert regardless of whether people visit the advertised site or not.

payware – Software that is sold rather than shared or given away free.
SEE ALSO: SHAREWARE, FREEWARE

PBX – See: **P**rivate **B**ranch **E**xchange

PC – See: **P**ersonal **C**omputer

pcANYWHERE – A popular remote control program for Windows from Symantec.
GO TO: www.symantec.com

PCB – See: **P**rinted **C**ircuit **B**oard

PC card – A lightweight, removable device about the size of a credit card that adds to a portable computer facilities and extras such as additional memory, modem connection, or network adapter.
SEE ALSO: PERSONAL COMPUTER MEMORY CARD INTERNATIONAL ASSOCIATION

PC chipset – Part of the *motherboard*, the PC chipset is a set of *microprocessors* that interfaces between all of the computer's subsystems. It enables the *buses* and electronics to allow the CPU, the memory and all input/output devices to interact with each other.

PC compatibility – Any software or hardware that will work with a standard IBM-compatible personal computer.

PC conflicts – The clash between devices and programs that are competing for the same resources in the PC.

PC Demo – See: demo software

PC-DOS - The *DOS* operating system that was developed by Microsoft and supplied by IBM on its PCs before the launch of Windows 95.

PC fax - **See:** fax modem

PCI - **See:** **P**eripheral **C**omponent **I**nterconnect

PCL - **See:** **P**rinter **C**ontrol **L**anguage

PCM - **See:** **P**ulse **C**ode **M**odulation

PCMCIA - 1. **See:** **P**ersonal **C**omputer **M**emory **C**ard **I**nternational **A**ssociation 2. An ironic acronym: **P**eople **C**annot **M**emorise **C**omputer **I**ndustry **A**cronyms.

PCS - **See:** **P**ersonal **C**ommunications **S**ervice

PC/TV - A personal computer that can also receive and display normal TV broadcasts.

PCX file - A popular way to store a *bitmap* image on disk. It enables images to be easily exchanged between different graphics programs.

PDA - **See:** **p**ersonal **d**igital **a**ssistant

PDC - **See:** **P**rimary **D**omain **C**ontroller

PDF - **See:** **P**ortable **D**ocument **F**ile

PDL - **See:** **P**age **D**escription **L**anguage

PDN - **See:** **P**ublic **D**ata **N**etwork

PeaceNet - An International network that promotes peace, justice, and human rights.

peak rate - This refers to the largest number of kilobits per second that are transportable over a *virtual circuit*.

peer - A computer linked on a peer-to-peer network. All peers can use the network resources and share files with other peers.

peer-to-peer network - Network consisting of computers able to exchange files without using a dedicated *server*. An egalitarian system where computers can, at any time, become *client* or server.

peering - The improvement of transmission efficiency by the arrangement of traffic exchange between *Internet Service Providers* (ISPs).

Pegasus - The code name used by Microsoft for *Windows CE*.

pel - **See:** Pixel

PEM - **See:** **P**rivacy **E**nhanced **M**ail

pen - Tool that can be used for inputting information into a computer, with output seen on screen.

pen/stylus computer - Keyboardless handheld computer using a pen to point to a display. Usually called a Palm Computer.

peon - Refers to a person with no privileges on a computer.

penetrate - To gain unauthorized access to a secure site or network.

penetration testing – Way of testing the security of a system by allowing hackers legal access into a computer system.

Pentium – The family name used by Intel for its 32 bit CPU microprocessors.
Go to: www.intel.com
SEE ALSO: PENTIUM MICROPROCESSOR

Pentium microprocessor – The family of Pentium microprocessors, launched in 1993, is the most widely used for commercial and home use. A PC may even be referred to as a Pentium PC.
• **Pentium (1993–96)** – the first, contained 3.1 million *transistors* and used a 66Mhz bus. Replaced the 486.
• **Pentium Pro (1995–97)** – used for high end PCs with massive memory increase and 5.5 million transistors.
• **Pentium MMX (97–99)** – extra multi-media functions and 4.5 million transistors
• **Celeron (98–2001)** – used for low end PCs and use up to 19 million transistors, up to 100Mhz system *bus*.
• **Pentium II (97–99)** – extra flexibility, up to 7.5 million transistors. Xeon models introduced for high-end servers.
• **Pentium III (99–01)** – more features, more speed with 28 million transistors and 133Mhz system *bus*.
• **Pentium IV – (2000)** – contains 42 million transistors and 400Mhz system bus. Uses *Netburst* technology to make it three times faster than Pentium III.

SEE ALSO: ITANIUM

Peoplesoft– A software company that specializes in producing programs that enable businesses to collaborate, both internally and externally, by the use of Internet technology.
Go to: www.peoplesoft.com

perceptual audio coding – A technique for further compressing digital sound by the elimination of those frequencies from the recording that cannot be perceived by the human ear. *MP3* technology uses perceptual audio coding dramatically to reduce the amount of digital data required on a music CD.

perfection image – A digitized image that gives the illusion of perfection.

performance – Refers to the effective functioning of a network in terms of the response time, throughput, output, and lack of bottlenecks.

performance rating (PR) – See: benchmark

peripheral – Short for *peripheral device*.

Peripheral Component Interconnect – Now installed on most new desktop computers, Peripheral Component Interconnect (PCI) is an interconnection system between a microprocessor or chip and attached hardware in which the expansion slots are spaced closely for high-speed operation.

peripheral device – This term is used to describe hardware that is connected to a computer but is located outside the unit in which the CPU, hard drive(s) and the memory chips are located. Examples of peripheral devices include: *keyboard, mouse, monitor, printer, scanner, disk* and *tape drives,* speaker, *joystick, plotter,* and *digital camera.*
SEE: FEATURE BOX

peripherals – 1. **See:** peripheral device
2. A derogatory term for so-called unimportant people in a business.

PERL – **See:** **P**ractical **E**xtraction and **R**eport **L**anguage

---

peripheral device

This shows the peripheral devices that most home computer users will have attached to their computers. (The PC Tower unit shown here is the main PC unit.)

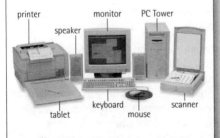

printer   monitor   PC Tower
    speaker

tablet   keyboard   mouse   scanner

---

permanent virtual circuit (PVC) – A *point-to-point* connection, established in advance. A PVC that is defined at the time of subscribing to a service is called a *virtual private network* (VPN).

permission – The facilities within a network that are available for use by an individual user; for example, the range of files a user may access.

permission marketing – Marketing information sent to those who have signed up in advance to receive such material.
SEE ALSO: OPT-IN, PUBLISH AND SUBSCRIBE, PULL ADVERTISING

persistent cookie – A *cookie* that stays on a computer system after the session on the originating web site has been terminated. Servers use this type of cookie to enable them to reuse information on a client. Such cookies may also be used by a web site to retain personal information so, when revisiting the site, the user will not have to provide all their details again; also used for monitoring and advertising purposes.
SEE ALSO: SESSION COOKIE

persistent URL (PURL) – PURLs are used for pages that are expected to move. The persistent *URL* redirects the request to the new page location.

personal area network (PAN) – A home-based network used to connect computers to TVs, burglar alarms, and lighting systems.

Personal Communications Services –
Wireless communications services that
use digital technology for transmission
and reception.

**personal
computer
(PC)** –
Any *IBM*-
compatible
computer
that is based on an *Intel* processor and
uses an *MS-DOS* or Windows-type
operating system.

**Personal Computer Memory Card
International Association (PCMCIA)** –
A non-profit trade association created to
standardize the connection of peripherals
to portable computers.

personal digital assistant (PDA) – A
palmtop computer that uses a *pen* for data
input. Often called a *hand-held computer*,
it was originally only used as an address
book and diary. Now it can also provide
Internet access.

personal firewall – A software application
used for protecting a single Internet-
connected computer from intruders.
Also called a desktop firewall.
SEE ALSO: FIREWALL

personal information manager (PIM) –
Records meetings and appointments, holds
a diary, address book, and personal data.

personal web site – A web site that is
produced by an individual, and which
provides content relating to that individual,
such as their CV, family profiles, interests,
and holiday snaps.
SEE: FEATURE BOX

personal web site builder – Software
that enables an experienced user to create
a *personal web site*, usually through the
use of a *wizard*.

Personal Home Page – See: **P**HP
Hypertext **P**reprocessor

Personal Web Server – Version of a
web server program from *Microsoft* that
is aimed at individual PC users who want
to share web pages and other files from
their computer's hard drive.

---

personal web site

Most personal web sites on the Internet feature
details, such as holiday photographs and
favorite personal items.

personalization – Customization of a web site or pages on a site to a particular customer's tastes. Often called one-to-one marketing, this is a kind of holy grail for many online retailers because it can ensure customer loyalty.

personalized services – Services that are customized to suit individual users; for example, the use of home pages which are tailored to the interests of the user and news services that alert the user to web pages that contain updated news and information on subjects of interest to that particular individual.

personalized newspaper – A *personalized service* that can provide the user simply with content that they have expressed an interest in receiving.
SEE ALSO: PERSONALIZED SERVICES

pervasive computing – Describes the never-ending advancement of computer technology and its invasiveness in society. Computers and microprocessors exist in everything from cars to washing machines, and many of the latest microprocessors are even wearable.

peta – Quadrillion; 10 to the power of 15.

petabyte – A quadrillion bytes; 1,000 terabytes.

PGA – See: Pin Grid Array

PgDn key – See: Page Down key

PGML – See: Precision Graphics Markup Language

PGP – See: Pretty Good Privacy

PgUp key – See: Page Up key

ph – Abbreviation for **ph**onebook

phantom dialing – 1. When a computer's auto-connect feature has been enabled and it attempts to dial out and establish an Internet connection on its own.
2. When a mobile phone user accidentally presses a pre-programmed auto-dial number on their keypad and initiates a phone call unintentionally. Many mobiles have lock functions on them to prevent this from happening.

phantom lines – Blurred lines on a computer screen that are made visible as dots or dashes to reveal the edges of objects that are hidden from view.

phase – 1. This is a period of time or a stage in a process.
2. Any one point or portion in a recurring series of changes, as in the changes of motion of one of the particles constituting a wave or vibration.

phase-alternate line (PAL) – The television broadcast standard throughout Europe (except in France). This standard broadcasts 625 lines of resolution, nearly 20 per cent more than the US standard, NTSC, of 525.

Philips – Philips' full title is Royal Philips Electronics. They are a commercial company with a long history, established in the Netherlands in 1891 by Gerard Philips. The company are now world leaders in LCD and *monitor* production.
GO TO: www.philips.com

phone hawk – A type of computer *hacker* who calls up a particular computer or network via a modem and either copies or destroys data.

phone-home – The capability of a server, PC, or other computing device to directly notify a repair center when it is failing; i.e., when it is starting to *fall over*. It is a reference to the Steven Speilberg film, *ET*.

phoneme – In electronic or synthetic speech programs a phoneme is a basic component of speech, such as "ph", "ch", and "sh". They are used to compose audio output and to analyze voice input recognizing words.

Phong shading – In three-dimensional graphics, a technique developed by Phong Bui-Tuong. Phong shading calculates a shaded surface based on the color and illumination at each individual *pixel*. This results in a more realistic look than *Gouraud* shading, but it requires much more computation and memory usage.

phono plug – The plug and socket connectors used to connect audio and video devices directly into the sound card of the computer.

phosphor – The light-emitting substance used to coat the standard *cathode ray tube* monitor. An electron scanning beam passes over tiny *phosphor dots* to produce an image.

phosphor dots – The small phosphor particles that lie in a film inside a monitor screen.

phosphor triad – To produce color images on a standard monitor, three *phosphor dots* in red, green, and blue are placed together to form a single screen pixel.

Photo CD – A system from Kodak that is used for storing up to one hundred 35mm slides or negatives on a CD-ROM.

photo scanner – A kind of *scanner* designed to read photographs up to 4" x 6" (10 x 18 cm). Generally designed for the home market.

photocomposition – Laying out a printed page, as in a book or magazine, by using electrophotographic devices such as image setters and laser printers.
SEE ALSO: PAGE MAKEUP, PAGINATION

photoconductivity – Electrical conductivity that is affected by exposure to light.

photodetector – A machine that senses the light pulses in an optical fiber and then converts them into electrical pulses.
SEE ALSO: PHOTON, PHOTOELECTRIC, PHOTOCONDUCTIVITY

photoelectric – Refers to the conversion of *photons* into electrons. Einstein discovered the photoelectric effect; i.e., that light was made of particles (photons) and that it carried an amount of energy exactly proportional to its frequency.
SEE ALSO: PHOTONICS, PHOTON, PHOTOELECTRIC, PHOTOCONDUCTIVITY

photography – 1. See: digital camera 2. SEE: FEATURE BOX

photo–library – A library of photographs that are available to view or download.
SEE ALSO: PHOTOGRAPHY

photon – A discrete subatomic particle having zero mass, no electric charge, and an indefinitely long lifetime.

photonic network – A type of communications network where information is transmitted entirely in the form of optical (light) or infra-red transmission signals. Also called an optical network.
SEE ALSO: OPTICAL NETWORKING

photooptic memory – Information storage technology that uses a laser beam to record data onto a photosensitive film.
SEE ALSO: PHOTOSENSITIVE

photopaint program – See: image editor

photorealistic – An image that has the quality of a photograph.

A photorealistic image of a beach scene.

photosensitive – A material that changes or reacts in a certain way when exposed to natural or artificial light.

photosensor – An electronic component that can detect the presence of visible light, ultraviolet (UV) light, and/or infra-red transmission (IR).

Photoshop – See: Adobe Photoshop

PHP – See: **P**ersonal **H**ome **P**age **H**ypertext **P**reprocessor

Personal Home Page Hypertext Preprocessor – Originally known as Personal Home Page, this a scripting language which is used to create web pages. Its primary use is to extract data out of a database and present it on the web page.

phreak – (slang) To hack into the phone system to make free telephone calls.

phreaker – (slang) One who phreaks.

PHTML – (**P**re-HTML) Some *HTML* documents contain embedded material that is not expressible in HTML. To enable the inclusion of this material, a program called PHTML is used with the file extension.

physical – Something that is actual as opposed to conceptual.

physical memory – Data stored on a physical medium such as a magnetic disk; e.g. a *floppy disk*.

Pi – The 16th letter of the Greek alphabet, which is used to represent the number 3.14159. It represents the ratio of a circle's circumference to its diameter and the value is the same regardless of the size of the circle. The decimal expansion of pi is a never-ending, no-repeating sequence of digits. This is called an irrational number.

PIC – Lotus picture file. A *file extension* for an image used by *Lotus* 1-2-3 in charts and graphs.

Pick – A well-renowned database management system for small to medium-size businesses, primarily based on a model of business data and its organization. Its main feature is that it allows developers to view information much as a business naturally views their data.

pick tool – This is an object used to specify an item from a displayed list; for example, a stylus.

picklist – A scrollable list of choices from which to pick.

pico – One trillionth.

picosecond (ps) – One trillionth of a second; one thousandth of a nanosecond.

PICT file format – The PICT is the native Macintosh graphics file format. When creating a screen capture on a Macintosh (by pressing Shift-Command-4) the graphics file produced will be a PICT file.

PICTIVE – See: **P**lastic **I**nterface for **C**ollaborative **T**echnology **I**nitiatives through **V**ideo **E**xploration

---

photography

The advent of digital photography and the Internet has increased the number of images available immeasurably. A number of large photo libraries have sprung up online and many are making a great deal of money by selling popular images. One of the biggest and best is www.corbis.com, founded by Bill Gates in 1989.

It is possible to store your digital photos at a specialist site, or a site where your friends and family can visit the virtual photo album. www.fotango.com is considered one of the best in this field.

pictograph – 1. A graph that represents statistics on a computer by way of images and pictures. 2. Synonym for *icon*.

picture element – The full name for a *pixel*; very rarely used.

picture quality scale (PQS) – A method of measuring the quality of an image as judged by the human eye, as opposed to the computer measuring differences in pixels.

piechart – A way of graphically displaying statistics where the percentages are represented as wedges of a pie.
SEE: FEATURE BOX

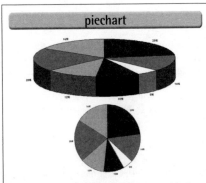

piechart

These two examples show different graphical representations of the same data: the lower is a 2D piechart, the upper is a 3D piechart.

PIF – **See:** Program Information File

PII/III – **See:** Pentium Microprocessor

piggyback attack – When an attacker watches the activities of a user on a network. Then, when the user logs off, the attacker cancels the request giving them access to the network using the original user's identity.

piggyback board – A small circuit board that plugs into a larger circuit board to extend its capabilities.

PIM – **See:** Personal Information Manager

pin – A metal conductor on a chip or other electronic device.

PIN – Personal Identification Number. The PIN is the number required for gaining access to a bank account when using a credit card or similar card which uses an electromagnetic strip. PINs are also needed for many other purposes when accessing networked systems.

Pin Grid Array (PGA) – A square microprocessor that looks rather like a bed of nails. It offers a high density of pins (200 pins can fit in 1.5" square), which allows it to support a large amount of input and output (I/O).

pincushion distortion – Distortion on a monitor whereby the edges of the image bend in toward the center of the screen.

PINE – Acronym for **P**ine **I**s **N**ot **E**lm or **P**rogram for **I**nternet **N**ews and **E**-mail. An e-mail client for *UNIX* systems that replaces an older program called Elm.

PING – See: **P**acket **In**ternet **G**roper

ping flooding – When a network is overwhelmed by the malicious transmission of *ping* messages.
<small>SEE ALSO: SMURFING</small>

ping of death – A form of attack where a very large *ping* is sent, causing the destination computer to crash.

Ping_Pong – A *computer virus* that randomly activates a Ping-Pong-like white ball and sends it bouncing around the screen of the infected computer. It only works on 8086 and 8088 *CPUs*.

ping storm – A term synonymous with *ping flooding*.

pinout – A description of the purpose of each specific *pin* in a multi-pin hardware connection interface. Not all pins are used in every connection.

pipe – 1. A kind of transmission line that provides a connection to the Internet. A fat pipe is a telephone line with a high capacity.
2. The link between two programs running on a single computer where the output of one is the input of the other.
<small>SEE ALSO: PIPELINE</small>

pipeline – 1. To carry out several simultaneous instructions at once to increase performance.
2. This means to carry out two processes at the same time; for example, to scan an image and to compress that same image while scanning.

pipeline burst cache – A *cache* that uses *RAM* in conjunction with pipeline processing to improve performance. It is used as a secondary cache in computers with high-speed processors to transfer large quantities of data.

piracy – The illegal copying of software and other media.

pirate – A person who makes *illegal* copies of software, music CDs, or video materials, often for profit.

pitch – 1. The frequency of sound.
2. The number of characters per inch in a typeface. Fixed-pitch types set the same width for each character, while in proportional-pitch type, some characters are wider than others. The pitch is the average character width.

Pixar – A multi-award winning graphics company who, with Disney, created films such as *Toy Story*, *A Bugs Life*, and *Monsters Inc*. It has a reputation for groundbreaking technology in the graphics and animation fields.
Go to: www.pixar.com

pixel - Short for picture element. A pixel is the smallest unit of visual display that can be used to build an image. Pixels are visible as the tiny squares seen when an image is enlarged. The higher the number of pixels in an image, the better its *resolution*.
SEE ALSO: BITMAP
SEE: FEATURE BOX

pixel depth - See: pixel

pixelated - A graphic image where the individual pixels are visible. Often occurs when an image is blown-up too large.
SEE ALSO: DPI

Pixie dust - A three atom thick magnetic coating comprising the element ruthenium, which is sandwiched between two magnetic layers. Pixie dust is an informal

name that *IBM* uses for its antiferromagnetically-coupled (AFC) media technology, which can increase the data capacity of hard drives by up to four times.

PKCS - See: Public Key Cryptography Standards

PKI - See: Public Key Infrastructure

PKUNZIP - See: PKWARE

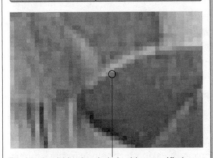

PKWARE - PKWARE Inc are responsible for a family of *compression* utility programs. Phil Katz developed the .ZIP standard compression program that is now used throughout the world. Their major programs act as follows.
• **PKZIP** compresses.
• **PKUNZIP** decompresses.
• **PKSFX** and **ZIP2EXE** create self-extracting archives that automatically decompress when run.
• **PKLITE** compresses only .EXE and .COM files, which decompress and run at the same time.
GO TO: www.pkware.com
SEE: FEATURE BOX

PKZIP - See: PKWARE

place - To import one file into another file.

plain old telephone service - (slang) The ordinary telephone service without any computer-enhanced upgrades. Commonly termed "pots."

The block within the circle in this magnified picture is one pixel, the smallest unit of display that can be used to build an image.

plain text – Text that is not encrypted and is available to be read by anyone, rather than *cipher text* which is encrypted prior to transmission.

plane – One layer within a graphic image that can be edited independently. Most graphics programs enable the user to create images constructed on several planes.

plasma display – Displays, found on some portable computers displays, that exploit the electroluminescence properties of certain gases.

Plastic Interface for Collaborative Technology Initiatives through Video Exploration (PICTIVE)– A way of building and representing a computer system or network by using non-computing materials such as paper, pen, and ink.

platen – The long cylinder on a printer which guides the paper and forms a surface for the printing process.

platform – Synonymous with *operating system*; so *Windows* and *Macintosh* are both platforms.

Platform for Internet Content Selection – A system of using labels to indicate Internet *content*. It aims to help parents and teachers limit what children access over the Internet, but is also used for *privacy* and *authentication* purposes.
SEE ALSO: PARENTAL CONTROLS

Platform for Privacy Preferences – See: P3P

platform independence – Software that can work on computers running any *operating system*.
SEE ALSO: PLATFORM

platter – This refers to a single disk in a *hard disk* drive. Most drives have between two and eight platters which spin around a central spindle.

play by e-mail – A game in which each player's moves are sent to the other player(s) through e-mailed messages.

playback – To play a multimedia clip such as music or video.

player – A device that is capable of reading and interpreting data; for example, a CD-ROM player is another term for a CD-drive.

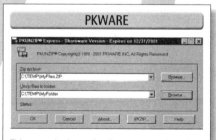

This example shows the shareware version of PKUNZIP Express, one of the many products from PKWARE's compression utility programs.

Playstation – A sophisticated games computer with 3D graphics, launched in 1994 by Sony. Playstation 2 (PS2) replaced it in 2000.
SEE ALSO: PLAYSTATION 2
GO TO: www.sony.com
SEE: FEATURE BOX

Playstation 2 – Launched in the year 2000 with huge media hype, Playstation 2 is a highly sophisticated games computer with additional features such as the capability to play DVD and audio CDs. One of its key benefits is that old games can still be played on it. It has a 128-bit CPU offering high resolution 3D graphics.
GO TO: www.sony.com

plenum–rated – Cabling that is safe to be used in the space between ceilings and drop down ceilings along with heating and electrical systems. Used to create local area networks (LANs) in office buildings.

Playstation

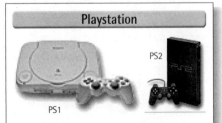

PS2

PS1

Playstation and Playstation 2 (PS2), the 3D games computers from Sony Corporation that were launched in 1994 and 2000 respectively.

plesiochronous – A term meaning almost synchronous. It specifically refers to a transmission where the devices sending and receiving information are synchronized, but set to different clocks to avoid blockages.

plot – To create an image by drawing a series of lines.

plotter – A type of printer that uses colored pens to draw lines. Popular for use in conjunction with *CAD* programs.

plug – Connector that plugs into a *socket*.
SEE ALSO: MALE CONNECTOR

Plug and Play – The *Windows* operating system's mechanism for the addition of new devices. The device is plugged into the computer and Windows will automatically take care of the configuration; e.g. to add a new printer, simply plug in and follow the screen instructions.

plug and pray – This term can be used when referring to the sometimes frustrating experience of installing additional peripheral devices on a PC.

plug and tell – Plug and tell refers to the installation of new peripheral devices in a PC and the use of a utility program that can help to configure the new device properly. Plug and tell utilities analyze the system and recommend which settings should be made.
SEE ALSO: PLUG AND PLAY, PLUG AND PRAY

plug compatible – Hardware that will work with any computer that is fitted with the correct sockets.

plugfest– A risky way of testing the operations of network devices by actually plugging them into a running network. It saves time in testing but there may be some damage done either to the device or the network.

Pluggable Authentication Modules – A *UNIX* programming interface that enables third-party security methods to be used.

plug-in – This term is used for describing the kinds of software that are widely employed for extending the existing functions of a web browser. For example, an audio/visual plug-in might be used for enabling video-conferencing; Adobe Acrobat may be downloaded, installed and then run in order to read an Adobe-formatted document.

plug-inless – A reference to a unique feature on a web site that does not require a *plug-in* to be downloaded, installed, and associated with the browser in order to use it. Advantages include saving time changing computers and a lower risk of infection from *computer viruses*.

p-mail – Old fashioned communications using printed paper and postage. Generally referred to as *snail mail*.

PMS – See: **P**antone **M**atching **S**ystem

PNG – See: **P**ortable **N**etwork **G**raphic

PnP – See: **P**lug and **P**lay

Pocket applications – This term refers to a suite of pared-down applications for *Pocket PCs* from Microsoft. This suite of applications includes versions of Microsoft's most popular programs, such as *Word*.

Pocket PC – A version of Windows developed by Microsoft for use in hand-held computers. It provides scaled-down versions of Microsoft's most commonly used applications.
Go to:
www.microsoft.com/mobile/pocketpc

pod – The bubble that encloses a player in a *virtual reality game*.

POD – See: **P**rint **o**n **D**emand

point – 1. To move the cursor to a location on the screen.
2. In typographical terms, the measurement for the height of a piece of type. One point is the equivalent of 1/72-inch.

point and shoot – An action such as selecting a menu option or activating a function by moving the cursor onto a line or object and pressing the return key or mouse button.

point of contact (POC) – The person at an Internet Service Provider's offices with whom a user can interact via telephone, e-mail or web site.

Point of Presence (POP) – The telephone number for access to an Internet Service Provider (ISP). POPs are provided in locations served by that ISP throughout the country in order to enable their customers to make use of local-rate phone charges. When traveling it is best to locate a POP in the area to keep telephone costs to a minimum.

point solution – The process of solving one particular problem without regard to related issues. In programming it may be used as a quick fix or short-term solution while a wider problem is being worked on.

pointer – The icon shown on screen that indicates the location of the *cursor*. Common forms include the I-beam pointer, arrow, or paintbrush.

pointing device – Any device that controls the input of the *pointer*, usually a *mouse*, but also keyboard instructions, *touchpads* and rollerballs on laptops, or a *pen* or *stylus* on hand-held devices.

point-of-sale system – Any computerized system that records sales; e.g. computerized cash registers or scanners.

point-to-point network – This kind of network is based on computers interlinking through other computers. The Internet and most *wide area networks* are examples of point-to-point networks. Contrast with broadcast network.

point-to-point protocol (PPP) – The rules governing transmission of data by a computer over the telephone line using *TCP-IP*. Without the point-to-point protocol, a computer would not be able to connect to the Internet.

Point-to-Point Tunneling Protocol (PPTP) – A system that allows remote users to access a local area network (LAN). It is useful if a business wishes to connect several offices via the Internet creating a *virtual private network*.

Poisson distribution – Developed by the 18th century French mathematician S. D. Poisson, this is a statistical process used for predicting the probable distribution of a series of events.

Policy Certification Authority – An organization that is authorized to issue *digital certificates*.

politeness window – This is the time used by a *spider* when visiting a *server* to access information for cataloging purposes.

polling – 1. When one program repeatedly checks with another program to see if it has data ready for it.
2. Checking hardware to see if a process has occurred, e.g. data transfer.

polycarbonate – A term covering a number of plastic materials used to make a wide range of products used in computing.

polygon – A common object used in computer graphics. It consists of a multi-sided object that can be filled with color and placed anywhere on the page.
SEE ALSO: POLYLINE

polyline – In computer graphics, a line that can be manipulated at several points.
SEE ALSO: POLYGON

polymorphic virus – A type of virus that changes each time it passes from one computer to another. This makes it difficult for *virus protection software* to discover. Also called a self-mutating virus.
SEE ALSO: COMPUTER VIRUS

ponzi scheme - **See:** pyramid scheme

POP – 1. **See:** Post Office Protocol
SEE ALSO: POP3
2. **See:** Point of Presence

POP3 – Post Office Protocol version 3. This is a way of receiving e-mail messages where the message is held on the *server* until the addressee picks it up. Once received by the user, they are deleted from the server's post box.
SEE ALSO: POST OFFICE PROTOCOL

pop-under – A *window* that is hidden beneath the window of a web site that the user is visiting. When the user leaves that site, the pop-under window becomes visible. Pop-unders are generally used for advertising purposes.
SEE ALSO: BANNER AD

pop-up – Windows, menus, etc. that instantly appear on-screen, usually as a result of clicking the mouse on an icon or using keys in combination.

pop-up menu – Menu that appears over the existing window, remaining active until a command is given or the menu is closed. It usually appears on clicking the mouse buttons or using key combinations. These menus are different from the *pull-down menus* located on the toolbars.

pop-up utility – Program that is run by pressing a special hot key, appearing regardless of which application is currently running and remaining in memory.

pop-up window – Small window, that appears over the active window, informing the user of an error or confirming a choice, such as, "do you really want to quit?" When the appropriate button is clicked, the pop-up disappears, leaving the original window.

pornography – One of the attractions of the Internet for some people is the uncensored access to pornography. For those that do not want to have pornographic sites displayed through search engines or want to restrict a child's access to such material, various *parental controls* are available. Software packages called *censorware* can be purchased to screen incoming material and *browsers* can be set to accept different levels of sex, violence, and language.

port – 1. The connection point where data can flow in and out of the computer to *peripherals*. Dedicated ports within the computer connect to specified services. 2. On the Internet, the number given to each application available on a *server*.
SEE ALSO: SERIAL PORT

port address – The number that identifies each port. They are divided into three families - Well Known Ports, Registered Ports, and Dynamic or Private Ports. There are over 65,000 registered by the Internet Assigned Number Authority.
SEE ALSO: PORT

port replicator – When a laptop is connected to a docking station, the ports available on the laptop are replicated on the docking station. This means such peripherals as the mouse, printer, and keyboard do not need to be attached every time.
SEE ALSO: LAPTOP, PERIPHERAL DEVICE

portable – This term describes any kind of hardware or software that can be taken from a computer and will work with different *operating systems*.
SEE ALSO: REMOTE COMPUTING

Portable Document File (PDF) – The *file format* used by *Adobe Acrobat*. It is popular with web site designers because it is *portable*, can be read by *browsers*, and is highly flexible.
SEE ALSO: ADOBE ACROBAT

Portable Network Graphics (PNG) – A compressed, bitmapped, graphic *file format* similar to the *GIF file*. The PNG format developed out of a copyright problem with CompuServe, who developed the GIF format. With its additional features, the Portable Network Graphics file format is expected to replace the GIF in popularity.

portal – The portal is a web site that acts as a *gateway* through which a user travels when they begin using the Internet. Portals offer much by way of content, e-mails, chat rooms, and personalization services. For example, a portal may be a search engine that provides additional services, a company such as AOL (which supplies Internet access and wide range of additional features), or a more specialist provider of content.

portrait – In printing, portrait is the term used for the orientation of the paper where the longer side is vertical and the shorter side is horizontal. The opposite orientation (longer side horizontal and shorter side vertical) is known as *landscape*.

POS – See: **P**oint **o**f **S**ale System

post – The act of sending a message (*posting*) to a *newsgroup*.

POST – **P**ower-**o**n **S**elf **T**est. The routine testing that the PC performs on its hardware, CPU, and memory when it is switched on.

Post Office Protocol – A basic protocol that operates between client and server to *download e-mail*. The most recent POP version is *POP3*.

postcardware – Software that is free to the user but is accompanied by a request from the software producer to receive a postcard showing the town where the user lives.
SEE ALSO: FREEWARE

posting – This is the common term describing any message sent for display on a *newsgroup server*. Responses to a posting on the Internet are referred to as follow-up postings, while a thread is the term used to describe a set of postings on the same topic.

postmaster – The postmaster is someone at the server who manages *e-mail* delivery. Most *ISP*s have a postmaster and problems or questions regarding e-mail should be directed to him or her.

PostScript – A page description language (PDL), created by *Adobe*, primarily to enable print accuracy on laser printers. It is used on all computer platforms and is considered the Industry standard to be used in commercial typesetting and publishing. PostScript gives great flexibility in color management and font selection.
GO TO: www.adobe.com

POTS – See: Plain Old Telephone Service

pound key – 1. Synonymous with the number key #.
2. The key that types the "£" symbol. On a British keyboard it is the Shift 3 key.

pound sign – The number sign # is also called the pound sign.

power cycle – To turn a computer off and then on in the hope of curing a fault such as *freezing*.

power down – To turn off the computer.

power line protection – A device that is plugged into a power socket to protect the computer from power surges which can cause irreparable harm to a system.
SEE ALSO: UNINTERRUPTIBLE POWER SUPPLY

Power Mac – A range of PCs from *Apple* first launched in 1994.
GO TO: www.apple.com

power supply – The electrical supply to the computer. It also refers to the subsytem that converts and regulates internal power.

power up – To switch on.

power user – Someone who needs the latest and fastest IT equipment.

PowerBook – *Apple's* trade name for its highly successful portable PCs.

PowerBuilder – Produced by Sybase, this is a widely used application development system for web client-server environments.
GO TO: www.sybase.com

PowerNow! – Technology from *AMD* that was used in notebook computers and laptop computers; it improves efficiency of the processor, enhances power conservation and extends the life of the battery inside.
Go to: www.amd.com

PowerPC – Family of *CPU microprocessors* designed by Apple, IBM and Motorola and introduced in 1993. PowerPCs are designed to be used in a range of computing devices from hand-helds to supercomputers; it is a Reduced Instruction Set Computer (*RISC)* chip and was first used in *PowerMac* PCs in 1994.

PowerPC REference Platform – A common but now outdated specification for PowerPCs from both IBM and Apple that allows them to run a number of different operating systems.

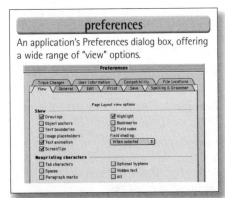

preferences

An application's Preferences dialog box, offering a wide range of "view" options.

Powerpoint – A program from *Microsoft*, which can be used to create presentations, handouts, visual aids and slides.
Go to:
www.microsoft.com/office/powerpoint

PowerStep – Power-saving device built into *Apple* laptops and notebooks. It helps the user to slow the processor speed.

p-p – **See:** peer-to-peer

ppm – Pages per minute.

PPP – **See:** Point-to-Point Protocol

Practical Extraction and Report Language
(PERL) – The programming language used to write *CGI* programs that enable a web server to interact with various applications such as form filling or searching. Increasingly being usurped by Java.
Go to: www.perl.com

precedence – Order for processing logical and mathematical data. In *Boolean* logic, usual order of precedence is NOT, AND, OR.

Precision Graphics Markup Language (PGML) – A *scalable* graphics *language* for the production of 2D graphics and their integration into documents. PGML is part of *XML.*

preconfigured – Devices or software that have been set up in advance and modified for the customer or situation. Some servers and computer manufacturers supply a set of preconfigured applications.

preemptive multitasking – A form of *multitasking* where the operating system can interrupt a currently running task in order to run another task. In cooperative multitasking, it is the application that decides on priorities.

preferences – A set of options within a program or operating system that the user can select. Within a browser this may include display options such as font and color schemes but also allow the user to select whether or not to accept cookies, set privacy and security options, select a homepage, and many other features.
SEE: FEATURE BOX

prefetch unit – The part of the processor that looks at data and decides which action to perform next.

Premiere® – A digital video-editing program from Adobe that, according to the manufacturers, offers a wide range

of features and provides cross-platform support for all the leading Web video formats.
Go to:
www.adobe.com/products/premiere

premium content – High quality or specialist content on the Web that is downloaded for a fee.

PReP – See: **P**owerPC **Re**ference **P**latform

preprocessor – A type of software that performs a certain level of preliminary processing on input, before it is processed by the program to be used.

prescan – This is a quick, low-memory scan that is produced by some scanners to enable the user to check that the final scan will be optimal.

presence – In *instant messaging*, being aware that another person is currently online and available.

presentation graphics – Computer-based presentations for business and educational purposes. The presentation can be viewed on the computer display, through an overhead projector or can be projected onto a screen.

press – 1. The newsmedia.
2. Short for printing press.

Pretty Good Privacy (PGP) – An encryption program based on *public-key cryptography*. Messages can only be read if the recipient has the encryption key with which the data was encrypted. It is used for secure e-mail transmissions, when sending credit card details, and for the creation of *digital signatures*.

pretzel – (slang) The Macintosh command key, which is so called because the logo on the key is pretzel-shaped.

preview – 1. Some programs, such as web page design packages, enable the user to see a preview of how the document will appear once displayed on screen or printed. 2. A short extract of a video, movie, or piece of music that is used for the purposes of demonstration.

Primary Domain Controller (PDC) – In *Windows NT*, a service that manages security for its local domain. Each domain has a PDC containing a list of usernames, passwords, and permissions.

primary mouse button – The right hand mouse button. This is the only button on older mice.

primary server – The first server that is visited when accessing an IP address. A secondary server (primary back-up server) is usually available if a problem occurs.

Primary Rate Interface – An enhanced version of *ISDN* transmission technology.

 primitive – The use of basic shapes (such as circles, squares, and triangles) to create more complex images.

print – To generate a paper copy of a computer-generated document.

print job – A file that is awaiting printing.

Print Manager – The software within *Windows* that manages print jobs.

Print on Demand – This phrase refers to the technology that allows for the printing of single copies or for the production of very low print runs (up to 2000) of books. It enables those publishers that use it to keep their stocks to a minimum and therefore to print in response to demand rather than needing to make an educated guess as to how many books will be needed. The term Print on Demand also means that books need never go completely out of print, as they can be stored digitally and then ordered and printed as necessary.

Print Screen key – A command that prints the current page on the computer screen. Within Windows the page is first sent to the *clipboard* and can be placed in other documents or viewed via the clipboard viewer in the system tools.

print server – A computer in a network that handles printing for other computers.

printed circuit board (PCB) – A board that contains *chips* and electronic components. It is not strictly printed but is rather an etched circuit. The main printed circuit board is the *motherboard*. Smaller *boards* or *cards* slot into the main printed circuit board.

printer - The printer is the device that makes paper copies of computer-generated documents.
SEE ALSO: DOT MATRIX PRINTER, IMPACT PRINTER, INKJET PRINTER, LASER PRINTER, NON-IMPACT PRINTER

printer buffer - The computer sends data to the printer faster than the printer can print. This data is held in an area of memory called the print buffer until it can be printed.

printer cable - A cable used for connecting the printer to the computer. Printer cables are usually connected to the PC's parallel port.

Printer Control Language (PCL) - A type of *page description language* introduced by Hewlett Packard and adopted by many of its competitors.

printout - A printed copy of a file. Also called a *hard copy*.

prisoner of Bill - This is a patronizing term used by non-Microsoft users to describe those computer users relying on Microsoft applications. Bill is Bill *Gates*, founder of Microsoft.

privacy - Within an online context, as elsewhere, this term refers to a person's right to maintain the privacy of personal information. Internet users are concerned about the unauthorized sharing of information, anonymous messaging, and of the right for Internet users' messages to be exchanged without unauthorized persons reading them.
SEE ALSO: ENCRYPTION, PRETTY GOOD PRIVACY, REMAILER, SPAM

Privacy Enhanced Mail (PEM) - A method of securing e-mail transmissions that ensures integrity and authentication. Privacy Enhanced Mail is now being supplanted by *Secure Multimedia Internet Mail Extensions (SMIME)*.

private automatic branch exchange (PABX or PBX) - This refers to an automatic telephone switching system operated by and within a business or within some private enterprise.

private branch exchange (PBX) - See: private automatic branch exchange

private chat - When a chat room is used for a private one-to-one *real-time* conversation it is described as private chat. In order to communicate, a user needs first to *log-on* to the chat *channel* and establish whether the second person is online. Most people choose to use an *instant messaging* program to facilitate private chat.

private data network – A network that is solely used by one organization or company. It can run over the Internet or consist of private lines.
SEE ALSO: PUBLIC DATA NETWORK, VIRTUAL PRIVATE NETWORK

private key – The code that is used by the originator of an encrypted message.
SEE ALSO: PRIVATE KEY ENCRYPTION, PUBLIC KEY, PUBLIC KEY ENCRYPTION

private key encryption – A system of *encryption* in which sender and receiver have the same key.
SEE ALSO: PRIVATE KEY

private packet radio – When a private wireless network is used to enable wireless network connections.

private web site – An *intranet*; a web site accessible by internal personnel only.

PRN – Abbreviation for *printer*.

pro – This is one of the proposed new domain names suggested in 2000 for use by a professional individual.

process – Any action performed by a user on a computer.

processor – Short for *central processing unit (CPU)*.

processor speed – The number of instructions a Central Processing Unit (CPU) can perform in a minute.

Prodigy – A commercial online service that provides access to the Internet, e-mail and a variety of databases. Prodigy was launched in 1988 as a partnership of IBM and Sears.

profile – 1. The rules that a filter uses to screen incoming material over the Internet. 2. Information about how a particular user wishes to set up the computer. Useful in situations where more than one person uses the machine.

program – 1. (noun) Software that enables the user to perform a task; for example, word-processing software, games software, photo-processing software.
2. (verb) To write a program for a computer.
SEE ALSO: PROGRAMMER, PROGRAMMING, PROGRAMMING LANGUAGE

program icon – The *shortcut icon* on the *desktop* representing a program. Double-click on the icon to run the program.

Program Information File (PIF) – A file within *Windows* that tells the operating program the type of *environment* needed for a program; i.e. the amount of memory required, type of graphics, and printer handling information.

program library – A cataloged collection of programs and related information.

programmable function – This refers to any *function* that is able to be given instructions (programmed).

programmable function key – Refers to any key on the keyboard that can be programmed to perform a function. The F (function) keys are one example, but combinations of shift, control, and alphanumeric keys are also commonly used to perform functions of various kinds.
SEE ALSO: FUNCTION KEYS

Programmable Read-Only Memory (PROM) – A kind of *memory chip* that can only be programmed once.
SEE ALSO: ROM, EPROM

Programmable Universal Micro Accelerator (PUMA) – A commercially available *chipset* that accelerates graphics operations for the screen and printer.

programmer – Someone who writes computer programs (instructions) is known as a programmer.
SEE ALSO: PROGRAM, PROGRAMMING, PROGRAMMING LANGUAGE

programming – This term refers to the process of designing and writing a computer program. The programmer must decide what the program needs to do, develop the logic of how to do it, and write instructions for the computer in a programming language that the computer can then translate into its own language and execute.
SEE ALSO: PROGRAM, PROGRAMMER, PROGRAMMING LANGUAGE

programming language – This refers to one of the many languages used for writing instructions for a computer. Programming languages come in a wide range of accessibility for the learner. The simpler ones are ideal stepping stones for moving on to the more powerful and sophisticated languages that are most commonly used by experienced programmers: both amateur and professional. Examples of the many programming languages include: COBOL, BASIC, AppleScript, Visual Basic, C, and C++. Programming languages that are used to write and automate web pages include *CGI, Java, JavaScript,* and *PERL.*
SEE ALSO: PROGRAM, PROGRAMMER, PROGRAMMING LANGUAGE

Progressive JPEG – Graphic images similar to JPEGs; but, as a progressive JPEG image is loaded, the viewer gradually sees the image emerging from a "fog" until it becomes totally clear. This effect is created by the fact that, whereas a normal JPEG image is displayed by creating one line after another from top to bottom, progressive JPEGs are displayed on screen in alternate lines, allowing the viewer to see part of the image at first. Then the missing lines are filled in on a second pass, creating the effect of an image coming into focus. (With some software, this focussing effect may be replaced by a kind of Venetian blind effect).

project – A discrete undertaking with definite objectives and constraints. For example, Project Gutenberg
SEE ALSO: PROJECT GUTENBERG

Project Gutenberg – This massive effort to provide free Internet access to 10,000 classic books by the year 2002. It was begun in 1971 when its first entry - the American Declaration of Independence - was made available to the world in a format in which all subsequent texts have also been posted: ASCII text. This means that the thousands of texts that are now available can be read on any computer.
Go TO: http://sailor.gutemberg.org
SEE ALSO: ELECTRONIC LIBRARY, E-BOOK

projection panel – See: LCD panel

prolly – An abbreviation for the word "probably," used in chat rooms and newsgroups.

properties

In Windows, right-click any file and choose Properties from the menu that appears to access the Properties dialog box.

This example shows the Properties box for a Microsoft Word file called Document 1.

PROM – See: Programmable Read-Only Memory

Promail.Trojan – A widely available and sinister *Trojan* horse program that can act as a normal *POP* client allowing a user to obtain e-mail from a designated POP server. However, the program also sends account information, including passwords, to an anonymous e-mail address, where it allows anyone with access to the anonymous e-mail address mailbox to read, delete, and manipulate the users POP mail. The file is generally distributed as a zip file named proml121.zip.

promiscuous mode – A networking *mode* in which crackers can read data from all *packets* traveling over a network regardless of their destination address.

promiscuous security policy – A policy that allows anyone on the Internet access to an organization's internal network.

prompt – A message from the computer asking the operator for input, e.g. to enter a password.

propagation delay – The time required for data to be transmitted to its destination over the Internet or other network.

propeller head – Synonymous with *geek*, someone with good IT knowledge.

properties – In *Windows,* the properties feature gives information about a file; for example, size, location, the date on which it was created and modified, and its attributes (e.g. whether the file is read-only, or hidden, etc.). The properties of the file depend on the nature of the file. For example, a file created within a Windows word-processing application is likely to reveal properties concerning its author, date of creation and modification, statistics, and content. The nature of the properties information, and the means by which it is accessed, will also vary according the operating system being used.
SEE: FEATURE BOX

proportional pitch – In typesetting, a typeface where some characters are wider than others; i.e. M is wider than N.
SEE: FEATURE BOX

proportional spacing – **See:** proportional pitch

proprietary – Software that is owned by a company or by an individual programmer. Proprietary programs are run by the user under license.
SEE ALSO: COPYRIGHT

protected distribution system – A transmission system (often fiber-optical) that has sufficient in-built security protection to make it possible to transmit unencrypted data.

protected mode – A *mode* of program operation using an Intel-based microprocessor. In protected mode much of the operating system code and the application programs are protected to ensure that essential data is not accidentally overwritten.

protocol – The rules or standards governing the way that computers on a network exchange information. For example, *HTTP* defines the relationship and sets out the mutually agreed rules of interaction between *client* and *server* that enables users to use a *browser* for the purpose of accessing web pages.
SEE ALSO: ARP, FTP, IMAP, IP, KERMIT, MIDI, NNTP, OSI, POP, PPP, SLIP, SMTP, SOCKS, TCP/IP, UUCP, WAP

protocol header – This is information contained within the *packet* that provides transmission details such as addresses and encoding data.

---

proportional pitch

proportional spacing **Proportional**

mono spacing **Proportional**

An example of proportional pitch at work where some characters are wider than others.

protocol stack – The term protocol stack refers to a hierarchy of protocols that provide services on a network. For example, OSI and TCP/IP.
SEE ALSO: LAYER

provider – **See:** Internet Service Provider

prowler – A *daemo*n or dormant program that is evoked to perform a maintenance routine, e.g. disk cleanup.

proxy – Something which acts as a substitute for something else and/or as a front for something.

proxy operator – A feature of some *search engines* that shows words that are in proximity to each other. So a search on "Java applet" would bring up all the files in which the words Java and applet appear close to each other in the searched text.

proxy server – A *server* program, that lies between a *client* application (most commonly a browser) and the server. It provides quick access to commonly requested files by holding them on a local *cache*. Another function is to allow Internet access from behind a *firewall*.

Prt Scr key – **See:** print screen key

PS – File extension for documents created in PostScript format.
SEE: APPENDIX 5 for file extenstions.

PS 2 – **See:** Playstation 2

PS/2 – A family of *plugs and sockets* used to connect mice and keyboards to a computer and audio devices. Sometimes referred to as a DIN connector.

pseudo – This refers to the false name and identity given by someone in a *newsgroup* or *chat room;* it is short for pseudonym.

pseudonymous profile – Information about a particular computer user that can identify that user either by his or her computer's IP address or by a nickname. It describes a user's interests, habits, online activities, etc and is often used for web site *personalization*, or for marketing purposes.

psychedelicware – Software that is used for creating the kind of moving images in bright colors that were popular in the psychedelic fashions of the 1960s.

PSTN – **See:** public switched telephone network

p-to-p – **See:** **p**eer to **p**eer/**p**erson to **p**erson

public carrier – A *carrier* that is obliged to accept all traffic, as opposed to a private carrier which can refuse to provide services.

public data network (PDN) – A communications network where the *carrier* company provides a service to a number of networks that are operating using several different *protocols*.
SEE ALSO: PRIVATE DATA NETWORK

public domain (PD) – Public domain means belonging to the public; not protected by copyright.

public domain software – Freely available programs for which ownership has been relinquished to the public at large.
SEE ALSO: FREEWARE, SHAREWARE

public directory – An area of the server that is accessible without the use of a password. Such files are available for anyone to use without constraints.

public file – The kind of file that is available to everyone who accesses a network or system.

public key – A code used to encrypt messages that is available for anyone to use. The decoding is done by a private key that is kept by the person originating the public key.
SEE ALSO: CRYPTOGRAPHY, ENCRYPTION, PUBLIC KEY ENCRYPTION, PRIVATE KEY ENCRYPTION

Public–Key Cryptography Standards (PKCS) – The set of rules governing the usage of *public key encryption*

public key encryption – A form of cryptography where messages are sent encrypted with the receiver's public key; the receiver decrypts them using the *private key*.
SEE ALSO: PUBLIC-KEY CRYPTOGRAPHY STANDARDS

public key infrastructure (PKI) – PKI is the published part of a *public key encryption* system.

public switched telephone network (PSTN) – Voice and data communications service for the general public which uses switched lines.

public web site – Refers to a site on the World Wide Web that can be accessed by anyone with a web browser and access to the Internet.

puck – A *pointing device* used in association with a *graphics tablet*.

public web site – A web site accessible to all users of the World Wide Web.

publish and subscribe – A service that offers information on a regular basis to anyone who subscribes. It may be free or a fee may be charged. E.g. Regular e-mails, newsletters, business advice, etc.

pull – Where the user decides to visit a web page or to download software. Contrast with push, where the user is automatically sent information.

pull advertising – Persuading users to visit an advertised web site by such means as *banner ads* and *hyperlinks* in a web pages.

pull technology – A specific request from a specified source; e.g. using the *browser* to locate a *URL* from the Internet.
SEE ALSO: PUSH TECHNOLOGY

pull-down – A function that expands downward on demand, usually a menu.

pull-down menu – **See:** drop-down menu

Pulse Amplitude Modulation – The first step in pulse code modulation, PAM is the conversion of audio wave samples to pulses. This is then followed by the conversion of the pulses to digital text.
SEE ALSO: PULSE CODE MODULATION (PCM)

pulse code modulation (PCM) – PCM provides a method for the storage of sound that is commonly used in high performance *sound cards.*

pulsing zombie – This is a computer whose security has been breached without the user's knowledge so that it intermittently carries out a *denial-of-service attack* on other computers in a network. A pulsing zombie weakens rather than paralyzes its victims.
SEE ALSO: ZOMBIE

PUMA – **See:** **P**rogrammable **U**niversal **M**icro **A**ccelerator

punched card – Punched cards were originally invented in the 1890s, and were the preferred data storage medium for almost 80 years. They consist of an oblong piece of thin cardboard that holds data as patterns of punched holes. The holes are punched by a keypunch machine and then fed into the computer by a card reader.

punter – This is a program that sends a very large *HTML* file by e-mail, causing the user's computer to freeze until the download is completed.

purge – To delete both data and all references to that data; e.g. emptying the recycle bin.

PURL – **See:** Persistent URL

push – To deliver data and services to a user's desktop automaticaally.

push advertising – To send advertising material automatically and without the user's request.
SEE ALSO: SPAMMING

push technology – Data delivery technology where information is delivered or "pushed" automatically to a user who subscribes to it. Contrast with pull technology where the user asks for data. Push technology is popular with services such as news delivery systems and stock market quotes.

pushware – A type of software that uses push technology to deliver information.
SEE ALSO: PUSH TECHNOLOGY

put – 1. To place in a specified location. 2. In programming, a request to store a current record in an output file.

PVC – **See:** **p**ermanent **v**irtual **c**ircuit

PVM – **See:** **P**arallel **V**irtual **M**achine

.pwl – A Windows password list file. When a user first types and saves a password while connecting to a password protected resource, Windows stores the password in the password list file.

PWS - See: Personal **W**eb **S**erver

pyramid scheme – An Internet scam that encourages users to recruit other users, who in turn recruit other users. Generally, such schemes revolve around selling an item for commission where part of the commission for every recruit is paid to the person who recruited that member. Eventually such schemes fold and the founder disappears. This is also called a ponzi scheme.

Python – Python is a popular, object-oriented scripting language invented by Guido van Rossum in Holland in the early 1990s. It was named after the BBC comedy series "Monty Python's Flying Circus." It is used for writing system utilities and Internet scripts and as a *glue* language for integrating components in C and C++.

QA – 1. **See:** quality assurance
2. An integrated *file manager* and word-processing program from the company Symantec.

Q&A – Short for **Q**uestions **and A**nswers, a popular format for displaying web site information.
SEE ALSO: FREQUENTLY ASKED QUESTIONS

QBASIC – A *BASIC* interpreter program from Microsoft.

QBE – **See:** query by example

QIC – **Q**uarter-**i**nch **C**artridge. *Magnetic tape* used to back up information. The quarter inch referred to the width of the original tape, these days the tapes are much larger.

QoS – **See:** quality of service

quad-speed CD-ROM drive – Drive that spins the disk four-times faster than a single *CD-ROM,* providing higher output at 600Kbps. Also known as 4xCD-ROM – most PCs are now up to 24x or 48xCD-ROM.

 Quake – A massively popular computer game launched in 1996. It was a successor to the popular Doom. It is a strategy game where players navigate their way around 32 levels of mazes while combating alien foe.
GO TO: www.idsoftware.com/quake/ for the official site.

quality assurance – A planned and systematic process with the aim to provide adequate confidence to the consumer that the final product or service meets industry standards and fulfils customers' expectations. E.g. That a computer is problem-free and able to perform the task for which it was designed.

quality of service – A measure of the ability of a company to deliver what it says it will or to get to an established standard. E.g. A network must offer predictable and guaranteed transmission speeds. Often abbreviated to QoS.

quarantine – Incoming messages that a *security* system suspects may contain a *computer virus* are moved to a quarantine area. A message will be sent to the originator of the transmission to alert them to the possibility that they have sent a virus.

QuarkXPress – A commercially available desktop publishing program from Quark, Inc., well regarded for its precision and advanced text and graphics handling.

Quark**XPress**

It is widely used by many book, magazine and newspaper publishers as well as by advertising and design companies.
GO TO: www.quark.com

query – To interrogate a web site, database, or network through the use of a search engine.

query by example (QBE) – A simple way to *search* a database by typing the search *keywords* into empty fields. The conditions are then entered that need to be included in the query. For example, to find all records where the Age field is greater than 30, you would enter *>30* in the Age field blank. Software then converts this field-based search into a *query language*, e.g. *SQL*, to activate the search.

query language – A specialized language used for extracting information from databases, with extensive use of QBE. *SQL* is a major Internet query language as is the use of *query by example*.
SEE ALSO: BOOLEAN SEARCH; KEYWORDS

query window – A window that appears when an error has occurred, usually requesting an action or input of data.

queue – The list of operations waiting to be completed; e.g. e-mails waiting to be sent or documents awaiting printing.

quick and dirty – (slang) A web site, program, or technological solution that is put together fast and without attention to detail.

QuickBASIC – A widely used BASIC compiler program from *Microsoft*. It adds advanced features to the BASIC language.

Quickcam (LOGITECH) – A commercially available digital camera from LogiTech, it can be used in video conferencing, animation, and video clips.
GO TO: www.quickcam.com

QuickDraw – The graphics display program built into *Macintosh* computers. It provides a consistent interface across all applications and draws objects on screen. The GX version offers more special effects and better print management.
GO TO: www.apple.com

QuickTime – A popular multimedia program developed originally by *Apple* for the *Macintosh*, it now works with *Windows* too. It allows for sound and video to be embedded in web pages and it also supports video-conferencing.
GO TO: www.apple.com/quicktime

QuickTime VR (Virtual Reality) – A *virtual reality* version of QuickTime. It allows subjects to be viewed on screen as if in 3D. Scenes are compiled from multiple still shots taken of all sides of whatever is being shown.

quit – To exit a program or system by choice, via the *menu, keyboard shortcut*, or appropriate dialog box.

quotation marks – When using a search engine, putting the query in quotation marks means that the search is conducted on the phrase rather than the individual words. E.g. Typing in computer dictionary will yield a list of computers and dictionaries, while "computer dictionary" will give you more precise results.

quote – When replying to e-mails, to include the text of the previous e-mail or e-mail *thread*.

QWERTY keyboard – The standard English language keyboard layout. QWERTY are the first six letters of the top line of letters.
See also: KEYBOARD

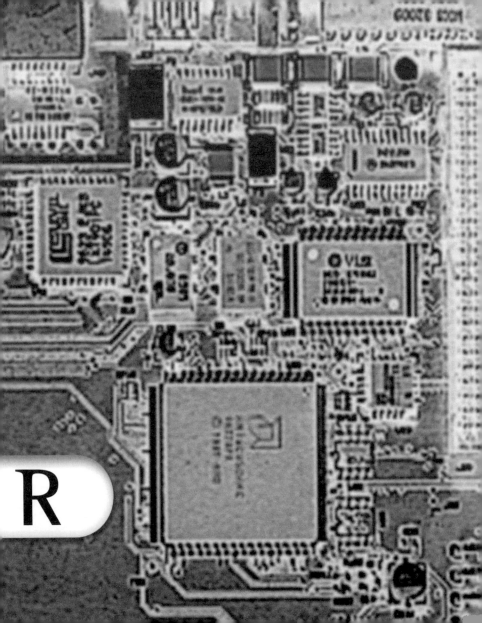

R/3 – Produced by SAP America, R/3 is an integrated series of client/server applications for businesses.
Go to: www.sap.com

ra – range

.ra – This extension indicates that the file is a *RealAudio* file. Real Audio is the online audio player used for live broadcasts.
See: Appendix 5 for a full list of file extensions.

rabbit – See: bacteria

race condition – A race condition occurs when two or more programs that are dependent on each other compete to finish a task even though they need each other to complete it. This condition can lead to problems concerning the accuracy of data and performance.

rack – A frame for hardware.

rack unit – A unit of measurement related to the height of a rack-mounted device. One rack unit, or RU, is 1.75 inches.

RAD – See: rapid application development

RAD tool – Description of a program or utility that speeds up the development and programming of an application. For example, using a visual programming tool to quickly develop graphical interfaces.

radial – Radiating from or converging to a common center.

radial fill – In a drawing application, a graded *fill* where two or more colors blend outward from a central point to a circular perimeter. By moving the center point and a single control point on the circle, the user can make changes to the fill effect on the object.

radial transfer – The transfer of data between two bits of software or hardware that are at different layers in a structured system.

radio – In an online context, radio refers to live audio broadcasting across the Net. The advent of virtual audio players, often available for free download and use, from companies such as RealNetworks and Microsoft has meant the availability of thousands of new radio channels that cater for a whole gamut of tastes and styles. Users can customize their radio players and consequently personalize their listening experiences.
Go to: www.radio-locator.com or www.web-radio.fm or www.radiotower.com
See also: Real Player

radio button This is a small, graphically depicted button that is used to present a number of options within a *web page* or *window*. The radio button normally exists in an on or off state; in a group of radio buttons only one of them is usually allowed to be on.

RADIO CORPORATION OF AMERICA (RCA) – An entertainment company now owned by Thomson Multimedia, who manufacture color TV sets, VCRs, digital satellite decoders, DVD players, camcorders, home audio systems, and many accessories.
GO TO: www.rca.com

radio frequency – Radio waves are transmitted on the electromagnetic spectrum at frequencies of between 3kHz and 300 GHz. The term radio frequency or RF covers the range of frequencies above our audio range to just below that of visible light.

---

ragged

This example shows a column of text that is displaying ragged text on the right. It can be referred to as left aligned, or in this case, ragged right.

The text lines up straight against the left margin.

INTRO TEXT GOES HERE Lorem ipsum dolor sit amet, consectetuer adipiscing elit, sed diam nonummy nibh euismod tincidunt ut laoreet dolore magna aliquam erat volutpat. Ut wisi enim ad minim veniam, quis nostrud exerci tation ullamcorper suscipit lobortis nisl ut aliquip ex ea commodo consequat. Duis autem vel eum iriure dolor in hendrerit in vulputate velit esse molestie consequat, vel illum dolore eu feugiat nulla facilisis at. GOES HERE Lorem ipsum dolor sit amet, consectetuer adipiscing elit, sed diam nonummy nibh euismod tincidunt ut laoreet dolore magna aliquam erat volutpat. Ut wisi enim ad minim veniam, quis nostrud exerci tation ullamcorper suscipit lobortis nisl ut aliquip ex ea commodo consequat.

The right hand ends of the lines are ragged.

If this column of text had an uneven margin on the left, it would be referred to as ragged left.

---

radio-frequency interference (RFI) – *Interference* caused by signals that are emitted by a piece of electrical equipment when it carries rapidly changing signals. RFI can affect unprotected circuits and cause them to malfunction.

radiosity – A computer simulation of light reflecting off one surface and onto another. Radiosity is a more accurate method of rendering light and shadows than ray tracing. It produces a much more realistic view of shadows, reflections, and soft lighting.

radix – The base value in a numbering system. In decimal the radix is 10, the radix point being the decimal point. Binary numbers have a radix of 2.

radix point – The specific point in a number that separates the integer from fraction; so, in the decimal system, the radix point is the decimal point.
SEE ALSO: RADIX SORT

radix sort – A way of sorting batches of numerical information one digit at a time. First data is sorted by the least significant digit. The result of this is sorted by the second least significant digit, and so on, until the batch of data is sorted on the most significant digit. The advantage of this method is that it requires a minimum amount of space and a minimum amount of data movement.
SEE ALSO: RADIX

ragged – In text processing, this refers to text that is not aligned along a margin. Ragged right means that each line ends at a different point on the right of the column of text. (This is also referred to as left aligned).
SEE ALSO: JUSTIFIED, ALIGN
SEE: FEATURE BOX

RAID – See: **R**edundant **A**rray of **I**nexpensive **D**isks

RAID Advisory Board – Founded in 1992, the RAID Advisory Board is an organization that is involved with the dissemination of information, and the standardization and classification of RAID storage systems. It is an open organization and welcomes any companies as members.
GO TO: www.raid-advisory.com
SEE ALSO: REDUNDANT ARRAY OF INEXPENSIVE DISKS

RAM – See: **r**andom-**a**ccess **m**emory

RAM cache – See: Level 2 cache

RAM chip – See: **R**andom **A**ccess **M**emory chip

RAM cram – A situation where there is insufficient memory to run applications. It is common in older computers with limited memory available.

RAM disk (virtual disk) – *Random access memory* arranged to simulate a *disk drive*. This enables faster working but once the power is turned off information on the RAM disk will be lost. Also called a RAM drive.

RAM doubler – A piece of software that compresses the contents of memory, thereby in theory doubling available memory capacity.

RAM latency – The time between initiating a request for a character in memory, and when it is retrieved.

RAM refresh – The recharging of dynamic *RAM* chips (many times per second) to keep the bit patterns valid.

RAM residents – Programs that remain in memory in order to interact with other programs or to be available when required by the user.
SEE ALSO: RANDOM ACCESS MEMORY

Rambus memory – See: RDRAM

RAMDAC – See: **R**andom **A**ccess **M**emory **D**igital-to-**A**nalog **C**onverter

ramp up – A term meaning to increase: for example: "We need to really ramp up production of those chips."

random – Without settled direction, aim, or purpose; without previous calculation; left to chance; haphazard; a guess. Without order.

random access – **See:** direct access

random access device – A piece of hardware whose ability to retrieve data at speed is not affected by the type or location of that data.

random access memory – A collection of memory chips that function as a computer's primary workspace. Random refers to the contents of each byte of storage in the chip; they can be directly accessed without regard to the bytes before or after it. RAM chips require power to maintain their content, which is why data must be saved onto disk before turning the computer off.
SEE ALSO: MEMORY

Random Access Memory chip – The correct term for a normal memory chip or for a microprocessor.

Random Access Memory Digital-to-Analog Converter (RAMDAC) – The video graphics control *chip* that maintains the color palette and converts data from memory into analog signals required for the monitor.

random number – A number that cannot be predicted.
SEE ALSO: RANDOM NUMBER GENERATOR

random number generator – A random number generator is a program that does exactly what its name suggests: it produces a random number, as required.

random processing – Random processing is the processing of information in the order it is required rather than in the order in which it was stored.

range – 1. The difference or interval between the smallest and largest point in a group of values.
2. In mathematics, the set of all values a given function may take on.
3. On spreadsheets, a series of cells that are worked on as a set or group.
4. A geographic distance.
5. A group of frequencies.
6. In music, the gamut of tones that a voice or instrument is capable of producing.
7. A series of objects or items.
8. Refers to a set amount between a minimum and a maximum.
9. Refers to a set of allowable values – a number range.

rank – To sort data, either alphabetically or by number. Usually associated with some quality aspect.

ransom note typography – The fault of using too many fonts in a document or presentation, like the text in a ransom note that is pasted together from words cut out of different magazines and newspapers.

Rapid Application Development – The process of developing systems and networks incrementally, delivering work piecemeal every three to four months, say, rather than waiting until the entire project is programmed before implementing it. The term can also apply to the development tools or to any features that make the process of programming easier.

rapid prototyping – The process of building a mock-up of a site at high speed, showing it to the customer and then progressing through a cycle of feedback and change until the customer is satisfied with the end result. A very common method of web site development.

RARP – See: **R**everse **ARP**

RAS – See: **R**emote **A**ccess **S**ervices

.ras – A filename extension for a *raster* file, usually a *bitmap* image.
SEE: APPENDIX 5 for file extensions.

raster – 1. A scanning pattern of parallel lines composed of pixels that form an image projected through the cathode-ray tube of a television set or display screen. 2. The rectangular area of a display screen actually being used to display images.

raster burn – (slang) Eyestrain brought on by too many hours of looking at low-res, poorly tuned, or glare-ridden monitors.

raster display – A display monitor that uses the raster scan method for creating the image on screen.

raster graphics – An image represented by a series of minute dots.
SEE ALSO: BITMAPPED GRAPHICS

raster image processor (RIP) – This is a combination of hardware and software that converts an image into a *bitmapped graphic* image.

raster operation (ROP) – An instruction that manipulates the bits of a *bitmapped graphic* image in some way.

rasterize – To prepare a page for display or printing using a *raster image processor.*

rating services – Sites and books that offer ratings and reviews of web sites or services such as *ISPs*. They rate according to criteria such as reliability, speed, *content*, and cost. Some sites pay customers to review items they have used, or buy products specifically to rate the service received.
Go to: www.dooyoo.com or www.kelkoo.com

Ravage – *Computer virus* that resides in two memory sectors - the *MBR* of a hard drive and the boot sector of a floppy disk.

rave – 1. An argument that is getting out of control or one person's impassioned plea that goes beyond reason. A common feature of *newsgroups* everywhere. 2. To discuss persistently a specific subject while knowing very little about it. 3. To annoy another person verbally on purpose. 4. Similar to *flame* but the participant is oblivious to the fact that he is annoying.

rave-on – In a chat room, to ask someone to continue raving. Usualy it is meant sarcastically as the participant is unlikely to be aware that they were raving.

raw – This is a reference to original and untouched material or data.
SEE ALSO: RAW DATA

raw data – Any information that has not been organized, formatted, analyzed, or manipulated in any way is referred to as raw data.

ray – 1. A thin line or narrow beam of light or other radiant energy; graphic or other representation of such a line. Radiance; light.
2. A straight line extending from a point. Also called half-line.
3. A structure or part having the form of a straight line extending from a point.

ray tracing – A highly advanced and onerous system for simulating the effects of light and shadow on images.
SEE ALSO: RAY

RBL – See: Realtime Blackhole List

RC5 – An algorithm called a block cipher, used in encryption programs, developed by the company RSA Security.
SEE ALSO: RSA

RCA – See: Radio Corporation of America

RDBMS – See: Remote Access Server

RDRAM – A faster *Dynamic RAM* owned and licensed by Rambus Inc. It is used primarily in computers but some advanced versions are used in computer and video games.
GO TO: www.rambus.com

read – 1. To look at printed words and understand their meaning.
2. To scan text.
3. To retrieve data.

readme file – A common kind of text file included in software disks containing essential information, last-minute updates, or errata that have not been printed in the documentation manual. On simple programs it may replace a manual.

ReadNews – This is a *newsreader* for *Usenet* newsgroups.

read-only – Describes a file that can be read but not manipulated. Most programs allow the user to make a file read-only.

read-only memory – A read-only memory *chip* permanently stores instructions and data. The contents of the RAM chip are created at the time of its manufacture and cannot to be altered later.
SEE ALSO: MEMORY

read-only user – (slang) Description of someone who uses a computer only for the purposes of reading Usenet and other newsgroups, bulletin boards, and/or e-mail.

readout – 1. A piece of computer paper containing information.
2. A small digital display.
3. Any screen information.

Read-rite – Read-rite is one of the world's largest suppliers of magnetic recording heads for the hard disk drive (HDD) market.
Go to: www.readrite.com

read-while-write – A type of tape drive that can write data and read it back for verification immediately; both the operations take place in the same pass.

read-write – A term applied to a device that can both input and output or transmit and receive. Sometimes written as read/write. When used as a prefix it denotes a two way transfer of data.

ready – Fit to be used, awaiting use.

real – Being or occurring in fact or actuality. An item having verifiable existence. True, not imaginary, alleged, or idealized. Not virtual.

real estate – (slang) Commonly used term for any resource measured in units of area.

real life – On the Internet, real life means having practical experience rather than theoretical or academic knowledge. Commonly used in *newsgroups*.

real mode – An operating *mode* for *Intel microprocessors* 80286 and later models. In this mode they imitate the operation of earlier models, but at much faster speeds.
See also: pentium

Real Mode driver – This is a PC driver limited to one megabyte of memory and written to the original 16-bit – *8086* and *8088* architecture. Real Mode drivers must run within the first megabyte of memory.

Real Name® – A system on the Internet that was developed to help users locate difficult-to-remember web site addresses (Universe Resource Locators) by using an easy-to-remember set of keywords. Users can search for companies using this site.
Go to: www.realnames.com

real number – A number that is rational or irrational, not imaginary. Usually represented by a floating point; e.g. 4 10-5.

RealAudio - A popular online audio (sound) player often used for *streaming* live broadcasts.
See also: RealPlayer
Go to: www.real.com

RealJukebox – A virtual jukebox that enables the user to download, play and organize music.
Go to: www.real.com

reality check – This refers to ensuring that a theoretical course is a realistic one. For example, during a project such as system development reality checks may be put in place to ensure that the project is being completed satisfactorily.

RealPlayer – A very popular multimedia player and browser *plug-in* from RealNetworks, Inc. It plays RealAudio and RealVideo transmissions.
Go TO: www.real.com

 Experience Entertainment

RealSystem – **See:** RealPlayer

real-time – An instant and immediate response to events as they happen.

Realtime Blackhole List – A service that enables people to blacklist sites that have been responsible for the generation of *spam* e-mail. This Realtime Blackhole list is available to e-mail transport programs and enables them to filter out spam mail from those sites.

real-time clock – An electronic circuit that maintains the correct time and works like an alarm clock, providing timing signals for certain key operations.

realtime credit card processing – When ordering online, an immediate authorization of a credit card purchase.

Real-Time Streaming Protocol (RTSP) – A specification developed by *Netscape* and Progressive Networks for the transmission of video, audio, and animation over the Internet. Real-Time Streaming Protocol supports live transmissions.

Real-Time Transport Protocol (RTP) – A widely used Internet Protocol (IP) that supports the real time transmission of voice and video.

realtime video – This provides the capability to transmit video live; in other words as "realtime" video without missing any frames.

RealVideo – A popular online video player often used for the transmission of *streaming* live broadcasts and for playing back downloaded video files.
Go TO: www.real.com
SEE ALSO: REALPLAYER

reasonable test – A form of testing to determine whether a value or result falls within a range that is considered normal or logical.

reboot – To start up or re-start a computer, usually after some error or damage has occurred or after maintenance has been carried out. After installing a new piece of software, you will often be advised that rebooting the computer is required before the new software will work.

rebuild – To build again, usually after equipment failure.

recall – 1. To bring back a previous file. 2. When a fault is found in an important piece of hardware the computer manufacturer may ask the consumer to send it back for repair.

receive only terminal – This describes a printing device only; there is no additional keyboard, or interaction.

receiver – In contrast to a transmitter, a receiver is a device that accepts signals.

reception (RX) – The condition or quality of signals received.

reciprocal link – An arrangement between two web sites, both of which promote each other's sites with hyperlinks.

recompile – The process of compiling a program again, usually after a change has been made to it, in order to test and run the revised version. The process of recompiling is likely to occur many times during a program's development.
SEE ALSO: COMPILER

reconstitute – The restoration of a corrupted file. The term reconstitute also describes the process of returning a file to a previous state.

record – A group of related fields (each one item of information) that store data about a subject or activity. A collection of records makes up a *file*.

records management – The organization and control of essential information, including back-up data or personal files, for any kind of organization or business. The records may be paper-based or computer-based.

recover – To restore a file or piece of information of any kind.

recovering erased files – Files are often not fully erased from the system when the delete button is pressed. In Windows they get sent to the *Recycle Bin* from which, under most circumstances, they can be retrieved. There are several commercial programs available which will help users recover any old, deleted and lost files. The process of recovering erased files is also known as "undelete."
GO TO: www.norton.com or www.microsoft.com or www.apple.com

rectifier – An electrical circuit used to convert AC into DC current; it is actually a *diode* that causes the current to flow in only one direction.

recursion – This is when a *program* or *subroutine* calls itself; for example, when requesting a service or information of some kind. Recursion is a memory sapping technique that can prove useful when solving large problems, especially those where large amounts of data need comparing or checking.

recursive – The function of *recursion*. If the call during recursion is via one or more other functions then this group of functions are called mutually recursive.

recycle – To re-use or reprocess the same material.

recycle bin – Introduced with the launch of Windows 95, the recycle bin is an icon of a wastebasket that is used for deleting files. The icon of any file or folder for deletion can be dragged to the wastebasket and released. Known as a trash can in Apple Macs. The deleted files are kept until the Recycle Bin is emptied.
SEE: FEATURE BOX

Red Book – The documentation of the US National Security Agency that defines the operating criteria for secure networks.

Red Green Blue – The term for the standard color model used for generating video on screen. The colors are displayed as varying intensities of red, green, and blue dots. A range of different colors are produced on the computer screen as the dots are mixed and the intensification is varied.

redaction – Editing sensitive documents before their release to the public. Redaction is a reference to the use of red ink for covering up any errors or sections of classified information.

redefine – To change the function or value that has been assigned to a *variable*.

redirect – Diverting data from its normal destination to another.

redlining – In word-processing, identifying text that has been changed by displaying it in a special color. It stems from the days when red ink was always used to mark changes to texts.

redo – To repeat an action or reverse an undo instruction.
SEE ALSO: UNDO

Reduced Instruction Set Computer (RISC) – A type of microprocessor that only works to a limited set of instructions, which enables those instructions to be carried out at a faster than normal rate. Pronounced "risk."

redundancy – The duplication of data, often intentionally, to make programs more robust.

recycle bin

Microsoft's Recycle Bin icon first appeared in its Windows 95 operating system. (Apple Macs use a trash can icon).

Double-clicking on this icon opens the Recycle Bin folder, showing the files that you have deleted.

Redundant Array of Independent Disks (RAID) – A class of disk drives mainly used on servers using two or more drives in combination. This lowers the risk of errors and faults, increases performance and drives down costs. There are several levels of **RAID**. The most widely used are:

RAID LEVEL 0 - interleaves data across multiple disks for improved performance, but does not protect against failure.

RAID LEVEL 1 - provides complete duplication of data. High reliability, but high storage cost.

RAID LEVEL 3 – As level 0 but all drives operate in parallel, achieving the highest data transfer speed.

RAID LEVEL 5 -Most widely used. Data is placed across three or more drives for performance, and a high degree of fault tolerance built in.

RAID contrasts with JBOD, which stands for Just a Bunch Of Disks, those without a controller and managment capabilities.

Go to: www.raid-advisory.com
See also: RAID advisory board

refresh – To re-draw or reload an image or web page on a screen. To update regularly.

Refresh button – Generally, the F5 key on a standard keyboard, it refreshes the page.
See: feature box

refresh rate – The number of times the data in a *Dynamic RAM* microprocessor has to be read and re-written, per second.

regional settings – The settings on a computer that allow it to match local time and date and work in the right language.

register – An area of memory that can be accessed rapidly, often built into the CPU.

registering a domain name – To adopt a *domain name* for personal or business use. Specialist companies exist to manage domain name registration, and many ISPs also offer this service.

registration – To notify the manufacturer that their product has been purchased. It usually results in guarantees being ratified or a number of other benefits such as free programs and information.

---

refresh button

A refresh button is available with Internet Explorer (similar to the Reload button with Netscape Navigator). Clicking these buttons reloads the contents of the web page.

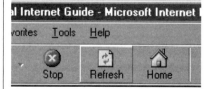

Refresh or reload buttons (or menu options) are built into the toolbars or menus of many applications.

Registration Editor – See: Registry

Registry – An organization or company responsible for allocating *domain names* for the Internet and *IP addresses*. The registry is also the dedicated database used in Windows for storing details on how operating programs have been set up.

rehi – In *newsgroups*, *chat rooms*, and *MUDS*, the term is used as a greeting, short for "Hello again."

relational database – This method of database organization links files by comparing and complementing data, such as account numbers, addresses and names. A relational database has the flexibility to take any two or more files and generate a new file from the records that meet the matching criteria. In practice, however, it can prove to be a slow system that requires extensive use of indexing.

relational database management system (RDBMS) – A program that looks after the organization, storage, retrieval facilities, security, and integrity of data in a database. It does this by using the principles and architecture of a relational database.

relative address – The location of a piece of data identified by indicating its distance from another address that is called the *base address.*
SEE ALSO: ABSOLUTE ADDRESS

relative link – A *hyperlink* that is not directed to the *URL* of the web page, but to the folder that contains it. This makes a link less susceptible to being lost in the event of changes in the web site.

release – To launch a version of a product in the marketplace. Often products are given a release number or version to assist in identifying the latest upgrades.

relevance feedback – Some *search engines* can provide users with feedback on the relevance of a document found in response to a query. The search engine then uses this information to search for other relevant documents.
SEE ALSO: WIDE AREA INFORMATION SERVICE

relevancy algorithm – The system used by a search engine to decide whether a page is relevant to a search. The exact scheme used by an individual search engine is kept a closely guarded secret to prevent unscrupulous web site developers from cheating and giving their site a higher *site ranking* than it might otherwise deserve.

reload – To close a piece of software and load it again; this is the first remedial step that should be taken if a program fails to function properly.

relocatable program – A program that can be run from any memory location.

remailer – See: anonymous remailer

remote – Not physically at the same location. The computer in the current location is known as *local*.

remote access – Accessing a network from a distant location by such means as *dial-up access*. This enables the user to use files and programs on the remote computer's hard disk. For example, home users access the Internet through remote access to an *Internet service provider*.

Remote Access Server (RAS) – The computer and software that is designated to manage users seeking access to network remotely. This server makes dial-up access to a network possible.

remote control software – The software that enables a user to connect to a remote computer and use its files via the Internet or other link. E.g. Accessing an office computer from home or from a laptop. Both computers need to be fitted with the same software.

Remote Job Entry (RJE) – Transmitting batches of transactions from a remote terminal or computer. The receiving computer processes the data and may transmit the results back to the RJE site for printing or viewing purposes.

remote login – To *login* to a remote computer, as if it were the local computer, by using a network connection. *Telnet* provides a popular route for remote login.

Remote Method Invocation (RMI) – A *Java* technology for *distributed objects* that enables two objects programmed in Java located on different computers to communicate with each other. For example, if a form is submitted by a user, the second computer could inform the first computer about that process.

remote monitoring (RMON) – The collection of information about the functioning of a network.

remote procedure call (RPC) – A means of writing code on one computer, which is to be executed on another computer. The results are returned to the initial computer and then used. In client/server systems, such as the Internet, this enables the client to make a request from the server, who returns a response.

remote server – The host computer within a *local area network* (LAN) that gives access to remote users via the host computer's modem.

Remote Shell – This is a *UNIX* command that enables a user to remotely log on to a server on a network and then to pass commands to it.

remote terminal – A terminal which is not directly connected to the computer that it is working off; e.g. *Telnet* is a *terminal emulator* which enables *remote login* and file access.

removable hard disk – A portable hard disk that can be taken out of one computer and transferred to another, or kept in a library. It is generally used for back-up, long-term storage, or for transferring large files.

removable storage – Storage media that is saved on the disk drive and removed when not required. Removable disks include floppy disks, optical disks, and tape.

render – A surface mapping technique that adds color and shading to a graphic object to make it look real. Such objects are usually created using a wire frame or vector system.

resample

Resampling of an image file is often carried out to reduce the number of pixels from which it is made. This reduces the file's storage requirements.

These two images show the same picture, the first with many pixels, the second with far fewer.

Altering the number of pixels used to create an image may be necessary to enable it to be printed.

repaginate – To reset a document's page numbering system.

repeat rate – The speed at which a character is repeated when its keyboard key is depressed.

repeater – An electronic device which boosts a signal during transmission. A network will contain a number of repeaters which enable signals to travel further.

repetitive sequence suppression – A form of *compression* that looks for repeated sequences of data and replaces them with a token that is used to represent the sequence.

replace – To substitute one object for another.

replicated web site – **See:** mirror site.

replication – To create a copy (or replica) of something.

reply button – Reply buttons are often found on an e-mail system, allowing the user to reply to the current message without the need to type in the address or subject. The content of the initial message is also included in the reply.

Request For Comment (document) – This is a document sent out by the *Internet Engineering Task Force* that sets out a proposed change to Internet protocols and allows interested parties to respond to the proposal before it is adopted.

Request for Price Quotation – A document created by the customer and delivered to the vendor or provider of a service that requests a price for hardware, software, or service.

request to send – Signal sent from a serial port to a modem or other device to indicate it is ready to receive more data.
SEE ALSO: HANDSHAKE

res – Short for *resolution*.
SEE ALSO: DPI

resample – To alter the number of pixels used to create an image. This may be necessary to enable an image to be printed or to reduce storage requirements.
SEE: FEATURE BOX

reseller – A merchant who buys computers and other information technology equipment, then adds value, for example, including premium software, and then resells to the consumer at a price that includes a decent profit.

reseller hosting – The provision of web hosting services to companies that then act as hosts for other companies. Usually such hosts add additional services such as web site design and site management services.
SEE ALSO: HOST

reserve price – In online auctions, the prices below which an item will not be sold. E.g. If the reserve price is $100, then a bid for $50 would be rejected.

reset button – A switch on a computer case that will reset the system without switching off completely.

resident font – A font that is permanently built into a printer's read-only memory (ROM). It is necessary to have the corresponding font within the computer's software to display it on screen.

resident program – A program that remains in the memory.

resize – To make an object smaller or larger.

resolution – The number of *pixels* in an object or *display*. The greater the number of pixels, the better the quality of the final image or display.
SEE ALSO: BITMAP

resolver – This is the program that enables the client computer to look up *domain names* and then obtain the *IP* address of other computers.

resource – Any device or application available to the user of a network. For example, a printer that is shared by several people is a resource.

resource leak – See: leak

reponse bot – An automatic program used in *chat room servers,* it replies to common questions, checks for bad language and responds to offending users accordingly.
SEE ALSO: BOT

response time – The time between a computer-generated request and its fulfilment by the network; e.g. the time between the requesting and loading of a web page.

restart – A *Windows* operation, available from the Start button, that reloads the operating system. This is different from using the *reset button* which also resets the system hardware.
SEE: FEATURE BOX

restore – To recall documents that have been placed in the trash or have been saved via automatic back-up, maybe as a result of a system crash.

---

restart

The dialog box (Shut Down Windows) is available from the Windows Start menu by clicking Shut Down or by pressing both the Alt and the F4 keys at any time.

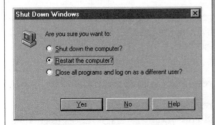

Choosing the middle option and clicking the Yes button reloads the Windows operating system.

---

resubmit – Repeatedly sending web pages to search engines for indexing. It may be done legitimately when the content of a web site has changed significantly. Resubmission may also be an attempt to increase the *site ranking* and in this way cheat the *relevancy algorithm.*

retouching – To alter an image to eliminate any flaws.

The right-hand image has been retouched to remove its stalk.

retransmission timeout – This occurs when data has been sent to a computer on a network and no acknowledgment has been received. Usually after a specific period of time the sender either retransmits it automatically or on a prompt.

retrieve – To request data that has been stored in a computer system.

retro – Of former times. Usually refers to old technology or fashions, or computer games that have been long overtaken by superior versions.

retrocomputing – Using and developing out-of-date software in order to keep old or obsolete computers running.

retronym – An entity or idea, which preceded newer versions; e.g. a biological virus is a retronym of a computer virus.

retrovirus – A *computer virus* that works its way through the system, finding its way to back-up copies of files and destroying or damaging them.

return – To create a line break. A *soft return* is a return of convenience, a flexible line break that is inserted into the text automatically; a *hard return* is inserted as a command by the user and is fixed.

return from the dead – A phrase used for a member of a newsgroup or chat room that has been absent for some time.

¶   ↵   **Return key** – This is the
hard soft large keyboard key that is
return return used for entering
information and creating a hard return. It is also known as the Enter key. Some keyboards actually label this key, Enter.

reusable – Some programming languages enable code written for one application to be reused in a different application.

reverse – Characters that are displayed in the opposite mode.

Reverse.948 – A simple memory-resident, *.com* and *.cxc* file-infecting virus that does nothing more then replicate.

Reverse Address Resolution Protocol – Part of the *TCP/IP* protocol which enables computers to find their own IP address; e.g. when an address has been assigned to the computer *on the fly.*

Reverse ARP – This is a *TCP/IP* protocol used by a diskless workstation to obtain its *IP address.*

reverse auction site – A web site that finds the products that a user wants at a price that he has specified.

reverse engineering – To take apart an object to see how it works.
1. Software may be reverse engineered to reproduce or enhance the program or to repair virus damage.
2. In 3D graphics, this may be to create a wire frame from an object.

reverse slash – More commonly known as *backslash:* the "/" character.

rewriteable – A storage medium that can be repeatedly overwritten. For example, CD-RW and *diskette.*

RF – **See:** **R**adio **F**requency

RFC – **See:** **R**equest **F**or **C**omment

RFI – **See:** **R**adio-**f**requency **I**nterference

RF shielding – This kind of material protects a device from electromagnetic radiation.

RGB – **See:** Red Green Blue

RGB color pallet – In the computer, the maximum number of colors that can be used for a color image; typically 24-bit color.
SEE ALSO: RED GREEN BLUE

RGB monitor - **R**ed, **G**reen **B**lue monitor. A high definition monitor that works with red, green, and blue input signals. Each colored pixel has a value of red, green and blue within it and these are reproduced with accuracy to create sharper and clearer pictures than a normal video display.
SEE ALSO: RED GREEN BLUE

Rhapsody - The code name given by *Apple* to its next-generation *operating system*, which eventually became *Mac OS X*.

rib site - This is a computer with a high-speed connection to a *backbone* that provides regional service for e-mail and newsgroup access.

ribbon bar - A flexible *toolbar* that displays different options, depending on the current active command.

rich e-mail - Refers to e-mail with attached voice messages.
SEE ALSO: ATTACHMENT

rich media - Information that is more storage, and bandwidth-intensive than ordinary text. Rich media can consist of any combination of graphics, audio, video, and animation.
SEE ALSO: RICH TEXT FORMAT

rich text format - This format stores all the textual details such as format, font, and page layout information. Versatile, it allows documents to be trasferred and opened within a wide variety of platforms and programs. If a document is unreadable to the recipient of an Internet transmission, sending the document in rich text format might help. The file extension for rich text format is .rtf.

right justify - Text that is aligned on the right margin.
SEE ALSO: JUSTIFIED, ALIGN

Right Thing - Something that is incontrovertibly correct or definitely the appropriate action. Usually capitalized to emphasize its correctness.

right-click - To *click* a right-hand *mouse* button. This is used in conjunction with many programs to evoke a limited menu. It is also used in many games.

rightsizing - The process of selecting the computer system, whether micro, mini, or mainframe, that best meets the needs of the application, or needs of the organization or person purchasing it.

ring network - Network *topology* where all the computers and devices such as printers are linked together with cable. Each device that is connected to the ring is called a *node*.
SEE ALSO: TOKEN RING

RIP - **See:** **R**aster **I**mage **P**rocessor

rip - To convert recorded music into digitized form for storage on a disk.
SEE ALSO: RIPPER

ripper – A program that is capable of transferring music from a *CD* and storing it directly on the computer without the need for reference to the computer's sound card.
SEE ALSO: MP3

Ripper – A *computer virus* that randomly corrupts the disk writes when active in memory. Approximately one in every 1,000 disk writes is affected, making the information that is written invalid.

ripping – 1. Using a raster image processor, ripping is the term used when the program prepares a page for display or printing. 2. The process of extracting the digital data from an audio CD.
SEE ALSO: RIPPER

RISC – See: Reduced Instruction Set Computer

riser card – An expansion card fitted to a fully loaded computer that enables additional cards or chips to be plugged in.

risk averse – A cautious or risk free approach. It is a common way of working for many programmers because it is able to minimize errors.

Risks digest – See: RISKS forum

RISKS forum – A popular online discussion forum that concerns itself with systems' problems.
GO TO: http://catless.ncl.ac.uk/Risks

RJ-11 connector Registered Jack 11 – A connector jack used in conjunction with telephone sockets in the US.

RJ 45 Registered Jack 45. – A serial connector, resembling a telephone connector, used with *Ethernet* and *Token Ring* networks.

RJE – See: Remote Job Entry

RL – See: Real Life

rlogin – See: Remote Login

RMI – See: Remote Method Invocation

RMON – See: Remote Monitoring

RMS – See: Root Mean Square

rn – See: ReadNews

road rage – (slang) A user's anger when they encounter difficulties on the web, such as slow or overloaded connections, busy servers, and missing links.

road warrior – A kind of person, such as a computer sales representative, who tends to travel a great deal with both a laptop and a mobile phone.

roaming To use a service in a number of locations. Many *Internet Service Providers* enable roaming access through the use of local *nodes* in world-wide locations. This means that the traveler can access the Internet through their laptop from most locations for the cost of a local phone call.

robot – A utility program with a defined task. For example. a program that trawls the Internet searching for pages that have changed significantly since the last visit. A *spider,* on the other hand, is a robot that specifically looks for indexing information. Abbreviated to *bot.*

robotics – The creation and use of robots.
SEE ALSO: ARTIFICIAL INTELLIGENCE

robust – A system or software that will perform well under exceptional conditions.

Rocket eBook – An *e-book* reader from Gemstar. It is roughly the size of a large paperback book, weighs 22 ounces, and holds about 10 paperbacks-worth of data. There is also a Pro model that holds the equivalent of 22 novels.
GO TO: www.rocket-ebook.com

rococo – (slang) Programs that are overly elaborate, with many unnecessary and memory-heavy enhancements.

rogue site – A site that has been established to serve some covert purpose; e.g. to act as a delivery agent for *spam,* for sending viruses, or for credit card fraud.

role-playing game – A computer game in which the players act out a different reality. Role-playing games are often based on fantasy or futuristic environments which are intended to challenge the player. The game is often overseen by a gamemaster or dungeonmaster who displays and

clarifies information and rules while also providing the challenges and tasks that players must undertake.

rollback – A very helpful feature built into database management systems, the rollback reverses the current transaction out of the database and returns the database to its former state. This can prove to be essential when a failure interrupts a half-completed transaction.

rollover – This facility within *JavaScript* changes the appearance of a hyperlinked graphic when a mouse event occurs. For example, one image may be replaced by another, or text may change color or animate when the mouse crosses its location. The principal function of the rollover is to alert the user to the existence of the *hyperlink.*

roll-up menu – A kind of menu that will reduce its height to nothing but the title bar when clicked.
SEE ALSO: DROP-DOWN MENU

ROM – See: **R**ead-**O**nly **M**emory

ROM BIOS – See: BIOS

roman – Abbreviation for *Times New Roman,* the most widely used font.

root – See: root directory.

root directory – The top directory in a computer system, from which all other branches sprout.

root mean square (RMS) – RMS is a measurement of the effective voltage or current of an AC wave.

root server – The *name server* that resolves *top-level domain names.*
SEE ALSO: RESOLVER

RO terminal – See: **R**eceive **O**nly terminal

ROP – See: **r**aster **op**eration

rot13 – **Rot**ate 13. A means of *encryption* that is used in *newsgroups* alerting users to the existence of offensive material within the posting. The message is encrypted using a simple formula. Each letter in the alphabet is assigned another letter 13 letters away from itself, with the end of the alphabet merging with the beginning. Newsreader software is capable of decrypting rot13 messages.

rotate – In graphics programs, to turn an object through 360 degrees or part thereof.

This image has been rotated 45 degrees counterclockwise.

round robin – A continuously repeating sequence; for example, requesting and gathering information, from several terminals by repeating the query. Used where reports are needed on data that changes continually.

roundtripping – The conversion of a document from one format such as *Microsoft Word* to a document in another format such as *HTML* and then back again – a process which can induce errors.

route – The path taken by a data *packet* from its source to its destination.

router – A device, usually a dedicated computer, that links together two *networks*. The router reads the address of a *packet* and directs it to its destination.

router cache – A database of addresses and forwarding information that are stored in a *router*.
SEE ALSO: CACHE

router droppings – The information provided by the router when it is unable to deliver an e-mail. This is incomprehensible to most people.

routine – A discrete chunk of a program that carries out a particular task.

routing – The process of deciding which *route* a *packet* should take to its destination.

Routing Information Protocol (RIP)
The Internet *protocol* used by *gateways* to determine the most efficient route for a *packet* to travel through the Internet.

routing protocol – A formula used by *routers* to determine the correct path onto which information should be forwarded.

routing switch – A *switch* that forwards *packets* by reading a destination address while acting as a *router*, forwarding the packets to the next router.

routing table – Database containing information about the *topology* of a network including *IP addresses*. Usually contains information on the current state of network traffic and the location of choke points, combining this information to determine the most efficient route a packet can take to its destination. Routing tables often work with *firewalls* to determine whether or not a packet should be rejected.

row – Horizontal set of components or data within a table, spreadsheet, or page.

RPC – **See:** **r**emote **p**rocedure **c**all

RPM – **R**evolutions **p**er **m**inute.

RPQ – **See:** **R**equest for **P**rice **Q**uotation

RS – **R**ecommended **S**tandard. Numbered documents suggesting optimal requirements for such things as interfaces and connector; e.g. RS-422 defines how serial devices are connected.

RSA encryption – **R**ivest, **S**hamir and **A**dleman encryption. A commercially available and very secure method of data encryption from RSA Data security. **Go to:** www.rsa.com

RSAC – **R**ecreational **S**oftware **A**dvisory **C**ouncil.

rsh – **See:** Remote Shell

rshd – **See:** Remote Shell

RTF – **See:** **R**ich **T**ext **F**ormat

.rtf – A filename extension for a *Rich Text Format* file.

RTP – **See:** **R**eal-**T**ime **T**ransport **P**rotocol

RTS – **See:** **R**equest **T**o **S**end

RTSP – **See:** **R**eal-**T**ime **S**treaming **P**rotocol

RU – **See:** **r**ack **u**nit

rubbage – (slang) A combination of garbage and rubbish; a term widely used in *newsgroups*.

rubber banding – In computer graphics, the moving of a line or object where one end of it stays fixed in position, while the other is moved, using the mouse, to where it is needed.

rude – (slang) In the sense that it offends, something that is poorly executed or fails to perform; e.g. a badly written program. A term used in *newsgroups*.

ruggedized PC – A computer that is designed for rough usage. A ruggedized PC is shockproof, waterproof, and will withstand dropping. It will also often have a removable hard drive. This kind of PC is regularly used by the armed forces, fire service, police, and by other services that may have hazardous working conditions.

rule – A system that is commonly used for screening incoming e-mail for specific information and then acting upon it. For example, the rule might place e-mails that have been received from different clients in different folders, or file e-mails in different folders by their subject matter, or date received.

ruler – The optional display toolbars that provide measurements to help ensure that the page will fit on a screen or to help with design and layout.

rules based – Using if-this, do-that rules to dictate actions. Rules-based products permit a great deal of flexibility in programs, enabling tasks and data to be easily changed by the replacement of one or more rules.

run – To execute a program.
SEE: FEATURE BOX

run length encoding – This data *compression* technique substitutes a character and a number for a run of identical characters.

run native – In contrast to running a program under some sort of emulation or simulation mode, to run native is to execute software written for the native mode of the computer. This is the most common way of working for computers, operating systems, and programs. However, this may change as emulation technology

improves, as it is easier to simulate something rather than build it from new.
SEE ALSO: EMULATOR

run under – To run under the control of a higher-level program.

running head – A *header* that is used at the top of every page in a document.

runt – A *packet* that proves to be too small to transmit.

runt filtering – The discarding of *runt* packets, which can clog up a network.

runtime – 1. The time during which a process is taking place.
2. The time that is taken for a process to be executed.

---

run

In the Open box of the Run dialog box (shown below) Microsoft Windows users can type the appropriate file name and location for the application they are intending to run.

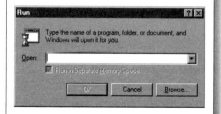

The Browse button can be used for searching on the local or network drives for the required program.

Rupe1.923 – A small, *encrypted* computer virus that infects only *.com* files. When an infected file is run, it searches the current directory for .com files and infects the first clean one that it finds. On July 18, before going into an infinite loop, the virus displays the following text:
!Hola! yo soy Ruperto y hoy 18 de Julio es el día de mi activación .com

Russian New Year Exploit – A type of attack which allows a malicious intruder to gain control of a system by visiting a web site. A function hidden in the HTML code, which enables a subprogram to temporarily gain control of the computer. The intruder may erase files or gain access to private information without the user ever being aware that an attack took place.

RX – **See:** reception

RXD – A code used in the context of modem technology meaning receiving data.

SAA – **See:** Systems Application Architecture

sabermetrician – A statistician who predicts the future performance of sports teams and players with the assistance of a computer.

sacrificial host – 1. A *server* outside the network that an organization uses to provide services which would compromise the internal security of the network.
2. A computer used to entrap attackers before they gain entry into a system.

SAD – **See:** Systems Analysis and Design

SadCase Trojan – A sinister *Trojan* horse that deletes everything on the C drive.

Safe For Kids – A system that rates Internet *content* suitable for children.

safe mode – In *Windows*, a simplified operating system that runs automatically if the computer detects a serious operating problem. Safe mode provides sufficient capability to detect and solve the problem.

SafeSurf – An organization devoted to making the Internet a safe place. They are especially concerned with protecting children from inadvertently accessing pornography and images of violence.
Go to: www.safesurf.com

sag – A drop in voltage from a power source. Contrast with *spike*.
SEE ALSO: BROWNOUT

salescritter – (slang) A patronizing term for a person who sells computers.

Salsa – A *Windows* application development system from Wall Data Inc. that uses predefined templates for common business functions.

salt – 1. In cryptography, a random number that is added to the *encryption* key to add another layer of protection.
2. To add random characters to a *password* to increase security.

Samba – Software that allows a *UNIX* server to act as a file server to clients using *Windows*.

sampling – Converting signals or movements emitted at regular intervals into digital code. Generally describes the operation of a sound card in converting sound waves into digitized data.
SEE ALSO: ANALOG TO DIGITAL CONVERSION

sampling rate – The frequency at which samples are digitized. A fast *sampling* rate and a large sample size results in a more accurate digitized sound.

Sampo – A *computer virus* that targets the boot record of the hard drive of a computer. The virus remains hidden in the memory after the user reboots successfully.

samurai – A computer specialist who is contracted out to perform legal *cracking* jobs, usually for lawyers.
SEE ALSO: STUPID, WHITE HAT

samuri – (slang) A skilled *hacker* who is hired out as a kind of "electronic locksmith." They are employed to perform legitimate *snooping* operations, e.g. in legal cases and some political situations.

sandbox – An *environment* in which certain specified functions are prohibited. Sandboxes are used on the Internet to isolate program elements that have come from an external source that is unknown or potentially damaging. E.g. *Java* have created a sandbox to provide security when downloading Java applets. They can be run from the browser and do not access the hard drive or network.

sans–serif – Typefaces where the riser and descender do not have a short horizontal line added at the top or bottom.
SEE ALSO: SERIF

SAP – See: Service Advertising Protocol

SAP – A Germany-based software company specializing in e-business systems.
GO TO: www.sap.com

SAPI – Speech API. A programming interface from *Microsoft* for *speech recognition* and synthesis. It enables applications to send text to and receive text from voice devices.

SATAN – Security Analysis Tool for Auditing Networks. A freeware utility that analyzes security vulnerability over the Internet and other networks.

satcom – SATellite COMmunication. All forms of communication that take place via a satellite.

satellite computer – A remote computer that is under the control of a host (master) computer. It can either function as a slave to the host computer or perform additional tasks offline.

satellite link – A signal that travels from the earth to a communications satellite and back. This is in contrast to a terrestrial link, which travels across the earth's surface.

satellite modem – A type of *modem* used to transmit and receive signals from a satellite transponder. It has to modulate digital signals from a *multiplexor* into a carrier frequency and then send to an upconverter, amplifier, and antenna. To receive data, it must reverse the process.

satellite phone – A telephone that transmits and receives signals via satellites. Satellite phones provide coverage around the world, and are often used in areas where there is little or no coverage from standard cellular networks.

satellite radio – Radio that is broadcast in digital format via satellites.

saturation – The amount of white contained in a color. E.g. A fully saturated yellow would be a pure yellow. The less saturated, the more pastel the appearance.
SEE ALSO: LUMINANCE, HUE

Saturday night special – (slang) A software program that has been created in a hurry without thorough checking for bugs and reliability.

 sausagetools.com – The company that produces the HotDog range of web authoring software.
SEE ALSO: HOTDOG
Go to: www.sausagetools.com

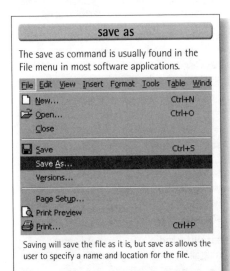

save as

The save as command is usually found in the File menu in most software applications.

File	Edit	View	Insert	Format	Tools	Table	Windc
New...						Ctrl+N	
Open...						Ctrl+O	
Close							
Save						Ctrl+S	
Save As...							
Versions...							
Page Setup...							
Print Preview							
Print...						Ctrl+P	

Saving will save the file as it is, but save as allows the user to specify a name and location for the file.

save – To place data in storage, either internally on a hard drive, or externally on a CD-ROM, floppy disk, or tape.

save as – To specify a *file* name and *address* location for data to be stored.
SEE: FEATURE BOX

SC connector – A device used to connect fiber-optic cables.

scag – The destruction of information that is stored on a hard disk.

SCAI – **S**witch-to-**C**omputer **A**pplications **I**nterface. A standard for integrating computers to a *PBX*.

scalable – A graphic or character that can be manipulated, enabling it to be displayed or printed in a range of sizes.

scalable font – A font that can be printed or displayed in a wide range of sizes. Non-scalable fonts may have a blurred or jagged appearance at some sizes.
SEE ALSO: JAGGIES, ALIASING

scalar – A single item or value; contrast with vector and array, which are both made up of multiple values.

scale – To resize an object or system to make it larger or smaller. Often used in reference to the expansion capabilities of hardware or software.

scaler – Products that can be upgraded to increase capacities or that will expand automatically to accommodate a much greater volume of data.

scan – To *digitize* an image or photograph and convert it to *bitmapped* data using a scanner. Scanned graphics are used extensively on web sites as they are easily manipulated and enhanced.

scan converter – A device that converts the video output from a computer to standard TV signals. This allows an ordinary TV to be used as a computer screen.

scan line – A horizontal line found in a graphics frame.

scan technology – A method for testing chips on a printed circuit board. The chips are designed with additional input and output pins for testing purposes.

ScanDisk – A utility in *Windows* and *DOS* that scans a disk for errors. It is found under the Accessories, System Tools menu and is part of the regular maintenance program of the system.

scanner – A device which *scans* any image, document, or photograph and converts it to digitized bitmap format. Most scanners operate by placing the document to be scanned on a flat plate. A beam then passes over the image and converts it to digitized data. Handheld scanners are also available.

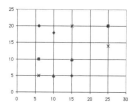

scatter diagram – A graph plotted with symbols at each data point. Also called a scatter chart or scattergraph. Scatter diagrams are used extensively by computer programmers to visualize data calculations and predict the results of the code that they are using to create applications.

scatter read – The facility for data to be entered into two or more locations of memory in one read operation.

scene description language – A method that uses a programming source code language to describe graphics objects. It helps to create a lifelike image. Contrast with a paint program, which uses graphical tools for creating images.

scheduler – The facility within an operating system to initiate and terminate tasks carried out within the computer.

scheduling algorithm – A method used to schedule jobs within the computer. It uses criteria such as priority, job queuing, and the availability of resources.

schema – Defines the structure and contents of a *database*.

sci – The designation for newsgroups with a scientific focus.

science fiction fandom – A computer subculture that is based on science fiction and fantasy literature. Related activities include web sites, newsgroups, and conventions which explore the culture and associated language.

scientific application – An application that simulates the real world using mathematics. Objects are turned into mathematical models and the actions of the objects are simulated by manipulating the formulas. Many of these applications take huge amounts of memory to function, e.g. flight simulation.

scientific computer – A computer specially designed for high-speed mathematical processing.

scientific language – A programming language specifically designed for use with mathematics, formulas, and matrices; e.g. Algol and Fortran.

scientific visualization – Computer-generated graphical representation of real-world objects. It is used to show such things as the shape of atoms, genetic modeling, and weather systems. It is especially helpful when explaining complex ideas to non-specialists.

scissor – To delete areas of a graphic or image which fall outside of a window.

scissors – The *icon* on a toolbar in most applications that represents the command "to cut."

SEE ALSO: CUT

Scoot.com – A popular online business directory based in the United Kingdom and northern Europe.

GO TO: www.scoot.com

SCOOT®

Scooter – The name of a *spider* program used by some *search engines*, notably *Alta Vista*.

scramble – To *encrypt*.

scrambling – In *cryptography*, to encode data and render it indecipherable.

Scrapbook – A feature of *Macintosh* computers, it is an area of memory that holds frequently used text and graphics objects.

scratchpad – An area of memory or a disk used for temporary storage. Sometimes known as the clipboard.

scream and die – (slang) Refers to the error message that is displayed before a program crashes.

screaming – A communications line that generates masses of incomprehensible data due to a malfunction.

screen – 1. A display on a computer, TV, or similar device.
2. A mesh placed over a computer display to reduce emissions and glare.

screen burn – When a static image is displayed on a screen for a long time, it sometimes burns into the phosphor, creating permanent damage. This problem has largely been eradicated in modern computer monitors.
SEE ALSO: SCREEN SAVER

screen capture – To store the current screen image. In *Windows*, this is done by pressing the *print screen key*, which places the present image in the clipboard or scratchpad. Sometimes called screen dump or screen grab.

screen dump – **See:** screen capture

screen grab – **See:** screen capture

screen name – The name adopted for use in an *IRC, MUD,* or other online service. This may or may not be the user's real name. Many Internet users like to use a screen name to preserve their anonymity for reasons of personal privacy and security. This is generally regarded as a sensible precaution when engaging in online actvities.

screen overlay – 1. A glare-reduction mesh screen that is placed in front of a video monitor.
2. A touch panel that enables screen

buttons to be activated.
3. A window that displays a temporary data screen. When the overlay is removed, the area of the screen that was overlaid is saved and restored.

screen reader – Software designed for the visually impaired that converts the text displayed on screen into speech.
SEE ALSO: TEXT-TO-SPEECH

screen resolution – **See:** resolution

screen saver – Software that creates continually moving images on the screen. It is activated after a specified time lag to prevent screen burn. Although this is not so much of a problem now, screen savers are popular because they are attractive and personalize the user's computer.
SEE ALSO: SCREEN BURN

screen shot – **See:** screen capture

ScreenCam – Screen-recording software developed by *Lotus*. It is used to make demos and training material by capturing software actions from the screen.

screenagers – (slang) A teenager who spends a lot of time on the Internet.

screened-host firewall system – A type of *firewall* which uses a *router* to filter incoming and outgoing connections before sending them on.

script – A set of instructions within a computer program.

script error – A *programming* error.

script kiddy – A derogative term for computer hacking by inexperienced people (often represented as bored teenagers) who use well-known *scripts*, programs, or routines to search for and exploit weaknesses in Internet-linked computers.

scripting host – The ability of a program to run another program. E.g. A browser is a scripting host that can execute instructions in languages such as *Java*.

scriptlet – A reusable *HTML* and script fragment that can be downloaded once, held in a cache, and referenced repeatedly by different HTML pages and scripts.

scroll – To move the displayed image or text up, down, left, or right to see an entire web page or document.
SEE ALSO: SCROLL BAR

scroll back buffer – Memory that holds transmitted data, which the user can recall.

scroll bar – The bar on the side of the display that enables the user to scroll the current display up, down, left, or right. The twin *scroll* arrows at the base of the vertical scroll bar enable page-by-page scrolling.
SEE ALSO: SCROLL BAR
SEE: FEATURE BOX

scroll mouse – See: wheel mouse

scrollable window – A window that contains too much data to be seen on the screen at once. The scroll bar is used to move the content horizontally or vertically, allowing the user to view it in its entirety.
SEE ALSO: SCROLL BAR

SCSI – **See: S**mall **C**omputer **S**ystems **I**nterface

scud e-mail – Defamatory e-mail that damages the reputation of the sender.

SD Card – **See: S**ecure **D**igital **C**ard

SDH – **See: S**ynchronous **D**igital **H**ierarchy

SDK – **See: S**oftware **D**evelopment **K**it

SDMI – **See: S**ecure **D**igital **M**usic **I**nitiative

---

scroll bar

The scroll bar is used to move the content of a window, so that it can be seen in its entirety.

The vertical bar is used to move the content up or down.

The horizontal bar moves the content to the left or right.

The twin scroll arrows move the content a page at a time.

S

SDSL - See: Symmetric **D**igital **S**ubscriber **L**ine

.sea - A self-extracting file. A condensed file system used by *Macintosh* computers.

seamless tiling - The use of a repeated image across and down a web page to provide background interest on the page. The server downloads only one image, and the repeats are created by the browser.

search - To seek out and find information over the Internet, the *World Wide Web*, or within a web site.
SEE: FEATURE BOX
SEE ALSO: SEARCH ENGINE

search agent - See: spider

search and replace - Within text processing programs, a facility that allows the user to find a certain word or phrase and replace it with another, throughout an entire document.

search box - The rectangular box, or field, that accepts typed-in text in order to facilitate a search.

search engine - A program that scans for specific or key words, then returns a list of documents where those words are to be found. There are many different types of search engine on the Internet. Many are directory sites that employ experts and volunteers to maintain and monitor the

sites on their database.. The best known directory search engine is *Yahoo!.* Some other types of search engine are entirely automated. These use *spider* programs to find relevant data; some are specialized and only look for data on a specific subject. *Altavista* is probably the best known of this type of search engine. It is worth trying several search engines, as different spiders and directories work in slightly different ways. Most search engines offer a number of advanced features, which allow the user to edit or refine their searches. This can help eliminate the frustration caused by searches that return large numbers of irrelevant hits. Most of the major search

search

Most browsers, including Microsoft's *Internet Explorer,* incorporate a search facility.

The magnifying glass icon opens the search menu.

Words to search for are entered in a dialog box.

Address   www.lycos.co.uk

Search   ×
New   Next   Customize
Choose a category for your search:
⊙ **Find a Web page**
○ Previous searches
○ Find a map

Find a Web page containing:

Brought to you by   Search
UK Plus

©2000 Microsoft Corporation. All rights reserved. Terms of Use

engines now have multiple sites, allowing searches restricted to documents that are based in, or are relevant to, a particular country or region. Many search engines also provide additional services, such as news, web-based e-mail, and Internet access. For most Internet users, search engines are their primary point of access to the often overwhelming amount of information that is available on the *World Wide Web*.

SEE: FEATURE BOX

search field – See: search box

search scope – The computer location where a search should be carried out. It can be a single folder, several folders, a disk, or several disks.

search site – A web site that searches other web sites for information.
SEE ALSO: SEARCH ENGINE

search tool – A search engine.

searchable database – A traditional database on the Web that can be searched for specific content.

searchenginewatch.com – This web site is worth a visit, as it lists all the search engines, tells you how they work, and offers advice on how to use them.
GO TO: www.searchenginewatch.com

search engine

This is the welcome page of *Lycos*, one of the most popular search engines on the Web.

This is the search box, into which the words or phrases to be searched for are entered.

The search is activated by clicking a button, or hitting the return key on the keyboard.

searchware – A class of program that searches data for specific information.
SEE ALSO: SPIDER

seat – On a network, a single *workstation* operated by one person at a time. The term is used in reference to how many seats a system can serve.

secondary mouse button – The left-hand *mouse* button. This button allows the mouse to be used to input commands from a limited menu choice.

secondary storage – All types of storage external to the hard drive, including disks, CD-ROM, and tape.

second-generation site – A web site that includes graphics, tables, forms, and *hypertext*. These features were not available on the earliest web sites before the widespread use of *HTML*.

second-level domain – In an *IP address*, the portion of the *Uniform Resource Locator* (URL) that identifies an individual domain. The second-level domain name includes the top-level domain name so that "dk.co.uk" is a second-level domain, containing within it the top-level domain "co." Second-level domains are sometimes subdivided into subdomains that indicate different departments, e.g. "books.dk.co.uk."

secret key cryptology – An *encryption* key that is used by a limited number of people.
SEE ALSO: PRIVATE KEY CRYPTOGRAPHY

sector – The smallest unit of storage that can be written to or read on a disk. For hard disks this is 512 bytes, for CD-ROMs, it is 2048 byttes.

secure – A site that has protection from attack by unauthorized users. Most use forms of *encryption* and SSL (*Secure Sockets Layer*) to create a *secure channel*. It is wise only to make payments for transactions through a secure site to protect personal information.
SEE ALSO: ACCESS CONTROL, DIGITAL CERTIFICATES, FIREWALL, PACKET SNIFFER, PROXY SERVER, VIRTUAL PRIVATE NETWORK

secure channel – A connection between a user and web site that is protected by a *Secure Socket Layer*.

Secure Digital Card – A flash memory card that provides secure storage for handheld devices such as *smart phones* and *personal digital assistants (PDA)*.

Secure Digital Music Initiative (SDMI) – An initiative that was established to protect music companies' copyrights on the Web, SDMI aims to develop a system for secure music transmission which prevents the unauthorized copying and distribution of music. The move was prompted by the problems caused by music sharing systems such as *Napster*.
GO TO: www.sdmi.org
SEE ALSO: MUSIC

Secure Electronic Transaction Standard (SETS) – A system developed by credit card companies, including MasterCard and Visa, that uses *digital certificates* to create a secure environment for credit card payments over the Internet.
SEE ALSO: SECURE TRANSACTION

Secure HyperText Transfer Protocol – See: SHTTP

secure messaging – A *messaging* system that has privacy and security measures built into the system.
SEE ALSO: INSTANT MESSAGING

Secure Multimedia Internet Mail Extensions (S/MIME) – A system for e-mail transmission that guarantees both security and integrity. It relies on a number of security measures, such as *digital certificates* and *public key encryption*.
SEE ALSO: PRIVACY ENHANCED MAIL

Secure Socket Layer (SSL) – A security system devised by *Netscape* to *encrypt* sensitive personal information, such as credit card details that are transmitted over the Web. Both the user and the site visited need to support SSL. When this happens, the secure nature of the site is indicated by the appearance of a small, closed padlock in the bottom left-hand corner of the browser's status bar. An open padlock indicates a site that is not secure.

secure transaction – A transaction that has been *encrypted* for the safe online transmission of sensitive data.
SEE: FEATURE BOX

secure URL – A *Uniform Resource Locator* that works in conjunction with a *Secure Socket Layer*. Such sites are indicated by the shttp: replacing the usual http: at the beginning of the URL.

security – The protection of equipment and data from theft or damage. Every PC should have a level of security protection, especially against virus attack. Obtaining a minimum level of security and preventing unauthorized access to your programs by the use of passwords is very simple, but viruses can undermine this. Free virus prevention and security software can be obtained from companies such as Zone Labs and AVG.
GO TO: www.grisoft.com and www.zonelabs.com

security certificate – **See:** digital certificate

security identifier (SID) – A unique moniker (name or alias) assigned to each network user or workgroup.

security officer – A person within a large organization who has responsibility for network and Internet security.

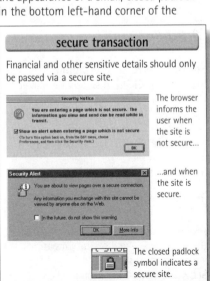

secure transaction

Financial and other sensitive details should only be passed via a secure site.

The browser informs the user when the site is not secure...

...and when the site is secure.

The closed padlock symbol indicates a secure site.

security zones - A feature of *Internet Explorer* that identifies four security zones on the status bar. The user sets the level of content security they desire and only sites that meet that criteria are displayed. The zones are: local intranet, trusted sites, Internet, restricted sites.

segment - 1. The amount of data in one *packet* sent over a *TCP/IP* network.
2. Section of a network that is bounded by bridges, routers, or switches.
3. In a *local area network* (LAN), a continuous electrical circuit that is often connected to other segments by repeaters.

select - To highlight an object or piece of text by placing the cursor on the item and clicking with the mouse. Selected items can then be manipulated.

select all - A command in the Edit menu of programs such as Word, which selects the entire document for manipulation. E.g. Enabling the type specifications to be changed throughout a document, or a list to be transformed into a table.
SEE: FEATURE BOX

selection area - The defined area around an image that is selected.

selection marquee - **See:** marquee

selection sort - A sort technique that begins by searching for the lowest or highest item (alphanumerically) in the list and moving it to the first position. The

process is repeated, starting with the second item, then the third, etc., until all of the items are in the required order.

selection tool - In drawing or paint programs, the icon in a toolbar that enables items to be selected.

selective calling - In communications, the ability of the transmitting station to indicate which station on the network is to receive the message.

self-extracting files - *Compressed* files that contain an executable program. This enables a *decompression* program to be activated to decompress the data.

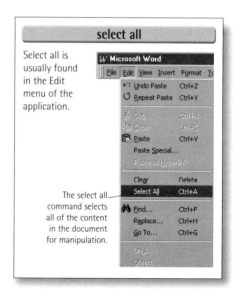

select all

Select all is usually found in the Edit menu of the application.

The select all command selects all of the content in the document for manipulation.

Self-Monitoring, Analysis, and Reporting Technology (SMART) – A drive technology that is able to automatically report an imminent failure back to the operating system.

Semantic Web – The idea that in the future, the Web will develop and become much more intelligent. The idea of a Semantic Web was proposed by Tim Berners-Lee, the inventor of the *World Wide Web*. In particular, he suggests that search engines will become far more precise and be better able to serve the user.
SEE ALSO: SEMANTICS

semantics – The study of the meaning of words and the relationship of symbols to their meanings.

semiconductor – A transistor is an example of a semiconductor. By definition, it changes state from non-conductive to conductive when charged with electricity or light. This creates an on/off switch.
SEE ALSO: CHIP

send – In e-mail, the act of transmitting the message. Most browsers and e-mail applications have a send button.

send to back/front – In paint, draw, and desktop-publishing programs, the facility to overlay one item upon another. A selected object can be placed on top of another: sent to the front; or placed beneath another object: sent to the back.
SEE: FEATURE BOX

sensitive information – In network and Internet security, information that should be protected because its misuse or destruction would cause harm to someone or something.

sequential – To be place in consecutive order; e.g. alphabetically, numerically, or chronologically.

sequential-access – The storing and retrieving of information in sequence. E.g. Data stored on magnetic tape is sequential, while that stored on a CD-ROM can be accessed at random.

serial – A process that deals with tasks, one at a time.

---

send to back/front

Send to back/front is a standard feature in most paint, draw, and desktop-publishing applications.

The white circle has been sent to the front; the black square has been sent to the back.

The white circle has been sent to the back; the black square has been sent to the front.

serial line – A transmission line that connects two serial ports. Data travels over networks sequentially in single bits, although a serial line may have two wires enabling data to be transmitted and retrieved simultaneously.

Serial Line Internet Protocol (SLIP) – A transmission *protocol* that enables *TCP/IP* over a telecommunications line (a serial line). This is an unsophisticated protocol that has been surpassed by *Point-to-Point Protocol*.

serial mouse – The most popular sort of *mouse*, which is plugged into a *serial port*.

serial port – A *socket* on a computer that is used to connect a mouse, scanner, or serial printer. It is a *male connector* and has nine or 25 pins. A serial port sends information reliably through a cable, one bit at a time. Contrast with a *parallel port*, which is faster – capable of sending data 8 bits at a time.
SEE ALSO: SERIAL TRANSMISSION

serial printer – A printer connected to the computer by a serial port.

serial transmission – In data transmission, when one bit at a time is sent over the *serial line*.
SEE ALSO: SERIAL PORT

serial-access device – Hardware that is connected to the computer through the *serial port*; e.g. a keyboard or printer.

serif – Typefaces where the riser and descender have a short horizontal line added at the top or bottom.
SEE ALSO: SANS-SERIF
SEE: FEATURE BOX

server – A computer and associated software that supplies services such as file transfer, database management, or printing to a *client* computer. Most are powerful and specialized computers designated to perform a particular task; e.g. a web server, database server, FTP server, network server.

server API – The software used by a server to provide a service to a client.
SEE ALSO: **API**

server application – Any program that runs on a server, sometimes specifically designed for this function.
SEE ALSO: CLIENT, SERVER

---

serif

This is an example of a serif typeface – each character has a line at the top and bottom.

serif
serif
SERIF

This is an example of a sans-serif typeface – the characters do not have lines.

sans serif
sans serif
sans serif

Serif and sans-serif are terms that describe the style of different typefaces, or fonts.

---

server farm – A group of linked computers acting as a server. On the Internet, this may be a web site that uses more than one server to handle requests, or a large Internet Service Provider that uses multiple servers to provide its Web-hosting services.

server mirroring – A duplicate of a busy server, which is maintained in order to reduce the load on the site and to speed up access for users.

server-centric – An operation that runs only on a server and not independently on networked workstations.

server-side – Services that are maintainedand provided only on the server and are not downloaded onto the client computer.

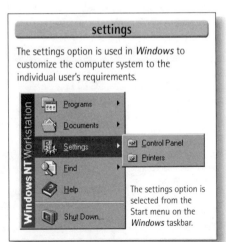

settings

The settings option is used in *Windows* to customize the computer system to the individual user's requirements.

The settings option is selected from the Start menu on the *Windows* taskbar.

server-side includes (SSI) – When files or portions of data from the server are placed inside an HTML document through the use of tags which link to the specified files. This can be used to keep the site current; e.g. by inserting modification dates. Now largely replaced by the use of *Java*.
SEE ALSO: ON THE FLY

service – The performance and/or fulfilment of expectations of a piece of equipment, software, or an organization. E.g. The service provided by an *Internet Service Provider* is measured by such things as reliability, speed of access to the network, support, content, etc.

Service Advertising Protocol (SAP) – Part of the *Internet Packet Exchange Protocol* that informs network clients of available network resources and services.

Service Level Agreement – The contract between an *Internet Service Provider* and a customer that specifies what level of services are to be provided.

service pack – A patch that augments a previously installed program either to extend its functionality or cure a bug. It can be downloaded from the developer's web site or may come on a CD-ROM.

service profile identifier (SPID) – The number used to identify a user's equipment for connecting to an ISDN (Integrated Services Digital Network) line.

service provider – See: Internet Service Provider

service space provider – An organization or person that provides storage space on a server for web pages, usually for a fee. Many *Internet Service Providers* provide free web space on their server as part of their service package.

servlet – An *applet* or small program that runs on a server. This usually refers to a *Java applet* that runs on a web server; e.g. form processing.

session – One single use of an application, or one instance of online connection.

session cookie – A file that collects information about a web site visitor that disappears when the browser is closed. This is in contrast to a *persistent cookie* that remains on the hard disk. Also called a *transient cookie*.

SET – See: **S**ecure **E**lectronic **T**ransactions

settings – In *Windows*, the option on the start menu that enables the user to customize the computer system.
SEE: FEATURE BOX

settlement rate – The cost charged by the local access carrier to terminate a call that has been made in another country.

setup string – The commands that automatically run to *initialize* a device, such as a scanner or printer.

SGCP – See: **S**imple **G**ateway **C**ontrol **P**rotocol

SGML – See: **S**tandard **G**eneralized **M**arkup **L**anguage

SGRAM – See: **S**ynchronous **G**raphic **R**andom **A**ccess **M**emory

shadow RAM – **S**hadow **R**andom **A**ccess **M**emory. When turning on the computer, data from the *ROM BIOS* is copied into the RAM for faster processing.

Shallow link – A *hyperlink* on a web site that is quickly accessed, such as a link to a home page, as opposed to a *deep link,* which is accessed after repeated clicking on higher-level hyperlinks.

share – The collaborative use of any resource such as equipment, files, or software made by several people on a network.

share ramping – To artificially cause the price of a share to be increased by talking it up using newsgroups and message boards. The practice was carried out prior to the existence of the Internet, but instant mass communication has made it more effective.

shared hosting – Web hosting where a service provider holds web pages for more that one web site, with each web site having its own Internet domain name. This is a cost-effective way to create a Web presence, but is insufficient for web sites with a high volume of traffic. Such sites need a dedicated Web server, either provided by a Web-hosting service or maintained in-house.

share-level security – The control of access to any shared network resource based on knowing the password of that resource. Share-level security provides less protection than user-level security, which is unique to each user on the network.

shareware – *Copyrighted* software that may be freely downloaded for a limited time period. After the time expires, the user is asked to pay for continued use. Many shareware products offer additional features to registered users.
SEE ALSO: FREEWARE

sharing violation – To try to open a file that is already being used by another application.

sheet feeder – A mechanism within a printer that automatically feeds sheets of paper from an input drawer to the printer head and roller.

shelfware – Software that is purchased but never used, often because it is of a poor quality.

shell – The software that provides the interface between the user and the computer's operating system. Shells generally try to make the interface between the user and system easier to use, e.g. the

mouse-based *graphical user interface* system used by Windows.

shell account – An account with an *Internet Service Provider* that uses *UNIX*.

shell out – To temporarily exit an application, go back to the operating system to perform a function, and then return to the application.

shell script – The file that contains the commands to be carried out by the *shell*.

shell site – A *back-up* facility that operates on the minimum amount of equipment necessary to be used in the event of a disaster.

shell virus – A *computer virus* that attaches itself to a *shell* command and is then executed each time that command is called up.

Sherlock – In *Apple* computers, a search utility that allows the user to search the local hard disk, the local network, and the Internet. From the fictional detective, Sherlock Holmes.

shift – The keyboard key that is held down to make all the letters print as capitals and the non-letter keys print other special characters such as the $ &*. The shift key is also used in combination with other keys to input a selection of commands.

shim – A small piece of data inserted into a web site for a particular purpose. .

shocked site – A web site that contains animations that require the *Shockwave* plug-ins to launch.

Shockwave - A very popular Web browser *plug-in* program that lets the user view animations produced by Macromedia's suite of visual software.

Go to: www.macromedia.com

shockwave.com

shopping cart – On a shopping web site, the name of the page containing the products the user has chosen to purchase. The user clicks on the items that they wish to buy and the information on those items is saved. When the purchaser has finished their selection, all the goods are listed together, the order is totalled and then confirmed on the checkout page.
See also: ADD TO CART

shopping online – Purchasing goods or services through a web site. The Internet has revolutionized the way we shop, bringing a much wider range of products to our doors. People can really indulge their interests and buy whatever suits them, at any time of day, often at a lower price, and have it delivered to their home. It hasn't led to the death of shopping malls or the traditional shopping street, but it has given a great deal of flexibility to many customers. Using a credit card to buy goods is safe providing that you use known

retailers and ensure that you are buying from a secure site (it will show either a padlock on the toolbar, or the prefix before the URL will begin https://) that uses encryption software.
See also: SECURE TRANSACTION, WEB APPLICATION MEETS BRICKS–AND–MORTAR

Short Messaging System (SMS) – The ability to transmit or receive short messages using a wireless phone.

shortcut – A short path to an operation that is faster than the regular way of doing the same operation. E.g. Clicking a desktop icon that enables a user to easily see and select a particular program without having to search through a directory.

shortcut key – Using keyboard character combinations to create a *shortcut*.

shorthand – Abbreviations and *acronyms* commonly used in e-mails, chat-rooms, and newsgroups that reduce the time taken to type a message.
See: APPENDIX 1

shouting – The use of ALL CAPITAL LETTERS in an e-mail, chat, or newsgroup message. This is considered very bad manners.

shovelware – 1. Information put on the Web so quickly that it is useless.
See also: QUICK AND DIRTY
2. Additional software placed on a *CD-ROM* to fill up extra space, but is not required by the main product.

show – In a graphical user interface, a menu selection that instructs the computer to show certain things on screen; e.g. balloon help, the toolbox, guidelines, etc. The opposite command is "hide."

shriek – The use of the exclamation mark (!) in newsgroup and similar postings..

shrink – To reduce the size of a window, image, or other object.

ShrinkWrap – A commercially available copying and *compression* program for *Macintosh* computers. Made by *Aladdin Systems*, ShrinkWrap allows the user to make exact copies of files for backup purposes and sharing with other users. **Go to:** www.aladdinsys.com

shrink–wrapped software – Refers to software that is bought off the shelf.

It is usually for a standard, widely supported platform.

SHS virus – A *computer virus* that arrives as an e-mail attachment or web site download with an .SHS *file extension*. As these are *Windows* scrap files and can be programmed to perform a wide variety of tasks, the virus can potentially do anything. **See: Appendix 5** for file extensions.

shtml – **S**erver-include **H**yper**T**ext **M**arkup **L**anguage. A file extension that indicates that the file includes some information that will be added *on the fly* by the server.

SHTTP – **S**ecure **H**yper**T**ext **T**ransfer **P**rotocol. A system for ensuring a safe connection between a user and an e-commerce site. **See also: HTTPS, secure transaction, security**

shunt – To bypass.

shut down – The command to exit the computer's operating system and switch off the power source. **See: feature box**

SIG – **See: S**pecial **I**nterest **G**roup

SIG block – **See:** signature file

SIG file – **See:** signature file

sig quote – A quotation, pithy saying, joke, or maxim that is included in a *signature file*.

shut down

In *Windows,* the user is presented with a few options before shutting down the computer.

The user selects the shut down option.

Clicking yes will shut down the system.

---

sign off/on – When a user exits an application, computer system, or network. The term is synonymous with *log on/off*.

signal – An *analog* or *digital waveform* that is generated to carry data. Control signals are used to carry messages that contain information about the operation of the transmission.

signaling – The use of control signals to start and stop a transmission or other similar network operation.
SEE ALSO: ACKNOWLEDGE

signaling gateway – A device within a network that converts controlling *signals* from one format to another.

signal-to-noise ratio – Technically, the amount of interference on a transmitted signal. It is also used to describe the amount of nonsense in relation to serious content found in a newsgroup. If the ratio is high, then the information is good.

signature – Information that the user opts to place at the end of every e-mail. It can be a name, telephone number, a pithy saying, or even ASCII art.

signature file – The short text file created to contain the user's *signature* information that is automatically appended to the end of e-mails or newsgroup postings.

signed document – A document authenticated by a *digital signature*.

silence suppression – In voice transmission over a *packet-switched* system, to encode the start and stop times of any silence within the communication. This minimizes wasted bandwidth capacity.

silicon chip – A thin slice of silicon that is used as the basis of integrated circuits used in computer technology.
SEE ALSO: CHIP

Silicon Valley – The area southwest of San Francisco, California, where many computer-related companies are located.

silly walk – (slang) A long-winded and stupid procedure that has to be undertaken to perform a relatively simple task.

silver surfer – (slang) An older user of the Internet. This sector has seen a rapid expansion in Internet access and use.
SEE ALSO: OVER-FIFTIES

SIMM – See: **S**ingle **I**n-line **M**emory Module

Simple Gateway Control Protocol (SGCP) – The first IP telephony protocol with a *master/slave* relationship.

Simple HTML Ontology Extension (SHOE) – An *HTML* extension enabling authors to include machine-readable *semantic* knowledge in web pages. It makes it possible for intelligent agents to obtain information about web pages and other documents more intelligently.

Simple Mail Transfer Protocol (SMTP) –
The standard protocol used on the Internet
for delivering e-mail. It identifies the server
through which an e-mail is routed and
then directs it to the correct mail server.
The e-mail is then held on the mail server
until the recipient logs on and claims the
message using *POP3* or *IMAP*.

**Simple Network Management Protocol
(SNMP)** – A standard for network
management. It regulates the operation of
network devices such as computers, hubs,
routers, and bridges, and provides a facility
for error detection.

Simple Object Access Protocol (SOAP) –
Provides a system for computers using
different types of operating systems to
communicate over the Internet. It exploits
the fact that all systems can communicate
with HTTP and Extensible Mark-up
language to provide cross-platform data
transmission; e.g. a *Windows* system
communicating with *Linux* or *UNIX*.

simplex – A communications channel that
can only transmit data in one direction.
SEE ALSO: DUPLEX

simulation – Creating a model of a real
system, to see how the system works.

**simultaneous voice and data
transmission** – The transmission of voice
and data by modem over a single *analog*
telephone line at the same time.

single in–line memory module (SIMM)
– A slim circuit board for *Random Access
Memory* (RAM) chips. SIMMs can be
plugged into a computer's *motherboard*
to add memory capacity.

single–density disk – The first generation
of floppy disks, now obsolete. Replaced by
double-density disks.

sink – Something that receives; e.g. a heat
sink, data sink, or message sink.

siphoning – To illegally route Internet
traffic to a particular site. This is often
achieved by submitting pages to a search
engine that have been maliciously
tampered with.

.sit – *File extension* for a *Macintosh* file
compressed using *Stuffit*.

site – Short for *web site*.

site license – A license that allows an
organization to use a software package on
multiple computers at a single site.
SEE ALSO: COPYRIGHT

site map – A description of a web site's
content that helps users navigate around
the site. It can be a simple *linked* list of
contents, or a more graphic representation.

site name – The unique *name* of a
computer system that is used to identify it
for electronic communication.
SEE ALSO: ADDRESS, DOMAIN NAME

site ranking – The order in which web sites are listed on a *search engine* as a result of a query.

site security – **See:** security

site submission – To make a site available to search engines for indexing purposes.
SEE ALSO: MULTIPLE SITE SUBMISSION

six degrees of freedom – In virtual reality, a term used to describe movement in three-dimensional space.

sizing – To manipulate an object by adjusting its dimensions. This is done to make it fit into a defined space.

skew – In drawing programs, a feature that changes the shape of objects by slanting, twisting, or variously altering them.

S/key – A security system from Bellcore that generates a series of passwords that are each only used once. This eliminates the need to send the same password over the network each time a user logs on.

skin – The way a program looks to the user. Some programs and operating systems allow the user to customize their appearance to suit various tastes or needs. The sound and appearance of game characters can be changed and skins for some applications and games can be downloaded over the Internet.

skinning – Designing a new look for a program, operating system, or game.
SEE ALSO: SKIN

skulking – **See:** lurking

skyscraper ad – An advertisement on a web site that is hung vertically on the page and is bigger than the usual horizontal *banner ad*.

slash – The *forward slash* "/" and the *backslash* "\".

slashdot effect – When a popular site (or other news source) posts a story that causes a surge of visitors to another web site. If the site receiving the rush of visitors is small, then it slows down and fails to operate properly.

slave – A computer that is controlled by another computer (the *master*), or a hard drive controlled by another hard drive.

SLED – **S**ingle **L**arge **E**xpensive **D**isk. The type of hard disk drive that was once used in minicomputers and mainframes. Such drives were used from the mid-1960s through the late 1980s. Today, all hard disks are small and inexpensive by comparison.

sleep mode – The mode a computer switches to after a period of inactivity. It turns off certain functions to reduce power consumption. The system reawakes when the mouse or keyboard is touched.

slide the talkways – (slang) To surf the Internet, visiting various *chat-rooms*.

sliding window – A communications technology that transmits multiple *packets* before acknowledgements are made. Both ends of the transmission are aware of the status of the packets in their respective windows.

slime – (slang) A derogatory term for a salesperson.
SEE ALSO: DWEEB, SALESCRITTER, SUIT

SLIP – See: **S**erial **L**ine **I**nternet **P**rotocol

slipstream – To repair a bug or add features to software without identifying such changes by creating a new version number for that software.

---

snap to grid

Snap to grid is a function in graphics programs, which assists with placement of objects.

Two objects (a block of text and a graphic) have been placed randomly on the page.

The objects have been aligned with each other by snapping them to the grid lines.

---

slot – A *socket* in a computer into which an expansion board can be plugged.

slow infector/virus – A *computer virus* that only operates when a file is being modified or created. This means that *anti-virus software* believes that the changes are legitimate.

slow mail – The regular postal service.
SEE ALSO: P–MAIL, SNAIL MAIL, DEAD TREE

small caps – A font option in which lowercase letters are replaced by small capital letters.

Small Computer System Interface (SCSI) – A fast PC-parallel interface that is used to communicate with peripherals such as printers and scanners.

smart – A program that is well designed and written and generally performs well.

SMART – See: **S**elf-**M**onitoring, **A**nalysis, and **R**eporting **T**echnology

smart book – A book in electronic format with searchable contents and the ability to jump between pages.
SEE ALSO: E-BOOK

smart browsing – Features within *browsers* that make it easier for the user to find a web page. E.g. Automatic entering of the http:// prefix or .com suffix, or offering previously visited URLs when the first few characters of an address have been typed.

smart card – A card containing a microchip that holds information. About the size of a credit card, they are used as a form of electronic cash, or for identification purposes (such as for private keys and certificates). To use a smart card, it is necessary to have a smart card reader attached to the computer, and the appropriate software.

smart phone – A digital cellular mobile telephone, which in addition to voice service offers any or all of the following facilities: e-mail, text messaging, paging, Internet access, personal organizer, and voice recognition.
SEE ALSO: **WAP**

SmartList – SmartList is an e-mail list management system.
GO TO: www.procmail.org

 **SmartMedia** – An ultra-compact flash memory card developed by Toshiba, it is very popular in digital cameras and allows capacities up to 128MB.

SMDS – See: **S**witched **M**ultimegabit **D**ata Service

smerf/smurf – A participant in a newsgroup or Usenet group who makes cute, silly contributions and who hasn't really appreciated the topic being discussed. It is generally used as an insult.

SMIL – See: **S**ynchronized **M**ultimedia **I**ntegration **L**anguage

 smiley – A graphic used in chat rooms to express happiness.
SEE ALSO: EMOTICON

S/MIME – See: **S**ecure **M**ultimedia **I**nternet **M**ail **E**xtensions

smoke test – (slang) A test for new equipment. If it smokes, it doesn't work.

SMS – See: **S**hort **M**essage **S**ervice

SMTP – See: **S**imple **M**ail **T**ransfer **P**rotocol

smurfing – To attack a network by *broadcasting ping* messages to cause *ping flooding*.

snail – The verb that is derived from the term *snail mail*. So to snail something is to send it by regular post.

snail mail – (slang) A derogatory term for the regular postal service.
SEE ALSO: P-MAIL, SLOW MAIL

snap to grid – In graphics, a function that assists with object placement. The object is locked onto an invisible matrix called a grid. This helps to align objects.
SEE: FEATURE BOX

snapshot tool – A program used by systems administrators to check for weaknesses in the security of a system, e.g. checks for easily cracked passwords.

snarf – (slang) To copy a file without the owner's consent.

sneaker net – (slang) To move files from one computer to another by means of a floppy disk or other transportable medium. The term derives from the sneakers worn by those carrying the disk between computers.

sniffer – Hardware and/or software that monitors the flow of data over a network. It can be used to manage traffic and identify problems but it is also used by attackers to try to capture credit card details and passwords.

SNMP – See: **S**imple **N**etwork **M**anagement **P**rotocol

snooping – 1. Using a *sniffer* to capture data to monitor Web activities. Used by employers to check up on the web sites employees visit, as well as any security breaches that they may create.
2. The malicious use of a sniffer.

snow – *Interference* on a monitor that looks like tiny white flecks of snow.

social engineering – (slang) A breach of security caused by exploiting weaknesses in *wetware* (humans) rather than in the computer system; e.g. tricking someone to disclose a password.

social filtering – A technique used by some web sites that automatically suggests information the user might be interested in.

sock puppet – (slang) When someone posting a message to a newsgroup writes more messages supporting the views of the first message under a pseudonym.

socket – 1. The holes into which a *plug* fits in order to make an electrical contact.
SEE ALSO: CONNECTOR, FEMALE CONNECTOR, MALE CONNECTOR
2. On a computer using *TCP/IP*, the exit or entry point for data that is located by programs in order to carry out the data transfer.

Socket server – A protocol for data transfer over a *TCP/IP* network using a *proxy server*. It enables users of a network to access the Internet over a shared connection. It also creates a *firewall* by hiding individual addresses and checking incoming and outgoing *packets*.

soft – Something that is flexible and changeable; e.g. software that can be reprogrammed.

soft goods – Software that is purchased online and downloaded directly to the computer, bypassing the need for the user to receive a CD-ROM copy.

soft page break – When the software begins a new page automatically, which will then move as additional text is added or deleted. Contrast with *forced page break* when the user specifies where a page is to end.

soft return – A return created by the software at the end of a line. When additional words are inserted, or words are removed, the line break will appear in different places.
SEE ALSO: RETURN

software – Computer *programs* or groups of programs designed to command the *hardware* to carry out a specific set of actions on a computer. Systems software provides operational commands, e.g. an operating system or printer driver software. Application software relates to what the computer is to do, e.g. word-processing, flight simulation, browsing the Internet.

software license – The agreement between the user and the *copyright* holder for the use of the software under defined conditions.

software development kit (SDK) –
1. Software issued for the use of other programmers so that they might extend the range of use of the program.
2. The software necessary to program computers in a specific programming language.

softy – (slang) Someone who has a thorough knowledge of software, but limited understanding of hardware.

SOHO – **S**mall **O**ffice, **H**ome **O**ffice. Description of products developed for use in a small business.

 Solaris (SunOS) – A *UNIX*-based operating system from Sun Systems. It allows for multitasking and multiprocessing and is well known for its sturdiness.
GO TO: www.sun.com

solution – A word used in a computer program name to indicate that the software can solve a problem; e.g. e-business solution.

sort – To arrange items in a particular order; e.g. date or alphabetical order.

sound card/board – The *expansion board* that converts analog sound waves into digitized data and vice versa, enabling the computer to play and receive sound.
SEE ALSO: MIDI, SAMPLING RATE, SOUNDBLASTER

sound clip – A short sound file that is embedded in a web page. The user activates the sound by clicking on a button or icon.

sound player – A *plug-in* that allows the user to hear sound clips downloaded on a web page.
SEE ALSO: SOUND CLIP, MP3, REAL PLAYER

 SoundBlaster – Type of sound card introduced by Creative Labs in 1989. The SoundBlaster is now the standard audio *protocol* for PCs.
GO TO: www.soundblaster.com

source – 1. To find, or search for data.
2. The origin of particular data, piece
of data, or news item.
3. To obtain equipment or parts.

source code – The *code* written by the
computer *programmer* that is then
converted into *machine language* by the
computer's *compiler*.

spaghetti code – Instructions that are
contorted and difficult to unravel.

spam – Unsolicited commercial e-mail, i.e.
e-mail that is broadcast to a list of e-mail
addresses. These lists are compiled by list
vendors who obtain addresses from areas
where a user has left personal
information. These include e-commerce
sites, Internet Service Providers, chat
rooms, newsgroups etc. The *bots* that
collect the addresses are known as address
harvesters, which act as *sniffers* looking
for address information on the Internet.
The origin of "spam" in this context is
hazy. Originally a type of spiced meat,
according to some it comes from the
Monty Python sketch in which a number
of Vikings demanded "spam, spam,
spam..." However, others in the industry
attribute the term to a quote made by a
Dallas newspaper editor, who said that
public relations is like "throwing
a can of Spam into an electric fan just to
see if any of it would stick to the unwary
passerby."

Tips to reduce the likelihood of
receiving spam:

- Avoid giving out your e-mail address
  whenever possible.
- If there is a check box offering not to
  disclose your personal details, always
  ensure that you check it.
- Have two e-mail addresses. Use the
  second address for use in chat rooms,
  newsgroups, and on commercial sites
  where you feel at risk of disclosure. That
  way, your principal account is kept clear
  of spam and those received in the second
  account can be deleted wholesale.
- Install anti-spam software.
- Use an anonymous e-mailer service
  for newsgroup postings.

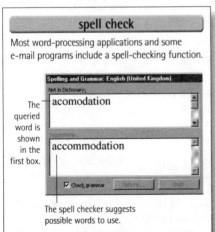

spell check

Most word-processing applications and some
e-mail programs include a spell-checking function.

The queried word is shown in the first box.

Spelling and Grammar: English (United Kingdom)

Not in Dictionary:
acomodation

Suggestions:
accommodation

☑ Check grammar   Options...   Undo

The spell checker suggests
possible words to use.

spam magnet – A service that provides a special e-mail address for sites which may divulge an address. This address is then used as a way of tracking the source of information being offered to companies who *spam*.

spamdexing – **See:** index spamming

spamhaus (slang) – An address list vendor who sells e-mail addresses to commercial organizations.

spammer – An organization or individual that sends *spam*.

spamvertise – To send spam as a way of advertising goods or services.

SPARC – **S**calable **P**rocessor **Arc**hitecture.

spawn – To launch one program from within another. The child program is spawned from the parent.

speaker recognition – To recognize a person by his or her spoken voice for security purposes. This is different from voice recognition, which is more flexible.

Special Interest Group (SIG) – A group of people with a common interest who use the Internet to exchange views and information.

specialized search engine – A search engine that specializes in areas of interest, e.g. golf, genetic research, or travel.

speech recognition – The ability of a computer to recognize human voice input in place of typed commands.

spell check – The facility within many text-processing programs, including browsers, to check the spelling in a document. Some e-mail programs allow an automatic spell check prior to sending mail. Many spell checkers will also check for grammar.
SEE: FEATURE BOX

spelling flame – An angry message, or *flame*, on a newsgroup that criticizes a user's poor spelling.

spew – To write large chunks of irrelevant text or repeat the same information in a *newsgroup posting*.
SEE ALSO: JABBER

SPID – **See: S**ervice **P**rofile **Id**entifier

spider – A program used by *search engines* that trawls the Internet looking for new web pages, updated pages, and deleted sites. Once a site becomes registered, the spider indexes it for inclusion in the search engine's database.

spider food – Keywords that are embedded into a web page to attract the *spiders* associated with *search engines*. The intention is to ensure that the web page is indexed and highly ranked by search engines.
SEE ALSO: SITE RANKING

spiffy – (slang) A program that is well-written, clever, and nicely presented. Can sometimes be used ironically for a program that is over-designed.

spike – A surge, or peak from a power source. Contrast with *sag*.

splash page – A web page, usually featuring the site's name and logo, which is shown for a few seconds when a site is launched. It is generally followed by the site's home page.

split screen – The function that allows two or more documents to be shown on the screen at the same time.
SEE: FEATURE BOX

---

split screen

Spilt screen allows two or more documents to be shown on the screen at once.

A word-processing document is shown in one half.

The browser displays a web page in the other half.

---

spod – A player in a multiuser dungeon game who is socially inept.

spoiler – A *newsgroup posting* that gives away the plot of a book or the end of a film. As a courtesy to other users, when posting a message containing such information, the word "spoiler" should be typed in the header.

spoofing – 1. To assume another's identity as a means of gaining unauthorized access onto a network. 2. Another name for index *spamming/spamdexing*.

spool – **S**imultaneous **P**eripheral **O**perations **O**nline. To store documents in a buffer for processing at another time. Most commonly used as a way of storing documents in a print queue.

 Spray can tool – In graphics and paint applications, a function that simulates the action of a can of spray paint. The tool can usually be calibrated to cover a small or large area.

spreadsheet – A worksheet in which columns of figures are summed for budgets and plans. On screen it appears as a matrix of rows and columns created as cells.
SEE: FEATURE BOX

sprite – An interactive animated graphic. E.g. A character in a computer game, such as Lara Croft in Tomb Raider, or the characters created in *The Simms*.

spyware – Any program that helps to gather information about a person or organization without their consent. Spyware can access a computer as a software virus or through a *cookie*, which a user may be aware of, but does not know the nature of the information that it seeks.

squammer – A person who purchases *domain names* in the hope that they may be able to sell them on at an inflated price. Often names of celebrities and company names are targeted by squammers.

SEE ALSO: DOMAIN NAME HOARDING

SQL – See: **S**tructured **Q**uery **L**anguage

SQL server – A database management system that uses *SQL* to respond to queries. The server interprets the query, carries out the task, then returns the results to the user.

SRAM – See: **S**tatic **RAM**

SSI – See: **S**erver-**S**ide **I**ncludes

SSL – See: **S**ecure **S**ocket **L**ayer

stack – 1. The different *layers* in the TCP/IP system through which *packets* must pass at both server and client ends.
2. The area of memory used while software is being run.

stage directions – In chat rooms, words used to indicate emotion, facial expressions, and body language. They are enclosed like this: <laugh> <cry>.

stand-alone – Something that works independently, e.g. a computer that is not attached to a network.

Standard Generalized Markup Language (SGML) – A programming language used to describe the format, structure, and storage of documents.

star – 1. When looking for a document or opening a document, it is used as a wildcard where * can mean any character or characters. So if you are looking for all the files with the extension .gif, *.gif can be entered into the find dialog box.
2. In stemming, where typing "typ* " would reveal words such as type, typing, typed, and typewriter. Also called "asterisk."

spreadsheet

Spreadsheet applications are most commonly used for financial plannning and calculations.

A spreadsheet is usually divided into columns and rows.

Data is entered into cells and a formula is used for calculations.

star dot star – *.* Used when searching for a file with any name and any extension. Useful if looking for text modified in a certain time span where the file name is unknown.

SEE ALSO: SEARCH

Start button – The button in the bottom left-hand corner of the Microsoft *Windows* screen, which provides a quick access route to the Start menu bar.

Start menu – The pull-up menu in a *Windows* system that contains links to the programs and documents on the computer. The user can customize the Start menu using the settings and taskbar options.

SEE: FEATURE BOX
SEE ALSO: START BUTTON

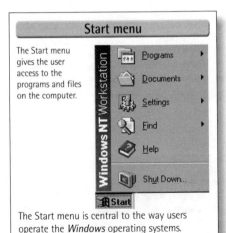

Start menu

The Start menu gives the user access to the programs and files on the computer.

Windows NT Workstation

- Programs ▸
- Documents ▸
- Settings ▸
- Find ▸
- Help
- Shut Down...

Start

The Start menu is central to the way users operate the *Windows* operating systems.

start page – The page that is opened in the browser as soon as the user logs on to the Internet. Generally, this is a home page, but the browser can be customized to start in any page.

startup disk – A disk containing the operating system and other programs necessary to start the computer. This is used as a back-up for use in the event of a system failure.

static – Stationary, as opposed to dynamic, which is moving or changing.

Static IP – This is a standard *IP address*, which remains the same, as opposed to a dynamic address, which is assigned as required.

Static RAM – **R**andom **A**ccess **M**emory that is available, so long as power is being sent to the system. This is faster and more expensive than dynamic RAM.

station – See: workstation

status – Information about the connection to the Internet, e.g. whether the line is active and how long the present connection has been live. In *Windows*, right-clicking on the connection icon on the toolbar provides the user with information on the connection status.

status bar – The toolbar, usually at the bottom of the screen which provides information on the present application.

Browser status bars provide information such as the locked/unlocked padlock to indicate the security of the current site, an icon to show if the connection is live, and a download bar to show the progress of a download.
SEE: FEATURE BOX

stealth – **See:** cloaking

steam powered – Something that is old, slow, and with limited storage capacity.

stemming – When using a *search engine*, the ability to recognize the stem of the word and generate all the forms of that word; e.g. if the word "type" was requested, then pages containing the words "typing" and "typed" would also be found.

stickiness – The ability of a commercial web site to keep its customers' interest. The more successful the site the "stickier" it is.

stochastic – Arrived at by guesswork or chance or generated randomly.

stop bit – The *bit* that is transmitted after every character in *asynchronous* communications.

stop-motion animation – The pre-computer graphics method by which each frame in an animated sequence was created and photographed independently.

storage – Another term for memory, generally used in relation to data storage.

store – 1. One of the new *domain names* introduced in 2000.
2. To place data into *memory*.
SEE ALSO: STORAGE

streaming – A way of sending data over the Internet in a continuous flow.

streaming audio – Audio that is transmitted over a network. This is a one-way transmission, which depends on the co-operation of the client and server. The client places a small section of sound in its buffers before it sends it to the speakers. Streaming audio is not *real time* and is not used in conferencing environments.
SEE ALSO: STREAMING, STREAMING MEDIA

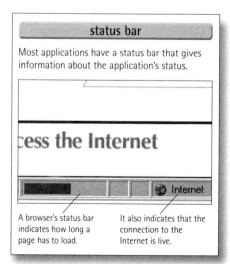

status bar

Most applications have a status bar that gives information about the application's status.

ːess the Internet

🌐 Internet

A browser's status bar indicates how long a page has to load.

It also indicates that the connection to the Internet is live.

streaming media – Audio and video data that is transmitted continuously over the Internet without any breaks. E.g. Radio and TV broadcasting over the Internet.

strudel – (slang) The "at" sign: @.

string – **See:** character string

Structured Query Language (SQL) – A computer language commonly used to question a *database*.

StuffIt! – A common shareware program from Aladdin Systems that compresses information to save storage and increase the speed of data transfer.
SEE ALSO: STUFFIT! EXPANDER, ALADDIN SYSTEMS, COMPRESSION
GO TO: www.stuffit.com

StuffIt The complete compression solution.

---

submit button

Information is entered in several fields.

Please provide the following contact information:

Name
Ext no
E-mail
Location

The submit button is then clicked.

Your Answer:

Submit Form   Reset Form

The submit button will be clicked in order to send information to a web site.

StuffIt! Expander – StuffIt Expander expands and decodes files downloaded from the Web or received via e-mail.
SEE ALSO: ALADDIN SYSTEMS
GO TO: www.stuffit.com

stunning – (slang) An unbelievably stupid or obvious suggestion.

stupid – Someone who employs a *samurai* for legal cracking jobs.

style guide – A set of guidelines set out by web site developers to ensure uniform presentation of content. E.g. A list of fonts and colors to use and for what purpose.

style sheet – These are often templates that describe the layout of a web page or document. E.g. There might be a standard format for a business letter and another for a personal letter. On the Web, this generally refers to a *cascading style sheet*.

subdirectory – A directory that is inside, or subordinate to, another directory. To reach a subdirectory, it is necessary to go through all directories above it.

subject – In an e-mail, the short line of type that indicates what the message is about. Some e-mail filtering programs can filter mail by subject line, so that all mail on a certain subject is filed, ranked by priority, or thrown out. Consequently, it is good practice to ensure that the subject line is accurate and descriptive.

submit – To send or *post* a message to a message board or newsgroup, or to return a completed form to a site; e.g. to confirm a purchase, or to send a request for financial services information.

submit button – This is the button on a web page that accompanies a form or other interactive object which has to be submitted to the site for processing.
SEE ALSO: SUBMIT
SEE: FEATURE BOX

subnet – Short for subnetwork. A discrete and identifiable part of a *network*; e.g. a *LAN* that operates in one building.

subnet mask – A number used to identify a subnet when an IP address is shared by multiple networks.

subroutine – A routine that carries out discrete processing operations in a program when called upon by the main routine. Once completed, the main routine takes over until another subroutine is required.

subscribe – 1. To sign up to an opt-in *mailing list*.
2. To add a newsgroup to the user's list of frequented newsgroups.

subwoofer – A large loudspeaker that is attached to a speaker system. It produces low frequency sound, which greatly improves the sound quality of the system.

suit – (slang) A patronizing term used by a non-suit wearer for an administrator or manager – someone who wears suits.

suite – A collection of related programs; e.g. *Microsoft Office*.

 **Sun Microsystems, Inc.** – One of the world's leading providers of hardware, software, and services, specializing in the Internet.
GO TO: www.sun.com

Sun workstations – A class of desktop solutions from Sun Microsystems consisting of PC peripherals and software.
GO TO: www.sun.com/desktop

SunOS – Sun's UNIX operating system.
SEE ALSO: SOLARIS

Sunsoft – A division of Sun Microsystems that specializes in selling software.

supercomputer – A computer that performs at the highest operational rate possible. They are generally used for scientific purposes, processing vast amounts of data, and carrying out a great amount of computation.

SuperDisk – A commercially available floppy disk drive, capable of holding up to 240MB of memory.
GO TO: www.superdisk.com

Super Visual Graphics Array (SVGA) – An enhanced graphics *display* system that allows *resolutions* of up to 800x600 *pixels* and 16 million colors.

super-video (S-Video) – An attempt by Chinese government-backed companies to produce a cheaper alternative to *DVD*. It is unclear whether it will be available outside China, although with the right software it is compatible with *DVD* players.

support – The help a manufacturer, ISP, or web site offers to people who need advice. This may come in the form of written manuals or telephone or e-mail support.

surf – (slang) To explore the *World Wide Web* either in a random fashion, or looking for precise information.

surf monkey – A safety-oriented and child-friendly online content provider.
Go to: www.surfmonkey.com

surface mapping – **See:** render

surface web – Web content that is easy to locate and has been indexed by search engines. Contrast with deep web, where information is available on the Web, but is embedded within databases.

Surfcontrol – An Internet content monitoring and filtering system.
Go to: www.surfcontrol.com

surge protector – A device that is fitted into an AC power line to prevent voltage "spikes" damaging computer equipment.

surround sound – **See:** Dolby Digital

SVDT – **See:** Simultaneous Voice and Data Transmission

SVGA – **See:** Super Visual Graphics Array

s/w – **See:** software

swap image – An image that changes when a mouse passes over it or is clicked upon it. They are used in the creation of *rollovers*.

swap file – A section of the hard drive, set aside to be used when the system demands more RAM.
SEE ALSO: VIRTUAL MEMORY

swap space attack – A *denial of service attack,* caused when the area of the hard drive used by the swap file becomes overloaded. This is caused by the browser sending huge amounts of data to be stored in the virtual memory, causing the system to slow and ultimately malfunction.

.swf – The file *extension* for Shockwave-formatted files.

Swiss cheese security – A *security* system, which is full of holes and is easily penetrated.

switch – In communications, a switch is a network device that selects a path or circuit

for transmitting data to its destination.
SEE ALSO: ROUTER

switched line – In communications, a link that is established in a switched network, such as the international dial-up telephone system, or ISDN.

Switched Multimegabit Data Service (SMDS) – A technology that allows the transmission of large amounts of data over a network on an intermittent basis.

switch-to-computer – To integrate voice, telephone, and database access. This is most commonly applied in customer service situations, where telephone services, such as automatic number identification (ANI) and automatic call distribution (ACD), can retrieve and route the customer's file to the next available human operator.

Symantec – The developer of the Norton range of Internet security programs. They provide software for things such as virus protection, firewalls, intrusion prevention, Internet content, and e-mail filtering systems for individual and corporate use. The site contains a useful list of viruses.
GO TO: www.symantec.com
SEE ALSO: FIREWALL, NORTON, PETER, NORTON UTILITIES

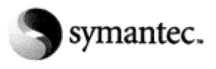

α β χ δ ε φ γ η
≈ θ κ λ ζ ν δ π
Ψ ρ σ τ ξ ƒ ξ γ
ζ α ω ÷ Δ ∇ ∓ Γ

A selection of symbol font characters.

symbol font – A font that has Greek and other special characters, especially useful for mathematical and scientific work and typing in foreign languages.

Symmetric Digital Subscriber Line (SDSL) – A communications technology that can send data at up to 3 Mbps over regular telephone lines. SDSL sends digital pulses in the high-frequency bandwidth not used by normal voice calls, enabling simultaneous voice and data transmissions over the same wires. It is symmetric in the sense that the same data transmission rates apply from server to client as from client to server. A special modem is necessary to use the system.
SEE ALSO: ADSL

synchronous – Communication between two devices that relies on a timed interval between the transmission of the previous character and transports data at the same speed in both directions. Synchronous transmission is faster than asynchronous transmission because there is no need for a start bit and stop bit on each character. However, most PCs use *asynchronous* data transmission.

Synchronous Digital Hierarchy (SDH) – A standard used for the transmission of *fiber-optic* data.

Synchronous Graphic Random Access Memory (SGRAM) – Memory used for graphics *applications,* such as 3D operations and full-motion video.

syndication – *Content* that is developed for sale to web sites. E.g. News content.

synonym ring – In a search operation, a way of looking for words with similar characteristics to broaden the scope of the search. This is useful when spelling is uncertain or when looking for a foreign or unusual placename.

syntax – The grammar and structure of words in both human language and computer language. Computer syntax is very clearly defined and inflexible.

syntax error – An error that occurs when a program cannot understand the command that has been entered.

synthesizer – A device that generates electronic sounds by creating waveforms or by accessing stored samples of musical instruments or sounds.
SEE ALSO: MIDI, WAVE FORM AUDIO

SyQuest – A Californian manufacturer of removable disk drives, founded in 1982 by Syed Iftikar (the name is derived from "Sy's Quest." It pioneered the removable hard disk industry for personal computers. Its drives are industry standard for the design, publishing, and printing sector.
GO TO: www.syquest.com

sysadmin – **See:** system administrator

sysop – **See:** system operator

system – A computer system includes all the hardware and software components that run together to process data and perform specific operations.

system administrator – The person in charge of a small networked computer system, also called sysadmin. They design the system and manage its use. The role is different to a network manager, who administers a larger network and is solely responsible for the networking operation and does not oversee the whole system.

system board – **See:** motherboard

system operator – 1. The person who runs the day-to-day operation of a server.
2. The moderator of a newsgroup or chat room. Abbreviated to sysop.

system software – Software that controls the computer and runs applications including operating systems, drivers, and communications and messaging protocols.

Systems Application Architecture (SAA) – Guidelines developed by *IBM* to stimulate the development of software that is able to operate regardless of hardware or operating system type.

systems analysis & design (SAD) – The review of a problem, and finding a solution to that problem. The most effective systems analysis is achieved when all sides of the problem are reviewed. Equally, systems design is most effective when more than one solution can be proposed.

systems analyst – The person responsible for systems analysis.

systems programmer – 1. In the IT department of a large organization, a technical expert on some or all of the computers' system software. They are responsible for the efficient performance of the computer systems. They do not usually write programs, but perform a lot of technical tasks with the software used by the organization. They will also act as technical advisors to other staff who work with the system.
2. In a computer hardware or software organization, a person who designs and writes system software.

T1 line/carrier – This is a leased-line connection that provides 24 channels of voice data; 23 if used for digital data transfer with the extra channel used for synchronization. T1 is the fastest carrier commonly used to connect.

T2 line/carrier – This is a leased-line connection that transmits the equivalent of four T1 lines.
SEE ALSO: MULTIPLEX

T3 line/carrier – A high-speed leased-line connection that transmits the equivalent of 28 T1 lines.
SEE ALSO: MULTIPLEX

T4 line/carrier – A high-speed leased-line connection that transmits the equivalent of six T3 lines.
SEE ALSO: MULTIPLEX

TA – See: Terminal Adapter

tab – 1. An abbreviation for tabulate. It is often used when referring to the use of prearranged *tab stops* to indent text or to organize text into columns.
2. In Microsoft *Windows*, to tab means to move from one field or button to another using the *tab key*

The tab key on a standard keyboard.

tab key – The keyboard key that is used for indenting text. On a standard keyboard, it is identified by the left- and right-facing arrows.
SEE ALSO: TAB

tab stops – These are the preset positions where the *cursor* will land when the *tab key* is depressed.

table – To arrange data in columns and rows. In Microsoft *Word*, the table button on the standard toolbar provides the necessary options for the creation and manipulation of tables. There is also an *HTML* command <TABLE> for the creation of tables within web sites.
SEE: FEATURE BOX

table of contents – Located at the start of a *CD-ROM* or *multimedia* package, it refers to the list of contents or headings, included with links to the relevant section.

tablet – See: graphics tablet

---

table

The table shown below was created in Microsoft Word using the Table menu in the standard toolbar.

	Holidays	Overtime	Illness	Total Days
Joanne	3	1	0	4
Sarah	6	2	0	8
Tom	1	0.5	1	2.5
Stephen	4	2	0	6
Adrienne	3	0.5	2	5.5
Michael	8	1	0	9

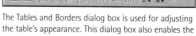

The Tables and Borders dialog box is used for adjusting the table's appearance. This dialog box also enables the user to format the information in alphabetical order.

TABLET – A type of query language.

tag – A tag is a coded command used in a *markup language* such as hypertext markup language (HTML). The command is placed within markers so that the program recognizes it as a formatting command or other command; e.g. <B> is the instruction tag within HTML to print the following text in bold typeface. </B> is the end tag that cancels that command.

tagged e-mail – Tagged e-mail refers to the kind of e-mail message where the subject line indicates the nature of that message. For example, the inclusion of the word "advertisement" in the subject line would indicate spam e-mail.
SEE: FEATURE BOX

---

tagged e-mail

The e-mail inbox shown below indicates that most of the e-mails are work-related or personal, but one is an advert.

This e-mail is tagged as an advertisement in the subject line. The user can choose to open it, or knowing what is in it already, can simply delete before reading.

Tagged Image File Format (TIFF) – A file format used to store monochrome or grayscale images and 8 and 24 bit color images. It is a useful format for the transfer of graphics between computers.

tailgating – Describes unauthorized eavesdropping on an interactive session, without being a participant. This is done by intercepting and canceling a user's log-out and then masquerading as that user. Similar to a *piggyback attack*.

talk – 1. This is a top-level newsgroup designation used for groups discussing controversial social issues.
2. **See:** talker

talk bomb – A program sent to a network, which generates random streams of characters which are displayed on the users' screens.

talker – A text-based, real-time chat environment. It often requires a *Telnet* connection although some browsers also enable talker. Sometimes called *live chat*.
SEE ALSO: INTERNET RELAY CHAT, MUD

tall – See: portrait

tamper – To alter data for devious purposes; e.g. to hide fraud or remove incriminating material.

tape – A high-capacity, external storage medium generally used for back-up purposes or long-term storage of data.

tape drive – This is an external drive that is necessary for reading and writing data on *tape*.

TAPI – **See:** **T**elephony **A**pplication **P**rogramming **I**nterface

.tar – The three letter .tar is the file *extension* for a compression format that is widely used in *Unix* systems. Tar is the acronym for the **T**ape **AR**chive format: a type of file archiving format that was regularly used for the transference and storage of files in Unix.

tar pit – A trap for spammers. A web site containing lists of user names and addresses is set up to attract the attention of spammers' address-harvesting software. Main server addresses are planted within the list, and these are programmed to take several days to respond to a request. This leaves the spammer's software *hanging* in limbo, and therefore traceable.
SEE ALSO: SPAMMER

target – This is a description of the user or group of users at whom a particular kind of web site might be aimed. It is a term that is frequently used in marketing circles. For example, the target market of a fashion e-zine might be women that are aged between 18 and 25.

target computer – Describes the computer that is the recipient of a *packet* or a fax transmission.

task – A single process or program that is being managed by the operating system. The task is assigned a task number by the operating system and is provided with system resources and disk space. A complex program may be split into several tasks, which is known as *multithreading*.

task switching – When several *tasks* are undertaken at a time, moving between operations is called task switching. This is easily achieved by clicking on the options displayed on the *taskbar*.

taskbar – The taskbar is the bar that runs by default along the bottom of the Microsoft *Windows* display screen and shows which task is currently active and which others are open and available for use. The systems tray section of the taskbar reveals programs that are opened automatically when Windows starts up. The taskbar can be moved to a different location simply by clicking and dragging it.
SEE: FEATURE BOX

---

taskbar

In Windows, the taskbar is situated at the bottom of the page, next to the Start button.

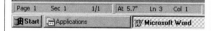

The programs that are open, Microsoft Word and the Applications folder, are shown at the bottom of the taskbar. Click on them to maximize them.

TCP – See: Transmission Control Protocol

TCP/IP – Transmission Control Protocol/Internet Protocol. This is the set of protocols that is used to manage the transmission of messages over the Internet. TCP/IP works by chopping the messages into small packages, each containing address information. It transmits these packages to the various networks on the Internet, and then reassembles them on receipt at their destination.

TCP/IP stack – This phrase refers to all the different components that go to make up the *TCP/IP* protocol.

TDMA – See: Time Division Multiple Access

teamware – See: groupware

tear-off menu – A tear-off menu is an on-screen menu or palette that a user is able to move and relocate to any part of the screen. Such menus are not made available with all kinds of applications as a default feature, and so has to be installed separately. The tear-off menu can often be provided as part of a program's built-in help facility.

techie – (slang) A term that is widely used when describing the kind of person who is believed to possess considerable Internet technology skills. In business environments, a techie often refers to a *technical support* person.
SEE ALSO: GEEK

technical support – The back-up service offered by *Internet Service Providers*, some web sites, and hardware and software manufacturers, to help clients who are experiencing operational difficulties. The quality of technical support, as reported by online reviews, reviewers in the computer press, and general word-of-mouth, can prove to be a key factor for many people when they are thinking of signing up with an Internet-based service.

technobabble – Text that is so littered with technical language and acronyms that it becomes almost meaningless.

technology butler – In a business hotel, the member of staff charged with sorting out guests' communications problems.

Technology Without An Interesting Name (TWAIN) – An interface that captures image data from a scanner or other *peripheral* device, while using a graphics application.

technophile – Someone who is greatly impressed by technology.

technophobe – Someone who is afraid of new technology.

Telco – A term used to describe a telecommunications or telephone company.

telecommunications – Any form of communication or data transfer that takes place over the telephone network.

telecommute – To work from a remote computer (usually at home) and be connected to a business computer network via a modem connection. This practice is also commonly referred to as teleworking.

teleconferencing – A computer-managed audio and video link that enables people in different locations to see and speak to each other in real time.

telecopy – To send a *fax*.

telecottage – An office that is completely computerized and Internet-linked. It can be a home office or a community resource, usually found in an isolated place.

telemedicine – Computerized medical applications, such as medical web sites, remote diagnostics used in isolated communities, and surgery directed by a surgeon from a remote location.

telephony – The standard that enables a computer to work in conjunction with the telecommunications lines to provide voice, messaging, and fax services.

Telephony Application Programming Interface (TAPI) – Software that enables Windows systems to work with telecommunications systems.

Telephony Server API (TSAPI) – A piece of equipment designed to improve operations between PCs and telephones. Go to: www.novell.com

television board – A television board is an *expansion board* for a PC that contains a television tuner. It works just like any television set but uses computer software for changing the channel and creating a *video overlay*.

teleworking – **See:** telecommute

Telnet – An *emulator* program, Telnet can be used for running a PC and connecting it to a server on a network or on the Internet. To use Telnet, the user needs to control the server and then enter commands through it. Many Web servers are managed in this way. Telnet also enables a user at a terminal to log on to a remote device and run a program.

template – Describes the kind of file that contains a format for a document type and carries preset information. It can be used to create a letter that the user may want to send out to many people – with only small changes for each person, such as address.

temporary file – This term refers to the kind of file that can be deleted when it is no longer required, in contrast to a permanent file.

tera- – This term denotes one trillion according to the US system. (In the US system tera- denotes one thousand billion. In the British system, tera- denotes one million million.) When referring to bytes, tera refers to 1,024 to the power of four.

terabyte – A terabyte, in approximate terms, relates to one thousand gigabytes (technically the figure is 1,024 x 1,024 gigabytes, or 1,024 to the power of two. When relating to megabytes, one terabyte is roughly one thousand thousand megabytes, or 1,024 to the power of three. When relating to bytes one terabyte is 1,024 to the power of four.
SEE ALSO: BIT, BYTE, MEGABYTE, GIGABYTE

terminal – A display and keyboard that is linked to a network and can be used to send data to other connected terminals.

terminal adapter – A device that adapts a computer to a digital *ISDN* line. The line plugs into the serial port of the computer or into an expansion slot.

---

text box

The text on this page can only sit in the designated text box, as shown. This paragraph of text is outlined by the box, which will not show up on printing.

> Intro text goes here Lorem ipsum dolor sit amet, consectetuer adipiscing elit, sed diam nonummy nibh euismod tincidunt ut laoreet dolore magna aliquam erat volutpat. Ut wisi enim ad minim veniam, quis nostrud exerci tation ullamcorper suscipit lobortis nisl ut aliquip ex ea commodo consequat. Duis autem vel eum iriure dolor in hendrerit in vulputate velit esse molestie consequat, vel illum dolore eu feugiat nulla facilisis at

This symbol in a box indicates that the user can insert text into the box, but not a graphic.

---

terminal emulator – When a computer acts as though it were only a terminal, i.e. it does not carry on any internal processing, but simply passes data to a network computer for processing.

terminal server – A *server* that provides *TCP/IP* services for *terminals*.

terminate and stay resident (TSR) – A *DOS utility* that stays in the memory after it is terminated and can be reactivated by pressing a hotkey or combination of keys, e.g. calculators and calendars.

tessellate – When a graphic image is converted into simple geometric shapes such as squares and circles in order to be manipulated or copied to another application.

A flower image that has been tessellated using hexagons

TeX – A typesetting language that embeds codes within the text of a document in order to initiate changes in layout. It is useful for its ability to describe elaborate scientific formulas.

texel – **TEX**ture **El**ement. The smallest unit of a texture map.
SEE ALSO: TEXTURE MAPPING

text – Words relating to a document; i.e. the words that belong to the main body of a document rather than those that appear in appendices or with the illustrations.

text box – This refers to a box that can either have visible or invisible outlines, into which text can be typed. Text boxes provide a common entry point for placing text into a web page or adjacent to an image.
SEE: FEATURE BOX

text editor – Refers to a text editing program – such as SimpleText provided with the Apple Macintosh operating system – that can be used for entering, changing, storing, and formatting text.

text file – A file that contains only text is referred to as a text file, whereas a file containing sound, graphics, or other multimedia elements would more likely be referred to as a sound or graphics file.

text messaging – This relates to mobile or cell phone technology that enables the user to send text messages via the telephone. These messages are inexpensive to send, but – owing to the small screen and the limited keyboard – the messages are kept short, often making wide use of acronyms.
SEE: APPENDIX 1

text mode – To operate the computer to show only text and no other images. E.g. MS-DOS works only in text mode.

text wrap – When graphics and text are used together, text wrap enables the author to place the text around the image, or to either side of it.
SEE: FEATURE BOX

text-based browser – This kind of *browser* can only read text files, not graphics or multimedia.

text-to-speech – The technology that converts text into computerized speech. This is often used by banks, utility customer service systems, and some web sites.

texture – The surface features of an object.

texture mapping – 1. This computer graphics effect reproduces the surface appearance of an object; e.g. water, wood, and marble.
2. It provides a plain image with an interesting or realistic appearance by overlaying a texture.

TFT – See: **t**hin **f**ilm **t**ransistor

TFTP – See: **T**rivial **F**ile **T**ransfer **P**rotocol

---

text wrap

This very simple example shows text wrapped around an image. The edge of the text assumes the same shape as the back of the koala bear.

INTRO TEXT GOES HERE Lorem ipsum dolor sit amet nonummy nibh euismod tincidunt ut laoreet dolor enim ad minim ullamcorper commodo co dolor in hendi consequat, ve at. Lorem i iscing elit, sed c ut laoreet dolor enim ad minim ve corper suscipit lo consequat. Duis in vulputate vel dolore eu feugia my nibh euism aliquam erat vo quis nostrud exe nisl ut aliquip ex vel eum iriure dol molestie consequat, sis at. Lorem ipsum di elit, sed diam nummy nil magna aliquam erat volutpat. nostrud exerci tation ullamco ea commodo consequat. Dui in vulputate velit esse molestie consequat, vel illur

thermal printer – A thermal printer is the kind of printer that uses heat to fix the image on the page.

thesaurus – A file containing lists of words that are linked to words with a similar meaning. *Search engines* often use a thesaurus to expand a search. Most of the current leading *word-processing* programs provide built-in thesaurus facilities.

thick client – **See:** fat client

thin client – Thin client refers to a computer that relies on a server to store, manage, and process applications. When such a computer is online it requires a *fat server* to provide it with processing power. The advantage of this is that the computer's memory is not overburdened with large and often outdated software.
SEE ALSO: THIN SERVER, FAT CLIENT

thin film transistor screen (TFT screen) – A screen that uses the kind of *liquid crystal display* that produces high-quality color displays for laptop computers.

thin server – This refers to a server in a client-server application where most of the program is resident on the client computer, known as a *fat client*.
SEE ALSO: THIN CLIENT

third-generation – The latest specification for cellular or mobile phones, which will enable high-speed Internet access and live video links.

third-generation web site – This identifies the kind of web site that contains text, graphics, animations, and video and sound clips, as well as interactive forms. Many web sites that were identified as third-generation were first introduced in the mid 1990s.

third-party processor – A company dedicated to the processing of credit cards for web sites.

third-party service provider – An *Internet Service Provider* that provides Internet access and associated services to a company or organization's members or employees. This arrangement proves advantageous to customers, since it dispels their need to set up routes for Internet access via their own networks.

thrash – 1. To use a disk extensively. 2. A problem with *virtual memory* that requires the *Central Processing Unit* to utilize excessive resources by moving data around between memory and disks.

thread – A strand of related messages. A thread is usually found in a *newsgroup* or on a *bulletin board,* where all the responses to a posted message on a particular topic are indented beneath the original message.

thread sled – (slang) The *browser* or software that is used for messaging.

threaded Internet newsreader – **See:** Tin

three-dimensional audio – Sound that seems to come from a number of different directions, creating the illusion of a three-dimensional space. The effect is often achieved using headphones. It is used in *virtual reality* environments.

three-dimensional graphics – A *graphic* or *image* that has within it the illusion of depth. Such images are more realistic than flat images.

three-dimensional spreadsheet – A spreadsheet where the data is organized by three criteria: row, column, and sheet. This enables the user to create large spreadsheets – moving between sheets to access data.

three-tier architecture – In this client-server model, used in database handling, the client is the first tier, the server is the second tier, and software acting as the go-between is the third-tier.

throwaway e-mail address – A secondary e mail address created by users for managing unwanted e-mails and reducing the amount of *spam* received by their main address, by directing it to the throwaway e-mail address. The user can choose to give out the throwaway e-mail address when an address is required on an Internet site.
SEE ALSO: SPAMDEXING

thumb – This describes the *elevator* slider on a *scroll bar*.

thumbnail – A small version of a larger image. These are often found on web sites when they are used as a hyperlink. When a thumbnail of this kind is clicked, a full-sized version of the image displayed by the thumbnail in miniature will be revealed. Thumbnails are very popular because they take considerably less time to load than the full image and they also provide the user with the option to see the enlarged image only when they request it. This is especially useful when the user is loading a web page containing a large number of thumbnails.
SEE: FEATURE BOX

tick box – This is a small box on a web page that allows a user to switch an option on or off; e.g. a *dialog box* which offers the option for information entered on a form to be remembered.

ticker tape – See: marquee

thumbnail

The two thumbnails here show pages of a book in perfect miniature. Some web sites, such as www.amazon.com, show thumbnails that the user can click on to see the book content in full.

tickler – An e-mail send to authenticate an e-mail address. Such e-mails usually require a confirmatory reply.

Tier 1 ISP – An *Internet Service Provider* that provides direct access to the Internet.

Tier n ISP – An *Internet Service Provider* that leases access lines to the Internet through a *Tier 1 ISP*.

TIF – **See:** Tagged Image File Format

.tiff – *Tagged Image File Format*. A graphics file format.
SEE: APPENDIX 5 for file extensions.

TIFF – **See:** Tagged Image File Format

---

tiled windows

Tiled windows enable the user to view at the same time all the programs they have running.

This user has four Word documents all displayed on the screen at once.

---

tight – This term can have a very wide range of meanings, usually with a very positive sense. In computing terms it is generally taken to mean a well-written and efficient program.

tilde – The ~ character, which is sometimes encountered in web site addresses. The tilde is also an accent that is frequently required over characters in certain languages such as Spanish and Portugese; e.g. above the "n" in señor.

tile – This is an image that is repeated across the display.

tiled windows – Describes a series of windows that are displayed side by side instead of overlapping.
SEE: FEATURE BOX

Time Division Multiple Access (TDMA) – A combination of satellite technology and cellular phone technology, which uses multiple digital signals, converted into a single high-speed channel.

Time Division Multiplexing (TDM) – A *multiplexing* technique used with satellites and cellular phones where the signals take turns in transmitting.
SEE ALSO: INTERLEAVE

time bomb – A type of attack where a program is sent to a computer to be activated at a certain time and/or date. E.g. A program left on the system by employees who have left a company.

time stamp – This describes information relating to the time of creation or the time of last modification (or the time of last access) that is attached to a file or message. It is usually possible to find the time stamp for any file by looking at the Properties dialog box for that file. For example, right-clicking any file in Microsoft Windows reveals the Properties box for that file. This box reveals the dates when the file was created, modified, and accessed. In the Apple Mac operating system, clicking any file and pressing the "i" key in combination with the function key reveals the info dialog box. This shows the dates on which that file was created and modified.

time stamped certificate – A *digital certificate* which guarantees that a certain event took place at a certain time on the Internet.

time to live (TTL) – This phrase is used to describe the amount of time a *packet* can be considered to exist within a network before it is destroyed.

time-out – Time-out describes when a connection has been terminated because there has been no activity within a specified period. Many Internet Service Providers and certain kinds of software packages automatically close down a connection that has been dormant for a certain amount of time – a period that is usually measured in minutes.

Times New Roman – This common *serif* typeface is often set as the *default* font within a system. Times New Roman can also be set as the default typeface by the user for many applications; for example, Microsoft Word's default font is Times New Roman. The same is true of the word-processor supplied with the Star Office suite developed by Sun Microsystems.
SEE: FEATURE BOX

Tin – A *Unix* newsreading program that is used for maintaining the message threads in an Internet newsgroup site. Tin is an acronym for **T**hreaded **I**nternet **N**ewsreader.

tint – This verb describes the addition of a shade to a specified color.

Times New Roman

Times New Roman is shown here in its four fonts:

normal
```
Times New Roman
ABCDEFGHIJKLMNOPQR...
abcdefghijklmnopqrstuvwxyz
1234567890!@#$%^&*()
```

bold
```
Times New Roman (bold)
ABCDEFGHIJKLMNOPQ...
abcdefghijklmnopqrstuvwxyz
1234567890!@#$%^&*()
```

italic
```
Times New Roman (italic)
ABCDEFGHIJKLMNOPQRS...
abcdefghijklmnopqrstuvwxyz
1234567890!@#$%^&*()
```

bold italic
```
Times New Roman (bold, italic)
ABCDEFGHIJKLMNOPQR...
abcdefghijklmnopqrstuvwxyz
1234567890!@#$%^&*()
```

title – The name of a document, file, or message – it appears on the *title bar*.

title bar – The horizontal bar that usually appears at the top of an application's window. It is used for displaying basic controls for the active program (minimize, maximize, and close) and identification details for the active file; e.g. the file's title and sometimes the application's name.

This title bar appears at the top of the Internet Explorer window.

TLD – **See: T**op-**l**evel **D**omain

TN – **See: T**el**n**et

TNEF – **See: T**ransport **N**eutral **E**ncapsulation **F**ormat

toast – (slang) A term used in a similar way to *fried*, meaning to *crash* a computer. It is also used in relation to a software failure.

toggle – To switch or fluctuate between two states; for example, between conditions of on or off.

toggle button – This kind of button offers just two states. For example, pressing F11 in Internet Explorer toggles between full-screen and regular views of the browser window.

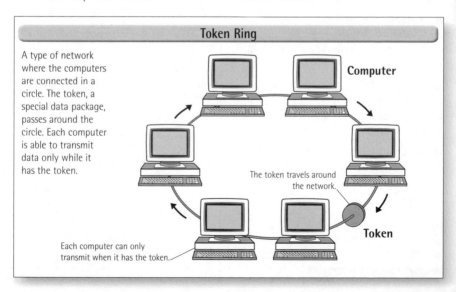

Token Ring

A type of network where the computers are connected in a circle. The token, a special data package, passes around the circle. Each computer is able to transmit data only while it has the token.

Computer

The token travels around the network.

Token

Each computer can only transmit when it has the token.

token – 1. A code used to control transmissions within a network.
SEE ALSO: TOKEN RING
2. A form of e-cash which can be used to make purchases over the Internet.

Token Ring – A *protocol* for *local area networks* developed by IBM. It works by passing packets of data tokens via each workstation in a network. The workstation cannot transmit until it receives the token; all stations are connected to a hub called a Multi-station Access Unit, through which the whole network can be managed.
SEE: FEATURE BOX

Token Ring network – **See:** Token Ring

toner – The finely powdered ink that is used in laser printers.

tool – Refers to any specific function within a program; for example, print, undo, cut, and paste. It can even refer to an application; e.g. a graphics program can be called a graphics tool and an application that maintains web site content can also be referred to as a tool.

toolbar – The bars that are located at the top, bottom, or side of a display that provide the buttons to activate the various tools quickly. E.g. The toolbar on a browser offers options to stop the transmission of a page and to go back to the last page and forward to the next. A floating toolbar is one which can be repositioned by the user.

toolbox – This is a box containing icons that represent the commands for an application. The toolbox can be moved or made to disappear.
SEE: FEATURE BOX

top-down programming – Top-down programming describes the kind of program where actions at a high level are defined. These definitions are then broken down into elements, which are in turn defined in greater detail.

top-level domain (TLD) – This describes that part of the domain name in the hierarchical naming scheme, the Internet Domain Name Service, that represents the top level. Widely used top level domains include the following examples: .net, .com, .edu, .gov, .org.

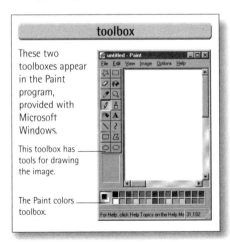

toolbox

These two toolboxes appear in the Paint program, provided with Microsoft Windows.

This toolbox has tools for drawing the image.

The Paint colors toolbox.

topic drift – This describes the tendency for *newsgroup threads* to drift away from the original subject under discussion.

topology – The way that a network or computer is set up in terms of its connections, types, and nodes. For example, *Token Ring* topography is a network that operates on a token ring system; star topography has each node connected to a central hub; and bus topography attaches the nodes to a single cable.

TOPS – **See:** **T**ransparent **Op**erating **S**ystem

tortoise site – The kind of web site that is so data heavy that it takes a very long time to download.

TOS – Abbreviation for **T**erms **o**f **S**ervice.

TOSsed out – This describes the kind of situation when someone is required to leave a chat room for violating the TOS (Terms of Service).

touchpad – The small touch-sensitive rectangular-shaped area on a *laptop* computer that can be used to control the *cursor* position on the screen.

touchscreen – A touch-sensitive display that can be used to control the *cursor* or to make selections.

tourist – A visitor to a *newsgroup* or *intranet* who has not been assigned an account but is given temporary access.

tower – Refers to the kind of housing case for a computer's internal operations – for example, the hard drive, the central processing unit (CPU), and boards – that stands upright.

TPI – **T**racks **P**er **I**nch

TPM – **T**ransactions **P**er **M**inute

trace – A method of verification for checking whether a program is functioning properly. A table of current status and contents of the *registers* and *variables* are displayed after each instruction.

traceroute – Software that tracks the route taken by packets transmitted from a user's computer to its destination.

tracert – This is a Microsoft *Windows* *traceroute* utility that can be run from the Start menu.

track – 1. A single song on a CD.
2. In *multimedia* software, the instructions that move an object in time.
3. In a *MIDI* file, track relates to the individual notes in music that can be distinguished either by the instrument, the part played, or the channel.

trackball – This provides a method of moving a *cursor* on the screen. Often found on the case of a portable computer, a trackball closely resembles the underside of a conventional *mouse*. It is moved with the fingers or parts of the hand.

tracker – This program monitors events and can be set up to inform users if something in which they are interested occurs. The most common form of tracker is part of a news service.

tracking – The movement of the mouse in relation to the movement of the cursor on screen. High tracking requires a small movement of the mouse to create a large movement on screen; low tracking is the opposite, which is better for detailed work.

traffic – The amount of data packets that are being transmitted over a network at any given time. The higher the traffic, the lower the transport speed.

transaction – A completed process, usually within a database or between a customer and an e-commerce site.

transaction certificate – A *digital certificate* that is issued as proof that a certain event has taken place.

transaction processing – The correct processing of *transactions*. Software is employed that ensures that all transactions leave the system in good order without interfering with other transactions processed concurrently.

transceiver/transmitter–receiver – A device that transmits and receives data.

transfer – The process of moving data from one location to another.

transfer interrupted – This kind of error message is displayed by a browser when the transfer of data is halted, usually as a result of technical difficulties.
SEE ALSO: INTERRUPT

transfer rate – The speed at which data is transferred from one location (such as a folder, a network, or a disk) to another.

transient cookie - A transient cookie is the same as a *session cookie*.
SEE ALSO: COOKIE

transistor – A device that contains a semiconductor and that has at least three electrical contacts, used in a circuit as an amplifier, detector, or switch.

transistor transistor logic (TTL) – A commonly employed type of digital circuit in which the output is derived from two *transistors*.

transition effect – In a presentation, the situation when one image dissolves into another one.

translator – Any kind of device that translates one language into another language.

Transmission Control Protocol – The part of the *TCP/IP* protocol that assembles data into packets and manages their transfer to another location over the Internet.

Transmission Control Protocol/Internet Protocol – See: TCP/IP

transmission line – A telecommunications (phone) line through which packets are sent by means of a *Wide Area Network*.
SEE ALSO: CIRCUIT, CHANNEL

transparency – 1. The illusion that the user is dealing directly with a web site or database without an awareness that they are using a network.
2. The technique of making a graphic appear as though it has been produced directly onto a web site.

transparent GIF – A GIF image that contains a color which, when displayed, enables the user to look straight through the color to the background beneath. This feature enables images to be placed on patterned backgrounds.
SEE ALSO: GRAPHICS INTERCHANGE FORMAT

transparent operating system (TOPS) – A type of *local area network* (LAN).
GO TO: www.sun.com

Transport Neutral Encapsulation Format (TNEF) – A format used by the Microsoft Exchange and Outlook e-mail clients when sending messages formatted as Rich Text Format (RTF). TNEF is usually pronounced "Tee-Neff."

transposition – A form of *encryption* that mixes up symbols in plain text. In those situations where this process occurs twice, it is referred to as double transposition.

trapdoor – Within an *encryption* system, this is a loophole that allows someone with an understanding of the process to read encrypted messages. E.g. Some people believe that there is a trapdoor within the *Data Encryption Standard* developed by the US government that enables authorized persons to read encrypted mail.

trapping – The process of capturing a piece of data, or testing for a particular condition in a running program.

  Trash – The area within the *browser* or on the *desktop* where unwanted documents and programs can be deposited for disposal.

Trash can empty.   Trash can full.

Travel – Booking flights and holidays online is one area where the Internet has flourished. There are great deals to be had, although it is best to shop around to get the top prices. The most well-established sites offer an efficient service almost as good as any travel agent. Information sites are also flourishing, with tourists often adding their tips and recommendations.
SEE ALSO: EXPEDIA.COM
GO TO: www.lonelyplanet.com for information and www.expedia.com for flights and holidays.

 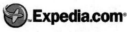

tree network – A network architecture that combines bus and star topology.
SEE ALSO: TOPOLOGY, BUS

tree structure – This type of organizational structure shows all the folders and subfolders within a system. In a PC, the main directory (folder) is usually known as the root directory while those directories connected to it can be seen in a graphical representation to resemble many branches growing from a tree.
SEE ALSO: BINARY TREE
SEE: FEATURE BOX

treeware – Any document, book, or other printed reading material that is produced on paper (i.e. the pulp made from chopped-down trees).

trep – (slang) Short for entrepreneur.

Trinitron Sony – This is a family of high-technology televisions from Sony.
GO TO: www.sony.com

triple data encryption standard (triple DES) – As its name suggests, this is a form of data *encryption* that uses the *Data Encryption Standard* three times in succession.

triplecast – The simultaneous transmission of a program on three media: television, Internet, and the radio.

trivial file transfer protocol (TFTP) – One of the most simple and efficient protocols for the transfer of files over the Internet. TFTP is generally used for the loading of an operating system onto a computer within a network. It has no error-checking facility, which limits its use for data transfer.

Trojan – A Trojan is a *computer virus* that is disguised as a program or as another standard attachment. The user can download the virus believing that it is something that they wish to receive. To help minimize the chance of opening a Trojan, it is generally considered to be good practice not to open *attachments* that have been received from an unknown sender. Also called a Trojan horse.
SEE ALSO: E-MAIL

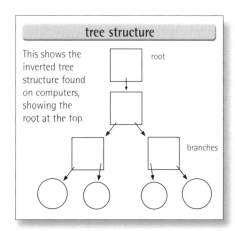

tree structure

This shows the inverted tree structure found on computers, showing the root at the top.

root

branches

troll – (slang) A participant in a *newsgroup* who intentionally makes inflammatory comments that provoke an angry response or even a *flame war*.
SEE ALSO: FLAMING

tron – A person who can only be contacted through e-mail or chat rooms; i.e. it is not possible to contact them through *snail mail* or on the telephone.

true color – This describes the capability to create realistic photographic images on a computer. True color is a representation that comprises a minimum of 24 bit color or, in other words, a minimum of 16,777,216 colors. This kind of color looks real in a video or in a photograph on a computer screen.

TrueSpeech – A *Netscape Navigator plug-in* that enables the transmission of *real-time* audio. In other words, TrueSpeech enables users to speak in real time across the Internet with any other user who is speaking through a computer that is suitably equipped with this software.

TrueType font – An *outline font* that is printed out exactly as it appears on screen and can also be scaled up and down to any size without losing definition or form.
SEE ALSO: FONT

Trumpet Winsock – Part of *TCP/IP* that enables systems using Microsoft Windows 3.1 to connect to the Internet.

truncation – This describes the process of cutting down a number so that it becomes a certain length. There is no element of rounding up or rounding down when truncating a number. The relevant numbers of digits are simply removed from the number without any further consideration. For example, to truncate two digits from 4.5687 makes it 4.56.

trunk – This is another name for a *transmission line*.

TSAPI – See: Telephony Server API

TSR – See: Terminate and Stay Resident

TTL – See: Time To Live

tune – In the context of computers and software, to tune usually means to set a system to its optimum performance level by careful adjustment.

tunneling – The enclosure of a *packet* of data from one type of network so that it can be sent without error to another type of network.

turbo- – This prefix is commonly used to denote an upgraded or more powerful version of an existing program.

Turbo C, Pascal – Commonly used *compiler* programs from *Borland*, who are largely responsible for making them commercially viable.
GO TO: www.borland.com

Turing, Alan – Born London 1912, Alan Turing was a mathematician, war hero, and the man credited with describing the first computers before the technology existed to build them.
SEE ALSO: TURING MACHINE, TURING TEST

Turing machine – Invented by *Alan Turing* in the early 1930s, the Turing machine would read a series of ones and zeros from a tape. These ones and zeros describe the steps needed to solve a particular problem or perform a certain task. It would read each of the steps and perform them in sequence, resulting in the proper answer.

Turing test – In 1950 *Alan Turing* wrote a paper describing a test that could tell whether a machine had developed true intelligence. This test involved asking questions via a keyboard to both a person and an "intelligent machine." Turing believed that if the questioner could not tell the machine apart from the person after a reasonable amount of time, the machine had some intelligence. Scientists and philosophers have been arguing about its relevance ever since.

turnkey system – This system was designed especially for a specific customer. The term – turnkey system – is based on the sentiment summed up in the following phrase: to operate it the customer simply has to turn a key.

TWAIN driver – See: **T**echnology **W**ithout **A**n **I**nteresting **N**ame

tweening – The process of graphically showing the progress of something. For example, on a web site design program, showing the process of an image breaking up into little pieces by using a series of different images. Tweening might be used in the fairly commonplace representation in which the progress of man from the apes is demonstrated in half a dozen steps – all using a slightly different image to show the evolutionary progress.

twiddle – To make small changes in a group of settings and parameters usually in order to personalize or customize the system in question.

twinning – The process of writing data to more than one storage medium for the purposes of safekeeping. Also referred to as *mirroring*.

two–tier – This describes a system that demonstrates two-way interaction. For example, a two-tier system describes a client/server where the interface is with the client but the data remains with the server.

type – 1. (verb) To write by means of a keyboard; either directly onto paper using a typewriter or onto a computer screen using a computer keyboard.
2. (noun) Type, as a noun, is commonly used as an abbreviation for typeface.

type style – The styling of the letters of a typeface. For example, the same typeface can be styled as normal, bold, italic, bold italic, underline, strikethrough, outline, shadow, and/or reverse.

Typeface
Typeface
Typeface
Typeface
Typeface
Typeface

typeface/size – The design of a complete set of type characters and their point size. For example, Times New Roman 12 point; Arial 16 point; Copperplate 10 point.

typesetting – To lay out text so that it is ready for printing.

typo – An abbreviation for typographical error. A typo can be a mistake made by not hitting the intended key.

typosquatter – Someone who reserves a domain name or one who slightly misspells the brand name in the hope of stealing customers who mistype the original name. For example, www.pengun.com instead of www.penguin.com.
SEE ALSO: CYBERSQUATTING

UART – See: **U**niversal **A**synchronous **R**eceiver-**T**ransmitter

UDF – See: **U**niversal **D**isk **F**ormat

UDP – See: **U**ser **D**atagram **P**rotocol

ugly code – A reference to programming that is so poorly written or complex that it is difficult to figure out what it does.

UHF – **U**ltra **H**igh **F**requency. It covers the range of electromagnetic frequencies from 300MHz to 3GHz.

UI – See: **U**ser **I**nterface

UID – See: **U**ser **ID** and username

u/lc – Commonly used abbreviation for upper and *lowercase* lettering.

ULSI – See: **U**ltra **L**arge-**S**cale **I**ntegration

undo

Clicking this button reverses commands or deletes the last entry typed.

Clicking this button reverses the previous action of the undo button.

Tools Table Window Help

The undo and redo button commands are found in Microsoft Word's Standard toolbar.

Ultra ATA – Ultra AT attachment. An upgraded version of the kind of IDE interface that is commonly used for connecting additional hard drives to a computer. Ultra ATA is capable of increasing the speeds of data transfer.

ultra large-scale integration (ULSI) – Achieving more than one million transistors on a microprocessor chip.

ultraviolet (UV) – The range of light (i.e. the invisible radiation wavelengths from about four nanometers to about 380 nanometers) a little beyond the violet in the visible spectrum.

UMA – See: upper memory

UMB – See: upper memory

UML – See: **U**nified **M**odeling **L**anguage

unbuffered memory – In unbuffered memory, the microprocessor controller is in direct contact with the memory. Buffered modules contain a buffer to help cope with the large electrical load required when the system has a lot of memory.

UNC – See: **U**nified **N**aming **C**onvention

underflow – 1. When the result of a computation turns out to be smaller than the smallest quantity that the computer is able to store.
2. When less data is transferred than expected in data communications.

Undernet – Undernet is probably the largest of the *Internet Relay Chat* (real-time) networks. According to information on Undernet's Web site, it has 45 servers that are capable of connecting more than 35 countries and over 1,000,000 users a week.
Go to: www.undernet.org

undo – 1. To annul, reverse or erase.
2. In the context of computer programs, to undo generally refers to restoring the last editing operation that has taken place, or reversing a command that has just been applied within the program. The undo command is commonly built in to any programs that contain image or text editing features. In most programs of this kind (Microsoft Word, for example) the undo feature is generally given its own button, appearing within the program's standard toolbars.
See: feature box

undocumented – Not supported by written materials.

unerase – See: recover

ungroup – To ungroup is to take an image or chart and split it or adapt parts of it to form several images; e.g. a pie chart can be ungrouped to show the separate chunks of the pie more clearly.

uni – A prefix meaning single or one.

Unicast – This refers to the transmission of a message to one receiver only, usually from a server to a workstation.
See also: multicast

Unicode – As a standard for the communication of characters as integers, Unicode was originated to cover all known languages and to break down nationality barriers. Its two-byte-per-character approach means that it has the capability to handle more than 65,000 characters.
Go to: www.unicode.org
See also: ASCII

Unified Modeling Language (UML) – UML is an object-oriented analysis and design language. It was created to enable the amalgamation of several diagramming processes.
See also: Object Management Group (OMG)
Go to: www.omg.com

Unified Naming Convention (UNC) – This is a standard system for identifying servers, printers, and other peripherals that make up a network. Unified Naming Convention originated from *UNIX* and it uses double slashes or backslashes to precede the name of the computer that is being identified.

uniform – 1. Unvarying.
2. Conforming to an agreed standard or protocol.
3. The same as another or others.

Uniform Resource Identifier (URI) – A generic term for the kinds of names and addresses that refer to destinations on the Internet. A *uniform resource locator* (URL) provides an example of a URI.

Uniform/Universal Resource Locator (URL) – **See:** URL

uninterruptible power supply (UPS) – Backup power, to be used when the electrical power fails. Whether uninterruptible power supply is provided by batteries or by a generator will depend on the importance of the system.

unique visitor – Online retailers and web advertisers use this term to describe a visitor who returns to one of their sites. Information provided by that visitor on a previous visit is used to reidentify them.

SEE ALSO: COOKIE

universal asynchronous receiver-transmitter (UART) – The electronic circuit that makes up and manages the *serial port.*

universal disk format (UDF) – A file system for optical disks, universal disk format was originally designed to enable read-write operations between all the key operating systems. UDF was also used for getting compatibility between rewrite and write-once compact disks. The widely used DVD is based on the UDF format.

SEE ALSO: COMPATIBLE

universal network – The idea or ideal of a single network that integrates existing telecommunications networks including the Internet, cable TV, data networks, and video broadcast networks so that they work together to provide the best service possible.

Universal Plug and Play – **See:** upnp

universal serial bus (USB) – A useful hardware interface for low-speed peripherals such as the keyboard, mouse, scanner, printer, or joystick. Its hot swap capability allows elements to be unplugged or plugged in without the need to turn off the system.

SEE ALSO: BUS

UNIX – A widely used and flexible multi-tasking *operating system*, originally developed by AT&T Bell, it was designed to run on almost any computer. It forms the basis for many of today's most successful programs, networks, and systems.

Unix to Unix Coding (UUcoding) – A popular way of transmitting non-text files via e-mail, the UUencode utility program encodes the files by converting 8-bit characters into 7-bit *ASCII* text, and the UUdecode utility program decodes it back at the receiving end.

SEE ALSO: MIME

Unix to Unix Copy Protocol (UUCP) – **See:** UUCP

U

Unix to Unix Decoding (UUDecode) –
See: Unix to Unix Coding

Unix to Unix Encoding (UUEncode) –
See: Unix to Unix Coding

unmoderated – Web page content, or other kinds of data, that is sent unchecked.

unmoderated newsgroup – This is a kind of Internet newsgroup that does not have a moderator to filter messages.
SEE ALSO: MODERATED NEWSGROUP

unpack – Unpacking describes the act of decompressing data.
SEE ALSO: PACK

unPC – This term is commonly used to describe something that is not considered to be politically correct. For example, a sexist would be described as unPC.

unzipping – This describes the act of decompressing a file that has been previously compressed using the popular *PKZIP* program.
SEE ALSO: PK WARE

upgrade – To improve performance, to update existing software to a newer version. Also refers to increasing memory.

upgrade fever – The ever-increasing desire to upgrade equipment and software, whether or not it is actually needed.

uplink – A telecommunications channel from Earth to a satellite.

uplink port – A *port* on a network switch that is used to connect to other switches.

upload – To transmit.
SEE ALSO: DOWNLOAD

upnp – Universal Plug and Play. A network architecture that provides compatibility between different software and peripherals. There are over 400 retailers and vendors that are involved in the Universal Plug and Play Forum.

upper memory area (UMA) – Refers to the memory in a PC between 640K and 1024K. The upper memory block (UMB) refers to the unused areas of memory in the UMA.

uppercase – CAPITAL letters (large letters) as opposed to lowercase (small letters). To produce an uppercase letter with a conventional typewriter keyboard, the shift key needs to be depressed at the same time as the appropriate letter.
SEE ALSO: LOWERCASE

A B C D E F G H I J K L M N
O P Q R S T U V W X Y Z

UPS – See: Uninterruptible Power Supply

upstream – The direction in which data travels from the customer to the *Internet Service Provider* (ISP). For example, a web page request travels upstream.

upward compatible – If new hardware or software is deemed to be compatible with succeeding versions it is usually referred to as upward compatible.

URI – See: **U**niform **R**esource **I**dentifier

URL (Uniform/Universal Resource Locator) – The URL system is used to identify and standardize the way electronic addresses are written, including those on the Internet. A typical URL is made from three main parts:
- The protocol – normally http
- The domain name – e.g. www.dk.com
- The directory or file name – e.g. UK or filename.htm

So, the URL for Dorling Kindersley's UK home page is http://www.dk.com/uk

URL hijacking – The process of clandestinely re-routing or re-using material from an established site. A URL hijacker often takes advantage of inadvertent typos (typographical errors) by creating a web address with a mis-spelled version of a well-known company.
SEE ALSO: TYPOSQUATTING, PAGEJACKING

URL minder – A program that tracks changes to URLs. This can prove very useful for keeping up-to-date *bookmarks* for subject and specific information, news, business updates and any other *favorite* site addresses.

USB – See: **u**niversal **s**erial **b**us

Usenet Newsgroups – A global bulletin board system that provides forums or newsgroups where anyone can post a message on a huge variety of subjects. GO TO: www.google.com for a list of news groups and a dedicated search facility.

user – A person using a computer.

User Datagram Protocol (UDP) – A *protocol* within the *TCP/IP* protocol suite that is used in place of TCP when a reliable delivery is not essential. It is often used for broadcasting messages over a network.

user-friendly – Easy to use; designed with the user in mind.

user group – Describes an organization or a loose collection of users. A user group may have a common interest or use the same system or network.

User ID – User **id**entification.
SEE ALSO: USERNAME

user interface – The combination of hardware or software designed to make it easy for the user to interact with the computer and its programs. Its importance is often overlooked in the rush to improve programs and computers.

username – The username (often called the user ID) is used for identification when a user is logging onto a computer system or online service. Often a password is required as well.

usr – Abbreviation for *user*.

utility – A useful program, a utility performs routine tasks such as copying files or sorting, and often specific mathematical functions.

UUcoding – **See:** Unix to Unix Coding

UUCP – Unix to Unix Copy Protocol. This is a UNIX utility program that copies a file from one computer to another.

UUDecode – **See:** Unix to Unix Coding

UUEncode – **See:** Unix to Unix Coding

UV – **See:** Ultraviolet

V

V. series – A series of small to medium-scale mainframe computers introduced in 1996 by Unisys.

V2V – An expression used in chat rooms and newsgroups (short for voice-to-voice) to propose a phone conversation or even a meeting between participants.

V.90 – An international standard for a modem that communicates at 56 Kbps downstream and 33.6 Kbps upstream.

v mail – **See:** video mail

vaccine – A program designed to detect and stop the progress of *computer viruses*.

vacuum – A space empty of matter.

value–added reseller (VAR) – A company that sells products (e.g. computers) made by another company after adding improvements, e.g. extra components or games software.

vampire tap – A cable connection that is made with a unit that clamps onto and bites into the cable.

VAN – **See:** Virtual Area Network

vandalware – Software that has been developed specifically to cause harm; e.g. virus software.

vanilla – (slang) Computer term meaning ordinary. It refers to a bottom-line piece of hardware or software that has no extra features – the "no frills" version.

vanilla branding – (slang) 1. The essence of a brand.
2. Ordinary or vague brand identity.

vanity domain – A *domain name* which has the same name as the individual who owns it.

vaporware – Software that is not completed on time. Often producers will announce a particular program launch only to find their programmers have vastly under-estimated how long it takes to build the program. Hence, it does not exist on the launch day.

VAR – **See:** value-added reseller

variable – 1. A character assigned to a number or value e.g. $y + z = x$.
2. In programming, variables are used to write flexible programs with the actual data added when the program is finished.

variable bit rate (VBR) – A type of *asynchronous transfer mode (ATM)* that provides a specified throughput even though data is not sent evenly. It is mainly used for voice and *videoconferencing* data.

variant – Another version, slightly different from the original.

VAX – **See:** Virtual Address Extension

VBNS – **See:** Very high-speed Backbone Network Service

VBR – **See:** Variable Bit Rate

VBScript – Microsoft **V**isual **B**asic Script. A programming language that enables the inclusion of interactive controls, such as buttons and scrollbars, on web pages. It is a simpler variant of Microsoft's *Visual Basic* and similar to *JavaScript.*

VCACHE – The disk *cache* system employed in Microsoft Windows 95 and 98. It is dynamic in that it can change the size of the disk *cache* depending on available disk space and application requirements.

vCard – A standard format for an electronic business or personal card that includes space for photos, sound and company logos. There are applications that allow vCards to be viewed and dropped into an e-mail address book.

VCD – **See:** **V**ideo **C**ompact **D**isk

VCM – **See:** **V**irtual **C**hannel **M**emory

VCPI – **See:** **V**irtual **C**ontrol **P**rogram **I**nterface

VCR – **See:** **V**ideo **C**assette **R**ecorder

VDU – **See:** **V**isual **D**isplay **U**nit

vector – 1. An address that directs a computer to a new location in the memory. 2. In computer graphics, a line point designated by its end points. It consists of coordinates made up of a direction and a magnitude. Used in *vector graphics.* 3. A one-row, one-column matrix.

vector graphics – A way of representing pictures and drawing lines or geometric shapes based on designated coordinates. For example, a circle would be made up of many small *vectors.*
SEE: FEATURE BOX

vector processor – A type of computer that performs multiple calculations on *vectors* simultaneously.

vendor – A seller or retailer.

Venn diagram – 1. Graphical representation of a system or circuit, and the relationships between the components. 2. A graph feature (like a pie chart) used to display statistical information in an impactful and eye-catching fashion.
SEE: FEATURE BOX

verify – To confirm, e.g. a password.

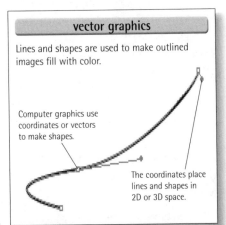

vector graphics

Lines and shapes are used to make outlined images fill with color.

Computer graphics use coordinates or vectors to make shapes.

The coordinates place lines and shapes in 2D or 3D space.

Veronica – A *search engine* looking for specific resources by description, not just file name. It is a successor to *Archie*, named for the character Veronica in the *Archie* comics.
SEE ALSO: GOPHER

vertical – Situated at right angles to the horizon, upright; e.g. a scroll bar.

vertical industry portal (vortal) – **See:** vertical portal

vertical justification – The adjustment of spacing between lines of text so that they fit the section of text into a page.

vertical portal – A site that specializes in providing information and services for a specific industry. Also known as a vortal.

vertical scrolling – **See:** scrolling

very high-speed backbone network service (VBNS) – A high-speed US network that interconnects supercomputer centers at 622 Mbps.

VESA – **See:** Video Electronics Standards Association

VFM – Marketing-speak for Value For Money. For example, a good shopping web site will offer VFM.

VGA – Video Graphics Adapter.
SEE ALSO: VIDEO CARD

VI – Visual Interface. A *UNIX* full-screen text editor utility program.

video – A very popular audio/visual recording and playback technology. On the Internet, video is used as a term for any audio-visual playback, no matter what technology was used to get it on screen.

video adapter – **See:** video card

video capture board – A board that plugs into the expansion socket of a PC allowing the user to capture a TV picture and store it in the memory. It digitizes the picture.

video card – A board that plugs into a PC and converts images created in it to the electronic signals required by the monitor. Also known as a display adapter.

video cassette recorder (VCR) – Standard videotape cassette recording and playback machine.

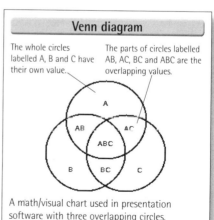

Venn diagram

The whole circles labelled A, B and C have their own value.

The parts of circles labelled AB, AC, BC and ABC are the overlapping values.

A math/visual chart used in presentation software with three overlapping circles.

video clip – A small video segment that is embedded in a web page and animated by means of a *plug-in*. Video clips can take up a lot of memory and slow down the downloading of a web site. *Video streaming* is the technology designed to deal with this problem.

video compact disk (VCD) – A compact disc format used to hold full-motion video. It uses *MPEG* technology.

video editing – The manipulation of video graphics.

Video Electronics Standards Association (VESA) – Founded in 1989, VESA is an organization that sets video interface standards for workstations and computers. Go to: www.vesa.org

VESA ☐ *Working to Make Electronics Work Together*

video graphics board – A combination of video card and video capture board that accepts analog NTSC video (the US standard) from a VCR player or camera.

video mail – Sending video clips as *attachments* to email messages.

video overlay – Placing a video window on the display screen. It can be viewed without changing the original display.

Video Random Access Memory (VRAM) – A type of memory within a video card. It is fast, enabling screen updates even while new data is being processed, giving good quality images.
SEE ALSO: RAM

video streaming – Playing video in *real time* as it is delivered to a *browser*. Load times are greatly improved over older .wav style files (which have to be downloaded in their entirety before any playback is possible).

videoconferencing – The linking of audio-visual technology – including video camera, microphones, and computers - usually with large monitors to enable "meetings" between several people or boardrooms to take place simultaneously around the globe. In the 1990s this was prohibitively expensive, but now it is commonly used by many multi-national organizations and other smaller companies. Videoconferencing software includes *CU seeMe*.

Video-on-Demand (VoD) – To deliver a video program to a web browser or TV whenever the user requests it.

view – 1. To look at what is displayed on the screen or desktop.
2. A pull-down menu feature in many applications, e.g. Microsoft Word, and in browser software, e.g. Netscape Navigator.

viewer – A utility program that allows the user to see what is in a file without having to start the program that created it.

vignette – An image without a hard or solid border, much used on web sites.
SEE: FEATURE BOX

viral marketing – A marketing term for a campaign that relies on an offer that is taken up almost without thinking. It has nothing to do with a computer virus.

virtual – A reference to a computer simulation of a real device, e.g. it can be used as though it really did exist. Now commonly used in technology as a prefix to refer to something imagined, not real. The Internet is considered a virtual world.
SEE ALSO: VIRTUAL REALITY

Virtual Address Extension (VAX) – A very successful family of 32-bit computers made by *Compaq* in the 1980s.

virtual area network (VAN) – A network on which users can share a virtual face-to-face experience through the use of high bandwidth connections. Potentially very useful for medical and legal consultations and business conferencing.

virtual channel memory (VCM) – A specialized form of add-on *Dynamic Random-Access Memory* that provides for high speed data transfers.
GO TO: www.nec.com

virtual circuit – Temporary communications path created between computers in a communications system that uses *switches*, e.g. for the duration of a call.

virtual classroom – An online class taught remotely over the Internet. Part of a remote learning package.
SEE ALSO: EDUCATION

virtual community – A community that exists online to pursue a common interest. For example, searching for family histories (genealogy) is a highly popular online pursuit.

virtual control program interface (VCPI) – An industry specification for managing memory beyond the first *megabyte* on PCs.

virtual desktop – A desktop expanded on screen by the use of *virtual devices*.

virtual device – A *peripheral* simulated by the operating system.

vignette

This design device can be used to create a nostalgic look. It also serves to enhance a rather plain image.

A vignetted picture shades off into the edges – frequently in a circular fashion.

virtual device driver – A particular type of *driver* that allows Microsoft *Windows* to perform functions via other applications that Windows could not otherwise control.

virtual dial-up – A way of connecting to the Internet that does not make use of the *TCP-IP* protocols.

virtual disk – A section of *RAM* that simulates a fast disk storage system.

virtual hosting – When a *server* contains more than one web site, each with its own *domain name*. Many organizations, companies, and individuals prefer to hire a hosted web space, rather than to own one, because of the cheaper costs involved in virtual hosting.

virtual LAN (VLAN) – A network of computers configured through software rather than hardware. Such computers act as if they are connected to the same lines, even though they may actually be physically located on different segments of a *local area network*. VLAN's main advantage is flexibility in that computers can be physically moved without disruption to the network.

virtual machine – An *IBM* mainframe *operating system*. It can run multiple operating systems within the computer simultaneously so that each one can run its own programs.

virtual machine environment (VME) – An operating system used by ICL for its series 39 computers.

virtual memory – The simulation of more memory in a computer than actually exists. Virtual memory can be turned off and on and the size increased or decreased. It can allow the computer to run larger programs by breaking up a program into small segments, called pages, and then bringing as many pages into virtual memory as will fit into a reserved area for that program.

virtual memory system (VMS) – Multiple user, multiple tasking operating system for the VAX computers made by *Compaq*.

virtual organization – An organization that is not dependent on location or time in its trading.

virtual private line – A telecommunications line which appears to the user to be a *dedicated* line but which in fact is not. Such lines offer comparable facilities at a reduced cost.

virtual private network (VPN) – A network used by a select group within a public network. For example, there are programs that allow the use of parts of the Internet for private use.

virtual reality – An artificial representation of reality using powerful and sophisticated computers and graphics programs. Also known as VR for short.

Virtual Reality Modeling Language (VRML) – A commonly used 3D graphics language. After downloading a VRML page from the Internet, its contents can be viewed, rotated and manipulated as required. The ability to "walk" into simulated rooms (as on web property pages or in computer games) is a commonly used application of VRML.

virtual server – **See:** virtual hosting

virtual storage – **See:** virtual memory

virtual storefront – The pages of an e-commerce site that offer merchandise for sale.

Virtual Telecommunications Access Method (VTAM) – Software used by IBM in its system network architecture for controlling communications.

virus – **See:** computer virus

virus protection software – A program that when updated regularly safeguards against common computer *viruses*.
SEE: FEATURE BOX

Visio 2002 – A program designed to facilitate the presentation of diagrams.
GO TO: www.microsoft.com/office/visio

visit – A word for going to a web page via the browser. One visit may result in several hits (though the words are often used to mean the same thing).
SEE ALSO: HIT

Visual Basic – A program tool used to develop Windows applications quickly by use of a *graphical user interface* (GUI).
GO TO: www.microsoft.com

Visual C++ – Program development software from Microsoft. It enables the creation of *Windows* applications by using graphics and C program code.

Microsoft®
Visual C++.net
Microsoft Visual Studio .NET Family Member

visual computing – The use of visual images (e.g. photographs, video sequences, or simple icons) to represent other things that are not necessarily visual themselves, e.g. certain computing systems.

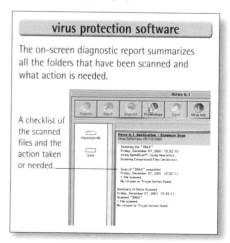

virus protection software

The on-screen diagnostic report summarizes all the folders that have been scanned and what action is needed.

A checklist of the scanned files and the action taken or needed.

visual display unit (VDU) – A terminal comprising a screen and a keyboard.

visualization – The act of representing abstract concepts such as business or scientific data in image form in order to make the concepts easier to understand, e.g. using a *venn diagram*.

Vivo – A commonly used format for sending video over the Internet.
Go to: www.vivo.com

VLAN – **See:** **V**irtual **LAN**

VME – **See:** **V**irtual **M**achine **E**nvironment

VMS – **See:** **V**irtual **M**emory **S**ystem

VoD – **See:** **V**ideo **o**n **D**emand

voice mail – A computerized telephone answering and message-taking service.

Voice over IP (VoIP) – A two-way audio transmission over the Internet, it specifically refers to transmission over a *TCP/IP* network, but the term is used more generally, too.

voice portal – A web site that can be reached by telephone, e.g. for information such as sport scores, or stock quotes. WAP cellular telephones connect to the Internet and also provide a small visual display.
See also: voice–activated e-mail

voice recognition – The ability of a computer (through a sound card and appropriate software) to recognize certain words or sounds and take the corresponding actions.

voice–activated e-mail – A way of accessing e-mail over the telephone. The user usually dials into a *voice portal* and then requests mail by saying, "get my e-mail." The messages are then read using speech synthesis software.

voice-enabled e-mail – **See:** voice-activated e-mail

volatile memory – Memory that will lose all data when power is switched off.

volatility – A reference to the number of records that are added or deleted from a system compared to that which is stored.

volt – A unit of electrical potential.

voltage – Force of electricity when expressed in volts.

voltage regulator module (VRM) – A device that provides steady output voltage, even if the input varies.

volume – 1. External data media, e.g. tape, discs or diskettes.
2. A loose measure of space occupied by data in memory.
3. Sound settings within a computer's operating system or separate software.

volume serial number (VSN) – A number automatically assigned to a floppy disk or hard disk that uniquely identifies it.

vortal – **See:** vertical industry portal

voxel – A voxel (from **VO**lume and pi**XEL**) is a three-dimensional version of a *pixel* defined by x, y and z coordinates. Voxels can be used in scientific and medical applications that process 3D images.

VPN – **See:** **v**irtual **p**rivate **n**etwork

VRAM – **See:** **V**ideo **R**andom **A**ccess **M**emory

VRM – **See:** **V**oltage **R**egulator **M**odule

VRML – **See:** **V**irtual **R**eality **M**odeling **L**anguage

VRWeb – VRweb is a browser for 3D objects modeled in the *Virtual Reality Modeling Language*. **Go to:** www.vrweb.net

VSN – **See:** **V**olume **S**erial **N**umber

VTAM – **See:** **V**irtual **T**elecommunications **A**ccess **M**ethod

VxD – **See:** **V**irtual device **d**river

Vxtreme – A format for the delivery of *streaming* videos.

W2K – **See:** Windows 2000

W3 – Short for *World Wide Web*.

W3C – **See:** World Wide Web Consortium

wabbit – A computer program that makes copies of itself every time it is run, eventually crashing the system. Technically a wabbit is neither a *virus* nor a *worm*.

WACK – **W**ait before sending ACK (**ack**nowledgement). The message sent to indicate that the destination computer is not ready to receive the ACK.

wafer – The thin sheet of semiconductor material used to form the substrate (base layer) for a microchip.

WAIS – **See:** **W**ide **A**rea **I**nformation **S**ervice

wait state – The delay in a powerful computer that enables slower memory components to retrieve data.

waiting time – The time lag between the initiation of a request for data and the moment it is received.

Wake on LAB – The facility for the power in a remote client location to be activated by the network. This allows upgrading and management tasks to take place out of office hours.

walled garden – A control that places limits on the user's access to Web content and services. The walled garden directs the user's browser to particular areas, allowing access to a selection of material, or preventing access to other material. This does not prevent users from navigating outside the walls, it simply makes it more difficult. For instance, browsers may place limits on the sites that they allow children to visit. Alternatively, they may direct users to certain sites in order to generate an income from those sites.

wallet – **See:** digital wallet

wallpaper – In Microsoft *Windows*, the pattern or picture that forms the background to the graphical user interface. It can be selected and altered through the Control Panel, Desktop Settings.
SEE: FEATURE BOX

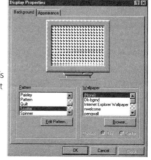

wallpaper

Wallpaper patterns are used to customize the look of a window or graphical user interface.

The Desktop Settings Control Panel is used to select wallpaper. The user can use almost any kind of pattern or picture.

Walsh code – A code that generates unique sets of numbers for encryption and cellular (mobile) communications. Also known as pseudo-random noise codes.

WAMBAM – **See:** **W**eb **a**pplication **m**eets **b**ricks-**a**nd-**m**ortar

WAN – **See:** **W**ide-**A**rea **N**etwork

wand – A computer-linked hand-held optical reader. It is most frequently used to read bar codes but can also read typewritten fonts, printed fonts, and OCR fonts.

WAP – **W**ireless **A**pplication **P**rotocol. A standard for applications developed for use over wireless communication networks. WAP phones and other handheld devices are able to connect to the Internet using this technology, which can transmit voice, data, graphics, and video using a simple *browser*. It's fair to say that WAP technology has not caught on as its designers hoped it would. Its use is limited by the size of the screen available on most mobiles. New technologies, such as *imode* and *GPRS* will eventually overtake it.

WAP Forum – An organization established to promote standards for delivering wireless e-mail, text-based web pages, and data to smart phones, pagers, PDAs and other mobile terminals.
Go to: www.wapforum.org
See also: WAP

war dialer – A computer program that dials phone numbers to establish which lines are connected to modems and fax machines. Often used maliciously.

warez – Software or files that are illegally made available by software pirates. Such files are sometimes found on FTP sites.

warez doodz – *Crackers* who illegally penetrate commercial sites to gain access to copyrighted software, which is then posted on *warez* sites for general access.

warlording – To remove a signature file from a user's mail. This may be done by the ISP because the file contains offensive content or is too large. The term is said to be the nickname of the first user to have his signature file deleted.

warm boot/start – To restart a computer that has previously been running and whose components are already warm. This is necessary after a computer has crashed.

warm swap – To exchange an old component from a system for a new one without turning the power off. However, the component concerned should not be active at the time of the exchange.

warmware – Human beings. Synonymous with wetware.

Warp – An IBM operating system. The client version is OS/2 Warp, and the server version is Warp Server for e-Business.

waster - The result of a search inquiry that is listed repeatedly.

watch icon - The Macintosh equivalent to the hourglass symbol, which indicates that the computer is processing something and unable to receive new commands.

waterfall - A description of a software program or web site that is under development but progresses one step at a time with each step being irreversible.

watermark - Similar to the watermark on expensive paper. Some computer files have digital watermarks embedded within them, which are not noticeable to the user. Such digital patterns can be used to authenticate documents and detect unauthorized copies.

watt - A unit of electrical power equal to one joule per second.

.wav/WAV - See: Wave Form Audio

wave - The oscillation or movement that transfers energy from point to point and is visualized as a succession of curves resembling waves. Signals such as light, sound, electricity, and radio travel in waves.

wave audio - See: digital audio

Wave file - A file that contains a sound signal in *digital* form. Such files have the .wav *file extension*.

Wave Form Audio (WAV) - A Windows sound file stored in digitized format.

wavelength - The distance between one point on a wave and the same point in the next cycle.

wavelength division multiplexing (WDM) - A means of transmitting multiple signals simultaneously over a single optical fiber. The signals travel within color bands, with one color band for each signal.

wavelet compression - The process used in the *lossy compression* method for graphics and video.

wavetable - The memory in a sound card that contains recordings of musical instruments. Some types of sound cards use FM synthesis, a method that relies on mathematical formulae to recreate the sound of the instrument.
SEE ALSO: FREQUENCY MODULATION

WDM - See: Wavelength Division Multiplexing

wearable computer - A computer that is worn on the body. Such computers are generally accessed via *voice recognition* and use a head mounted display to provide the user with screen-like visual input. Many computers are used in challenging work environments and have to be adapted for use. Wearable computers are also used for *virtual reality* games.

weasel - An inexperienced or uninformed user of the Internet.
SEE ALSO: NEWBIE

weasel text – The message found on a web site that tells the user that a part of the site has been removed, and why.

Weather Observation Definition Format – An Extensible Markup Language (*XML*) application used for weather observation reports and forecasts. It is also called Weather Observation Markup Format (WOMF).

Web – A shorthand term for *World Wide Web*.

web accelerator – A software utility designed to increase the speed at which web pages are retrieved.
SEE ALSO: PLUG–IN

web address – The unique *URL address* that enables users to locate a page on the *World Wide Web*.
SEE ALSO: ADDRESS

Web aggregator – An organization that compiles news, sports scores, weather forecasts, and reference materials from a number of sources and distributes it to customers via the Internet.
SEE ALSO: CONTENT

web anonymizer – See: anonymizer

Web application meets bricks-and-mortar (WAMBAM) – Refers to conventional commercial organizations that introduce a web presence, for

web design

Good web design is essential for a successful web site. Web designers and developers use web authoring software such as *Dreamweaver* to create web pages. The software creates the *HTML* code necessary to publish the pages on the *World Wide Web*, and allows the designer to combine a variety of media.

Pictures and animations can be generated and manipulated using tools of the web-authoring software.

Text can be generated within the web authoring software, or imported from another application.

Images, graphics and text are then combined with *HTML* code to produce the final pages.

example, traditional bookshops and clothing retailers.

web authoring software – Software used to create web sites and web pages. It is the Internet equivalent of a desktop publishing application. Web authoring software generates the *HTML* code required for web site programming and shows the user a clear page layout while they are working. *Dreamweaver* is one example.

web browser – **See:** browser

web bug – A way of passing information from a user's computer to a third party. Web bugs often work in conjunction with *cookies* to gather and track information. The web bug itself is usually a single-pixel, transparent *GIF* image and uses its associated *HTML* code to point to a third party web site, which will retrieve the GIF image. It then passes information gleaned from the user's computer to the web site.

web cam – **See:** webcam

web chat – **See:** chat

web design – The way that a web page looks, and is laid out and structured. It can also describe how the speed with which it downloads affects its attractiveness, functionality, and the user's desire to visit the site again. A well-designed site is vital to the success of any online activity.
SEE: FEATURE BOX
SEE ALSO: WEB AUTHORING SOFTWARE

web designer – **See:** web developer

web developer – Someone with the technical skills to create a web page. This includes a knowledge of web design programs such as *HTML* and *Java* as well as knowledge about the various *protocols* that govern the functioning of the Internet.

web e-mail – **See:** e-mail

web end – A web site that has no functional *links*.

web farm – **See:** server farm

web filter – **See:** filter

web graffiti – Alterations to a *web site* that have been carried out without the consent of the owner or site developer.

web guru – Someone with an exceptionally good knowledge of the Web, e.g. an organization's web developer.

web hosting: – **See:** host

web log file – A file maintained by a web server that records the web pages visited by a user, including time of access, duration, etc. This information is then used by the webmaster to optimize the service offered.

web navigation – **See:** navigation

web objects – Each of the various elements that combine to make a web page; e.g. text, graphics, URLs, audio/video clips, and scripts.

web page – One page of a document posted on the *World Wide Web*. Each page has a unique address and is usually written in *HTML* and stored as a file on a *server* to enable users to access it. Most web pages have *links,* either internally to other pages of the same document, or externally to web pages that form parts of other documents.

web page design – **See:** web design

web page editor – Software used to create and modify HTML-based web pages and documents.

web page title – Synonymous with *Internet domain name.*

web payment service – The management and transfer of funds from a user to an e-commerce site. The money could come from a *digital wallet,* from a credit card stored on a digital wallet service or from a prepaid account.
SEE ALSO: E-CASH

web police – Volunteers in the US who search the Web looking for violations of Internet protocol, security, or laws. When criminal activity is discovered, they pass this information on to the authorities.

web portal – **See:** portal

web producer – **See:** web developer

web publishing – The creation of documents that are made available on the *World Wide Web.* Such documents can contain multimedia in the form of graphics, sound, video clips, animation, and interactive forms, as well as text. Documents published on the Web must be stored on a computer that acts as a *server.* It in turn should publicize its existence through a directory listing or *links* from other related web sites.

web rage – Anger that is generated by the frustrations of using the Web. This may be caused by slow access, missing links, poorly designed or maintained web sites, or failure of searches to come up with good results.

web ring – A collection of related web sites that are accessed via a common homepage. E.g. Rings set up by voluntary groups on a specific disease or those run by a town's chamber of commerce to promote commercial and social groups in the town.

web rot – What happens to a site that is poorly served and contains out of date or dysfunctional links.
SEE ALSO: COBWEB

Web Search – A flexible *metasearch engine* which can be customized by the user.
GO TO: www.web-search.com

web server – **See:** server

web server farm – **See:** server farm

web site – A collection of *web pages* that are thematically or commercially related and linked together via a *homepage*.

web slate – **See:** webpad

web TV – A means of accessing the Internet via a television set, a set-top box, an ordinary telephone line, and a subscription-based online service.

web wrap agreement – The contract entered into by an Internet user prior to downloading some software.

web-based – Software that interacts with a web site.

web-based application – In a *client/server* environment, any *application* that is *downloaded* from a web site each time it is run. These programs leave the client computer's memory clear and allow the application to be upgraded without reference to the client.

Webcam – The Internet can bring out the voyeur in us all. One of its most fascinating aspects is to be able to tap into CCTV, or specially set up cameras from all over the world, showing anything from the weather in the Arctic to wildlife in the African national parks.
Go to: www.camcentral.com as a starting point.

webcast – To *broadcast* information, music or video over the *World Wide Web*.

web-centric – A world view that is based on the World Wide Web. It usually refers to a program or facility that has been designed with the Web in mind.

WebCrawler – A simple-to-use *search engine* and web site directory. It works by searching the other search sites, then coming back with a summary of results.
Go to: www.webcrawler.com

webhead – (slang) Someone who regularly posts material on the *World Wide Web*.

webhippie – (slang) A person who thinks that the widespread use of the Internet heralds a new age of freedom and self-expression.

webify – To transfer a document from either hard copy or computer-generated material to the *World Wide Web*.

webinar – **Web**-based sem**inar**. An interactive seminar or lecture presented over the Web.

webisodics – Internet-based soap opera stories that are updated on a regular basis, just like their TV counterparts. They can be text based, or have multimedia elements.

weblication – Any *application* that runs on the Web.

weblish – A composite word formed from **web** and Eng**lish**. It is used to describe the language of the Internet, particularly that used in e-mails and jargon. Weblish is often noted for its poor spelling and grammar.

webmail – Synonymous with *e-mail*.

webmaster – The person who administers a web site. Most Internet Service Providers have a webmaster who can be contacted about any problems, usually by sending an e-mail to <u>webmaster@name of ISP</u>.

webmonkey – Someone who attempts web design without the necessary skills.

webonomics – E-commerce or any other means of generating money using the *World Wide Web*.

webpad – A hand-held, wireless computer that can be customized for Internet use. It is very small, lightweight, and uses a touch screen for input. Also called a web slate or *graphics tablet* computer.

websmith – Someone who develops and maintains a web site.

web-to-phone – Making a phone call by using a computer connected to the Internet. The computer speakers and a microphone, or a PC headset, replace the telephone handset. A *Java applet* is used to dial the number, either via the system's *browser* or stand-alone software. Voice-to-IP interfaces convert the IP packets into voice streams.

webtrap – **See:** tar pit

webvertizing – A composite word for web site advertizing.

webzine – **See:** e-zine

wedging – Flooding a system or network with *worms*.

weenie – In a chat room, an enthusiastic but immature participant who disrupts the flow of the discussion.

welcome page – An initial page on a web site that welcomes users to the site, confirms the site's identity and reinforces its brand, products, services, or logo.
See: FEATURE BOX

---

welcome page

The welcome page of a web site is the first point of access to a site for most Web users.

The company's name is clearly displayed on the welcome page. The web page displays the products and services available.

well-behaved – Refers to software applications which function as expected and conform to all the standards.

we-mail – E-mail sent from an address shared by two people.

wetware – Human beings.

WFM – See: Wired for Management

whack a mole – To close down unsolicited advertising windows that appear repeatedly and clutter the screen. Often the user has to click quickly to keep closing the windows as soon as they appear - rather like playing the game "Whack a Mole."

whacker – An incompetent hacker; one who modifies files and programs without really understanding how they work.

What You See Is What You Get (WYSIWYG) – The presentation of a page layout on a computer screen that shows how the actual page will look when it is published on the Web. An example of a WYSIWYG editor is Microsoft Frontpage, as it lets the user publish a page on the Web, without the user having to know HTML or another programming language. What the user draws on the screen is exactly what the program allows the user to publish.

What You See Is What You Print (WYSIWYP) – An image or page display in the same colors and resolution that will be produced by the printer.

wheel – A privileged user on a computer system; someone whose use of the system takes priority over other users and/or has access to parts of the network or functions that are not common to all users.

wheel mouse – A mouse that has a rubber wheel in the center used to scroll around the page. It is useful for working on the Web, where whole pages cannot always been seen in the window at one time. Some wheel mice also have a button, which when depressed, will return the user to the previous page.

whispers – Private conversations that take place in a *chat room*.

white book – The documentation that accompanies a video CD.

white hat – A hacker who is hired to prevent others from gaining unauthorized access to a network, or a hacker who gains unauthorized entry to a site and then informs the owner. Generally these are seen as good guys.
SEE ALSO: BLACK HAT

white noise – Broadband interference generated by the electricity in a communications line, sounding like a hiss.

White Pages – A directory service similar to the white pages in a telephone directory, providing information on e-mail addresses, street addresses, and telephone numbers.
GO TO: www.bigfoot.com

white paper – A short document that is designed to educate the reader on some technical matter.

white space – The blank space on a printed page. Denoted by spaces, tabs, and line feeds.

whiteboard – The equivalent of a blackboard, but on a computer screen. A whiteboard allows one or more users to draw on the screen while others on the network watch. It can be used for instruction in the same way that a blackboard is used in a classroom.

whois – An Internet directory service. Whois can be used to find information about users registered on a server, or other information about the network.

Wide Area Information Server (WAIS) – A type of database that contains indexes to documents that reside on the Internet. Text files can be searched using keywords. The entire contents of documents can be searched, rather than simply the titles.

wide distribution – When an e-mail or other document has been sent to a large number of different computers.

wide-area network (WAN) – A *network* that connects computers that are located in different areas. They are usually connected to each other via telephone lines and satellite communication links. Contrast with *local area network* (LAN).

wideband – A communications channel with transmission speeds from 64 Kbps to 2 Mbps; e.g. ADSL and T-1 lines. Sometimes used synonymously with *broadband*.

widget – An icon that appears on a web site and acts as a shortcut to a program operation; e.g. a button or toggle.

widow – When the final word of a paragraph is stranded at the bottom of a page. Widows are best avoided as they are considered stylistically poor.

wildcard character – Sometimes written as *.*, a character that is used like a wild card in a card game. In computers, a * represents any character or symbol, while "*.*" can be substituted for any file name; e.g. "*.html" would mean any file saved in html format.

WIMP interface – (slang) **W**indows, **I**cons, **M**ouse, **P**ull-down menus. A slang term for a *graphical user interface*.

Win32 – An *application-programming interface* (API) for programming 32-bit Windows operating systems, including Windows NT, 95, 98 and 2000.

Win32s – An extension of Win32 for Windows 3.1 that allows it to run 32-bit applications.

window – A section of a computer display screen, which operates as a single unit and can be opened, closed, manipulated, and moved around on the screen independently. Several windows in different applications can be open at any given time and can be overlapped or viewed simultaneously. The active window appears as the top window and contains the cursor.

window attack – A *denial of service* attack that creates a large number of *windows* and other *widgets,* all of which consume a large amount of computing resources. The computer becomes unable to cope with such demands and will crash.

window cascading – **See:** cascading windows

Windows – When the word Windows is written with a capital W, it stands for Microsoft Windows.

Windows 2000 – An update on Microsoft *Windows NT* that offered more stability and made adding peripherals much easier.

Windows 2K – **See:** Windows 2000

Windows 3 – The first version of *Microsoft* Windows to gain wide popularity. It was able to manage larger amounts of memory than previous versions, and ran 16-bit *DOS* and *Windows* applications. Windows 3.1 was an improvement that included *Object Linking*

and Embedding (OLE) and *multimedia* capability. With the Win32s extension, *Windows 3.1* can run 32-bit applications.

Windows 95 – Released in August 1995, the highly popular Microsoft Windows 95 was a 32-bit operating system designed to replace Windows 3.1. It offered a completely new user interface, adding among other treats a *Start menu, Taskbar,* improved memory, *Plug and Play, threading, multitasking,* and built-in *networking.*

Windows 98 – Microsoft's update on *Windows 95.* At the time, it supported many new technologies including FAT32, *multimedia extensions (MMX), universal serial bus (USB), Advanced Configuration and Power Interface, Accelerated Graphics Port,* and of course, *DVD.* However, the most obvious new feature of Win98 was the *Active Desktop,* which integrated the Web browser, Internet Explorer, with the operating system.

Windows 9x – A reference to Microsoft *Windows 95, 98* and *ME.*

Windows CE – Introduced in 1996, this is Microsoft's version of *Windows* designed for use in handheld computers and embedded systems. Windows CE-based PDAs use scaled down versions of Word, Excel and other *Windows* applications, which are known as "Pocket" applications. SEE ALSO: POCKET PC

**Windows Internet Naming Service
(WINS)** – A facility within *Microsoft
Windows* that finds the *IP address* for
computers linked within a network. In
many systems each computer has a
different IP address each time it is switched
on and WINS provides name resolution
for such systems. *DNS* provides the same
service for computers that have a fixed
IP address.

Windows ME – Windows Millennium
Edition is an upgrade of *Windows 98*. It
added more support for digital cameras,
multi-player games on the Internet and
home networking.

Windows Media Audio (WMA) – **See:**
Media Player

Windows Media Player – **See:**
Media Player

Windows Metafile Format (WMF) –
A Windows file format that holds vector
graphics, bitmaps and text. The file
extension used is .wmf.

**Windows NT
(Windows
New
Technology)** – A popular 32-bit operating
system from Microsoft for high-end
workstations, servers, and networks. It offers
a high degree of security and also has built-
in networking, multitasking, threading,
memory protection, and fault tolerance.

Windows Socket (winsock) – Utility
software that enables a connection
between a *Windows application* and
TCP/IP. Winsock is included in *Windows 95*
and newer versions, and automatically
configures with Internet software when
this is installed.

Windows Washer – A commercially
available program that allows the user to
clear *caches* and Internet history storage,
so eliminating the traces of web sites that
have been visited.

Windows XP – An upgraded client version
of *Windows 2000,* Microsoft released XP in
2001. It provides a multitude of changes
including new Start menu, Taskbar and
control panels, plus enhancements
including Internet Explorer 6, improved
connection sharing and a built-in firewall.
It also massively improves support for
playing games, digital photography, instant
messaging and wireless networking. The
Home Edition is designed for the consumer,
while XP Professional is aimed at the office
worker, with added security and
administrative options.

WinGate – A facility that allows users of a
local area network to share a modem and
Internet connection.

WinProxy – Synonymous with *WinGate*.

WINS – **See:** Windows Internet
Naming Service

Winsock - See: Windows Socket

Wintel - (slang) A composite word for *Windows* and *Intel* used to describe any computer which uses an Intel processor in combination with *Windows* software. Such combinations are called *platforms*.

 WinZip - A handy Windows-based utility program used for *zipping* and *unzipping* compressed files.
GO TO: www.winzip.com

wired - A computer that is wired is connected to the Internet.

Wired - A magazine dedicated to the Internet. One of the first magazines in the field, Wired was very influential in the first years of widespread Internet use.

Wired for Management (WFM) - A method of configuring and updating client computers on a network from the server. This is particularly useful for systems offering mobile Internet access.
SEE ALSO: WAP

wire-feet - The distance in wiring used (in imperial feet), rather than distance in a straight line. Also called wire-meters.

wireframe modeling - In computer graphics, representing a three-dimensional image by showing the outlines in lines and arcs, as if the object were made from wires.

wireless application protocol - See: WAP

wireless bitmap - A *bitmap* graphic format that was designed for use with wireless computers.

wireless communication - Networks that are connected by radio channels, as opposed to telecommunications wires. They rely on technologies such as packet radio, cellular technology, satellites, and microwave towers.

wireless LAN - A local area network that is not physically connected by wires, but relies on such technologies as *intra-red* and *packet radio*.

wireless local loop (WLL) - *Wireless* devices or systems in a fixed location, such as an office or home. Contrast with mobile wireless devices such as WAP phones.

Wireless Markup Language (WML) - A language that is used by *WAP* devices to connect to the Internet. Web sites that are written in HTML have to be translated into WML in order to be received by mobile WAP devices.

wireless modem - A modem that enables WAP devices to connect to the Internet.

wireless phone - A telephone service that is transmitted without using wires, e.g. *cellular* (mobile) *phones* and *personal communications* systems.

wireless–infra-red – **See:** infra-red, wireless communication

wizard – 1. A utility that provides interactive help by taking the user through a task, step-by-step. E.g. Installing new software or sending a fax.
2. An expert who understands computer technology really well.

wizzywig – **See:** WYSIWYG (**W**hat **Y**ou **S**ee **I**s **W**hat **Y**ou **G**et)

WLL – **See:** **w**ireless **l**ocal **l**oop

WMA – **See:** **W**indows **M**edia **A**udio

WMF – **See:** **W**indows **M**etafile **F**ormat

WML – **See:** **W**ireless **M**arkup **L**anguage

w/o – Abbreviation for **w**ith**o**ut.

Word – **See:** Microsoft Word

word of mouse – The distribution of information and ideas through the World Wide Web.
SEE ALSO: WEBINAR

word-processing – The writing and presentation of text documents. Features provided by most word processing software include text editing, spelling and grammar checking, word wrap, type styling, page formatting, search and replace, style sheets, and mail merge. *Microsoft Word* and *WordPerfect* are two of the most commonly used word-processing packages.

word spamming – The repeated use of key words on a web page in order to attract the attention of web *spiders* and ensure that the site is prominently located on the list of sites retrieved by a search engine. Generally, this is considered to be poor practice.
SEE ALSO: SPAMDEXING

word wrap – Most text editing systems include the facility to continuously type without line breaks. When the right margin is reached, the next word automatically moves down to begin a new line.
SEE ALSO: WORD-PROCESSING

WordPerfect – A once leading word-processing program from Corel, later versions include desktop publishing, fax, e-mail, and spreadsheet functions. Largely being replaced by Word.

workgroup – Two or more computer users who are networked together and share data and files.

working directory – The *directory* that is currently open.

worksheet – **See:** spreadsheet

workstation – 1. A powerful computer that is used for graphics, scientific and engineering computing, CAD, and other applications that require high performance and memory.
2. A terminal in a network.
3. A terminal or PC used by one person.

world wide wait - An expression used by those who have a low speed Internet connection and have to wait a while for sites to download, or by people experiencing slow download times due to web traffic overload.

SEE ALSO: GRAY BAR LAND

World Wide Web (WWW) - The collective term for the millions of *web sites* that use *Hypertext Transfer Protocol* and are posted on the Internet. It is called the Web, because of the intricacy of the links between sites. By clicking on *hyperlinks* embedded in the web pages, the user is able to travel from one page to another, or one site to another with great ease. Web sites can be accessed, and the World Wide Web *navigated,* by using *browsers,* which also enable *multimedia* effects to be incorporated into web pages. The World Wide Web is at the very heart of the Internet and is the most visible part of it, although the Internet also includes *e-mail, newsgroups, chat rooms,* and *Usenet.* Many people confuse the Internet with the World Wide Web. The difference between the two is that the Internet refers to the international network of computers that are linked together by telecommunications lines or wireless communication technology. The World Wide Web consists of millions of web sites and web pages, and is just one facility offered to users of the Internet.

World Wide Web Consortium (W3C) - W3 Consortium/W3C/ W3O. The organization that controls the standards and protocols used on the *World Wide Web.* It is based at the Massachusetts Institute of Technology (MIT).

GO TO: www.w3.org

W3C WORLD WIDE WEB consortium

Leading the Web to its Full Potential...

worm - 1. A computer program that can make copies of itself and spread from one computer to another through connected systems. Worms use up resources and may cause damage or overload the affected systems.
2. A computer program on the Internet that catalogs web sites.

SEE ALSO: SPIDER

WORM (Write **O**nce, **R**ead **M**any times**)** - A storage medium that can be written to only once, but can be read many times; e.g. optical disks.

Worm.ExploreZip virus - A *worm* found in 1999 that sends an automatic reply to the sender of an incoming message that says "Hi <name of person>! I received your e-mail and I will send you a reply ASAP. Till then, take a look at the attached zipped DOCs. Bye." It then proceeds to destroy the contents of all Microsoft files and some files in the C drive, leaving just the file names.

wormhole – An intentional hole in a system's security, which is created to provide access for maintenance technicians.

worst of the web – A web site that singles out the worst pages on the Web. It is worth visiting one of these sites before designing a web page, so as to avoid the pitfalls of web design.

Wozniak, Steve – Known as the Wizard of Woz, Wozniak co-founded *Apple,* along with Steve *Jobs* in 1983. Wozniak invented the Apple II personal computer.

wrap – **See:** word wrap

wrapper software – 1. Software that is wrapped around or based on older software so that it can be used on newer systems. 2. Software that is wrapped around files distributed over the Internet. It may contain security features to prevent unauthorized copying or compression software to reduce the size of the file.

wrist rest – A device used to raise the wrist above the level of the keyboard to prevent repetitive strain injury when typing.

write – To record data onto a disk, tape, or other storage medium.
SEE ALSO: WRITE OVER

write once – A means of storage where the data can be written only once; it cannot be erased or rewritten.
SEE ALSO: **WORM, CD-R**

write over – 1. The ability of some text processing programs to type over text that has been previously written. 2. To write data on a storage medium which has held other data; contrast with write once. E.g. A floppy disk allows write over.

write–protect – A means of preventing data from being written to a disk or other medium. A floppy disk, for instance, has a small sliding tab in the top right-hand corner, which prevents new data being written onto the disk.

WS_FTP – A *FTP* client program that uses a *graphical user interface.*

WWW – Common abbreviation for *World Wide Web.*

WYSIWYG – **See: W**hat **Y**ou **S**ee **I**s **W**hat **Y**ou **G**et

WYSIWYP – **See: W**hat **Y**ou **S**ee **I**s **W**hat **Y**ou **P**rint

X2 – Technology developed by US Robotics that enables high-speed data transmission over phone lines. X2 transmits digital data at up to 56 Kbps without analog conversion to the receiving modem for decoding.

X.400 – E-mail messaging standards specified by the *International Telecommunications Union*. It is an alternative to the more popular *Simple Mail Transfer Protocol* (SMTP). X.400 is used in Europe and Canada.

X.500 – A standard format for an electronic directory of people within an organization that can be incorporated into a global directory posted onto the *World Wide Web*. The format includes different levels for each piece of data, e.g. country, state or county, city, and so on. Compatible with *X.400*.
SEE ALSO: WHITE PAGES

x-axis – In an X-Y matrix the x-axis is the horizontal row.
SEE ALSO: Y-AXIS
SEE: FEATURE BOX

xDSL – A general term used to refer to *Digital Subscriber Line* (DSL) services.

Xeon – A line of *Pentium* II *chipsets* from *Intel* introduced in 1998, which allow faster data transfer between *CPU* and *Level1 cache*.

Xerox – Xerox Corporation is a manufacturer of copy machines, computer printers, and many other document management systems.
GO TO: www.xerox.com

XGA – EXtended Graphics Array. A display screen resolution of 1,024 x 768 pixels introduced by *IBM* in 1990.

x-height – In typography, the height of the letter "x" in lower case.
SEE ALSO: POINT, ASCENDER, DESCENDER

XHTML – See: Extensible Hypertext Mark-up Language.
SEE ALSO: EXTENSIBLE MARK-UP LANGUAGE

XL – See: Excel

---

x-axis

The x-y matrix has an x-axis and a y-axis, and is the framework for two-dimensional structures. This is a very basic X-Y matrix.

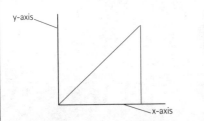

The horizontal axis in an x-y coordinate system is the x-axis. The vertical axis is the y-axis.

Xlink – **See:** XML Linking Language

XLR cable – **See:** XLR connector

XLR connector – An audio plug and socket used in professional and high-end audio equipment. It uses a balanced connection that locks into the socket.

XML – **See:** eXtensible Markup Language

XML Linking Language – The rules governing the attachment of *hyperlinks* to *XML* documents.

XModem – A protocol for the transfer of files over a dial-up access telephone line. It has an in-built error detection facility.
SEE ALSO: ZMODEM

X-OFF, X-ON – A means of controlling the flow of data between two devices, usually the modem and computer. X-OFF, X-ON uses software to send and decode messages which are incorporated into the data *packets*.
SEE ALSO: CTS, FLOW CONTROL, REQUEST TO SEND

XOR – In *Boolean* operations, an exclusive **OR** (XOR) is true if only one of the inputs is true, but not if both are true.

Xpath – **See:** XML Linking Language

XSL – **X**ML **S**tylesheet **L**anguage. Used to separate style from content when creating *HTML* or *XML* pages.

XUL – **E**xtensible **U**ser-interface **L**anguage

X-Window System – *Software* for shared network applications that allows displays of text and graphics and use of a mouse. It runs under *UNIX* and all major operating systems. Developed by MIT (Massachusetts Institute of Technology).

Y2K – Shorthand, much touted by the computing industry and media, for the year 2000 (the K standing for a thousand). It was used particularly in the advertising and marketing of *Y2K compliant* computers.

Y2K compliant – Computers manufactured or modified to deal with the date problem associated with the change of the millennium. Older PCs were programmed to accept that the year would always begin with 19xx and so only required the last two digits of the number to change automatically. When the year changed to 2000, computers could not recognize the '00' (was it 1900 or 2000?). They could not complete calculations that involved the year field, and would then malfunction. Governments and businesses spent millions to avoid this so-called millennium bug.

Yahoo! – Short for **Y**et **A**nother **H**ierarchical **O**fficious **O**racle!, Yahoo! is one of the most popular *search engines* and one of the most visited sites on the Internet. In Yahoo! it is possible to search under specific topics as well as generalized searches. Yahoo! relies on people to index and categorize the sites listed rather than automated *spiders*. It was started as a hobby in 1994 by two Stanford University graduate students, David Filo and Jerry Yang, as a directory of web sites. Yahoo! has many country and

regional offerings, as well as a broadcast site with links to over 500 radio stations and over 60 TV stations.
GO TO: www.yahoo.com and www.broadcast.com

Yahoo! Mail – *Yahoo!'s* webmail facility.

Yahooligans! – The *Yahoo!* search directory designed for children. All the content of Yahooligans! is guaranteed safe and approved for children to use.
GO TO: www.yahooligans.com

y-axis – In an X-Y matrix the y-axis is the vertical row.
SEE ALSO: X-AXIS

yell.com – BT's (British Telecommunications) web site version of its *yellow pages,* listing over 1.7 million UK suppliers of goods and services. The site is linked to the US Yellow Book site (which was yellowbook.com but is also now yell.com). Entries can be searched by type of business (e.g. florist, plumber), location, or name of company. They can also be accessed via *WAP* cellular phones.
GO TO: www.yell.com

Yellow Book – The standards set by the CD-ROM industry.

Yellow Book, USA – US-based book and website (yellowbook.com) company producing 30 million *yellow pages* directories of goods and services. In 1999 the company was acquired by British Telecommunications plc (one of the world's leading telecommunications companies and largest directory publishers) and yellowbook.com was later absorbed into BT's *yellow pages* Internet site *www.yell.com.*
Go to: www.yell.com
See also: YELL.COM

yellow pages – Services provided by some web sites, e.g. *yell.com*, which serve the same function as the yellow pages in a telephone directory. They provide trade and business directory facilities organized by services, location, and by name.

yes tv – *Broadband* portal offering Internet television programs, films, and video as well as e-mail and web site material via *ADSL*-connected phone line and cable.
Go to: www.yestv.co.uk

YModem – A modification to the *X-modem* system for transferring data over telephone lines, which takes into account the improved reliability of modems. Data is transferred in larger *packets* resulting in faster data transfer.

yottabyte (yb) – Two to the power of 80 bytes. A yottabyte (from yotta, the second-to-last Latin alphabet letter) is equal to 1,024 *zettabytes*.
See also: EXABYTE

yo–yo mode – When a computer repeatedly crashes and then is restored for use.

zap – 1. To electronically destroy something.
2. To fix a bug in a program by overlaying (zapping) a new code on top of the faulty code. The new code is called a zap.
3. In some games, to throw an electronic beam with the intention of hitting something.

ZAW – See: Zero Administration Windows

Z-buffering – In *three-dimensional graphics*, Z-buffering is used to ensure that perspective in the virtual world mimics that of the real world. This achieves effects such as a foreground object blocking the view of a background object.

zen mail – E-mail that arrives but contains no message.

Zero Administration Windows (ZAW) – *Microsoft's* initiative to make its operating systems simpler to install and manage. It is aimed at networked computers so that administrative functions such as upgrades can be carried out on one computer and delivered to all computers on the network.

zero content – Used in *newsgroups* to indicate a message that adds nothing to the recipient's knowledge on a subject.

Zero Insertion Force Socket (ZIF) – A socket on a computer's *motherboard* that uses small levers to enable processor chips to be inserted securely into the board without force.

zero wait state – Systems that have no wait states. This means the microprocessor is able to operate at its maximum speed without waiting for slower memory chips.

zettabyte – Two to the power of 70.

ZIF socket – See: Zero Insertion Force Socket

Zimmermann, Phillip – Encryption specialist who invented and released the *Pretty Good Privacy* program.

zine – See: e-zine

ZIP – See: WINZIP

zip code – Post codes within the US. Many web site forms require the user's zip code. Non-US residents should enter their own postal code.

Zip disk – See: Zip drive

Zip drive – A portable *disk drive*, which is usually used for backing up and archiving personal computer files. It can store almost 100 megabytes on a 3.5" disk.

Zip file – A file that has been compressed and also saved using the *WINZIP* compression format.

zip software – A general term for any compression software as well as specifically referring to *WINZIP* software.

zipperhead – (slang) Someone whose mind is closed to new ideas.

zipping – Compressing a file using *WINZIP*.

Zmodem – A *protocol* for the transfer of data using dial-up access lines. A Zmodem takes into consideration the improved reliability of *modems* and enables data to be transferred in larger packets, and consequently at faster speeds, than that used by the *Xmodem* protocol.

zombie – 1. A form of *denial of service attack*, a zombie site will receive a malicious message, which generates an overwhelming number of requests, eventually crashing the site or making it unable to respond to other requests.
SEE ALSO: PULSING ZOMBIE
2. A ghost web site; one that has been abandoned and left to rot.
3. In a *newsgroup* or *chat room*, a zombie occurs when a user has terminated their session, but the server believes (mistakenly) that the connection is still active.

zone of authority – An area where rules apply as agreed to a specified standard.

zoo – A web site that stores *computer viruses*. Such sites are illegal in certain countries round the world.

zoom in – To enlarge an area of the display to see the details more clearly. This is particularly useful when handling graphics.
SEE: FEATURE BOX

zoom out – To increase the area of the display to enable the user to view either the whole page at once, or a larger portion of a page. This is essential to achieve a balanced page design.
SEE: FEATURE BOX

zoomed video port – See: ZV port

zooming – To progressively scale the entire display image, either to increase or to decrease the magnification of the image.

Zuse, Konrad – German inventor, born in 1910 and died in 1995. He invented the binary digital computer, the Z1, in 1938.

ZV port – A technology that enables the delivery of multimedia and full-screen motion video to *notebook* computers.

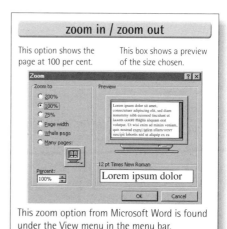

zoom in / zoom out

This option shows the page at 100 per cent.

This box shows a preview of the size chosen.

This zoom option from Microsoft Word is found under the View menu in the menu bar.

appendices

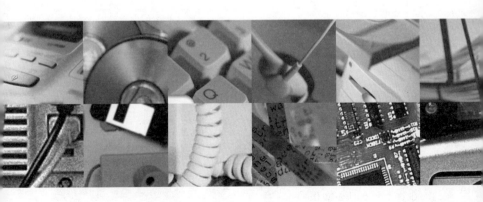

Appendix 1: Acronyms

These abbreviations are used in chat sessions, newsgroup postings, and e-mails to represent commonly used phrases. They have proved extremely popular, because they make Internet communication easy, quick, and more fun.

2U2   To You Too

AAMOF   As A Matter Of Fact

ABENT   Absent By Enforced Net Deprivation

ADN   Any Day Now

AFAIC   As Far As I'm Concerned

AFAIK   As Far As I Know

AFAIR   As Far As I Remember

AFJ   April Fool's Joke

AFK   Away From Keyboard

AIAMU   And I'm A Monkey's Uncle

AISI   As I See It

AKA   Also Known As

AMBW   All My Best Wishes

ANFAWFOWS
             And Now For A Word From Our Web Sponsors

ANFSCD   And Now For Something Completely Different

AOAS   All Of A Sudden

AS   Another Subject

ASAP   As Soon As Possible

ATSL   Along The Same Lines

ATST   At The Same Time

AWC   After While, Crocodile

AWGTHTGTWTA?
             Are We Going To Have To Go Through With This Again?

AYSOS   Are You Stupid Or Something?

B4   Before

B4N   Bye For Now

BAK   Back At Keyboard

BBFN   Bye Bye For Now

BBIAB   Be Back In A Bit

BBIAF	Be Back In A Few (minutes)	**BTW**	By The Way
BBL	Be Back Late	**BTWBO**	Be There With Bells On
BBN	Bye Bye Now	**BWDIK?**	But What Do I Know?
BBR	Burnt Beyond Repair	**BWL**	Bursting With Laughter
BCNU	Be Seein' You	**BWQ**	Buzz Word Quotient
BEG	Big Evil Grin	**BYE?**	Are You Ready To Say Goodbye?
BF	Boy Friend	**BYKT**	But You Knew That
BFN	Bye For Now	**BYOB**	Bring Your Own Bottle
BION	Believe It Or Not	**C4N**	Ciao For Now
BITD	Back In The Day	**C&G**	Chuckle And Grin
BITMT	But In The Meantime	**CADET**	Can't Add, Doesn't Even Try
BOF	Birds Of a Feather	**CFD**	Call For Discussion
BOT	Back On Topic	**CFV**	Call For Vote
BRB	Be Right Back	**CID**	1. Consider It Done 2. Crying In Disgrace
BRT	Be Right There	**CIO**	Check It Out
BTA	But Then Again	**CMIIW**	Correct Me If I'm Wrong
BTAIM	Be That As It May	**CO**	1. Conference 2. Company
BTHOM	Beats The Hell Outta Me		
BTOBD	Be There Or Be Dead	**CSG**	Chuckle, Snicker, Grin

CTS   Clear To Send

CU   See You

CU2   See You, Too

CUCME   See You See Me
(video discussion)

CUL8R   See You Later

CULA   See You Later, Alligator

CWOT   Complete Waste Of Time

CWYL   Chat With You Later

CYA   1. Cover Your Ass
2. See Ya

DAMIFINO
Damned If I Know

DBEYR   Don't Believe Everything You Read

DGT   Don't Go There

DHYB   Don't Hold Your Breath

DIIK   Damned If I Know

DIKU?   Do I Know You?

DIY   Do It Yourself

DK   Don't Know

DKDC   Don't Know, Don't Care

DLTBBB   Don't Let The Bed Bugs Bite

DQYDJ   Don't Quit Your Day Job

DTRT   Do The Right Thing

DWIMNWIS
Do What I Mean, Not What I Say

DWL   Dying With Laughter

EFLA   Extended Four Letter Acronym

EG   Evil Grin

EMFBI   Excuse Me For Butting In

EMFJI   Excuse Me For Jumping In

EOD   End Of Discussion

EOM   End Of Message

EOT   1. End Of Thread
2. End Of Transmission

ESO   Equipment Smarter
than Operator

ETLA   Extended Three Letter Acronym

F2F   Face To Face

FAI   Frequently Argued Issue

FAQ   Frequently Asked Question

FBKS   Failure Between Keyboard and Seat

FBOW   For Better Or Worse

FC   Fingers Crossed

FCFS   First Come, First Served

FIFO   First-In-First-Out

FISH   First In, Still Here

FMTYEWTK
   Far More Than You Ever Want To Know

FOAF   Friend Of A Friend

FOMCL   Falling Off My Chair Laughing

FS   For Sale

FTASB   Faster Than A Speeding Bullet

FTBOMH   From The Bottom Of My Heart

FTL   Faster Than Light

FUBAB   Fouled Up Beyond All Belief

FUBAR   Fouled Up Beyond All Reason/Recognition/Repair

FUD   Fear, Uncertainty, and Doubt

FWIW   For What It's Worth

FYA   For Your Amusement

FYE   For Your Entertainment

FYI   For Your Information

GA   Go Ahead

GAL   Get A Life

GBTW   Get Back To Work

GD&R   Grinning, Ducking, and Running

GD&WVVF
   Grinning, Ducking, and Walking Very, Very Fast

GF   Girl Friend

GFC   Going For Coffee

GFETE   Grinning From Ear To Ear

GFN   Gone For Now

GFR   Grim File Reaper

GG   1. Good Game
2. Gotta Go

GIGO   Garbage In, Garbage Out

GIWIST   Gee, I Wish I'd Said That

GLGH	Good Luck and Good Hunting	**IAC**	In Any Case
GLLA	Great Lovers Love Alike	**IAE**	In Any Event
GMTA	Great Minds Think Alike	**IAITS**	It's All In The Subject
GOWI	Get On With It	**IANAL**	I Am Not A Lawyer
GR8	Great	**IAW**	In Accordance With
GRMBL	Grumble	**IBTD**	I Beg To Differ
GTG	Got To Go	**IC**	I See
GTSY	Great To See You	**IDGI**	I Don't Get It
HAK (H&K) Hugs And Kisses		**IIABDFI**	If It Ain't Broke, Don't Fix It
HAND	Have A Nice Day	**IIRC**	If I Recall/Remember Correctly
HHIS	Hanging Head In Shame	**IIWM**	If It Were Me
HHOJ	Ha, Ha, Only Joking	**IJWTK**	I Just Want To Know
HHOK	Ha, Ha, Only Kidding	**IJWTS**	I Just Want To Say
HHO1/2K Ha, Ha, Only Half Kidding		**IKWUM**	I Know What You Mean
HHTYAY	Happy Holidays To You And Yours	**ILT**	I Liked That
HOYEW	Hanging On Your Every Word	**ILY**	I Love You
HSIK?	How Should I Know?	**IMA**	I Might Add
HTH	Hope That Helps	**IMCO**	In My Considered Opinion
		IME	In My Experience

IMHO	In My Humble Opinion	**JC**	Just Checking
IMO	In My Opinion	**JIC**	Just In Case
INPO	In No Particular Order	**JK**	JoKe/Just Kidding
IOH	I'm Outta Here	**JMO**	Just My Opinion
IOW	In Other Words	**JTLYK**	Just To Let You Know
IRL	In Real Life	**JW**	Just Wondering
ISO	In Search Of	**K**	Okay
ISSYGTI	I'm So Sure You Get The Idea	**KFY**	Kiss For You
ISTR	I Seem To Recall	**KHYF**	Know How You Feel
ISWIM	If (you) See What I Mean	**KISS**	1. Keep It Short and Simple
ITFA	In The Final Analysis		2. Keep It Simple, Stupid
ITSFWI	If The Shoe Fits, Wear It	**KIT**	Keep In Touch
IYKWIM	If You Know What I Mean	**KMA**	Kiss My Ass
IYSS	If You Say So	**KWIM**	Know What I Mean?
IYSWIM	If You See What I Mean	**KYFC**	Keep Your Fingers Crossed
IWALU	I Will Always Love You	**L**	Laugh
IWBNI	It Would Be Nice If	**L8R**	Later
JAM	Just A Minute	**LABATYD**	Life's A Bitch And Then You Die
JAS	Just A Second	**LDR**	Long Distance Relationship

LJBF — Let's Just Be Friends

LMHO — Laughing My Head Off

LOL — 1. Laughing Out Loud
2. Lots Of Love

LSHMBA
Laughing So Hard
My Belly Aches

LTNS — Long Time No See

LTNT — Long Time No Type

LTS — Laughing To Self

LUWAMH
Love You With All My Heart

LY — Love You

LYL — Love You Lots

M8 — Mate

MB — Message Board

MLA — Multiple Letter Acronym

MMF — Make Money Fast

MOF — Matter Of Fact

MORF — Male or Female

MOTAS — Member Of The Appropriate Sex

MOTD — Message Of The Day

MOTOS — Member Of The Opposite Sex

MOTSS — Member Of The Same Sex

MRU — Most Recently Used

MSSG — Message

MTBJ — Mean Time Between Jams

MTCW — My Two Cents' Worth

MYOB — Mind Your Own Business

NADT — Not A Darn Thing

NAVY — Never Again Volunteer Yourself

NBD — No Big Deal

NBIF — No Basis In Fact

NBSP — Non-Breathing SPace

NC — No Comment

NFF — No Fault Found

NHOH — Never Heard Of Him/Her

NIMBY — Not In My Back Yard

NINO — Nothing In, Nothing Out

NM — Never Mind

NOP	No OPeration
NOYB	None Of Your Business
NP	No Problem
NQA	No Questions Asked
NRG	Energy
NRN	No Reply Necessary
NTIM	Not That It Matters
NTIMM	Not That It Matters Much
NTW	Not To Worry
NTYMI	Now That You Mention It
NW	No Way
O	Over
OATUS	On A Totally Unrelated Subject
OAUS	On An Unrelated Subject
OBO	1. Or Best Offer 2. On Behalf Of
OBTW	Oh, By The Way
OIC	Oh, I See
OMDB	Over My Dead Body
OMG	Oh My Gosh

ONNA	Oh No, Not Again
ONNTA	Oh No, Not This Again
OO	Over and Out
OOC	Out Of Character
OOTB	Out Of The Blue
OOTC	Obligatory On Topic Content
OT	Off Topic
OTFL	On The Floor Laughing
OTL	Out To Lunch
OTOH	On The Other Hand
OTT	Over The Top
OTTOMH	Off The Top Of My Head
OWTTE	Or Words To That Effect
PAHFOI	Put A Happy Face On It
PANS	Pretty Awful New Stuff
PCM	Please Call Me
PDA	Public Display of Affection
PDS	Please Don't Shout

PEBKAC Problem Exists Between Keyboard And Chair

PF Personal Favorite

PFY Pimply Faced Youth

PITA Pain In The Ass

PLOKTA Press Lots Of Keys To Abort

PLONK Person with Little Or No Knowledge

PLS Please

PM Private Message

PMBI Pardon My Butting In

PMF Pardon My French

PMFJI Pardon Me For Jumping In

PMIGBOM
Put Mind In Gear Before Opening Mouth

PMJI Pardon My Jumping In

PMP Peeing My Pants

PNCAH Please, No Cursing Allowed Here

POV Point Of View

PPL People

PTB Powers That Be

PTMM Please Tell Me More

QBE Query By Example

RAEBNC Read And Enjoyed, But No Comment

RBTL Read Between The Lines

RE I. RE-greet; Hello again
2. In regard to

REHI Hello again

RHIP Rank Has Its Privileges

RIW Read It and Weep

RL Real Life

RLCO Real Life COnference

RLF Real Life Friend

RML Read My Lips

RN Right Now

ROF Rolling On Floor

ROFUTS Rolling On the Floor Unable To Speak

ROTFL Rolling On The Floor Laughing

ROTFLAHMS

Rolling On The Floor Laughing And Holding My Sides

ROTFLMAO

Rolling On The Floor Laughing My Ass Off

RRQ Return Receipt reQuest

RSN Real Soon Now

RSVP Respondez S'il Vous Plait (French for "please reply")

RTFF Read The Freaking FAQ

RTFM Read The Friendly Manual

RTM Read The Manual

RU Are You?

R U THERE?

Are You There?

RYFM Read Your Friendly Manual

RYS Read Your Screen

RX 1. To Receive
2. Regards

S Smile

SAPFU Surpassing All Previous Foul Ups

SB Smile Back

SEC wait a SECond

SEP Someone Else's Problem

SETE Smiling Ear To Ear

SFLA Stupid Four Letter Acronym

SHID Slaps Head In Disgust

SHTSI Somebody Had To Say It

SITD Still In The Dark

SLM See Last Mail

SMOP Small Matter Of Programming

SNAFU Situation Normal: All Fouled Up

SO Significant Other

SOHF Sense Of Humor Failure

SOS 1. Same Old Stuff
2. Help

SOW Speaking Of Which

STW Search The Web

SUFID Screwing Up Face In Disgust

SWAG Scientific Wild Ass Guess

SWDYT   So What Do You Think

SWIM   See What I Mean?

SWL   Screaming With Laughter

SWMBO She Who Must Be Obeyed

SYS   See You Soon

TAF   That's All Folks

TAFN   That's All For Now

TANJ   There Ain't No Justice

TANSTAAFL
> There Ain't No Such Thing
> As A Free Lunch

TARFU   Things Are Really Fouled Up

TAS   Taking A Shower

TBH   To Be Honest

TBYB   Try Before You Buy

TCO   Total Cost of Ownership

TCOY   Take Care Of Yourself

TFH   Thread From Hell

TFN   Thanks For Nothing

TFS   Three Finger Salute (Ctl-Alt-Del)

TFTHAOT
> Thanks For The Help
> Ahead Of Time

TFTT   Thanks For The Thought

TGAL   Think Globally, Act Locally

THX   Thanx

TIA   Thanks In Advance

TIAIL   Think I Am In Love

TIC   Tongue In Cheek

TILIS   Tell It Like It Is

TINWIS That Is Not What I Said

TLA   Three Letter
Acronym/Abbreviation

TLGO   The List Goes On

TMI   Too Much Internet

TMTOWTDI
> There's More Than
> One Way To Do It

TNT   To the Next Time

TNTL   Trying Not To Laugh

TNX   Thanx

TNXE6	Thanx a million (E6 is 10 to the 6th power – a million)
TOBAL	There Oughta Be A Law
TOBG	This Oughta Be Good
TOPCA	Till Our Paths Cross Again
TOS	Terms Of Service
TOY	Thinking Of You
TPTB	The Powers That Be
TRDMC	Tears Running Down My Cheeks
TSR	Totally Stupid Rules
TSWC	Tell Someone Who Cares
TTBOMK	To The Best Of My Knowledge
TTFN	Ta Ta For Now
TTKSF	Trying To Keep a Straight Face
TTYAWFN	
	Talk To You A While From Now
TTYL/TTYL8R	
	Talk To You Later
TTYT	Talk To You Tomorrow
TWIMC	To Whom It May Concern
TXT	Text

TY	Thank You
TYCLO	Turn Your Caps Lock Off (stop shouting)
TYVM	Thank You Very Much
UOK?	You OK?
V	Very
VBG	Very Big Grin
WB	Welcome Back
WIBLI	Wouldn't It Be Lovely If
WIIWD	What It Is We Do
WRT	With Regard To
WTG	Way To Go
WTMI	Way Too Much Information
WYSIWYG	
	What You See Is What You Get
XM	Excuse Me
YA	Yet Another
YAFIYGI	You Ask For It, You Get It
YGWYPF	You Get What You Pay For
YW	You're Welcome
ZZZ	Sleeping, bored, tired

Appendix 2: Emoticons

Also known as smileys, emoticons are a unique aspect of web language. Viewed sideways they show faces expressing different emotions or characteristics. They minimize word usage for speedier communication.

* :-o	Alarmed	|-o	Bored
%-}	Amused	%-6	Brain dead
>:-II	Angry	(:-...	Broken heart
>:-@	Angry	:^)	Broken nose
;-(	Angry/Black eye	}|{	Butterfly
|-|	Asleep	~=	Candle
~:-o	Baby (crying)	C=:-)	Chef
(:-)	Bald	:-~[	Cold
~~c___	Beach	%-)	Confused
-)#	Beard	8-)	Cool
%+|	Beaten up	]:o	Cow
C:-)	Big brain	X-)	Cross-eyed
:°-(	Big tear	:,(	Crying
:-(=)	Big teeth/Goofy	:'-(	Crying
;-(=)	Big-toothed grin	S:-)	Curly hair
(:-D	Blabbermouth	%-)	Dazed/Staring at screen too long
!-(	Black eye	:-|:-|	Déjà vu
:-{}	Blowing a kiss	>:>	Devilish/naughty
:-r	Blowing a raspberry	:-e	Disappointed
:-(	Boo hoo	>:-|	Disgusted

:)~	Drooling	:^)	Happy
:*)	Drunk	:-~|	Has a cold
<:)	Dunce	:-#	Has just said something that shouldn't have been said
_/	Empty glass		
}-)	Evil	|-)	Hee hee
>:-)	Evil grin	(_8-(|)	Homer Simpson
:-#	Fat lip	[]	Hug
:)3	Female	(((H)))	Hug
o+	Female	%*@:-(	Hungover
(O--<	Fishy	%-\	Hungover
@;-)	Flirt	;-S	I kind of like it
:'"-)	Floods of tears	(:-$	Ill
:-<	Forlorn	:-|	Indifferent
:-(	Frown (anger or displeasure)	:-]	Jaw dropping
:(	Frowning	:-x	Kiss
\~/	Full glass	:-*	Kiss/Sorry, didn't mean that
~:-(	Fuming	:D	Laughing
:-D	Funny/Laugh/Comedy moment	:-D	Laughing
>>:-<<	Furious	(-D	Laughing
8^|	Grim	(-:	Left hand
:-)	Ha-ha	:------)	Liar
:-)	Happy	:-9	Licking lips
^L^	Happy	:^D	Like it!
		8:-)	Little girl

>-<	Livid
>:-<	Mad/Annoyed
:)8-	Male
o->	Male
@@@:-)	Marge Simpson
)-::-(	Married
0>-<(=	Message of interest to women
#:-)	Messy hair
:-<)	Mustache
:-{)	Mustache
:-X	Mute
:-#	My lips are sealed
~~:[	Net flame
:/i	No smoking
:~)	Nose
%-{	Not amused
:-]	Obnoxious
:-o	Oh!
8-O	Oh my God!
.-)	One-eyed
:-O	Oops
:-!	Oops, foot in mouth
#-)	Partied all night

0:-)	Pea brain
:-/	Perplexed/Skeptical
[:-)	Personal stereo
:8)	Pig
P-(	Pirate
-:-)	Punk
:-"	Pursed lips
(-::-)	Putting heads together
:-I	Puzzled
:[	Real downer
:~/	Really mixed-up
[:-]	Robot
[:]	Robot
@}--->--->	Rose
:-(	Sad
:(	Sad
:-|	Sad
8^(	Sad
%-{	Sad
>:-(	Sad, angry
0:-)	Saint
0:)	Saint
M:-)	Salute

*<:-)>	Santa	:-w	Speaks with forked tongue
:->	Sarcastic	:-p	Sticking tongue out
:-Y	Saying it with a smile	*-)	Stoned
(:+(	Scared	:-T	Straight-faced
:@	Scream	<:-)?	Stupid question
(-_-)	Secret smile	(o) (o)	Surprise
$_$	Sees money	:-X	Swear
:o	Shocked	:X	Sworn to secrecy
=:-o	Shocked	&-(	Tearful
=:-)	Shocked	,':-)	That's a really interesting idea
:-( )	Shouting/Talking	:^)	Tongue-in-cheek
|-)	Sleeping	:-J	Tongue-in-cheek
^_^	Smile	:&	Tongue-tied
:-)	Smiley	:-s	Tongue-tied
:-!	Smoker	<:>==	Turkey
:-Q	Smoking	:-\	Undecided
~~8}	Snake	:-(	Unhappy
|^o	Snoring	:-E	Vampire
?-(	Sorry, I don't know what went wrong	:-[	Vampire
...---...	SOS	%*}	Very drunk
:-3	Sour, eaten a lemon	:-))	Very happy/double chin
:-M	Speak no evil	:-((	Very sad
:-v	Speaking	(:-\	Very sad

|-(	Very tired
{:-{	Very unhappy
:-(*)	Vomiting/Been sick
:-{X	Wearing a bow tie
:-#	Wearing a brace
d:-)	Wearing a cap
@:-)	Wearing a turban
{:-)	Wearing a wig
::-)	Wearing glasses
8-)	Wearing sunglasses
:.-(	Weeping
:-"	Whistling
;-)	Winking
%-|	Working too hard
:-}	Wry smile
:-(O)	Yelling
(@@)	You're kidding!
|-P	Yuk
>=^p	Yuk
$-)	Yuppie
:-o ^^^^:	Zipped up fly too fast

Appendix 3: Domain Suffixes

These domain name suffixes signify a category of web site or the country from which the web site originates.

.ac	Top-level domain name for an educational network (same as .edu)	.ba	Bosnia/Herzegovina
		.bb	Barbados
.ad	Andorra	.bd	Bangladesh
.ae	United Arab Emirates	.be	Belgium
.af	Afghanistan	.bf	Burkina Faso
.ag	Antigua and Barbuda	.bg	Bulgaria
.ai	Anguilla	.bh	Bahrain
.al	Albania	.bi	Burundi
.am	Armenia	.bj	Benin
.an	Netherlands Antilles	.bm	Bermuda
.ao	Angola	.bn	Brunei Darussalam
.aq	Antarctica	.bo	Bolivia
.ar	Argentina	.br	Brazil
.arpa	A top-level domain name used for ArpaNet sites	.bs	Bahamas
		.bt	Bhutan
.as	American Samoa	.bv	Bouvet Island
.at	Austria	.bw	Botswana
.au	Australia	.by	1. Belarus 2. Byelorussia
.aw	Aruba		
.az	Azerbaijan	.bz	Belize

.ca	Canada	.dj	Djibouti
.cc	Cocos Islands - Keelings	.dk	Denmark
.cf	Central African Republic	.dm	Dominica
.cg	Congo	.do	Dominican Republic
.ch	Switzerland	.dz	Algeria
.ci	Cote D'Ivoire, or Ivory Coast	.ec	Ecuador
.ck	Cook Islands	.edu	A top-level domain name used for educational sites
.cl	Chile		
.cm	Cameroon	.ee	Estonia
.cn	China	.eg	Egypt
.co	1. Colombia 2. Top-level domain name for some commercial networks, same as .com	.eh	Western Sahara
		.er	Eritrea
		.es	Spain
.com	Pronounced "dotcom." A top-level domain name used for commercial Internet sites	.et	Ethiopia
		.fi	Finland
		.firm	An ending of an address for an Internet site for a business
.cr	Costa Rica		
.cs	Czechoslovakia (former)	.fj	Fiji
.cu	Cuba	.fk	Falkland Islands/Malvinas
.cv	Cape Verde	.fm	Micronesia
.cx	Christmas Island	.fo	Faroe Islands
.cy	Cyprus	.fr	France
.cz	Czech Republic	.fx	Metropolitan France
.de	Germany	.ga	Gabon

Suffix	Country	Suffix	Country
.gb	Great Britain	.ht	Haiti
.gd	Grenada	.hu	Hungary
.ge	Georgia	.id	Indonesia
.gf	French Guiana	.ie	Ireland
.gh	Ghana	.il	Israel
.gi	Gibraltar	.in	India
.gl	Greenland	.int	A top-level domain name used for international institutions
.gm	Gambia		
.gn	Guinea	.io	British Indian Ocean Territory
.gov	A domain name used for a government site on the Internet	.iq	Iraq
		.ir	Iran
.gp	Guadeloupe	.is	Iceland
.gq	Equatorial Guinea	.it	Italy
.gr	Greece	.jm	Jamaica
.gs	South Georgia and South Sandwich Islands	.jo	Jordan
		.jp	Japan
.gt	Guatemala	.ke	Kenya
.gu	Guam	.kg	Kyrgyzstan
.gw	Guinea-Bissau	.kh	Cambodia
.gy	Guyana	.ki	Kiribati
.hk	Hong Kong	.km	Comoros
.hm	Heard and McDonald Islands	.kn	Saint Kitts and Nevis
.hn	Honduras	.kp	North Korea
.hr	Croatia/Hrvatska		

.kr	South Korea		**.ml**	Mali
.kw	Kuwait		**.mm**	Myanmar
.ky	Cayman Islands		**.mn**	Mongolia
.kz	Kazakhstan		**.mo**	Macau
.la	Laos		**.mp**	Northern Mariana Islands
.lb	Lebanon		**.mq**	Martinique
.lc	Saint Lucia		**.mr**	Mauritania
.li	Liechtenstein		**.ms**	Montserrat
.lk	Sri Lanka		**.mt**	Malta
.lr	Liberia		**.mu**	Mauritius
.ls	Lesotho		**.mv**	Maldives
.lt	Lithuania		**.mw**	Malawi
.lu	Luxembourg		**.mx**	Mexico
.lv	Latvia		**.my**	Malaysia
.ly	Libya		**.mz**	Mozambique
.ma	Morocco		**.na**	Namibia
.mc	Monaco		**.nato**	A top-level domain name used for NATO sites
.md	Moldova			
.mg	Madagascar		**.nc**	New Caledonia
.mh	Marshall Islands		**.ne**	Niger
.mil	A top-level domain name for a US military site on the Internet		**.net**	A top-level domain name used for Internet administrative sites
.mk	Macedonia		**.nf**	Norfolk Island
			.ng	Nigeria

.ni	Nicaragua	.pw	Palau
.nl	Netherlands	.py	Paraguay
.no	Norway	.qa	Qatar
.nom	An ending of an address for a personal site on the Internet	.re	Reunion
		.ro	Romania
.np	Nepal	.ru	Russian Federation
.nr	Nauru	.rw	Rwanda
.nt	Neutral Zone	.sa	Saudi Arabia
.nu	Niue	.sb	Solomon Islands
.nz	New Zealand (Aotearoa)	.sc	Seychelles
.om	Oman	.sd	Sudan
.org	A top-level domain name for organizational Internet sites	.se	Sweden
		.sg	Singapore
.pa	Panama	.sh	Saint Helena
.pe	Peru	.si	Slovenia
.pf	French Polynesia	.sj	Svalbard and Jan Mayen Islands
.pg	Papua New Guinea	.sk	Slovakia
.ph	Philippines	.sl	Sierra Leone
.pk	Pakistan	.sm	San Marino
.pl	Poland	.sn	Senegal
.pm	Saint Pierre and Miquelon	.so	Somalia
.pn	Pitcairn	.sr	Suriname
.pr	Puerto Rico	.st	Sao Tomé and Principe
.pt	Portugal		

.store	A domain name for a retail business web site
.su	Former USSR
.sv	El Salvador
.sy	Syria
.sz	Swaziland
.tc	Turks and Caicos Islands
.td	Chad
.tf	French Southern Territory
.tg	Togo
.th	Thailand
.tj	Tajikistan
.tk	Tokelau
.tm	Turkmenistan
.tn	Tunisia
.to	Tonga
.tp	East Timor
.tr	Turkey
.tt	Trinidad and Tobago
.tv	Tuvalu
.tw	Taiwan
.tz	Tanzania
.ua	Ukraine
.ug	Uganda
.uk	United Kingdom
.um	US Minor Outlying Islands
.us	United States
.uy	Uruguay
.uz	Uzbekistan
.va	Vatican City State
.vc	Saint Vincent and the Grenadines
.ve	Venezuela
.vg	British Virgin Islands
.vi	US Virgin Islands
.vn	Vietnam
.vu	Vanuatu
.web	An ending of an address for an Internet site that is about the World Wide Web
.wf	Wallis and Futuna Islands
.ws	Samoa
.ye	Yemen
.yt	Mayotte
.yu	Yugoslavia
.za	South Africa
.zm	Zambia
.zr	Zaire
.zw	Zimbabwe

Appendix 4: Number Definitions

There are many terms connected with the Internet that are represented by numbers. The most common are listed below with their definitions.

0k – Zero kilobytes.

0x – Used in programming, the symbol for a *hexadecimal* number.

10_Past_3 – A *computer virus* that causes no intentional damage. On specified dates, the virus alters some hardware and software interrupts, which prevents them from working. It also alters keystroke commands at certain times of the day. The .789 variant displays the following message on the 22nd of every month:
"Ah Ah ** Ah Ah ** Ah Therese** Ah ** Ah Ah Ah Ah." It then reboots the computer.

15_Years – A *computer virus* with a triggering mechanism that causes irreparable damage to any disk that is accessed. The virus is activated by date recognition and overwrites any file that is read, losing all the data from that sector.

100BaseT – Any of several fast *Ethernet* standards for twisted pair cables.

100BaseTX – The most used form of fast *Ethernet* - it runs over two pairs of wires in *category* 5 cable.

120 reset – A term referring to voltage in the US, meaning to cycle power on a computer in order to reset or un-jam it.

1-2-3 – A reference to *Lotus 1-2-3*.

16-bit – A program or hardware that can process 16 *bits* of information at a time.

16-bit sound card – A sound card that works on 16-bit *samples*. The 16-bit sound card produces high-fidelity sound and music for multimedia.

2D – Two dimensions or planes, e.g. height and width.

2-digit-year – The representation of the year in two digits such as 91 for 1991. This became a problem at the change of the millennium.
SEE ALSO: Y2K, 4-DIGIT-YEAR FORMAT

2G – Second generation wireless service that is also called Personal Communications Services (PCS). This is the current standard for wireless transmission in North America.

2.5G – Second-and-a-half generation wireless service. Most carriers move to this type of packet-switched service prior to making the more dramatic leap to 3G. The move to 2.5G will noticeably improve transmission speeds.

24/7 – All day, everyday. Many online retailers boast that they are "open 24/7."

3D – Three dimensions or planes, e.g. height, width, and depth.

32-bit – A program or hardware that can process 32 *bits* of information at a time.

386 – The nickname used for the 32-bit processor developed by *Intel* and used in PCs during the 1980s.

3G – Third-generation wireless transmission. It enables the transmission of high-quality wireless audio and video, and increases wireless transmission speeds to 2 Mbps.

3GL – Third-generation assembly language such as Pascal or Fortran.

3W – Short for *World Wide Web*.

4-bit color – A monitor that is capable of 4-bit color can only display 16 colors. This is too limited for most forms of graphic representation.

4-digit-year format – To write the year in a date using all four numbers, such as 2002.
SEE ALSO: 2-DIGIT-YEAR FORMAT

4004 – The name of the very first microprocessor or chip, designed by Marcian E. "Ted" Hoff at *Intel* in 1971.

404 – Someone who is uninformed, inexperienced, or just plain stupid. It refers to the 404-error message that is displayed when a browser cannot find a web page.

486 – The fourth generation of the *Intel* x86 family of CPU chips, introduced in 1989. It is often used to refer to the PC that uses it.

4GL – The fourth-generation assembly language. It is more advanced and closer to normal speech than its predecessors.

5Lo – A *computer virus* that changes the infected program's time and date to that at the time of infection. 5Lo does little more than replicate itself.

56k line – A transmission line that transmits data at up to 56,000 bps.

501 – An expression used in chat rooms and newsgroups for an argument that is full of holes. The allusion is to the Levi jeans of the same name.

586 – A reference to chips of the same class as the *Intel Pentium* family. However, they are not made by them.

686 – A reference to chips of the same class as the *Intel Pentium* Pro microprocessor. However, they are not made by them.

6800 series – Microprocessors that are developed by Motorola, and used in *Apple* computers.

6DOF – **See:** six degrees of freedom

701 – The name of IBM's first ever computer, made in 1952.

8-bit – A program or hardware that can process 8 *bits* of information at a time.

8mm – Eight-millimeter-wide magnetic tape technology that is used in analog and digital camcorders, and also in data-storage applications.

8.3 – Shorthand for the limits on filename length imposed by the file system used by MS-DOS and Microsoft Windows: up to eight characters, followed by a dot, followed by a filename extension of up to three characters.

802.11 – A set of protocols developed by the *IEEE* for *wireless local area network* technology.

8086 – Introduced in 1978 and arguably the most important microprocessor, it defines the base architecture of *Intel*'s x86 family that led to the *Pentium* series. It is a 16-bit microprocessor and contains 29,000 transistors addressing 1MB of memory.

8088 – A slower version of the 8086, this *Intel CPU* microprocessor is used in first-generation PCs, which were used for business applications in the 1980s. It uses an 8-bit data bus and contains 25,000 transistors.

90-90 rule – A programming aphorism attributed to Tom Cargill of Bell Labs – "The first 90 per cent of the code accounts for the first 90 per cent of the development time. The remaining 10 per cent of the code accounts for the other 90 per cent of the development time."

98lite – A *shareware* program from Shane Brooks that separates Windows 98 from Internet Explorer.

Appendix 5: File Extensions

The following chart shows the many different types of file extensions, describes what they mean, and also what applications are needed to open the files. Where there are two or more file extension names, it means that the file can be labelled as any of these.

File Ext.	Format Description	How To Open It
.aiff	A not-so-common sound format.	Use Sound Player, or Waveform Hold and Modify to play it.
.arc	Macintosh Hierarchical Archive.	Download as MacBinary. Use StuffIt! Expander for Windows.
.asp	An Active Server Page. This is a server-side customized html page.	View it in your browser.
.au	A once common sound format found on the Web.	Use Sound Player, or Waveform Hold and Modify to play it.
.bat	DOS batch file. A series of line commands, similar to a shell script. To run, simply name the file at the command line. AUTOEXEC.BAT runs when you boot your Win2000 PC.	Use any text editor.
.bin	MacBinary II Encoded File. Make sure to download as MacBinary or Binary.	Use StuffIt! Expander to turn back into a usable Macintosh file, if it isn't already.

File Ext.	Format Description	How To Open It
.cgi	Common Gateway Interface. A cgi script. Probably written in C but maybe Perl. If it is in C and compiled, then you probably can't edit it. You will know right away when you try to open it in a text editor.	Use any text editor.
.dat	Generally a data file, written by an application.	Use Microsoft Word, Simple Text, BBEdit, or any text editor.
.dbx	May be a Microsoft Visual Foxpro table file.	Use Foxpro, or import it to any other relational database.
.dll	Dynamic Link Library. This is a compiled set of procedures and/or drivers called by another program.	Compiled file – do not move or alter.
.doc **.dot**	May be a Microsoft Word or Wordpad document. .dot is a Microsoft Word template.	Use MS Word, or WordView to quickly display MS Word documents.
.eml	May be an Outlook Express saved message. This extension is assigned when you choose file|save in Outlook.	Use Outlook or a text editor.
.exe	May be a DOS/Windows program or a DOS/Windows Self Extracting Archive.	You need to run this in a DOS/Windows emulator such as RealPC Download and launch it in its own temporary directory; it may spawn a number of files and directories. Self-extracting.

File Ext.	Format Description	How To Open It
.gif	Graphical Interchange Format. Though not the most economical, this is the most common graphics format found on the Internet.	Use GIF Converter, JPEG View, Lview Pro, or PolyView to view these graphics.
.gz	.gz is the Gnu version of zip. It is a compression method developed for use on UNIX systems.	Use macgzip or WinZip to view and extract archives.
.hlp	This is a Windows help file. Windows provides some annotating features to modify the file, but as they are compiled files, they cannot be edited without a great deal of difficulty.	Use Helpmaker Plus to create your own help files.
.html **.htm**	HTML (Hypertext Mark-up Language), the code of simple web pages. Plain text file.	Use Netscape for Macintosh, Netscape for Windows 3.1, Netscape for Windows95, and Windows NT to view the file.
.hqx	BinHex 4.0 – Encodes a Macintosh file into 7-bit text so it can be safely transferred. Most Mac files appear in .hqx	Use Stufflt! Expander. To un-BinHex it in a DOS window, use BinHex 13.
.image	Macintosh Disk Image, most commonly found on Apple's FTP sites.	Use ShrinkWrap to mount the disk image, and deal with it like you would a floppy.

File Ext.	Format Description	How To Open It
.ini	Initialization file. Typically from earlier versions of Windows. These are software settings, and environment variables. You can alter them with a text editor, but keep a backup copy.	Use any text editor.
.jpg .jpeg .jfif	JPEG/JFIF, a 24-bit graphic format.	Use JPEG View, Lview Pro, or Polyview to see these graphics.
.max	May be a Paperport file.	Use Paperport Viewer.
.mdb .mde	Microsoft Access Database.	Use Microsoft Access.
.mim .mime	Multi-Purpose Internet Mail Extensions.	Use your e-mail client or a text editor.
.mpg .mpeg	MPEG, a standard Internet movie platform.	Use VMPEG with win32s, Ladybug, or Sparkle to play MPEGs or to convert them to QuickTime.
.mov .qt .movie .moov	QuickTime Movie, Apple Macintosh native movie platform.	Use Sparkle, FastPlayer, MoviePlayer, SimpleText, Microsoft Word, QuickTime for Windows, and many others. If the movie appears totally white, you may need to use the Apple QuickTime VR Player to see it.

File Ext.	Format Description	How To Open It
.pdf	Adobe Acrobat Portable Document Format. Download as binary.	Use Adobe Acrobat Reader or Adobe Acrobat.
.pfc	AOL Personal File Cabinet.	Manage from inside AOL.
.pl	Perl Script. Runs on UNIX-type platforms. ASCII file.	Use any text editor.
.pps **.ppt**	.pps may be Microsoft PowerPoint Slide Show, .ppt may be Microsoft PowerPoint Presentation.	Use Microsoft PowerPoint.
.ps	Postscript file. Plain text file, but not really human-readable.	Send to a Postscript printer with Laserwriter Font Utility or view it onscreen using Ghostscript.
.rm	Real Movie.	Download RealPlayer.
.rtf	Rich Text Format.	Use any word processor or editor which features Use Wordpad.
.sit	StuffIt! archive – binary.	Download as MacBinary, and use StuffIt! Expander for Windows. Use UnSit in a DOS window.
.sea	Macintosh Self Extracting Archive.	Download and launch as MacBinary. Use StuffIt! Expander for Windows.

File Ext.	Format Description	How To Open It
.smi	ShrinkWrap Disk Image File.	Use ShrinkWrap.
.swp	This is probably a Win95 "swap" file where Windows swaps out information from the memory to the disk. You should not mess with this file. If it is over 200 megs, look into "swap space" in your Windows configuration.	Use any text editor.
.sys	Probably a DOS/Windows system file; you should only edit these if you know exactly what you are doing.	Download and use Tar. Use WinZIP to view and extract archives.
.tar .tar.Z .tar.gz .tgz	UNIX tar program takes separate files and turns them into one file – often also compressed. Extensions such as .tar.Z, .tar.gz, and .tgz (latter two are equivalent) require decompression first, then un-tar. Some UNIX ftp servers will un-tar a file if you request it without the ".tar" extension.	
.tiff .tif	TIFF is a very large, high-quality image format.	Use JPEG View, Lview Pro, or PolyView to see these graphics.
.txt	A plain text file.	Use Microsoft Word, Simple Text, BBEdit, or any text editor. Open in Notepad or any text editor.
.uu .uue	A uuencoded file. Typically this is done on a UNIX command line: *uuencode OriginalFileName SecondFilename >*	Use UU Undo, WinCode, or ESS-Code to uudecode it.

File Ext.	Format Description	How To Open It
	EncodedFile.uu. A file is generated named *SecondFileName.* Using .uu as the extension is not required but is considered polite. Increasing numbers of desktop mail and newsreading programs will handle this type of encoding on the fly.	
.vsd	Visio Drawing File.	Use Visio.
.wav	Windows Wave format sound file.	Use Waveform Hold and Modify or SoundApp.
.wk1 **.wk3** **.wk4**	Lotus Worksheets. Can often be converted by Excel.	Use Lotus.
.wpd	WordPerfect Document.	Use WordPerfect.
.xls **.xlw** **.xlt**	Microsoft Excel Spreadsheet, Excel Workbook, Excel Template.	Use Microsoft Excel.
.Z		If you are downloading via ftp, most ftp servers will uncompress for you if you drop the ".Z." Otherwise use StuffIt! Expander w/EE or WinZIP to view and extract archives.
.zip	pkzip, a common DOS/Windows compression format.	Use ZipIt, StuffIt! Expander w/EE, or MacUnZip. Use WinZIP to view and extract archives.

Appendix 6: Useful Web Sites

This is a selection of commonly used, accredited web sites covering a range of topics. They have been selected to help make browsing the Web safe and easy.

Search Engines

www.altavista.com

www.askjeeves.com

www.bigfoot.com

www.excite.com

www.google.com

www.hotbot.com

www.infoseek.com

www.lycos.com

www.northernlight.com

www.smartpages.com

www.superpages.com

Metasearch engines

www.1blink.com

www.2trom.com

www.c4.com

www.dogpile.com

www.ixquick.com

www.mamma.com

www.metacrawler.com

www.oneseek.com

www.profusion.com

www.search.com

www.searchrunner.com

General

www.aol.com

http://family.go.com

www.ivillage.com

www.msn.com

www.netscape.com

www.ntl.com

www.yahoo.com

Entertainment

http://entertainment.connectonline.com/

www.eonline.com

www.ew.com

www.ign.com

www.pagesix.com

http://people.aol.com

Reference

www.biography.com

www.brittanica.com

www.clearinghouse.net

www.dictionary.com

www.encarta.msn.com

www.encyclopedia.com

www.infoplease.com

www.libraryspot.com

www.m-w.com

www.refdesk.com

www.worldtimeserver.com

www.xe.com/ucc/

www.yourdictionary.com

Jobs

www.careerbuilder.com

www.careerlab.com

www.hotjobs.com

www.jobfind.com

www.monster.com

www.stepstone.com

www.totaljobs.com

www.wetfeet.com

News

http://abcnews.go.com

www.agencefrancepresse.com/english/home/

www.ananova.com

www.ap.org

www.cbsnews.com

www.cnn.com

www.economist.com

www.enn.com

www.euronews.com

www.foxnews.com

www.ft.com

www.iht.com

www.itv.com/news

http://news.bbc.co.uk

www.referl.com

www.reuters.com

www.time.com

www.usatoday.com

Children's search engines

www.ajkids.com
www.aol.com/netfind/kids
www.beritsbest.com
http://home.edview.com
www.kidsdomain.com
http://lycoszone.lycos.com
www.netmom.com
http://sunsite.berkeley.edu/KidsClick!
www.yahooligans.com

Charity

www.alertnet.org
www.amnesty.org
www.care.org
www.charitynet.org
www.conservation.org
www.give.org
www.icrc.org
www.msf.org
www.oxfam.org
www.savethechildren.org
www.supportunicef.org
www.wwf.org

Sports

www.allsports.com
www.cbssportsline.com
www.espn.com
www.extremesports.com
www.fia.com
www.kidzworld.com/
www.sport.com
http://sport.news.com.au/
www.sportingnews.com
www.sportquest.com
www.sports.com
http://sports.yahoo.com
www.sportserver.com/
http://sportsillustrated.cnn.com
www.sportsnetwork.com

Health

www.allhealth.com
www.healthatoz.com
www.healthcentral.com
www.healthfinder.gov
www.my.webmd.com
www.oxygen.com/topic/health/

Shopping

www.all-internet.com
www.amazon.com
www.asseenonscreen.com
www.buy.com
www.buyagift.com
www.cdnow.com
www.cybershop.com
www.dealtime.com
www.ebay.com
www.gifts.com
www.harrods.com
www.interflora.com
www.laredonte.com
www.memorizethis.com
www.netmarket.com
http://onlineshopping.about.com
www.outtasites.com/shopping
www.qvc.com
www.safeshopping.org
http://shopping.yahoo.com
www.top20shopping.com
www.towerrecords.com
www.worldofshopping.com
www.worldshopping.com

Travel

www.cityhunt.com
www.concierge.com
www.ebookers.com
www.expedia.com
www.fco.gov.uk/travel/
www.fodors.com
www.frommers.com
www.letsgo.com
www.lonelyplanet.com
www.priceline.com
www.roughguides.com
www.statravel.com
www.travel.org
www.travel.discovery.com
http://travel.lycos.com
http://travel.yahoo.com
www.travelcity.com
www.travelholiday.com
www.travelnotes.org
www.travelsource.com
www.travmed.com
www.uniglobe.com
www.vtourist.com
www.worldtravelguide.net

Acknowledgments

Dorling Kindersley would like to thank the following:

AltaVista logo reproduced with the permission of AltaVista Internet Operations Limited. All rights reserved. Ananova logo © Ananova Ltd. 2001. Reproduced by permission. All rights reserved. BBCi is a trademark of the British Broadcasting Corporation and is used under licence. Cisco Systems and the Cisco Systems logo are registered trademarks of Cisco Systems Inc., and/or its affiliates in certain other countries. Demon is part of THUS plc. Dolby and the double-D symbol are trademarks of Dolby Laboratories Licensing Corporation. The eBay logo is a trademark of eBay Inc. Energy Star is a US registered trademark. Divider images courtesy of Eyewire. Google Brand Features are trademarks of Google, Inc. HotBot® is a registered trademark and/or service mark of Wired Ventures, Inc., a Lycos company. All rights reserved. HP is a registered trademark of the Hewlett-Packard Company. 2001. ICQ screenshots © 1998-2001 ICQ, Inc. Used with permission. Linux logo used with permission from Linux Online, Inc, © 2001 (special thanks to Larry Ewing for his work on Tux). Lycos logo © 2001 Lycos, Inc. Lycos ® is a registered trademark of Carnegie Mellon University. All rights reserved. McAfee® is a registered trademark of Network Associates.McAfee.com Inc. and/or its affiliates in the US and/or other countries. Microsoft® is a registered trademark of Microsoft Corporation in the United States and/or other countries. NCSA logo courtesy of the National Center for Supercomputing Applications (NCSA) and the Board of Trustees of the University of Illinois. Netscape Communicator browser window © 1999 Netscape Communications Corporation. Netscape Navigator is a registered trademark of Netscape Communications Corporation. Paint Shop Pro and Jasc are registered trademarks of Jasc Software, Inc. Pentium is a registered trademark of the Intel Corporation. Symantec®, the Symantec logo, Norton AntiVirus®, Norton CleanSweep®, and Norton Utilities® are registered trademarks of Symantec Corporation. Norton SystemWorks and Speed Disk are trademarks of Symantec Corporation. WinZip logo Copyright 1991-2001 WinZip Computing, Inc. WinZip® is a registered trademark of WinZip Computing, Inc. WinZip is available from www.winzip.com. WinZip logo reproduced with permission of WinZip Computing, Inc.